Emissions Trading

Ralf Antes · Bernd Hansjürgens ·
Peter Letmathe · Stefan Pickl
Editors

Emissions Trading

Institutional Design, Decision Making
and Corporate Strategies

Second Edition

 Springer

Editors
Prof. Dr. Ralf Antes
Universität Halle-Wittenberg
LS Betriebliches
Umweltmanagement
Große Steinstr. 73
06099 Halle
Germany
antes@wiwi.uni-halle.de

Prof. Dr. Peter Letmathe
Universität Siegen
FB 05 Wirtschaftswissenschaften
LS für
Wertschöpfungsmanagement
Hölderlinstr. 3
57076 Siegen
Germany
peter.letmathe@uni-siegen.de

Prof. Dr. Bernd Hansjürgens
UFZ Umweltforschungszentrum
Leipzig-Halle GmbH
Permoserstr. 15
04318 Leipzig
Germany
bernd.hansjuergens@ufz.de

Prof. Stefan Pickl
Universität der Bundeswehr
München
Fakultät für Informatik
Werner-Heisenberg-Weg 39
85577 Neubiberg
Germany
stefan.pickl@unibw.de

ISBN 978-3-642-20591-0   e-ISBN 978-3-642-20592-7
DOI 10.1007/978-3-642-20592-7
Springer Heidelberg Dordrecht London New York

Library of Congress Control Number: 2011935231

© Springer-Verlag Berlin Heidelberg 2008, 2011
This work is subject to copyright. All rights are reserved, whether the whole or part of the material is concerned, specifically the rights of translation, reprinting, reuse of illustrations, recitation, broadcasting, reproduction on microfilm or in any other way, and storage in data banks. Duplication of this publication or parts thereof is permitted only under the provisions of the German Copyright Law of September 9, 1965, in its current version, and permission for use must always be obtained from Springer. Violations are liable to prosecution under the German Copyright Law.
The use of general descriptive names, registered names, trademarks, etc. in this publication does not imply, even in the absence of a specific statement, that such names are exempt from the relevant protective laws and regulations and therefore free for general use.

Printed on acid-free paper

Springer is part of Springer Science+Business Media (www.springer.com)

Contents

Introduction 1
Ralf Antes, Bernd Hansjürgens, Peter Letmathe, and Stefan Pickl

Part A   Emisions Trading Markets

Intertemporal Emissions Trading and Market Power:
Modeling a Dominant Firm with a Competitive Fringe 9
Julien Chevallier

International Emissions Trading: A Pricing Model Based
on System Dynamical Simulations 33
Bo Hu and Stefan Pickl

Comparative Analysis of Alternative Post-2012 Climate
Policies and Ancillary Benefits for Ukraine: A General
Equilibrium Approach 45
Olga Diukanova

Design of Emission Allocation Plans and Their Effects
on Production and Investment Planning
in the Electricity Sector 71
Dominik Möst, Massimo Genoese, Anke Eßer-Frey, and Otto Rentz

The Negotiation Process to Include International Aviation
in a Post-2012 Climate Regime 85
Odette Deuber

Part B Greenhouse Gas Management, Emissions Trading and Business Strategies

Corporate Social Responsibility Programs for Emissions-Trading
Risk Management in Canadian Banks 109
Brian Robertson

How Does Emissions Trading Influence Corporate Risk
Management? 127
Edeltraud Günther, Martin Nowack, and Gabriel Weber

A Model for the Valuation of Carbon Price Risk 141
Henry Dannenberg and Wilfried Ehrenfeld

Integration of a New Emission-Efficiency Ratio
into Industrial Decision-Making Processes – A Case Study
on the Textile Chain 163
Grit Walther, Britta Engel, and Thomas Spengler

Offensive GHG Management and Small
and Medium-Sized Enterprises 181
Charlotte Hesselbarth and Barbara Castrellon Gutierrez

Part C New Technologies and Instruments in the Field of Emissions Trading

The Potential of Ocean Iron Fertilization as an Option
for Mitigating Climate Change 195
Christine Bertram

A New Sector Mechanism for Clean Coal Technologies
in a Carbon Constrained World 209
John Kessels

Post-Kyoto GHG-Offset Project Eligibility Criteria 227
Brian Robertson

Voluntary Carbon Offsets – Empirical Findings
of an International Survey 243
Stefanie Brinkel and Ralf Antes

Climate Change and the Clean Development Mechanism
in Indonesia: An Appraisal 263
Nicole Dathe

Contributors

Ralf Antes Department of Economics, University of Cooperative Education Gera, Weg der Freundschaft 4A, 07546 Gera, Germany, ralf.antes@ba-gera.de

Christine Bertram Kiel Institute for the World Economy, Duesternbrooker Weg 120, 24105 Kiel, Germany, christine.bertram@ifw-kiel.de

Stefanie Brinkel Martin-Luther-University, Faculty of Law and Economics, Chair of Corporate Environmental Management, Große Steinstraße 73, 06108 Halle (Saale), Germany, stefanie.brinkel@wiwi.uni-halle.de

Barbara Castrellon Gutierrez Centre for Emissions Trading, Martin-Luther-University Halle-Wittenberg, Große Steinstraße 73, 06099 Halle, Germany, barbara.castrellon-gutierrez@wiwi.uni-halle.de

Julien Chevallier EconomiX-CNRS, University of Paris, 10 Department of Economics, Office G-307a, 200 avenue de la République, 92001 Nanterre Cedex, France, jchevall@u-paris10.fr

Henry Dannenberg Halle Institute for Economic Research (IWH), Kleine Märkerstr. 8, 06108 Halle, Germany

Nicole Dathe Pfotenhauerstr. 74, 01307 Dresden, Germany, Nicole.dathe@hotmail.com

Odette Deuber Mathildenstr. 44, 72072 Tübingen, odettedeuber@gmx.de

Olga Diukanova Fondazione Eni Enrico Mattei (FEEM) Castello, 5252 - I-30123 Venice, Italy, olga.diukanova@feem.it

Anke Eßer-Frey Institute for Industrial Production, Universität Karlsruhe (TH), Hertzstraße 14, 76131 Karlsruhe, Germany

Wilfried Ehrenfeld Halle Institute for Economic Research (IWH), Kleine Märkerstr. 8, 06108 Halle, Germany, wilfried.ehrenfeld@iwh-halle.de

Britta Engel Braunschweig University of Technology, Katharinenstr. 3, 38106 Braunschweig, Germany, aip-pl@tu-braunschweig.de

Massimo Genoese Institute for Industrial Production, Universität Karlsruhe (TH), Hertzstraße 14, 76131 Karlsruhe, Germany

Edeltraud Günther Technische Universität Dresden, 01062 Dresden, Germany; University of Virginia, McIntire School of Commerce, bu@mailbox.tu-dresden.de

Bernd Hansjürgens UFZ Umweltforschungszentrum, Leipzig-Halle GmbH, Permoserstr. 15, 04318 Leipzig, Germany, bernd.hansjuergens@ufz.de

Charlotte Hesselbarth Centre for Sustainability Management, Leuphana University Lueneburg, Scharnhorststraße 1, 21335, Lueneburg, hesselbarth@uni.leuphana.de

Bo Hu Universität der Bundeswehr München, D-85577 Neubiberg, Germany, bo.hu@unibw.de

John Kessels IEA Clean Coal Centre, SW15 6AA London, United Kingdom, john.kessels@iea-coal.org.uk

Peter Letmathe Universität Siegen, Fachbereich 05, Hölderlinstr. 3, 57076 Siegen, Germany, peter.letmathe@uni-siegen.de

Dominik Möst Institute for Industrial Production, Universität Karlsruhe (TH), Hertzstraße 14, 76131 Karlsruhe, Germany, Dominik.Moest@kit.edu

Martin Nowack Technische Universität Dresden, 01062 Dresden, Germany, bu@mailbox.tu-dresden.de

Stefan Pickl Universität der Bundeswehr München, D-85577 Neubiberg, Germany, stefan.pickl@unibw.de

Otto Rentz Institute for Industrial Production, Universität Karlsruhe (TH), Hertzstraße 14, 76131 Karlsruhe, Germany

Brian Robertson SolTerra Capital Corp., Toronto, Canada, brianrobertson@solterracapital.com

Thomas Spengler Braunschweig University of Technology, Katharinenstr. 3, 38106 Braunschweig, Germany

Grit Walther Schumpeter School of Business and Economics, Bergische Universität Wuppertal, Rainer-Gruenter-Str. 21, 42119 Wuppertal, Germany, walther@wiwi.uni-wuppertal.de

Gabriel Weber Technische Universität Dresden, 01062 Dresden, Germany, bu@mailbox.tu-dresden.de

Introduction

Ralf Antes, Bernd Hansjürgens, Peter Letmathe, and Stefan Pickl

Climate change is related to dramatic alterations in weather conditions, causing extreme weather events all around the world. Glaciers are shrinking at an unprecedented rate and 2010 was the warmest year on record in earth's recent history. In spite of these alarming tendencies, governments were still not able to agree on a binding Post-Kyoto treaty. However, even without a Post-Kyoto agreement, some political blocks such as the European Union (EU) have agreed on reducing greenhouse gas emissions with carbon dioxide as the most important perpetrator of climate change. Since 2005, emissions trading has been a major instrument in the EU for limiting greenhouse gas emissions and it is expected that emissions trading will take on an even greater role in the future. For this reason, it is worth analysing current emissions trading markets, their functionality, their real impact, and their drawbacks in more depth. Better knowledge can help to avoid defective behavior of market participants, to reduce the overall costs of emissions trading and might even increase the competitiveness of companies involved in the emissions trading market.

R. Antes (✉)
Department of Economics, University of Cooperative Education Gera, Weg der Freundschaft 4A, 07546 Gera, Germany
e-mail: ralf.antes@ba-gera.de

B. Hansjürgens
UFZ Umweltforschungszentrum, Leipzig-Halle GmbH, Permoserstr. 15, 04318 Leipzig, Germany
e-mail: bernd.hansjuergens@ufz.de

P. Letmathe
Universität Siegen, Fachbereich 05, Hölderlinstr. 3, 57076 Siegen, Germany
e-mail: peter.letmathe@uni-siegen.de

S. Pickl
Universität der Bundeswehr München, D-85577 Neubiberg, Germany
e-mail: stefan.pickl@unibw.de

This book looks at emissions trading mainly from a business perspective. Part A analyzes the functioning of emissions trading markets in the absence of optimal market conditions in different industry sectors, and countries, whereas Part B focuses on corporate responses to emissions trading. This part discusses the interplay of emissions trading and corporate responsibility programs, the influence of emissions trading on corporate risks, and how emissions trading relates to efficiency changes in the industrial sector. Part C broadens the perspective by taking new instruments and technologies into account. Ocean iron fertilization and clean coal technologies represent potential new markets for innovative companies and potential contributions to climate change mitigation. Carbon offsetting including Clean Development Mechanisms are new instruments in the field of emissions trading. They can reduce the costs of greenhouse gas reduction but are also prone to greenhouse gas leakages, undermining the effectiveness of emissions trading.

1 Overview of the Book

1.1 Part A: Emissions Trading Markets

Julien Chevalier (University of Paris, France) analyzes the consequences of banking and borrowing emission allowances in an imperfect market. He argues that market power and the dynamic aspects of emissions trading have a strong influence on market efficiency. Through extensive modelling of the EU emissions trading market and simulations with real-world data it is shown that the degree of inefficiencies can be minimized by properly allocating emission rights over time.

Bo Hu and Stefan Pickl (Universität der Bundeswehr München, Germany) present a dynamic pricing model, which enables the prices of emission allowances to be forecasted when different scenarios are considered. To model the main influences, they adopt a systems dynamic approach and develop a stock and flow diagram of energy demand and supply.

Olga Diukanova (Fondazione Eni Enrico Mattei, Italy) evaluates alternative post-2012 carbon dioxide reduction targets for the Ukraine. By means of a Ramsey-Cass-Koopmans model, she demonstrates how setting up an emissions trading market in the Ukraine is of national interest. Emissions trading can contribute to efficiency gains in the energy sector, reduce levels of other hazardous emissions, and promote long-term changes in the industrial sector resulting in a higher competitiveness of the country's economy.

Dominik Möst, Massimo Genoese, Anke Eßler and Otto Rentz (Universität Karlsruhe, Germany) apply agent-based models to illustrate the effect of different allocation schemes and prices of emission allowances on investment planning in the electricity sector. Their results are based on the PERSEUS-NAP model, which includes electricity grid models covering 42 regions in Western, Central and Eastern

European countries. Interconnections are also considered between the different regions. Besides forecasting increasing electricity costs, the authors point out that gas- and lignite-fired power plants will be a preferred investment option in the most likely scenarios.

Odette Deuber (Tübingen, Germany) discusses the options for including the aviation sector in the emissions trading market. Her article focuses on sector-specific challenges caused by the non-national nature and asymmetric negation power of different actors. She concludes that a global sectoral approach would be most promising to overcome institutional and market-related burdens.

1.2 Part B: Greenhouse Gas Management, Emissions Trading and Business Strategies

Brian Robertson (NexTerra Capital, Toronto / Canada) shows how Canadian banks tackle risks related to emissions trading in the absence of a national emissions trading scheme. He categorizes these risks into regulatory, physical, legal, reputational, competitive and project risks. While many banks apply normative criteria defined in corporate social responsibility programs, they do not have fully developed risk management approaches in place.

Edeltraud Günther, Martin Nowack and Gabriel Weber (Technische Universität Dresden, Germany) derive a six-step risk management approach, which enables climate change risks to be incorporated into overall corporate risk management. The authors use a case study on the multinational energy company Vattenfall to illustrate interconnections of climate change and traditional risks. For Vattenfall, as well as for other companies, identifying climate change and emissions trading risks, then actively managing these risks (risk reduction, accurate calculation of their impacts, integrating risks into corporate decisions) and their related liabilities is most important when risk exposure is high.

Henry Dannenberg and Wilfried Ehrenfeld (Halle Institute for Economic Research, Germany) use a mean reversion process to model the price risk of emission allowances. While long-term marginal emission abatement costs set the lower limit for the allowance price, the penalty price codified in the European emissions trading regulation enables the upper price limit to be determined. Within this range, the authors find "erratic" price changes, which can be explained by the Markovian Pricing model published by Benz and Türck and their own long-term risk assessment model.

Grit Walther (Bergische Universität Wuppertal, Germany), Britta Engel and Thomas Spengler (both Technische Universität Braunschweig, Germany) develop a concept that is suitable to measure the ratio of costs and emissions on different aggregation levels. With the radial efficiency measure, decision makers can determine efficient frontiers that disclose potential cost and environmental gains when a firm is located within a feasible range but can still realize increases in efficiency.

The theoretical concept is highlighted by a case study from the textile industry showing a significant potential to reduce carbon dioxide emissions cost-efficiently.

Charlotte Hesselbarth and Barbara Castrellon Gutierrez (Martin-Luther Universität Halle-Wittenberg, Germany) deal with opportunities of offensive greenhouse gas (GHG) management of small and medium-sized enterprises. After analyzing resource constraints, they develop a typology of GHG management strategies. They highlight the opportunities of offensive GHG management strategies, which enable small and medium-sized enterprises to benefit from economic opportunities in existing and new market niches as well as pursuing a higher level of sustainability.

1.3 Part C: New Technologies and Instruments in the Field of Emissions Trading

Christine Bertram (Kiel Institute for the World Economy, Germany) discusses ocean iron fertilization, which can potentially stimulate the growth of phytoplankton in the ocean and enhance carbon dioxide uptake. Although several companies expressed interest in this new technology for mitigating climate change, many environmentalists adopt a critical view of what they see as an irresponsible experiment. Christine Bertram provides factual support for the latter position and finds only limited potential of ocean iron fertilization with high costs involved and severe side effects on ecosystems. She also discusses the legal issues of ocean iron fertilization and the difficulties associated with integrating this new form of technology into CDM regulations.

John Kessels (IEA Clean Coal Centre, United Kingdom) deliberates about the premises of clean coal technologies. Coal is relatively inexpensive, will be available for a long time, and will hence remain a major energy source in the future. However, coal has relatively high carbon dioxide emission coefficients and burning coal is one of the major causes of climate change. Therefore, John Kessels takes a closer look at clean coal technologies with a special focus on carbon capture and storage technologies. He argues that a balanced technology mix can contribute to climate change mitigation at relatively low costs.

Brian Robertson (NexTerra Capital, Toronto / Canada) takes a closer look at GHG offsetting mechanisms. He particularly highlights the clean development mechanisms (CDM) as a strong and pioneering instrument for offsetting greenhouse gas emissions but also argues that related standards have to become more stringent. On the one hand, more narrow interpretations of requirements will extend the positive impact on the environment. On the other hand, stricter rules will also increase investor confidence and proliferate the types and numbers of successful projects seen as beneficial investments.

Stefanie Brinkel (Martin-Luther University Halle-Wittenberg, Germany) and Ralf Antes (University of Cooperative Education Gera, Germany) consider voluntary carbon offsets as offered by many organizations worldwide. Their empirical study shows that the main motivators for such initiatives are marketing, climate change mitigation, general economic advantages and corporate social responsibility. Although several institutions involved with voluntary carbon offsets adopt standards from the field of climate change mitigation, e.g. CDM standards, the authors conclude that methodical improvements leading to better measurability and transparency are necessary.

Nicole Dathe (Dresden, Germany) focuses on CDM in Indonesia as one of the target countries of carbon offsetting instruments. She provides a comprehensive overview of the CDM market in Indonesia compared to other countries. With 30 registered projects by September 30, 2009, Indonesia's share in the number of projects is only 1.6 percent and 1.1 percent of the expected numbers of annual credited emission reductions (CER). Nicole Dathe shows that Indonesia only exploits a small proportion of its CDM potential and politicians aim for a 400 percent increase in projects with 94 projects already in the pipeline. The overall CDM potential is estimated to be 235 million CER equivalent to an economic value of more than two billion Euros per year.

Acknowledgements This book would not have been possible without the help of many. First of all, we thank the authors who submitted their dedicated work to be published in this book. We also thank the reviewers who decided on the articles suitable for publication and who provided their very valuable insights on how to improve the articles included in the three parts of the book through their valuable comments. Furthermore, we thank Dr. Werner Müller and Christian Rauscher from Springer who patiently supported the book's publication in each phase of its creation. This is already the third book, resulting from our long-lasting cooperation with Springer. The first book "Emissions Trading and Business" was published in 2006, and the second book "Emissions Trading – Institutional Design, Decision Making and Corporate Strategies" in 2008. Both anthologies were excellently received by scientists and practitioners in the field of emissions trading. We also express our gratitude to Sarah Gwillym-Margianto (www.info@der-fachuebersetzer.com) who proofread all articles and did an excellent job of improving the writing of the authors who are mostly non-native speakers of English. Deepthi Mohan supported us with valuable remarks and advice during the final publication process. Last but not least, we thank Monika Wagner who diligently worked on the layout of the book and far beyond her obligations made several suggestions on how to improve the graphics and figures.

Part A
Emisions Trading Markets

Intertemporal Emissions Trading and Market Power: Modeling a Dominant Firm with a Competitive Fringe

Julien Chevallier

Abstract In international emissions trading schemes such as the Kyoto Protocol and the European Union Emissions Trading Scheme, the suboptimal negotiation of the cap with respect to total pollution minimization leads us to critically examine the proposition that a generous allocation of grandfathered permits by the regulator based on recent emissions might pave the way for dominant positions. Stemming from this politically given market imperfection, this chapter develops a differential Stackelberg game with two types of non-cooperative agents: a large potentially dominant agent, and a competitive fringe the size of which are exogenously determined. Strategic interactions are modeled on an intra-industry permits market where agents can freely bank and borrow permits. This chapter contributes to the debate on the allocation of initial permits and market power by focusing on the effects of allowing banking and borrowing. A documented appraisal on whether or not such provisions should be included is frequently overlooked by the debate on whether or not to introduce the permits market itself among other environmental regulation tools. Numerical simulations provide a quantitative illustration of the results obtained.

Keywords Banking • borrowing • emissions trading • market power

JEL Codes C73, L11, Q52

J. Chevallier (✉)
EconomiX-CNRS, University of Paris, 10 Department of Economics, Office G-307a, 200 avenue de la République, 92001 Nanterre Cedex, France
e-mail: jchevall@u-paris10.fr

1 Introduction

What happens on a tradable permits market when distortions occur as a consequence of the initial allocation? Whereas Hahn (1984) first contributed to this debate by demonstrating the non-neutrality of allocating permits to an agent able to exert market power[1] in a static context and only concerning the spatial exchange of permits, this chapter addresses the critical aspect in the initial allocation of permits in a dynamic context and with respect to inter-temporal emissions trading. Theoretical analyses remain scarce in this domain, even if the properties of banking (i.e., the ability to stock permits for future use) and borrowing (i.e., the ability to borrow permits from future periods) have been detailed. In a continuous time model under certainty, Rubin (1996) shows that an intertemporal equilibrium exists on a permits market from the viewpoint of the regulator and the firm, and that banking and borrowing allow firms to smooth emissions. Under uncertainty, Schennach (2000) shows that the price of the permits may rise at a rate that is lower than the discount rate and new public information may cause jumps in the price and emissions paths, among other major contributions.

This chapter builds on the intertemporal emissions trading literature with market imperfections. It aims at filling the gap in the literature between the pros and cons of authorizing banking and borrowing in permit trading programs – a topic which is typically not debated enough when deciding whether to adopt such an environmental regulation system. Against this background, it attempts to shed some light on the ability of a large agent to move dynamic markets when permits are grandfathered.

Liski and Montero (2005b) study the effect of market power on the equilibrium of a permits market by introducing a large potentially dominant agent and a competitive fringe. Based upon two cases, their analysis firstly reveals that the large agent might manipulate the market by banking allowances when it owns the entire stock of permits and secondly that when the fringe receives the entire stock of permits, the large agent has an incentive to exchange permits at the competitive price and to build a permits bank for the next period. While previous papers restricted their analysis to banking only,[2] both banking and borrowing are allowed without restrictions in a continuous time setting.

The model enhances the regulatory economics literature with a realistic description of relationships between agents on a tradable permits market with information asymmetry. As Liski and Montero (2005b) did not impose a particular game structure, the Stackelberg game structure was adopted that enables one to deal with strategic interactions between two types of agents: a leader with an information advantage associated with a large agent, and a follower associated with a competitive fringe.

---

[1]For an exhaustive literature review on permits trading and market power, see Petrakis and Xepapadeas (2003).

[2]In fact, no major international agreement on greenhouse gases allowed borrowing to a full extent at that date.

The market imperfection arises from the free distribution of permits on the basis of past emissions, while the product market is assumed to remain competitive.[3] I explicitly include the Hotelling conditions[4] that must apply if permits are considered to be an exhaustible resource.

The chapter is structured as follows: firstly, the institutional framework of current permit trading programs is described, namely the Kyoto Protocol (KP) and the European Union Emissions Trading Scheme (EU ETS); secondly the Stackelberg game is developed and an expression derived for market power; thirdly numerical simulations for the price distortion condition are computed.

2 Institutional Framework

In this section, I describe how the model hinges on critical design issues of existing international emissions trading schemes, namely the KP and the EU ETS. I also attempt to provide a balanced picture of the EU ETS and KP market power concerns.

2.1 The Kyoto Protocol

The Kyoto Protocol came into force on February 2005 following the ratification of Iceland, and aims to reduce the emissions of six greenhouse gases (GHG) considered to be the main cause of climate change. Among the Members of Annex B, these agreements include the reduction of CO_2 emissions for 38 industrialized countries, with a global reduction of CO_2 emissions by 5.2%. One hundred and seventy-four countries, with Australia being the latest on December 3, 2007, have ratified the Protocol, with the notorious exception of the United States. The first commitment period of the Kyoto Protocol runs from January 1, 2008 to December 31, 2012.

The Kyoto Protocol is often referred to as "unfinished business." Very heterogeneous sectors were included under the same regulation, which could be detrimental in finding the right method for allocating permits depending on price elasticities between sectors.

The intra-industry structure adopted in this chapter may be seen as a simplification of the KP. However it may propose useful policy recommendations when dealing with such an international scheme. In the following, the focus is on the negotiation phase, the special case of Russia and the prospective use of banking and borrowing.

---

[3]For a distinction between the permits market and industry structure imperfections, see Sartzetakis (1997; 2004).
[4]Namely, the exhaustion and terminal conditions.

2.1.1 Negotiation Phase

Since no historical data is available on the cost of carbon emission reductions, it may prove particularly difficult to induce a cost-effective allocation of the initial quotas to participating countries. In the context of the KP, the case of countries supplied with allocations in excess of their actual needs has been coined as *Hot Air* in the literature.[5] The distribution of a large number of permits to the Former Soviet Union (FSU) and Eastern European countries (with Russia and the Ukraine accounting for two thirds) may indeed be seen as an imperfection of the KP, as those countries were given generous allocations to foster agreement during the first phase (2008–2012). Market power concerns arise as industrial companies may benefit from the gap between the allocation of their initial permits (based on 1990 production levels) and their real emission needs in 2008 (after a period of recession), and the use of these permit surpluses remains unclear. If a pure monopoly emerges, a single seller may price its output at a higher level than its marginal cost of production. Under international emissions trading, the case of relatively large buyers or cartels exerting market power sounds more relevant.[6]

This situation emerged as a conflict between the internal and the external consistency of the permits market:

- The *internal* consistency refers to the situation where agents freely receive or bid for permits according to their real needs. The regulator may be interested however in distributing more permits to a country than is strictly needed (according to business as usual emissions or a benchmark for instance) in order to ensure participation in the permits market.[7] As a consequence, one agent may achieve a dominant position, which in turn threatens the efficiency of the permits market itself.
- The *external* consistency of the permits market is linked to the broader debate of climate change as the purchase of a "global public good."[8] This altruistic view embodies the notions of "Burden Sharing" or "common but differentiated responsibilities"[9] attached to the KP, whereby developed countries agree to spend a higher share of their income on fighting climate change compared to developing countries.[10]

---

[5] See Baron (1999), Burniaux (1999), Bernard et al. (2003), Bohringer and Loschel (2003), Holtsmark (2003).

[6] One could symmetrically evoke the case of monopsony power whereby large buyers would lower the permit price from its level under perfect competition. Outlooks for the KP however do not match this perspective. Indeed, market power is likely to come from sellers than from buyers.

[7] This kind of negotiation with Russia was a determining factor for the KP to come into force on February 16, 2005.

[8] See Guesnerie (2006).

[9] See Muller (2002).

[10] Note that the implicit assumptions of the existence of such an Environmental Kuznets Curve (the environment is a superior good and environmental regulation becomes stricter through time at higher levels of GDP per capita) has been left out of the debate.

These conflicting views undermine the negotiation of the cap, which is fixed at a suboptimal level compared to what would be needed to minimize the total damage to the environment. GHG emission targets under the KP represent a mere 5% reduction below 1990 levels. Now, if early movers such as the EU countries are willing to bring the cap down a gear, little progress can be achieved without the involvement of major players such as the USA, India and China. Thus, many difficulties arise in uncovering the "veil of uncertainty" that surrounds international negotiation.[11]

Uncertainty also affects the nature and the size of individual market participants. As Klepper and Peterson (2005) put it: "The Kyoto Protocol and its related decisions do not explicitly state who is actually supposed to be trading. Probably we will observe both government and firm trading. Under the former, market power might indeed become a relevant issue." Therefore, the risk of market power is higher if governments are trading large amounts of permits in a centralized manner.

The fact that the creation of a permits market gives some countries the opportunity to draw a financial advantage without any direct environmental gain (i.e., in the absence of effective emissions abatement) may be puzzling. Yet as stated by Maeda (2003), "[this debate] seems misguided because it focuses on the political importance of the issue, rather than addressing it from an economic perspective." For this reason I will investigate in this chapter how permit price manipulation strategies may incur additional economic costs to achieve the same level of abatement as under perfect competition.

Overall, the hypothesis that generous allocations that broaden the scope of a cap-and-trade program might also elicit dominant positions shall not be neglected. This leads me to comment on the case of Russia in more detail.

2.1.2 Will Russia Be a Net Seller of Permits?

Russia seems to provide the best example for investigating potential market power within the KP according to Korppoo et al. (2006): "Given the collapse of its emissions in the course of its economic transition, Russia is the country with by far the largest potential surplus of emission allowances for sale under the Kyoto international trading mechanisms. It is also generally considered to be the country with the greatest potential for continuing emission-reducing improvements in energy efficiency. Indeed, in the first commitment period under the Kyoto Protocol it could be described as the Saudi Arabia of the emerging carbon market, with the potential to try to manipulate the market through strategic decisions as to when and how it releases it surplus – if there are buyers willing to deal."

Empirical evidence gathered by Grubb (2004), Liski and Montero (2005a)[12] and Korppoo et al. (2006) suggested that Russia would be a net seller of allowances during the first phase of the KP. Different projections for Russian CO_2 emissions and surplus are provided in Tables 1 and 2.

---

[11]See Kolstad (2005).
[12]Based on the MIT-EPPA database that aggregates FSU countries.

Table 1 A survey of projections for Russian carbon dioxide emissions Adapted from Decaux and Ellerman 1998; Loschel and Zhang 2002; Korppoo et al. 2006)

Source	Year of estimate	Percentage of 1990 levels	Period
Decaux and Ellerman[a]	1998	73	2010
Russian energy strategy	2000	76–93	2012
Loschel and Zhang[b]	2002	83.6	2010
IEA[c] World Energy Outlook	2004	72	2008–2012
CEPA[d]	2004	75	2008–2012

[a]Scenario with Annex B Trading
[b]Scenario assuming trading without the United States
[c]International Energy Agency
[d]Cambridge Economic Policy Associates. Scenario with a 2% energy intensity reduction

Table 2 A survey of projections for Russia's surplus under the KP (Adapted from Decaux and Ellerman 1998; Loschel and Zhang 2002; Korppoo et al. 2006)

Source	Year of estimate	Size of the surplus[a]	Period
Decaux and Ellerman	1998	111[b]	2010
Loschel and Zhang[c]	2002	157.8	2010
Russian Ministry of Economic Development and Trade[d]	2003	408–545	2008–2012
Russian forecast to the UNFCCC[e]	2003	456–913	2008–2012
CEPA[f]	2004	400	2008–2012
Klepper and Peterson	2005	410	2010
Bohringer et al.	2006	246[g]	2008–2012

[a]In million tonnes of carbon equivalent (Mt Ce)
[b]Mt CO_2
[c]Scenario assuming trading without the United States
[d]Adapted from Korppoo et al. (2006)
[e]United Nations framework convention on climate change
[f]Cambridge Economic Policy Associates. Scenario with a 2% energy intensity reduction
[g]Mt CO_2

The key finding in Table 1 is that under all scenarios Russia would meet its Kyoto targets, as its CO_2 emissions projections consistently achieve levels well below its 1990 levels. The room for interpreting Table 2 is limited by the wide variation in surplus estimates with the lowest value of 111 Mt CO_2 found by Decaux and Ellerman (1998) and, as expressed above, by the current absence of clearly defined international trading rules to monetize such a surplus.

Further projections regarding Russia's own energy demand after the first period of the KP, are needed to determine whether or not Russian industrial companies might actually benefit from their *Hot Air*. Besides, the way in which *Hot Air* is dealt with also requires some consideration about a potential "leakage"[13] of emissions to

---

[13]As documented by Decaux and Ellerman (1998), the net effect of potential market power associated with Hot Air depends on the compensating emissions that might "leak" to regions unconstrained by the KP.

other regions that are not covered by the KP and additional allowances from the Clean Development Mechanism or Joint Implementation[14] that might compete with Russian allowances.[15]

2.1.3 Prospective Use of Banking and Borrowing in the KP

This section offers a description of the possible use of banking borrowing in the KP. On the one hand, provisions on banking are explained by Klepper and Peterson (2005): "Assigned Amount Units (AAUs) resulting from the Kyoto commitment can be banked without a time constraint. Credits from Joint Implementation (JI) or Clean Development Mechanism (CDM) can be banked up to a limit of, respectively, 2.5% and 5% of a Party's initial assigned amount. Sink credits cannot be banked."

On the other hand, implicit provisions on borrowing may be found in the United Nations Framework Convention on Climate Change (UNFCCC 2000) report.[16] As explained by Newell et al. (2005): "International climate policy discussions have implicitly included borrowing within possible consequences for noncompliance under the Kyoto Protocol, through the payback of excess tons with a penalty (i.e., interest)." This penalty could be fixed at 40% of additional emissions reduction for the next period of the Kyoto Protocol despite uncertainties regarding the enforcement of this particular provision. This question has been addressed in detail by Alberola and Chevallier (2009).

2.2 *The European Union Emissions Trading Scheme*

The European Union Emissions Trading Scheme (EU ETS) was launched on January 1, 2005 to reduce CO_2 emissions in the European Union by 8% by 2012, compared to 1990 emissions levels. The introduction of a tradable permits market was decided upon to help Member States achieve their targets for the Kyoto Protocol.

In the following, I comment on two critical aspects of the EU ETS. Firstly, I deal with possible design flaws in the allocation of permits that might pave the way for dominant positions during the first phase and secondly, I provide an overview of the prospective use of banking and borrowing.

---

[14]Conservative estimates range from a lower bound of 800 Mt CO_2 according to UKERC (2006) to an upper bound of 1,000 Mt CO_2 according to Point Carbon.

[15]As Baron (1999) put it, trading based on projects may reduce the risk of market power or shift it to other regions, which already host a large number of CDM projects such as China.

[16]UNFCCC (2000).

2.2.1 Over-Allocation or Relative Success?

The EU ETS imposes gentle constraints on emissions (8% reduction for EU-15) so as to start with a low carbon price. However the debate has now shifted towards a possible over-allocation of permits during the first phase. The production decisions of private actors are under scrutiny: do permit surpluses constitute a relative success (i.e., have companies reduced their emissions above projected levels?) or do they reflect an imperfection in the design of the system?

The CO_2 emissions reduction target of each Member State has been converted into a National Allocation Plans (NAP). Each government is in charge of deciding the amount of quotas available for trading, after negotiating with industrial companies, and after validation from the European Commission. The role of the Environment DG is central in this scheme in order to harmonize NAPs among Member States, and to recommend stricter validation criteria for NAPs. The NAPs that are submitted may be rejected by the European Commission, and sent back to Member States for revision before a final decision is granted. The sum of NAPs determines the number of quotas distributed to installations in the EU ETS.

Between 2005 and 2007, 2.2 billion allowances per year were distributed. Between 2008 and 2012, 2.08 billion allowances per year will be distributed, corresponding to a more restrictive allocation, given some changes in the scope of the market with the inclusion of new Member States.

Figure 1 represents the share of 2005 European Union Allowance Units (EUAs in million metric tons of CO_2 equivalent) among countries, where Germany, Poland, Italy, the UK and Spain stand out as the most important actors by accounting for about two thirds of the total allowances. Data is taken from CDC (2006)[17] and the *Community Independent Transaction Log* (CITL) administered by the European Commission.[18]

Figure 2 represents the share of quotas (in million metric tons of CO_2 equivalent) between Member States over the commitment period from 2008 to 2012. Germany, Poland, Italy, the UK and Spain make up for around two thirds of the allowances distributed.

While it is not our goal to comment on the structure of the European carbon market here, it is however interesting to look at the possible surplus with which those countries were endowed.

Figure 3 portrays the emissions reported for 2005 and, if any, the size of the surplus. The sum of the two bars is equivalent to the 2005 allocation of permits for a given country. Its main finding lies in the fact that most countries seemed to favor

---

[17] Tendances Carbone is published by the Caisse des Depots, and is available at: www.caissedesdepots.fr

[18] Available at http://ec.europa.eu/environment/ets

Intertemporal Emissions Trading and Market Power

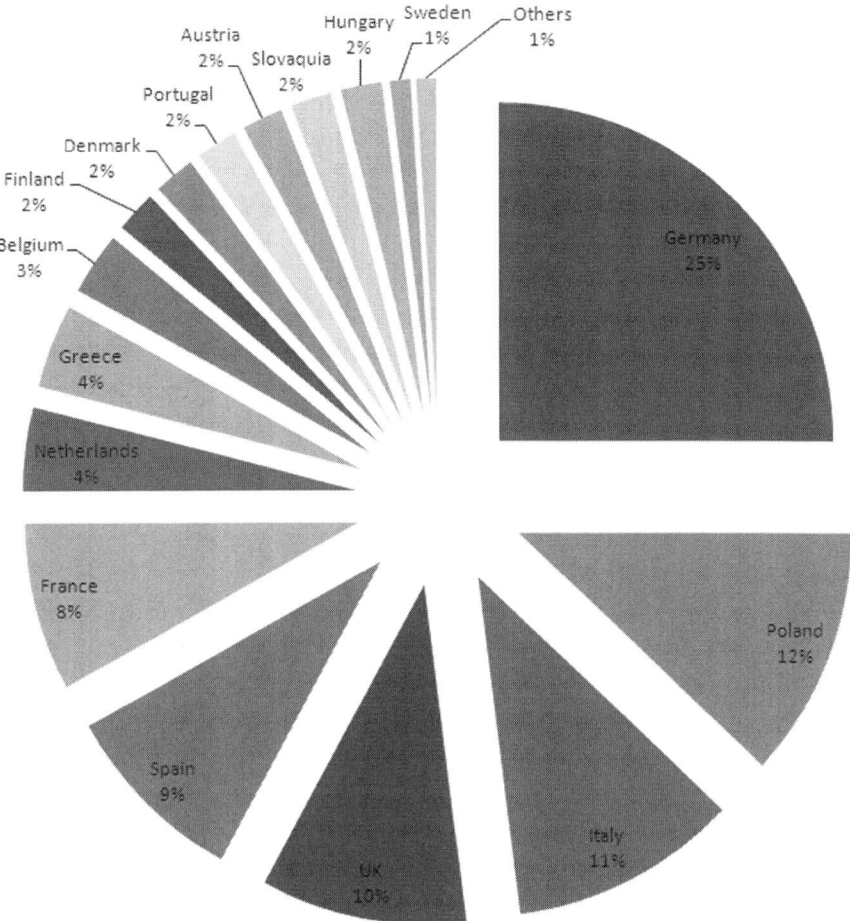

Fig. 1 EU ETS national allocation lans – phase 1 (2005–2007) (CITL 2007; CDC 2006)

generous allocations during the first phase of the EU ETS.[19] Surpluses also reflect to a limited degree reserves for new entrants, which are included in the data used.

Figure 4 takes a closer look at the allowance surpluses as a percentage of the allocation. It reflects a wide variety of cases among market participants as a conglomeration of countries (Poland, France, Finland, Denmark, Slovakia,

---

[19]Apart from the EU ETS, there is a need to be cautious here with the notions of "over allocating" and conversely "under-allocating" permits depending on the country. Their meaning depends on the reference point (business as usual plus some abatement for instance). If other trading schemes implement a per capita distribution for instance, it may appear less relevant to talk about "over allocation."

Fig. 2 EU ETS national allocation plans – phase II (2008–2012) (CITL 2008; CDC 2008)

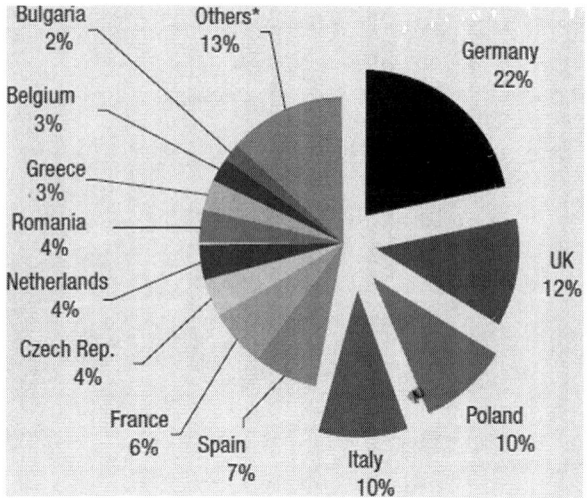

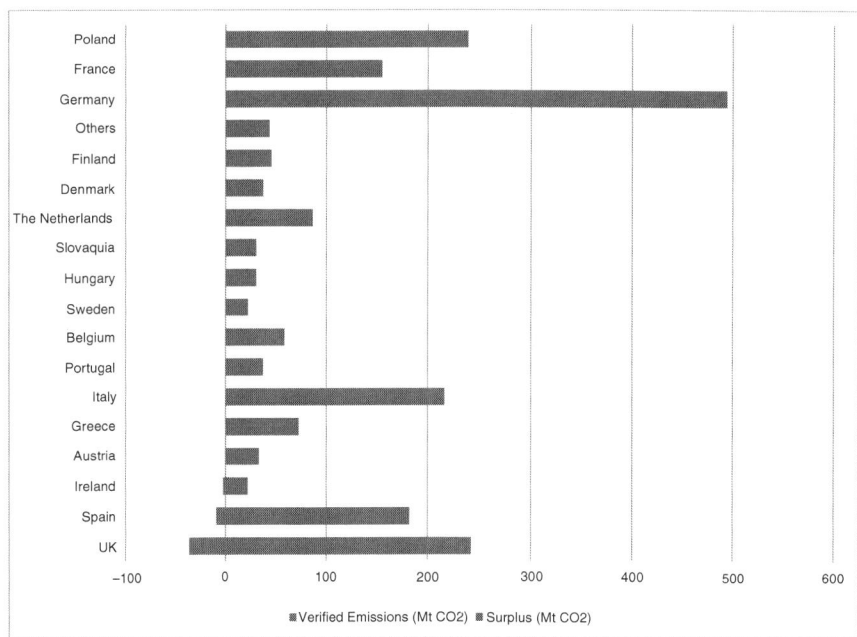

Fig. 3 Potential for market power by country (in absolute terms) (CITL 2007; CDC 2006)

Hungary) was able to build up a surplus of permits of more than 15%, while others (the UK, Ireland) are more than 15% short of permits.

The biggest player, Germany does not appear to be in a position to exert its market power with less than 5% of excess allowances. Poland's surplus should not

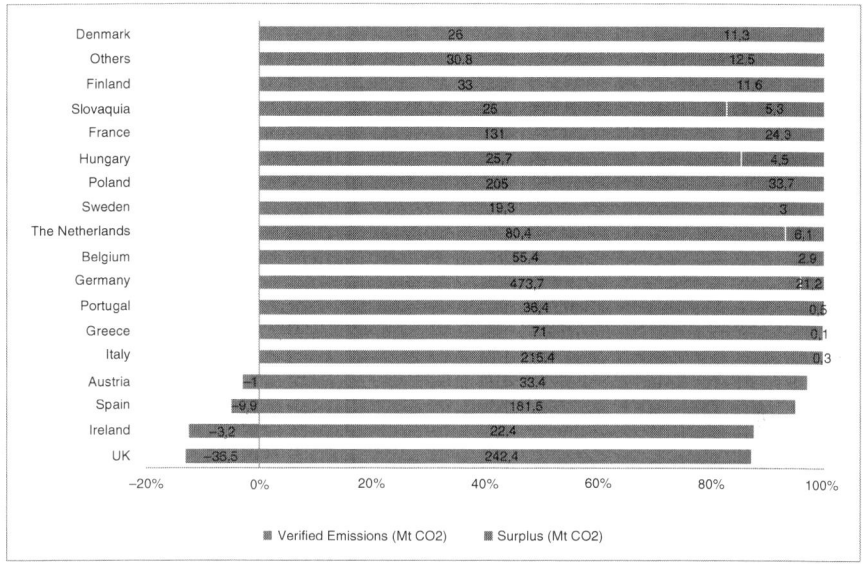

Fig. 4 Potential for market power by country (in percentage) (CITL 2007; CDC 2006)

be overstated either since the use of 10% of allowances is missing in the CITL. Portugal, Greece, Italy and Austria form a group of countries where the regulator strived to allocate permits optimally. On the contrary, stricter emissions reductions were enforced in the case of the UK, Ireland and Spain.

How could one explain those contrasting patterns in actual emissions for EU ETS participants in 2005? Part of the answer may be found in the decision making process within each National Allocation Plan (NAP). Godard (2003; 2005) describe the logic behind the French NAP when allocating shares of recent emissions baselines: non-electric utilities were supplied with their projected need for permits, while greater constraints were imposed upon electric utilities. This situation may be justified by the perceived abatement potential of the electricity industry, but overall reveals the necessary arbitrages to be made due to sector heterogeneity and a stringent cap.

As long as governments continue to allocate allowances to existing facilities based on historic emissions, the scheme will be flawed by a contrary "updating" incentive (Grubb and Neuhoff 2006). Indeed companies have no incentive to implement abatement technologies too early since higher emissions today will be rewarded with bigger allocations in future periods. Ellerman and Buchner (2008) provide a first empirical assessment of the EU ETS allocation process based on emissions data from 2005. They estimate a slight over-allocation of 4% during the first period of allocation, although there are strong signs that some emissions abatement measures have occurred. The analysis is not straightforward however since "a long position is not per se evidence of over-allocation." The difference between the 2005 allocation and verified emissions suggests that too many allowances were allocated, but the benchmark from which this conclusion is derived may be biased due to insufficient data reporting on emissions before 2005 and a lack of comparability measures at the EU-level. Companies may also be long because of differences in marginal abatement costs (MACs) or in expectations (regarding economic activity, energy prices, etc.) under uncertainty.

Overall, we can state that in the period from 2005 to 2007, the allowances that were allocated more than covered the verified emissions, with a net cumulated surplus of 156 million tons. This surplus however decreased from 83 million tons in 2005 to 37 million tons in 2006, and finally to 36 million tons in 2007. Emissions increased by 0.4% in 2007 compared to 2006, and reached 2,043 million tons compared to the 2,080 million allowances that were distributed.

Market power positions in the EU ETS should not solely be derived from analyses at the country level, but rather in conjunction with analyses at the installation level. For French installations subject to the Directive 2003/87/CE, an estimation based on 1,402 installations totaling 185.3 Mt CO_2 taken from the Register for Polluting Emissions (iREP)[20] revealed that almost 50% of permits were distributed to four players, with the first ten holders of permits accounting for 60% of permits accounting for the total allocation of permits.

Furthermore, Convery et al. (2008) point out a strong concentration of EU ETS installations, with 10% of 4,019 installations in surplus representing 75% of the total surplus (totaling 145 Mt) and 2% of installations representing 2% of the surplus.[21] Each of these big players might exert a dominant position in its own sector if permits are distributed freely based on recent emissions, as modeled in this chapter.

2.2.2 Prospective Use of Banking and Borrowing in the EU ETS

Member states have allowed banking and borrowing without restrictions within each compliance period. However, the possibility to carry over EUAs from the 2005–2007 period to the 2008–2012 period was restricted, even by France and Poland who allowed it to a certain extent in the first place.[22] A more detailed analysis of the consequences of banning banking from one period to another on the price of permits and the behavior of companies can be found in Alberola and Chevallier (2009). Moreover, preliminary analyses of the 2005–2007 data concerning the extent of the use of banking in the EU ETS can be found in Ellerman and Trotignon (2008) and Chevallier et al. (2008).

---

[20]The iREP is monitored by the Minister of the Environment and displays public information at www.pollutionsindustrielles.ecologie.gouv.fr/IREP/index.php

[21]Note however that Convery and Redmond (2007) compute a very low Herfindahl–Hirschman Index for the electricity-generating sector, which indicates an unconcentrated market. Thus, market observers are overall less wary of market power concerns in the EU ETS than in the KP, even if the Directive explicitly allows installations to "pool" allowances at the sector level.

[22]Permits that were bought cannot be banked. Besides, only "green" companies that have effectively reduced emissions may bank allowances in Poland.

This section provided an overview of two major markets for tradable permits along with their allocation methodology. It revealed a wide range of opportunities for strategic behavior in the design of international permit trading regimes. The presence of countries with large holdings of permits increases the probability of price manipulation and the risk of lower efficiency in the allocation of abatement efforts between countries. This background information is used as the basis for modeling a differential game with hierarchical play in this chapter.

3 The Model

This section outlines the features of the model. Firstly, the design of the cap-and-trade program is explained. Secondly, the industry and information structures are examined. Thirdly, an intertemporal constraint to emissions trading is defined and fourthly, the Hotelling conditions are described. Finally, the properties of the abatement cost function are explained.

3.1 Design of the Cap-and-Trade Program

The regulator sets a cap $\overline{E}$ on emissions of a given pollutant that corresponds to a specific environmental goal. The fix endowment is therefore exogenous to the model, and may be broken down into the individual allocation of permits $\overline{e}_i$ mandatory for each agent i.

Agents are split further into two types:

1. Agent $\{i = 1\}$ is a large polluting agent, who is initially allocated a large number of permits;
2. Agents $\{i = 2, \ldots, N\}$ aggregate many small polluting agents, who are assumed to be comparatively smaller holders of permits, belonging to the competitive fringe.

An agent may be a country, a company or a cartel.[23] The competitive market price is determined by the abatement costs of the fringe agents.

Market imperfection arises from the distribution of free permits on the basis of recent emissions.[24] The premise of the chapter is that the large agent may be able to

---

[23]For instance, within the KP permits may be exchanged from party-to-party, but also from company-to-company if Annex B members delegate this ability to private actors. In the third case, collusive behavior may arise either between parties or between companies (Liski and Montero 2005b).

[24]See Ellerman and Parsons (2006) for a review concerning the use of projections, benchmarking and intensity targets. While it is beyond the scope of this chapter to study the relative merits of grandfathering and auctioning, theoretical analyses stress the superiority of auctioning as in Jouvet et al. (2005). According to the Public Choice Theory, the free allocation of permits may also be seen by some companies as a means to extract more permits as a scarcity rent, and therefore lobbying takes place. However it also imposes liabilities on companies that are reflected in their

exert market power. I do not include the effects of incorporating a safety valve[25] into the model.

3.2 Industry Structure

This partial equilibrium model features an intra-industry permit market in a single good economy. I tend to neglect the interaction with the output market.

Market power is defined by Burniaux (1999) as "the capacity of a firm/country to influence the transaction price of traded permits" (referred to as a "cost minimizing manipulation"). Therefore, I do not address exclusionary manipulation strategies[26] that occur when the dominant agent uses its market power on the permits market to raise entry barriers or exclude agents on the output market.

3.3 Information Structure

A differential game[27] played in continuous time was modeled where all players have the possibility of influencing the rate of change of the permits bank through their current actions. It is therefore assumed that they adopt a Markovian strategy.

The common knowledge includes the fact that all players need to comply with the environmental constraint that is exogenously set by the regulator. The game unfolds in two steps. Firstly, the follower's reaction function is derived from any action announced by the leader through the fringe agents' cost minimization problem at the competitive price. Secondly, it is observed how the leader might exercise market power as a large agent integrates the reaction function into his own cost minimization problem, and decides how to adjust his emissions level. All other parameters are kept constant.[28]

---

balance sheets. As highlighted by Raymond (1996), the initial allocation of permits reveals social norms embedded by newly created permits. The free distribution of permits may be seen as an entitlement to an environmental resource. As conceptions evolve and auctioning might become predominant, the question arises as to whether the probability of achieving a dominant position will increase or decrease.

[25]A safety valve may be defined as a hybrid instrument to limit the cost of capping emissions at a certain target level, whereby the regulator offers to sell permits in whatever quantity at a pre-determined price.

[26]See Misiolek and Elder (1989).

[27]See Dockner et al. (2000) for an overview of differential games.

[28]For instance, agents do not incur information costs.

3.4 Intertemporal Emissions Trading

Agents may bank and borrow permits without restrictions. Let $B_i(t)$ be the permits bank, with $B_i(t) > 0$ in case of banking, and $B_i(t) < 0$ in case of borrowing.

Any change in the permits bank is equal to the difference between $\overline{e_i}(t)$ and $e_i(t)$, respectively an agent's i permit allocation and his emission level at time t. The banking and borrowing constraint may be written as

$$\dot{B}_i(t) = \overline{e_i}(t) - e_i(t) \tag{1}$$

with $B_i(0) = 0$ as an initial condition.

3.5 Hotelling Conditions

Notwithstanding differences between a permit and an exhaustible resource,[29] it is assumed in the literature that the Hotelling conditions for exhaustible resources must apply on a permits market. Consequently, the terminal and exhaustion conditions are detailed below.

3.5.1 Terminal Condition

Let [0, T] be the continuous time planning horizon.[30] At time T, cumulated emissions must be equal to the sum of each agent's depollution objective and therefore to the global cap $\overline{E}$ set by the regulator[31]:

---

[29] According to Liski and Montero (2006), the following differences may be highlighted. First, in a permits market with banking, the market still remains after the permits bank has been exhausted; while the market of a non-renewable resource vanishes after the last unit of extraction. Secondly, permits extraction and storage costs are equal to zero; while those costs are generally positive for a non-renewable resource. Thirdly, the demand for an extra permit usually comes from the demand derived from other companies that also hold permits; while the demand for an extra unit of a non-renewable resource more often comes from a demand derived from another actor (e.g., a consumer).

[30] This planning period seems appropriate for a theoretical study of intertemporal emissions trading. Alternative time settings including distinct phases may be found in Montero and Ellerman (1998), Schennach (2000) or Ellerman and Montero (2002), but they reflect the specific requirements of the Acid Rain Program (USA).

[31] See also Leiby and Rubin (2001).

$$\int_0^T \sum_{i=1}^N e_i(t)dt = \sum_{i=1}^N \overline{e_i} = \overline{E} \qquad (2)$$

3.5.2 Exhaustion Condition

At time T, there is no more permit in the bank (either stocked or borrowed):

$$\sum_{i=1}^N B_i(T) = 0 \qquad (3)$$

These conditions ensure that agents gradually meet their depollution objective so that the marginal cost of depollution is equalized at the current value over the time period, and the permit bank is cleared in the end.

There is typically a truncation problem at the end of the period:

- if $B_i(T) > 0$, surplus allowances are worthless and agents waste their permits;
- if $B_i(T) < 0$, agents need to pay a penalty.[32]

3.6 Abatement Cost Function

Let $C_i[e_i(t)]$ be the abatement cost function[33] incurred by agent i in order to comply with his allocation of permits $\overline{e_i}$. $C_i[e_i(t)]$ is defined on $\Re \to \Re$ continuously and is of class $C^2[0, T]$, i.e. twice continuously differentiable. The classical assumption[34] of strictly increasing abatement costs leads to $C_i[e_i(t)]$ being convex, with $C_i'[e_i(t)] < 0$ and $C_i''[e_i(t)] > 0$. $C_i[e_i(0)]$ can be set to 0.

An agent's i MACs are associated with a one-unit reduction from his emission level e_i at time t, and are noted as $-C_i'[e_i(t)] > 0$. At the equilibrium of a permits market in a static framework,[35] price-taking agents adjust emissions until the aggregated MAC is equal to the price P at time t:

---

[32]For instance, the penalty is equal to 40€ and 100€ per unit plus a compensating allowance for the first two periods of the EU ETS, and can add up to 40% of additional emissions during the first period of the Kyoto Protocol.

[33]Compared to a situation where profits are unconstrained, abatement costs are introduced in order to meet the emission cap.

[34]Stated first by Montgomery (1972). The conditions given by Leiby and Rubin (2001) include the output $q(t)$ where $C_i[q_i(t), e_i(t), t]$ is strongly convex with $C_i'[q_i(t)] > 0$ and $C_i''[q_i(t)] > 0$. Properties of non-convex abatement cost functions may be found in Godby (2000).

[35]See Hahn (1984).

$$P_t = -C'_i[e_i(t)] \tag{4}$$

4 The Stackelberg Game

In what follows, the dominant agent sets the price at a level, which corresponds to the maximization of the difference between revenues from the sale of permits and its abatement costs. All other agents behave as price takers, i.e. they minimize their abatement and trading costs given the permit price set by the dominant agent. It is interesting here to evaluate how the dominant agent will set the permit price higher and abate less (or sell fewer permits) compared to the competitive solution. This differential game with hierarchical play is solved by backward induction.

4.1 The Fringe Agents' Reaction Function

The first step of the game is concerned with developing the strategy of the fringe. Fringe agents choose their optimal emissions level according to the possibility of banking and borrowing permits in constraint (1). The cost minimization program may be written as follows:

$$\begin{cases} \min\limits_{e_i} \int\limits_0^T e^{-rt} \{C_i[e_i(t)] + P(t)[e_i(t) - \overline{e_i}(t)]\} dt \\ \dot{B}_i(t) = \overline{e_i}(t) - e_i(t) \\ B_i(0) = 0 \\ C_i[e_i(0)] = 0 \end{cases}$$

Two possible forms of the fringe agents' reaction function $P_t = -C'_i[e_i(t)]$ and $P_t = -C'_i[e_i(t)] + \lambda(t)$ may be highlighted depending on the net banking/borrowing position of fringe agents at the end of the period. See Chevallier (2008) for the formal resolution of this optimization program.

In the next step the large agent's behavior is incorporated and how he integrates the two possible cases of reaction function into his own optimization program.

4.2 Behavior of the Dominant Agent

In the second step of the game, the first-order conditions of the fringe problem are used as the constraints in the leader's problem. The large agent strategically adjusts his optimal emissions levels according to its initial allocation $\overline{e_1}$ as expressed by (2) and the banking borrowing constraint (1). The cost minimization program for agent $\{i = 1\}$ is

$$\begin{cases} \min\limits_{e_1} \int_0^T e^{-rt}\{C_1[e_1(t)] + P_t[e_1(t) - \overline{e_1}(t)]\}dt \\ \dot{B}_1(t) = \overline{e_1}(t) - e_1(t) \\ \overline{E} = \int_0^T e_1(t)dt + \int_0^T \sum_{i=2}^N e_i(t)dt \\ B_1(0) = 0 \\ C_1(0) = 0 \end{cases}$$

By replacing P_t with both forms of the fringe agents' reaction function as shown above, it is possible to identify the following price distortion condition[36]:

$$-C_1'[e_1(t)] = P(t) + \left[1 + \varepsilon_i \sum_{i=2}^N e_i(t)\right] \quad (5)$$

The large agent's MAC is equal to the competitive permits price plus an element of price distortion ε_i defined as the fringe agents' elasticity:

$$\varepsilon_i = \frac{C_i''(e_i)}{C_i'(e_i)} = \frac{dC_i'}{dC_i} \quad (6)$$

Thus, a manipulation of the price of permits results in higher total abatement costs than under perfect competition. Market power is a function of the fringe agents' elasticity and of the large agent's number of permits:

$$\varepsilon_i = \sum_{i=2}^N e_i(t) = \varepsilon_i[e_1(t) - \overline{e_1}(t)] \quad (7)$$

Due to the convexity assumption, the fringe agents' elasticity is negative, and emphasizes the possibility for the leader to negatively affect the fringe agents' behavior. The large agent's MAC is *lower* than under perfect competition. Since he enjoys a dominant position and has the ability to influence the price of permits, the large agent may be characterized overall as a net gainer and the fringe agents as net losers.

In either case where both agents have a net banking or borrowing position in the terminal period, the large agent is able to negatively affect the fringe agent's MAC through the number of permits he holds in excess of his emissions. This condition holds when both agents clear their permits bank in the terminal period, whereby

---

[36]See Chevallier (2008) for the formal resolution.

the large agent is still able to negatively affect the fringe agent's MAC. One can therefore confirm the possibility of strategic manipulation for both forms of the fringe agents' reaction function.

In the next section, numerical simulations are provided to illustrate these results.

5 Numerical Simulations

This section attempts to provide quantitative estimates of the degree of price distortions induced by dominant behavior on existing emissions trading schemes. More precisely, data on MAC curves is used provided by Decaux and Ellerman (1998) using the MIT EPPA model, and Loschel and Zhang (2002) using the world energy system model POLES (Criqui et al. 1996) to simulate the effect of a price distortion condition as shown individually in (5)–(7).

On the one hand, the MAC cost curves given by Decaux and Ellerman (1998) have the following functional form:

$$Y = \alpha X^2 + \beta X \qquad (8)$$

where Y is the marginal cost of carbon in 1985 in US\$, X is the extent of abatement in million metric tons of carbon (Mton), and where α and β are parameters.

On the other hand, Loschel and Zhang (2002) kept the following specification:

$$Y = \alpha(X)^\beta \qquad (9)$$

where Y is the MAC, X is the amount of abatement, and where α and β are parameters.

Several scenarios may be used in order to derive numerical estimates of the market power condition. In what follows, a situation is simulated where Foreign Soviet Union countries form a cartel, and attempt to distort the prices based on the *Hot Air* created by the political market imperfection at the negotiation stage of the Kyoto Protocol.

The values given for all parameters are displayed in Tables 3 and 4. Plugging these values into the price distortion condition (5), the following results are obtained:

From Tables 3 and 4, quantitative estimates are obtained on the degree of price distortions induced by the Stackelberg game. It is indeed striking to observe that, based on data provided by Decaux and Ellerman (1998), price distortions and efficiency losses based on the fringe agents' elasticities and the large agent's permit endowment range from 13% to 35% in the context of the *Hot Air* discussion underlying the Kyoto Protocol. These estimates are even wider when based on the data from Loschel and Zhang (2002), ranging from 33% to 229%. Notwithstanding the presence of outliers in our numerical simulations, these results globally illustrate the risk of market power and associated economic inefficiencies due to the initial allocation of emission rights, as pointed out by Hahn (1984).

Table 3 Simulated price distortions based on data provided by Decaux and Ellerman (1998) (Adapted from Decaux and Ellerman 1998)

Country	α	β	X	MAC'/MAC	$e_i - \bar{e}_i$	P_t	Price distortion (%)
USA	0.0005	0.0398	571	0.0033	571	127	−7.23
JAP	0.0155	1.8160	144	0.0108	144	127	−23.70
EU	0.0024	0.1503	308	0.0059	308	127	−13.08
OECD	0.0085	−0.0986	171	0.0121	171	127	−26.67
EUC	0.0079	0.0486	122	0.0160	122	127	−35.20
FSU	0.0023	0.0042	−110	−0.0183	−110	127	

The price distortion is computed using (5)–(7) *USA* United States, *JAP* Japan, *EU* European Union, *OECD* member countries of the organisation for economic co-operation and development, *EUC* Eastern European countries, *FSU* Foreign Soviet Union countries

Table 4 Simulated price distortions based on data provided by Loschel and Zhang (2002) (Adapted from Loschel and Zhang 2002)

Country	α	β	X	MAC'/MAC	$e_i - \bar{e}_i$	P_t	Price distortion (%)
AUN	0.6750	1.4420	24	0.0601	15.6	65.9	−150.93
JAP	0.7180	1.3380	29.3	0.0457	18.5	65.9	−114.71
EU	0.1140	1.3690	104.1	0.0132	66.4	65.9	−33.03
CAN	1.5670	1.3790	15.1	0.0913	9.6	65.9	−229.41
FSU	0.0460	1.4820	−125.6	−0.0118	−125.6	65.9	

The price distortion is computed using (5)–(7) *AUN* Australia and New Zealand, *JAP* Japan, *EU* European Union, *CAN* Canada, *FSU* Foreign Soviet Union countries

However, the specter of a large agent achieving a market power position may be averted by a careful design of the cap-and-trade program. As illustrated by the ongoing debate on the EU ETS NAPs, there is a need for further research to assess the best solution for allocating permits efficiently (whether this be through output-based methods, benchmarking, minimum price auctioning, etc.).

6 Conclusion

The description of the institutional framework on which the model hinges provided a balanced picture of market power concerns in existing international emissions trading schemes. As for the Kyoto Protocol and trading rules in the making, projections preclude from reaching a definitive conclusion; however our analysis also reveals the possibility of moving an international permits market in a dynamic context. A global conclusion concerning EU ETS market power concerns gears towards a prudent approach: if some firms have received more permits than projected, they might very well end up with a shortage of permits at the end of the first period because of an increase in emissions. The EU Commission is particularly careful when validating NAPs for their stringency and the fact that there will be no *ex-post* adjustment. Still, there are strong signs of concentration at the installation level. Both schemes allow a full banking and borrowing intra-period.

To capture the distortions induced by initial allocation, a differential game was introduced where agents differ in terms of their exogenous permit endowment and a Markovian strategy was adopted. The main result consists in a price distortion condition based on the fringe agents' elasticity and the large agent's permits endowment that explains how the large agent is able to negatively affect the fringe agents' MACs. In both cases where agents either compensate their net banking/borrowing positions or clear their permits bank at the end of the period, it is possible to identify *net losers* (i.e., fringe agents) and a *net gainer* (i.e., the large agent) as the large agent benefits from a *lower* MAC than it would do under perfect competition.

Since the price set by the dominant agent directly depends upon the amount of permits initially allocated to that agent, this chapter contributes to the link between distributional aspects and the overall efficiency of tradable permit markets. It extends Hahn's analysis from Hahn (1984) on market power in a dynamic framework and builds upon Liski and Montero (2005b, 2006) by modeling strategic interactions after a Stackelberg game and providing a full characterization of the effects of unrestricted banking and borrowing. The numerical simulations computed for the price distortion condition based on data from Decaux and Ellerman (1998) and Loschel and Zhang (2002) provide a quantitative illustration of the results obtained. They also reveal the magnitude of the economic inefficiencies induced by the initial allocation of emission rights.

However, the spectre of market power need not arise if the cap-and-trade program appears properly designed. The negotiation process of each NAP at the Member State level is typically an example of a manipulable rule whereby industries may conduct lobbying activities to extract more permits as a monopoly rent. With reference to the debate "rules vs. discretion" in monetary economics, this unhealthy lobbying on behalf of major industries calls for further research to ascertain the conditions under which it would be optimal to delegate the determination of the cap and the distribution of permits to an independent agency (Helm et al. 2003; Grubb and Neuhoff 2006).

The model could be extended by the adoption of an intertemporal trading ratio specific to borrowing as discussed by Kling and Rubin (1997),[37] allowing for a better understanding of the possibilities presented by intertemporal emissions trading. It may also be interesting to look at another source of heterogeneity between agents, for instance based on their emissions reduction function.

As a final comment, one could say that a greater reliance on banking and limited borrowing (i.e., with a specific discounting factor) should be promoted to allow firms to smooth their emissions and make investment decisions on abatement technologies with a better capacity to react to the evolution of the carbon constraint over time.

---

[37]The adoption of a discount rate penalizing borrowing may remove some of the perverse incentives whereby agents concentrate emissions on early periods, which is not socially optimal.

References

Alberola E, Chevallier J (2009) European carbon prices and banking restrictions: evidence from phase I (2005–2007). Energy J 30(3):107–136

Baron R (1999) Market power and market access in international GHG emission trading. IEA information paper. International Energy Agency, Paris, France

Bernard A, Paltsev S, Reilly JM, Vielle M, Viguier L (2003) Russia's role in the Kyoto protocol. MIT joint program on the science of policy and global change, report number 98, Massachusetts Institute of Technology, Boston, USA

Bohringer C, Loschel A (2003) Market power and Hot Air in international emissions trading: the impact of the US withdrawal from the Kyoto protocol. Appl Econ 35(6):651–663

Burniaux J M (1999) How important is market power in achieving Kyoto? An assessment based on the GREEN model. OECD workshop on the "Economic Modelling of Climate Change" Organization for Economic Co-operation and Development, Paris, France

CDC (2006) Note d'étude de la Mission Climat de la Caisse des Dépôts. Number 8, Caisse des Depôts et Consignations, Paris, France

CDC (2008) Note d'étude de la Mission Climat de la Caisse des Dépôts. Number 20, Caisse des Depôts et Consignations, Paris, France

Chevallier J (2008) Strategic manipulation on emissions trading banking program with fixed horizon. Econ Bull 17(14):1–9

Chevallier J, Etner J, Jouvet PA (2008) Bankable pollution permits under uncertainty and optimal risk-management rules: theory and empirical evidence. Working paper EconomiX-CNRS 2008-25

CITL (2007) Community independent transaction log administered by the European Commission. http://ec.europa.eu/environment/ets, Accessed on June 2008

CITL (2008) Community independent transaction log administered by the European Commission. http://ec.europa.eu/environment/ets, Accessed on June 2008

Convery F, Redmond L (2007) Market and price developments in the European union emissions trading scheme. Rev Environ Econ Policy 1(1):88–111

Convery F, Ellerman D, de Perthuis C (2008) The European carbon market in action: lessons from the first trading period. Interim report. MIT-CEEPR, Mission Climat Caisse des Dépôts and UCD

Criqui P, Cattier F, Menanteau P, Quidoz M-C (1996) POLES 2.2. Reference Guide, Institute of Energy Policy and Economics, Grenoble, France

Decaux A, Ellerman D (1998) Analysis of post-Kyoto CO_2 emissions trading using marginal abatement curves. MIT EPPR, report number 40

Dockner E, Jorgensen S, Van Long N, Sorger G (2000) Differential games in economics and management science. Cambridge University Press, Cambridge

Ellerman D, Buchner B (2008) Over-allocation or abatement? A preliminary analysis of the EU ETS based on 2005 emissions data. Environ Resour Econ 41:267–287

Ellerman D, Montero J P (2002) The temporal efficiency of SO_2 emissions trading. CMI working paper 13, Cambridge MIT Institute

Ellerman D, Parsons J (2006) Shortage, inter-period pricing, and banking. Tendances Carbone 5, pages 1–4, Caisse des Dépôts et Consignations, Paris, France

Ellerman D, Trotignon R (2008) Compliance behavior in the EU ETS: cross border trading, banking and borrowing. MIT-CEEPR working paper 2008-12

Godard O (2003) L'allocation initiale des quotas d'émission de CO_2 aux entreprises à la lumière de l'analyse économique. Cahier, 2003(008). Chaire Developement Durable Ecole Polytechnique – EDF

Godard O (2005) Politique de l'effet de serre: une évaluation du plan francais de quotas de CO_2. Rev Fr d'Econ 19(4):147–186

Godby RW (2000) Market power and emissions trading: theory and laboratory results. Pac Econ Rev 5:349–363

Grubb M (2004) Russian energy and CO_2 emission prospects: evidence from domestic analyses and international comparisons. Briefing note. Royal Institute of International Affairs

Grubb M, Neuhoff K (2006) Allocation and competitiveness in the EU emissions trading scheme: policy overview. Clim Policy 6:7–30

Guesnerie R (2006) The design of post-Kyoto climate schemes: an introductory analytical assessment. Working paper 2006-11

Hahn RW (1984) Market power and transferable property rights. Q J Econ 99:753–765

Helm D, Hepburn C, Mash R (2003) Credible carbon policy. Oxford Rev Econ Policy 19(3):438–450

Holtsmark B (2003) Russian behaviour in the market for permits under the Kyoto protocol. Clim Policy 3:399–415

Jouvet PA, Michel P, Rotillon G (2005) Optimal growth with pollution: how to use pollution permits? J Econ Dyn Control 29:1597–1609

Klepper G, Peterson S (2005) Trading Hot Air. The influence of permit allocation rules, market power and the US withdrawal from the Kyoto protocol. Environ Resour Econ 32:205–227

Kling C, Rubin J (1997) Bankable permits for the control of environmental pollution. J Public Econ 64:101–115

Kolstad CD (2005) Piercing the veil of uncertainty in transboundary pollution agreements. Environ Resour Econ 31:21–34

Korppoo A, Karas J, Grubb M (2006) Russia and the Kyoto protocol: opportunities and challenges. Royal Institute Of International Affairs Edn, Chatham House, London

Leiby P, Rubin J (2001) Intertemporal permit trading for the control of greenhouse gas emissions. Environ Resour Econ 19:229–256

Liski M, Montero JP (2005a) Market power in a storable-good market: theory and applications to carbon and sulfur trading. MIT CEEPR

Liski M, Montero JP (2005b) A note on market power in an emissions permit market with banking. Environ Resour Econ 31(2):159–173

Liski M, Montero JP (2006) On pollution permit banking and market power. J Regul Econ 29(3):283–302

Loschel A, Zhang Z (2002) The economics and environmental implications of US repudiation of the Kyoto protocol and the subsequent deals in Bonn and Marrakech. FEEM Nota Di Lavoro 23.2002

Maeda A (2003) The emergence of market power in emission rights markets: the role of initial permit distribution. J Regul Econ 24(3):293–314

Misiolek WS, Elder HW (1989) Exclusionary manipulation of markets for pollution rights. J Environ Econ Manage 16:156–166

Montero JP, Ellerman AD (1998) Explaining low sulfur dioxide allowance prices: the effect of expectation errors and irreversibility. MIT CEEPR, 98011

Montgomery WD (1972) Markets in licenses and efficient pollution control programs. J Econ Theory 5:395–418

Muller B (2002) Equity in climate change: the great divide. Working paper number EV31, Oxford Institute for Energy Studies

Newell R, Pizer W, Zhang J (2005) Managing permit markets to stabilize prices. Environ Resour Econ 31:133–157

Petrakis E, Xepapadeas A (2003) Location decisions of a polluting firm and the time consistency of environmental policy. Resour Energy Econ 25(2):197–214

Raymond L (1996) Private rights in public resources: equity and property allocation in market-based environmental policy. Resources for the Future

Rubin J (1996) A model of intertemporal emission trading, banking, and borrowing. J Environ Econ Manage 31:269–286

Sartzetakis ES (1997) Tradeable emission permits regulations in the presence of imperfectly competitive product markets: welfare implications. Environ Resour Econ 9:65–81

Sartzetakis ES (2004) On the efficiency of competitive markets for emission permits. Environ Resour Econ 27:01–19
Schennach SM (2000) The economics of pollution permit banking in the context of title IV of the 1990 Clean Air Act Amendments. J Environ Econ Manage 40:189–210
UKERC (2006) Implementing Kyoto – does it all add up? UK energy research centre workshop report, University of Oxford
UNFCCC (2000) Procedures and mechanisms relating to compliance under the Kyoto protocol: note by the co-Chairmen of the joint working group on compliance, Bonn

International Emissions Trading: A Pricing Model Based on System Dynamical Simulations

Bo Hu and Stefan Pickl

Abstract According to our System Dynamics model for international emissions trading the price of permits differs strongly between different countries as a function of national economic structure. A fair international emissions trading can only be conducted with the use of protective duties. A comparatively high price which evokes emission reduction inevitably has an inhibiting effect on economic growth.

Keywords Ecological economics • Emissions trading • System dynamics modeling

1 Introduction

Reducing greenhouse gas emissions is one of the global challenges of environmental protection which is one of the common goals of the international community alongside overcoming poverty and promoting development (see, e.g., UN Public Information 2008). However, it is difficult to achieve such goals without causing conflicts between them. Not only developing countries but also some developed countries like the United States are anxious that a strict environmental standard might substantially slow down economic growth. As a result, the Kyoto Protocol (UNFCCC 2009) which came into effect in 2005 does allow increasing CO_2 emissions for some signatory countries. Furthermore, many other countries ("Non-Annex I parties") are almost completely exempt from the original "Cap-and-Trade" principle, whereby no emission limits have been defined for these countries at all. At the same time it is possible for them to take part in global emission permits trading. This "inconsistent" regulation, at least from the point of view of the USA, is considered to be one of the main reasons for the USA not signing the Kyoto Protocol (see Byrd and Hagel 1997).

B. Hu (✉) • S. Pickl
Universität der Bundeswehr München, D-85577 Neubiberg, Germany
e-mail: bo.hu@unibw.de; stefan.pickl@unibw.de

Taking this into account this contribution attempts to answer the following questions using system dynamics simulations: (1) Does a trade in emission permits with Non-Annex I countries make sense given the economic development of those countries and the reduction of greenhouse gas emissions? (2) How does the price of emission permits influence economic development and furthermore how is the price influenced by economic factors?

Statistical data describing economic developments in different countries such as Germany, the USA and China between 1990 and 2005 are the basis of the modeling. The sources of data as well as reference literature are presented in Sect. 2. In Sect. 3 a Causal Loop Diagram (CLD) is introduced, which illustrates possible coherences of energy supply and economic development. Subsequently a Stock and Flow model is constructed and the results of this simulation are compared to the real data. In the following various scenarios are calculated. A discussion concludes this contribution (Sect. 4).

2 Related Works and Data Sources

As already mentioned this paper wishes to examine the effects of international emissions trading on climate protection and economic development with the help of system dynamics modeling.

Various climate-economic models have already been presented using system dynamic models (see Fiddaman 1997). The graphical rendering being used by system dynamics modeling helps decisively pointing to interdisciplinary approaches to find solutions to the problem (see Boulanger 2005). CLDs are able to clarify the differences in approaches such as "Carbon Tax" or "Cap-and-Trade." It is quite interesting to state that there will be pressure on politicians to issue more permits when there is a short term rise in the prices of emission permits (Fiddaman 2007).

As a matter of fact there are quite a lot of publications on the possible room for maneuver for a national administration concerning the total amount and the pricing of tradable emission permits. It has been stated, for example, that the critical line for the Japanese economy is reached at 5,000–6,000 Yen (41–49€ at present) for each ton of CO_2 (see Matsumoto et al. 2007, Matsumoto on Simulation Analysis of the Critical Price for Greenhouse Gases Emission Permits). Other calculations show that national administrations that are concerned about the competitive ability of national companies should issue more emission permits (see Pratlong 2005). Meanwhile emissions trading is in full swing. Depending on market conditions CO_2 has been traded at 10–30€ per ton of CO_2 over recent months on the European market (Cozijnsen 2009). In Australia the national price for CO_2 has been announced at A$23 (11.78€ per ton of CO_2) (see Australian Government 2008). Different sources report a price of 6€ per ton of CO_2 when trading emission permits between two Chinese companies and the World Bank in the year 2006 with a total volume of US$1.02 billion (see The World Bank 2006; Zhao 2006).

Emissions trading is strongly connected to economic development. While there are great fears about a conformity of emissions trading and "immiserizing growth" in the sense of Bhagwati (see Babiker et al. 2002), various research groups have tried to assess the coherencies between the strength of the economy, energy consumption and CO_2 emissions in different countries using statistical methods. A coherence between economic growth and an increase in energy consumption can indeed be statistically proven with 87% of the 30 members of the OECD as well as with 65% of 78 non-OECD-countries (see Chontanawat et al. 2006). Furthermore, in fast growing countries such as Brazil, Russia, India and China (BRIC) the economies grow at the expense of energy efficiency (see Chousa et al. 2008). The correlation between energy consumption and economic growth is the starting point of this contribution. The figures and data used for the simulation originate from a publicly accessible data pool (Gapminder Foundation 2008). They include the following statistical data per capita and year: CO_2 emissions in tons, energy consumption in kg oil equivalence as well as income in "purchasing power parity $" (PPP$).

3 System Dynamics Modeling

This section first introduces a CLD which presents a simple correlation between economic development, energy consumption and CO_2-emissions (Sect. 3.1). Based upon this diagram a Stock and Flow model will be developed (Sect. 3.2), which is able to produce simulations using real data (Sect. 3.3) and can thus be calibrated. In a final step different scenarios can be calculated with the help of those calibrated models (Sect. 3.4), disclosing various possibilities for influencing pricing for international emissions trading.

3.1 The Causal Loop Diagram

The correlation between energy supply and a national economy can be depicted in a CLD shown in Fig. 1. Economic power and energy consumption are directly correlated through the energy efficiency factor. When an economy experiences growth there will be a rise in energy consumption (see Chontanawat et al. 2006). Furthermore it is obvious that if an economy experiences rapid growth it could potentially evoke an energy shortage. At the same time a shortage of energy inhibits the development of the economy as has been observed with numerous developing nations as well as with developed countries in times of energy crises (B1).

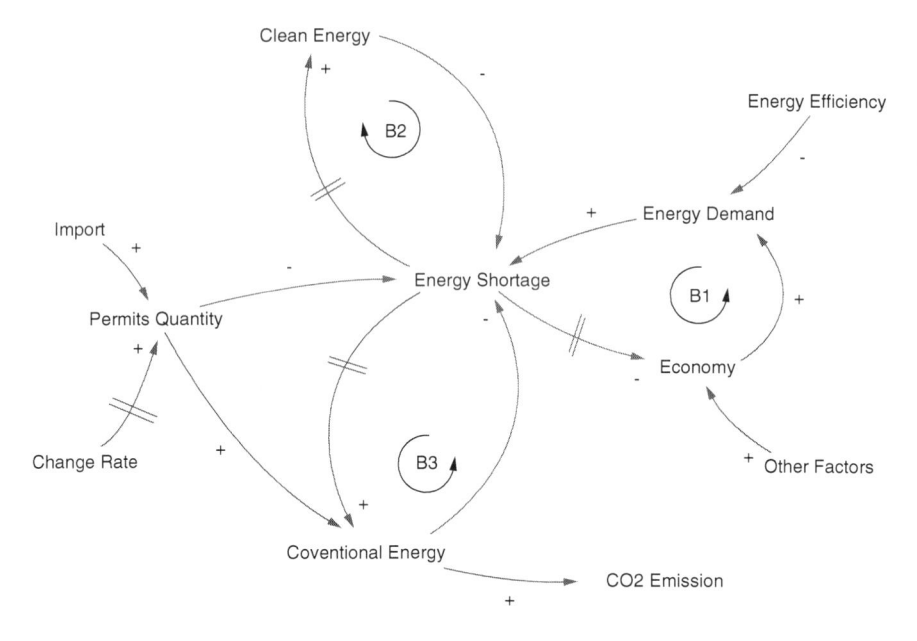

Fig. 1 Causal Loop diagram of energy demand and supply

Energy suppliers in turn react to energy shortages. As in our model in this present contribution we will differentiate between "clean energy" which is free of emissions and "conventional energy" with an emission intensity that can be defined as

$$\kappa_{\max} = 4 \frac{\text{kg CO}_2}{\text{kg oil equivalent}}$$

since the ratio between CO_2-emissions and energy consumption is lower than 4 in most countries (see Gapminder Foundation 2008). Each energy supply is in fact a combination of both clean energy and conventional energy which both react to energy shortages. While growth in the provision of clean energy can be evaluated positively from the point of view of economic development and emissions reduction (B2), the target of emissions reduction can be achieved when the market authority controls the feedback loop for conventional energy by limiting emission permits (B3). Assigning the total amount of emission permits confines the total amount of conventional energy on the market and thus inhibits its growth respectively enforcing a reduction in conventional energy by constantly reducing the amount of emission permits.

The present model takes into account the fact that the total amount of emission permits on a given national or supranational market may be influenced by permit import or export. The central issue of this contribution is how the import or export of emission permits will have an effect on economic dynamics and how knowledge about this influence may be used for pricing emissions trading.

3.2 The Stock and Flow Model

On the basis of the CLD introduced in Sect. 3.1, a Stock and Flow model can be constructed (Fig. 2). This diagram allows the development of a country to be understood within a given period of time through numerical simulation. The results of the simulation concerning the growth of the economy, energy consumption and the amount of emissions may be compared to data from the known data pool by Gapminder Foundation (2008). Input data are the following indicators:

1. Purchasing Power Parity in US Dollars (PPP$) per capita and year at the beginning of a given period of time (PPP$ Start)
2. CO_2 emissions in kg per capita and year at the beginning of a given period of time (kg CO_2 Start)
3. PPP$ pro consumed energy in kg oil equivalent at the beginning of a given period of time (PPP$ per Oil Start)
4. Average annual rate of improvement of the PPP$ per kg oil equivalent (PPP$ per Oil Slope)

With the help of the last two indicators the development of energy efficiency of a national economy can be presented. To check the validity of the diagram real data may be employed.

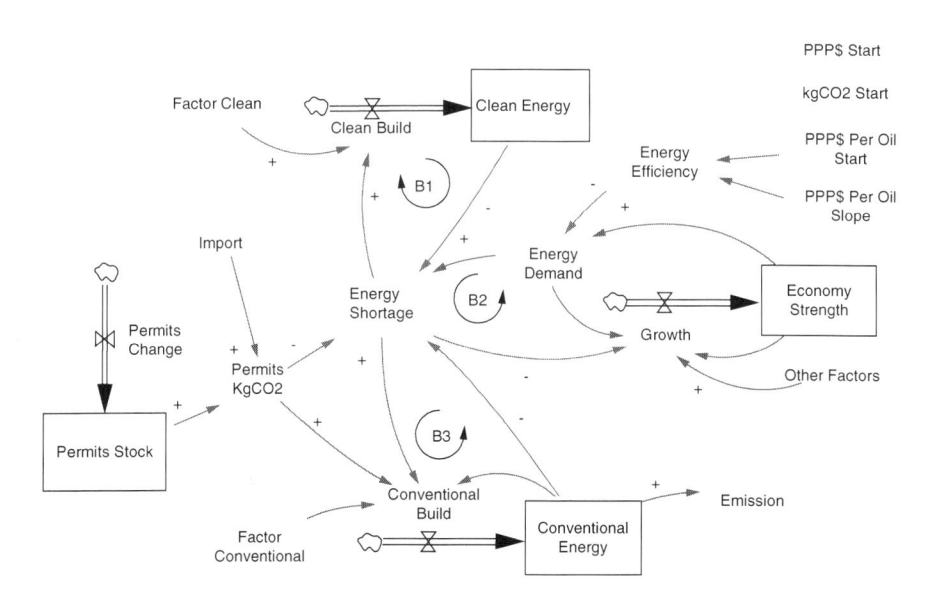

Fig. 2 Stock and Flow diagram of energy demand and supply

It is to be expected that the simulated strength of the economy in the form of PPP$ (Economy Strength) and the CO_2 emissions (Emission) correspond to the real data. There are three fitting parameters:

1. Reaction speed of the energy suppliers regarding a given shortage of conventional energy in year^{-1} (Factor Conventional)
2. Reaction speed of the energy suppliers regarding a given shortage of clean energy in year^{-1} (Factor Clean)
3. External, not ascertained factors, which promote economic development (Other Factors)

A third parameter is necessary to indicate national economies growing at different speeds. Real economic data can be used instead. In this case only the first two fitting parameters are needed to attain the target value CO_2 emission.

Additionally two parameters are introduced to show the different alternatives for a decision:

1. Changes in the total amount of emission permits stipulated by the market authority in kg CO_2 per capita and year (Permits Change)
2. The annual imported or exported emission permits in kg CO_2 per capita and year (Import)

The initial amount of emission permits complies with the actual amount ("grandfathered permits") as is general practice in Europe.

3.3 Simulation Results for the Period 1990–2005

Since the Kyoto protocol takes the year 1990 as a baseline for calculation and because the relevant data for most nations since 1990 is accessible (Gapminder Foundation 2008) the period 1990–2005 has been chosen to calibrate the parameters.

In a first step we want to find out how energy suppliers react to changes on the market. For that purpose known data on income development (PPP$ per capita), energy efficiency (PPP$/Oil) and CO_2 emissions (kg per capita) is fed into the model.

When fitting the parameters it becomes apparent that both China and India being the countries with the largest population in the world, showed similarities in behavior regarding CO_2 emissions over the given period of time. No measures have been taken to develop emission-reduced forms of energy (Factor Clean = 0). At the same time the development of energy without any remarkable emission reduction kept pace with the tremendous rates of economic growth (Factor Conventional = 3).

The three countries USA, Japan and Brazil as different as they are, show similarities in their energy systems regarding CO_2 reduction: Both the share of clean energy and conventional energy reacted to the same degree to market changes. The

International Emissions Trading: A Pricing Model Based on System 39

Table 1 Data and simulation

	Dimension	DE	CN	US	IN	FR	BR	JP
Income, 1990 (data)	PPP$/capita	24,996	1,466	31,744	1,137	24,037	7,247	25,870
CO_2 emissions (data)	kg/capita	11,740	2,150	19,180	830	6,650	1,365	8,770
Income p. energy cons. (oil eq., data)	PPP$/kg	5.57	1.93	4.11	3.02	5.99	8.09	7.19
Dito, change rate (aver. 1990–2005)	PPP$/kg·a	0.115	0.079	0.078	0.088	0.037	−0.028	0.0073
Other factors (fitting parameter)	1/a	0.018	0.081	0.019	0.048	0.022	0.0185	0.012
Factor Clean (fitting parameter)	1/a	3	0	3	0	3	3	3
Emission permits, change rate	kg/capita·a	−170				−50		
Factor Conv. (fitting parameter)	1/a		3	3	3		3	3
Income per capita, 2005 (data)	PPP$	30,496	4,091	41,850	2,126	29,644	8,596	30,290
CO_2 emissions (data)	kg/capita	9,500	4,260	19,530	1,300	6,200	1,700	9,650
Income per capita, 2005 (simulation)	PPP$	30,459	4,082	42,008	2,119	29,606	8,504	30,259
CO_2 emissions (simulation)	kg/capita	9,510	4,341	19,636	1,300	6,200	1,787	9,852

relation of clean energy supply and conventional energy supply did not vary within the observed period of time. A positive economic growth resulted in a positive growth of CO_2 emissions over the same period.

In France and Germany however the CO_2 emissions per capita decreased over the given period of time, whereas the clean energy supply increased. This was evoked through cutting down on CO_2 emissions and a targeted stimulation of producing CO_2-free forms of energy (solar-, wind- and nuclear energy) by market authorities. This situation is represented in the model through a reduction of emission permits of annually 170 kg per capita resp. 50 kg per capita in Germany resp. France.

Table 1 summarizes all data and parameters for the use in a model simulation. The comparison between the real data and simulated figures show a fairly good match.

3.4 Scenarios 2005–2020

The building and calibration of models so far answer the purpose of checking different decision options with the help of simulated calculations. Already the model in Fig. 1 shows that emissions trading only makes sense if both trading partners have use of a limited amount of emission permits which may be traded.

Otherwise, emissions can neither be cut down by trading nor can an emissions pricing be made effectively.

Therefore it seems reasonable to recommend a strategy for curbing CO_2 emissions by defining an emissions limit for every nation, even if the limit itself prospectively does not directly mean a reduction. In our *Basis Scenario* in Table 2 an annually increasing amount of emissions is calculated for all countries (except France and Germany) which does not hinder the economic development ("Business as Usual" or BAU). Nevertheless by doing so it is possible to calculate the fall in income through (massively) exporting emission permits. This fall in income adds up to an average of 376–679 PPP$ per ton CO_2 depending on the country or – again depending on the country – 198–616 US$ per ton CO_2 referring to the exchange rates of 2005.

If it is targeted to set the increase in emissions of all listed countries (except France and Germany) to 0 (Scenario 1), it may be assumed that there will be a comparable loss of income per ton of reduced CO_2 emission. China, for example, would have to compensate a loss of income of approximately 6,400 Bil. US$ within 15 years.

In the long run China and India have the possibility to reduce such a vast amount of loss of income by stimulating the production of clean energy. As Scenario 2 shows, those losses can be reduced by 40%, if the level of clean energy supply from other countries can be acquired.

All above scenarios assume, that an upper emissions limit has been set. If this is not the case Scenario 3 is of interest. By simply cutting 100 kg oil equivalent per capita off the Chinese capacity of conventional energy supply in the sixth year of the period of time under consideration, a reduction of 1.52 tons of CO_2 per capita can be achieved. The fall in income would then be about 539 PPP$ per ton CO_2. Table 2 comprises the main results.

4 Concluding Discussion

In Sect. 3.4 the loss of income per ton of CO_2 emission reduction has been calculated for different countries in different scenarios. According to our model the emission reduction of 1 ton of CO_2 (see Sect. 3.1) is associated with the saving of 250 kg oil equivalent. Therefore the energy costs are to be deducted when pricing CO_2 emission permits. Assuming an oil price of 50$ per barrel or about 400$ per ton of oil equivalent the following prices per ton of CO_2 emissions are conceivable for national trade:

The obvious difference in prices for emission permits shown in Table 3 can only partially be explained by the differences in energy efficiency. The US$ exchange rate also plays a vital role. Although Brazil, for example, has one of the highest energy efficiency rates and one of the lowest CO_2 emission rates it would still aspire to sell a large amount of emission permits to developed countries, since the price level in Brazil is generally much lower than that of developed countries. In

Table 2 Scenarios 2005–2020

	Dimension	DE	CN	US	IN	FR	BR	JP
Basis scenario								
Income, 2005 (data)	PPP$/cap.	30,496	4,091	41,850	2,126	29,644	8,596	30,290
CO_2 emissions (data)	kg/capita	9,500	4,300	20,000	1,300	6,200	1,700	9,650
Income per energy use (oil eq., data)	PPP$/kg	7.30	3.11	5.28	4.33	6.54	7.66	7.30
Dito, change rate (aver. 1990–2005)	PPP$/kg·a	0.115	0.079	0.078	0.088	0.037	−0.028	0.0073
Other factors (average 1990–2005)	1/a	0.018	0.081	0.019	0.048	0.022	0.0185	0.012
Factor Clean (scenario assumption)	1/a	3	1	3	1	3	3	3
Permits change (scenario assumpt.)	kg/cap.·a	−135	275	150	60	−30	40	100
Factor Conv. (aver. 1990–2005)	1/a	–	3	3	3	–	3	3
Income p. cap., 2020 (simul., BAU)	PPP$	38,237	11,536	55,378	3,995	37,827	10,750	35,425
CO_2 emissions (simulation, BAU)	kg/capita	7,520	8,300	22,000	1,936	5,760	2,287	10,896
Income change per CO_2 (simul.)	PPP$/t	522	559	376	679	468	509	475
Dito, in real price of 2005	US$/t	411	198	336	191	370	235	616
Scenario 1: setting permit quantity to constant in China, USA, India, Brazil and Japan								
Reduction of CO_2 2005–2020	t/capita		25.86	7.98	4.31		4.30	9.00
Income change per CO_2 (simul.)	PPP$/t		534	374	660		484	464
Scenario 2: speeding up clean energy development in China and Brazil								
Factor Clean (scenario assumption)	1/a		3				3	
Income change per CO_2 (simul.)	PPP$/t		314				362	
Scenario 3: shutting down conventional energy capacity in 6th year								
Capacity shut down (oil equivalent)	kg/capita		100					
Factor Clean (scenario assumption)	1/a		1					
Reduction of CO_2 2005–2020	t/capita		1.52					
Income change per CO_2 emissions	PPP$/t		539					

Table 3 Pricing on a national market according to the basis scenario

	Dimension	DE	CN	US	IN	FR	BR	JP
Domestic price (basis scenario)	US$/t CO_2	311	98	236	91	270	135	516

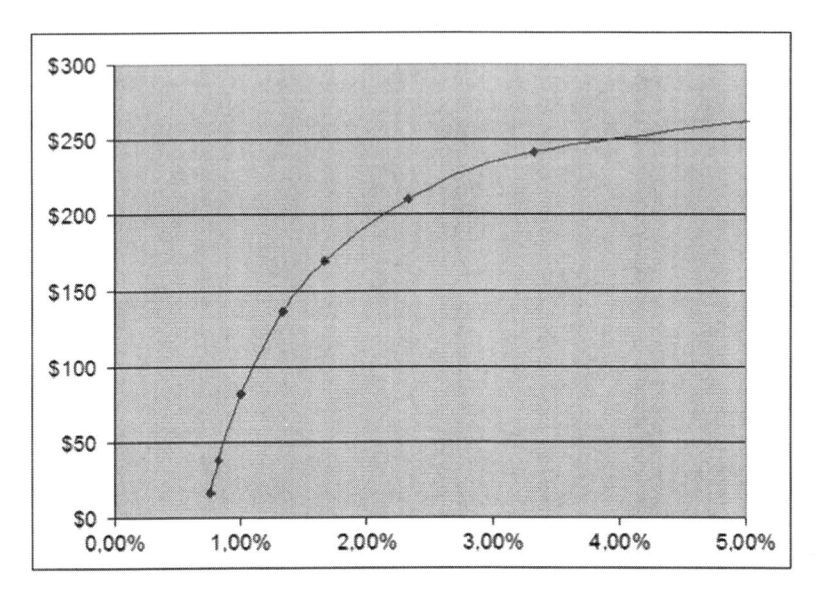

Fig. 3 Model calculation: emission permit per ton of CO_2 at the price from 2005 for the USA

developed countries a large volume of imported emission permits could on the other hand thwart the original emission policy as well as the development policy.

Since emissions trading is not subject to any natural limiting factors such as physical transportation it is to be expected that developed countries will introduce an import duty and developing countries will introduce an export duty of about 100 US$ per ton CO_2 to protect the national prices listed in Table 3.

The prices mentioned here are distinctly higher than the ones in Sect. 2. The reason for this is that a loss of income and reduction of CO_2 emissions are both non-linear functions of the quantity of emission permits. Our system dynamics model simulation shows for example that a price above 200 US$ per ton CO_2 can only be expected when the US market is lacking more than 2% of the emission permits needed, as depicted in Fig. 3.

From the present point of view it can be concluded that a fair international emissions trading can only be conducted with the use of protective duties. Furthermore, a comparatively high price which evokes emissions reduction inevitably has an inhibiting effect on economic growth according to our model. As expected it is not without difficulty to find a balance between economic growth and emissions reduction. More research work is necessary to verify the model presented in this contribution and in particular the fitting parameters introduced in Sect. 3.3.

References

Australian Government (2008) Emission prices. Australia's low pollution future fact sheet. http://www.treasury.gov.au/lowpollutionfuture/factSheets/downloads/Emission_Prices_Fact_Sheet.pdf. Accessed 23 Feb 2009

Babiker MHM, Reilly JM, Viguier LL (2002) Is international emissions trading always beneficial? DSpace at MIT: MIT's online institutional repository, MIT, 2002–12. http://dspace.mit.edu/handle/1721.1/3628. Accessed 23 Feb 2009

Boulanger PM, Bréchet T (2005) Models for policy-making in sustainable development: The state of the art and perspectives for research. Ecological Economics 55:337–350

Byrd R, Hagel SC (1997) Byrd-Hagel resolution (S. Res. 98). July 25, 1997. http://www.nationalcenter.org/KyotoSenate.html. Accessed 02 Mar 2009

Chontanawat J, Hunt LC, Pierse R (2006) Causality between energy consumption and GDP: evidence from 30 OECD and 78 Non-OECD countries. Surrey Energy Economics Centre (SEEC), Department of Economics Discussion Papers (SEEDS), 113, Department of Economics, University of Surrey, Surrey, UK. http://ideas.repec.org/p/sur/seedps/113.html. Accessed 23 Feb 2009

Chousa JP, Tamazian A, Vadlamannati KC (2008) Rapid economic growth at the cost of environment degradation? – Panel data evidence from Bric economies. William Davidson Institute Working Papers Series, wp908, William Davidson Institute at the University of Michigan Stephen M. Ross Business School. http://ideas.repec.org/p/wdi/papers/2008-908.html. Accessed 23 Feb 2009

Cozijnsen J (2009) EU CO_2 market snapshot. http://www.emissierechten.nl/. Accessed 03 Mar 2009

Fiddaman TS (1997) Feedback complexity in integrated climate-economy models. Thesis (Ph.D.), MIT, Sloan School of Management. http://dspace.mit.edu/handle/1721.1/10154. Accessed 03 Mar 2009

Fiddaman T (2007) Dynamics of climate policy. Syst Dyn Rev 23(1):21–34, 27 Apr 2007 (http://www3.interscience.wiley.com/journal/114229045/abstract?CRETRY=1&SRETRY=0)

Gapminder (2008) Gapminder Foundation. http://www.gapminder.org/. Accessed 24 Feb 2009

Matsumoto T, Uchida S, Mizunoya T, Higano Y (2007) Simulation analysis of the critical price for greenhouse gases emission permits. Stud Reg Sci 37(3):647–659, http://region.hse.tut.ac.jp/jsrsai/srs/vol37no3/37_647abst.pdf

Pratlong F (2005) Does the distribution of emission permits matter for international competitiveness? Cahiers de la Maison des Sciences Economiques, number v05011, Jan 2005. ftp://mse.univ-paris1.fr/pub/mse/cahiers2005/V05011.pdf. Accessed 20 Feb 2009

The World Bank (2006) Umbrella carbon facility completes allocation of first tranche. The World Bank Press Releases, The World Bank, August 29, 2006. http://go.worldbank.org/VN7JWFT170. Accessed 05 Mar 2009

UN Public Information (2008) Image & reality: questions and answers. About the United Nations, United Nations Web Services Section, Department of Public Information. http://www.un.org/geninfo/ir/index.asp. Accessed 22 Feb 2009

UNFCCC (2009) Kyoto protocol. UNFCCC, 14.01.2009. http://unfccc.int/kyoto_protocol/items/2830.php. Accessed 02 Mar 2009

Zhao H (2006) Two Chinese companies got $ 1,000,000,000 of greenhouse gas emissions trading. First Financial Daily, 27 Oct 2006. http://finance.sina.com.cn/chanjing/b/20060830/01582867116.shtml. Accessed 04 Mar 2009

Comparative Analysis of Alternative Post-2012 Climate Policies and Ancillary Benefits for Ukraine: A General Equilibrium Approach

Olga Diukanova

Abstract The goal of this study is to evaluate alternative post-2012 carbon dioxide reduction targets for Ukraine. In order to assist national policymakers in the adoption of a feasible and effective policy, a special focus is made on the assessment of ancillary benefits associated with CO_2 reduction. These benefits are defined as health benefits due to a simultaneous reduction of energy-related NO_X, SO_X and TSP air pollutants. The methodology is based on a forward-looking dynamic multi-sectoral computable general equilibrium model of a Ramsey–Cass–Koopmans type. The model employs domestic emissions trading as an instrument for CO_2 reductions in the country. Model results show that CO_2 abatement corresponds to the national interests of Ukraine. First, an imposed cost on carbon stimulates energy efficiency. Second, it promotes structural changes in favour of the country's least-energy intensive industries, supporting both mid-term and long-term strategies of the country's development. Third, it results in a substantial reduction in the mortality and morbidity statistics from air pollution. The magnitude of these effects strongly depends on the stringency of CO_2 reduction.

Keywords Ancillary benefits • computable general equilibrium model • Emissions trading • post-2012 emission policies

JEL Classification Q53, D58, Q56

The research leading to these results has received funding from the European Community's Seventh Framework Programme FP7/2007–2013 under grant agreement no. PIIF-GA-2008-220852. The author would like to thank Dr. Francesco Bosello (Fondazione Eni Enrico Mattei) for his comments and suggestions.

O. Diukanova (✉)
Fondazione Eni Enrico Mattei (FEEM) Castello, 5252-I-30123 Venice, Italy
e-mail: olga.diukanova@feem.it

1 Introduction

An inadequate economic structure, an inefficiently run energy sector and lax environmental legislation cause numerous environmental problems that substantially affect Ukraine's economic performance and the health of its population. A large proportion of the national economy is represented by resource-oriented industries that operate outdated industrial infrastructure that can only be updated with significant investment. Ukraine was ranked as one of the most energy- and carbon-intensive countries in the world in terms of intensity per capita and per unit of GDP (PPP and exchange rates), (IEA 2009). At the same time however the Ukrainian economy is largely dependent on imported energy. Currently 77% of its oil and 72% of its gas are imported from Russia and Central Asia, State Statistics Committee of Ukraine (2009).

The energy sector is a major contributor to local and transboundary air pollution. It is responsible for 65% of non-methane volatile organic compounds (NMVOC), 96% of nitrogen oxide (NO_X) and 93% of sulfur oxide (SO_X) emissions, Ministry of Environmental Protection of Ukraine (2009) and for 50% of discharges of total suspended particles (TSP) (EMEP 2008). Concentrations of these compounds exceed the maximum permitted levels by several times in most Ukrainian cities (Ministry of Environmental Protection of Ukraine 2008). The Ukrainian energy sector is the source of 70% of domestic greenhouse gases (GHGs), 78% of which are CO_2, Ministry of Environmental Protection of Ukraine (2009).

The knock-on effect of air pollution on human health is linked to a wide range of cardiovascular, respiratory and genetic disorders. Besides which air pollution causes substantial damage to ecosystems and materials.

According to estimates of the World Bank Project "Ukraine Energy Sector Review: Environmental Issues," Droste-Franke and Friedrich (2004), about 64% of the damage from NO_X, SO_X and PM_{10} air pollution occurs inside Ukraine and 36% outside of the country. The majority of domestic damages was estimated to be caused by PM_{10} followed by NO_X and SO_X, whereas damage outside the country is predominantly caused by SO_X-related effects. Annual human mortality from these pollutants was estimated to be equivalent to 192,000 years of life lost (YOLL).

Another study undertaken by Strukova et al. (2006) indicates that according to the conservative estimates $PM_{2.5}$ pollutants cause 6% of mortality in Ukraine, whereas the economic damage related to mortality from air pollution exceeds 4% of the GDP.

Nevertheless, state regulation of air pollution is highly inadequate and energy-intensive plants are often exempt from pollution charges (United Nations 2007); (Copsey and Shapovalova 2008).

According to the National Strategy Study for Joint Implementation and Emissions Trading in Ukraine, World Bank (2003), about 750 Mt of CO_2 equivalents ($CO_{2\text{-eq}}$) can be reduced with a marginal abatement cost (MAC) below $\$_{2003}$ 8/t $CO_{2\text{-eq}}$. One third of this emissions reduction can be achieved through energy efficiency.

However, GHG emissions have never been regulated in the country and the national government is not willing to start an abatement plan. During negotiations on post-2012 targets at the seventh session of AWG-KP meeting in Bonn, the Ukrainian delegation announced that the country "is ready to commit to the GHG emissions reduction by 20% by 2020 and by 50% by 2050 taking 1990 as a baseline year. Imposing stricter obligations will not only render economic growth impossible, but will also prevent the social and economic recovery of the country" (UNFCCC 2009). The target was confirmed on COP-15 in Copenhagen, UNFCCC (2010).

Obviously, these targets do not reflect the national emission reduction potential or forecasted emissions trends. In 2007 Ukrainian GHG emissions were half of the 1990 level (Ministry of Environmental Protection of Ukraine 2009). In 2020 national GHGs were estimated to average 55–65% of the 1990 level (Ministry of Environmental Protection of Ukraine 2006). The percentage is likely to be lower, because these estimates did not account for the devastating effect of the global economic crisis of 2008 on the Ukrainian economy. In 2009 its energy-intensive production slumped by more than a third (yoy). Because of the crisis, national GDP is expected to grow moderately and slightly exceed the level of 1990 in 2020 (Ministry of Economy of Ukraine 2009a).

According to various estimates of post-2012 emission reduction efforts among the Annex I countries: IIASA (2008a), Netherlands Environmental Assessment Agency (2009a, b), Energy Research Centre (2009), by 2020 Ukraine can achieve a 50–60% reduction in its GHG from the level of 1990 at no net welfare cost. These estimates were based on multiple criteria such as the GDP indexes, the technological potential to reduce emissions, the dynamics of population growth and historical responsibility.

Although the primary benefits from the abatement of GHGs are associated with the mitigation of global climate change impacts, the Ukrainian government tends to discount the future damages from climate change. Furthermore, because of its geographical position the impact of global warming on Ukraine is expected to be rather moderate. Thus, after discounting for time and uncertainty, primary benefits have a weak influence on climate policy decisions in Ukraine.

For this reason the study considers additional benefits of CO_2 reduction, which can be observed in the short term and with a high degree of certainty. Among these benefits are the promotion of energy efficiency, structural changes towards the least energy-intensive industries, a reduction in air pollution and the adverse health effects caused by it. This kind of integrated assessment is intended to assist national policymakers in adopting an effective and feasible post-2012 abatement target.

2 Literature Review

There are a number of studies focusing on the evaluation of GHG reduction policies and the ancillary benefits associated with these that employ the computable general equilibrium (CGE) approach.

Bosello et al. (2006) evaluated the climate-change-induced effects on human health. Changes in morbidity and mortality were interpreted as changes in labor productivity and demand for health care. Their results showed that GDP, welfare and investment all fall (rise) in regions with net negative (positive) health impacts. The study concluded that direct cost estimates, common in climate change impact studies, tend to underestimate true welfare losses.

Chu et al. (2002) employed a 28-sector static CGE model to evaluate the impact of SO_X, NO_X, and VOC reduction in Taiwan. They found that although strict air pollution control raises costs and thereby reduces the conventional GNP, the Green GNP increases and the regulation of air pollution promotes structural changes towards less polluting industries.

Nilsson and Huhtala (2000) in a CGE-modeling framework studied the Swedish environmental target to comply with the Kyoto Protocol in a CGE-modeling framework by abating GHG, and introducing two national goals to reduce acidification and eutrophication by abating SO_2 and NO_X pollutants. Their results indicated that when secondary benefits are taken into account, it could still be in the government's interest to decrease CO_2 at the national level.

Y. Wan et al. (2006) employed a CGE model for a macroeconomic assessment of the impact of air pollution on the Chinese economy and on human health. They found that an implementation of air pollution control policies could result in GDP losses, but at the same time provide significant health benefits.

Dessus and O'Connor (2003) estimated the health benefits for residents of Santiago de Chile due to a reduction in local air pollution. Their results suggest that even with the most conservative assumptions, Chile could reduce CO_2 emissions by almost 20% from the baseline at no net welfare loss, although a 10% reduction is closer to "optimal." If instead Chile were to target a 20% reduction in the concentration of TSP, a TSP tax would incur slightly lower costs than an equivalent carbon tax to achieve the same health benefits.

This study builds on the existing literature on the use of a dynamic forward-looking CGE model of a Ramsey–Cass–Koopmans type to quantify the economic and health impacts of the alternative post-2012 CO_2 abatement policies.

3 Policy Scenarios

In order to prevent catastrophic consequences of climate change, the global GHGs have to be stabilized at a level that is less than 550 ppm by 2100. This target is equivalent to a CO_2 stabilisation at a level of 450 ppm and a reduction of other GHGs at similar rates. To stabilize CO_2 at 450 ppm, according to different estimates global carbon dioxide emissions have to be reduced by approximately 30% in 2050 compared to 1990 levels (IPCC 2007; Ecofys 2006; Criqui et al. 2003). This study develops and evaluates a range of alternative post-2012 carbon abatement policies for Ukraine according to the global CO_2 stabilization target of 450 ppm.

The UNFCCC determined two key criteria for global policy architecture. First, achieving a long-term global temperature stabilization goal by adopting GHG reduction targets for the short-term (environmental sufficiency criterion). Second, maintaining equity and justice by determining national allocations (equity criterion) (United Nations 1992). Under the UNFCCC nations developed specific principles that constitute "equitable" reductions. The following were among the basic principles for the attention of the international community:

- Egalitarian: each person has an equal right to use the atmosphere.
- Sovereignty and acquired rights: all countries have a right to use the atmosphere and current emissions constitute a "status quo right."
- Historical responsibility and Polluter pays principle: the greater the contribution to the global warming, the greater the share in the mitigation.
- Capability: the greater the ability to pay for emissions reduction, the greater the share in the mitigation.

When policy-makers consider CO_2 emissions targets, it is important that they are aware of the economic consequences of their implementation. Building on the UNFCCC principles, this study considers the following carbon reduction scenarios for Ukraine:

- **ET90** scenario reflects the official pledge of the Ukrainian government that was proclaimed at the seventh session of the AWG-KP meeting in Bonn, UNFCCC (2009) to reduce national CO_2 emissions by 20% in 2020 and by 50% in 2050 compared to the level of 1990. Although this scenario can be associated with the Sovereignty and acquired rights principle, it was ranked by the international community as inadequate, since Ukrainian commitments by 2020 are well beyond business-as-usual projections (Ecofys 2009). However this scenario was considered in this study to provide a contrast to the stricter targets.
- **ET06** scenario considers a 20% reduction of CO_2 by 2020 and a 50% reduction by 2050 below the 2006 level. It reflects the estimated target for Ukraine according to the Netherlands Environmental Assessment Agency (2009a, b), Energy Research Centre (2009) and IIASA (2008a) studies. These estimates were based on a combination of different criteria such as the ability to pay, historical and per capita emissions, the potential and cost of emissions reduction.
- **Hist** scenario reflects the Historical responsibility principle that bases allocations upon each country's historical contribution to global warming. Over the 1850–2008 period Ukrainian energy-related CO_2 emissions were about 2% of the global energy-related CO_2 (CAIT 2010). Based on CAIT data it was estimated that the historical responsibility principle allows Ukraine a 22% increase in CO_2 emissions by 2050 compared to the 2007 level.
- **MAC** scenario is based on an equalization of the marginal emission abatement costs among the nations in order to achieve a common stabilization target (the Capability Principle). The global marginal abatement cost of meeting a 450 ppm CO_2 stabilization target was estimated according to Van Vuuren et al. (2006) as being the equivalent of 66€/t CO_2 in 2050. Simulations with the model

developed in this study have shown that an equalization of Ukrainian MAC with the global one by 2050 allows for a 14% increase in national CO_2 from the 2007 level.

- **pCap** scenario foresees an equalization of per capita emissions between the countries by 2050 according to the common 450 ppm CO_2 stabilization target (the Egalitarian principle). Based on the statistical data of CO_2 per capita in different countries (Energy Information Administration 2009a) and projections of global population until 2050, United Nations (2009) it was estimated that this target would require a 77% reduction of Ukrainian CO_2 by 2050 compared to 2007.

These scenarios were compared with a baseline trajectory under the absence of CO_2 reduction (**BAU scenario**).

CO_2 emissions limit. Since Ukraine has a surplus of "emission rights" equal to 1,350 mln. t of $CO_{2\text{-eq}}$ over the first commitment period of the Kyoto Protocol, emission reduction targets specified by the model scenarios were applied starting from 2012.

4 The Methodology

To quantify the economy-wide costs of post-2012 carbon reduction policies and the ancillary benefits associated with them, a dynamic forward-looking general equilibrium model of Ramsey–Cass–Koopmans type was developed in this study. Since most of the dynamic CGEs are built on the premise of a steady-state economic growth over the model horizon, the application of this framework would lead to an overestimation of economic impacts from CO_2 abatement in Ukraine. Therefore the CGE developed in this study features the long-term demographic crisis in the country along with the economic crisis of 2008–2009. The model was formulated as a mixed complimentarily problem (MCP) and programmed in GAMS/MPSGE software with PATH solver (Ferris and Munson 2000; Rutherford 1999).

There are three categories of economic agents acting within the model: consumers, producers and the government all of which operate in perfectly competitive markets. Producers maximize their profits; consumers maximize utility from consumption according to their budget constraints. Labor and capital can move freely within domestic borders. Ukraine is treated as a small, open economy relative to the international market.

The structure diagram of the general equilibrium model for Ukraine is shown in Fig. 1.

A single representative household (C) is endowed with labor (L) and capital (K). Its disposable income consists of the factors income and governmental transfers. A households' decision regarding consumption and savings depends on real interest rates. The capital accumulation function K equates the current capital stock to the

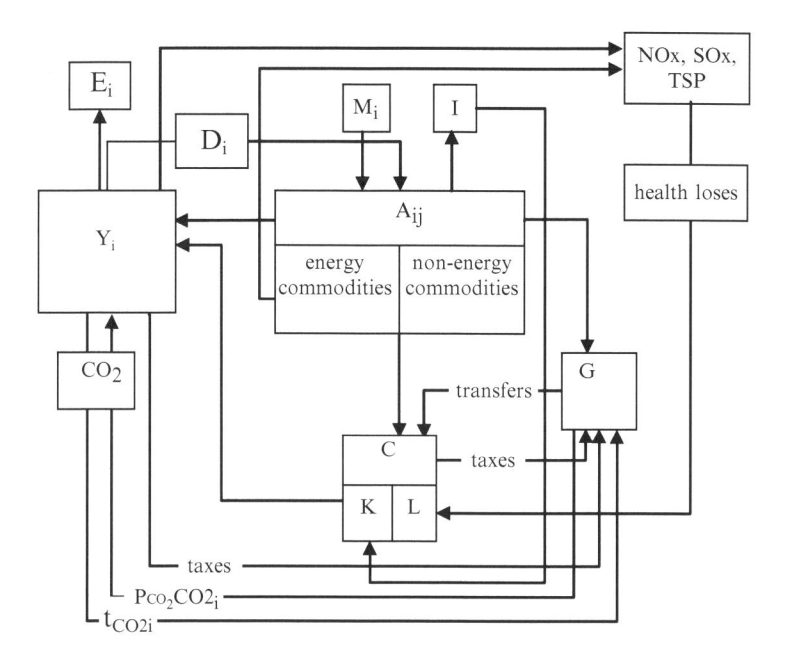

Comparative Analysis of Alternative Post-2012 Climate Policies

Fig. 1 The structure diagram of the CGE model for Ukraine

depreciated stock inherited from the previous period and is augmented by the gross investment I.

The output of sector i (denoted Y_i) is derived from the capital, labor and intermediate inputs. Sector i's consumption of intermediate input j is made up of domestic (D_j) and imported (M_j) varieties of good j that make up the Armington aggregate (A_{ij}). According to the Armington assumption (Armington 1969), which is employed in the model, there is an imperfect substitution between imported and domestic varieties of the same good and an imperfect transformation between domestic consumption and export. The Armington aggregate enters a sectors' production (Y_i), household consumption (C), government consumption (G) and investment (I). Produced output (Y_i) is divided into domestic consumption (D_i) and export (E_i). It was assumed in the model that the balance of payments surplus/deficit is fixed and that the exchange rate is flexible.

The government is allocated carbon emission permits $\sum P_{CO_2}CO_{2i}$, which it distributes among the sectors in accordance with the selected allocation scheme. The government collects income from taxes and auctioned emission permits and uses this income to finance public consumption and to pay transfers to households. Governmental revenue-neutrality is maintained in the model, so that proceeds from the auctioning of permits are redistributed as a lump-sum payment to households.

Although most of the dynamic CGE models employ the assumption of a steady-state economic growth, it is incompatible with the evolution of the Ukrainian economy. The current economic crisis led to a sharp economic slowdown in Ukraine in

2008–2009. The country faces a strong demographic crisis with a 0.68% annual rate of population decline, State Statistics Committee of Ukraine (2010). For these reasons necessary adjustments were made to reflect the unsteady economic growth in the country. First, a time-dependent growth rate was introduced into the model. It was calibrated to the observed and forecasted GDP growth rates (Ministry of Economy of Ukraine 2009b). Since there are no national forecasts beyond 2020, an assumed 3% annual growth between 2021 and 2050 was employed. Second, two components were defined for the investment sector: investments aimed at the accumulation of productive capital and investments intended for non-productive use in final consumption. Equations of capital accumulation, investments and final demand were adjusted to accommodate these changes. Energy productivity was modelled via the autonomous energy efficiency improvement (aeei) factor, which defines a 1% annual increase in energy efficiency. Following McKinsey (2009) a 2.3% increase in annual labor productivity was assumed. This alleviates to a certain extent the negative impact of the demographic crisis.

The CGE model for Ukraine has 16 production sectors: metallurgy, electricity, coke production, transport, the chemical industry, coal mining, mineral production, building and construction, agriculture, the production of hydrocarbons, petroleum refinement, non-energy extraction, pulp and paper production, machinery, food processing and the remaining least energy-intensive sectors aggregated (ROI). All sectors were assumed to operate under a cost optimization production technology.

Substitution possibilities among various inputs were reflected in the nested production functions.

The sectors' production functions have five levels of nesting. The first level reflects substitution between the aggregates of non-energy inputs and the energy-value-added. The second level shows a substitution between the energy and value-added aggregates, and among the non-energy inputs. On the third level labor is substituted with capital and electricity is substituted with the aggregate of fuels (petroleum, coal and hydrocarbons). The fourth level features a substitution between petroleum and the fossil fuels aggregate. The fifth level defines a substitution between coal and hydrocarbons. Levels of nesting were defined by the constant elasticity of substitution (CES) functions.

Since coal is a sector-specific resource in coal mining and coke production, hydrocarbons are a necessary resource in petroleum refinement and the production of hydrocarbons, and petroleum is a necessary resource for the transport sector, for the clarity of analysis an additional top-level nesting was employed in these sectors' production functions to define complementarity between the sector-specific energy resources and the remaining inputs.

Household and governmental preferences were established through the production function with three levels of nesting. The first level represents substitution possibilities between the energy aggregate and the composite of non-energy goods. The second level reflects a substitution between: (a) electricity and the fuels composite, and (b) among the non-energy goods. The third level combines different types of fuels. Levels of nesting were reflected by CES functions.

CO_2 emissions from fossil fuels were linked to the consumption of coal, hydrocarbons and petroleum from different sectors. Emission coefficients were estimated according to the data of the Ukrainian GHG Inventory, Ministry of Environmental Protection of Ukraine (2009) and the data of annual CO_2 emissions from coal, natural gas and petroleum consumption in the country (Energy Information Administration 2009b).

The model employs emissions trading as a main instrument for CO_2 reduction in Ukraine. Emissions trading is widely recognized as the most effective instrument to ensure the lowest cost in emission abatement. There are two basic options for allocating emission permits among the sectors. First, to provide them for free (the so-called "grandfathering" scheme) according to a certain metric, e.g. output, level of emissions, energy intensity, etc. Second, to sell them from the governmental auction. Although grandfathering is based on an implicit subsidization of emitting industries where the metrics of allocation determines the subsidized parameter, it has been criticized for undermining the efficiency of environmental regulation. However, in order to provide some adjustment period for Ukrainian industries to operate under the carbon constraint, the model starts with 100% grandfathering based on the output from 2007. The amount of grandfathered permits is gradually decreased in order to make the transition to 100% auctioning by 2050.

According to the output-based grandfathering scheme employed in the model, each sector's allocation is determined by the share of its output in total production. Since this type of allocation is linked to the level of production, it performs as an implicit subsidy to output. The sector-specific subsidization rate was determined as the ratio of permits' value that was allocated to the sector to its revenue.

The model does not account for potential revenues from joint implementation projects and international emissions trading since the rules that will guide these mechanisms after 2012 are currently still not well-defined.

Emissions of NO_X, SO_X and TSP were projected over the model horizon as a function of activity levels and fossil fuel consumption. Data on air pollutants were taken from the national submissions to the EMEP Centre on Emission Inventories and Projections (EMEP 2008). The coefficients of NO_X, SO_X and TSP emissions according to fuel type were estimated following the CORINAIR methodology (EMEP 2009). All emission coefficients were calibrated to the 2007 base year. Emissions of air pollutants were adjusted to the baseline growth trajectory according to the forecasts of IIASA (2008b).

For a comprehensive analysis of the ancillary benefits of carbon reduction policies it would be necessary to model the following links between: (a) CO_2 abatement and changes in discharges of air pollutants; (b) the emissions of air pollutants and their ambient concentrations; and (c) the concentrations of air pollutants and their exposure on human health and ecosystems. The link (a) is covered by the CGE model that is built into this study. Links (b) and (c) require sophisticated bottom-up dispersion models for each pollutant that translate emissions from the point sources to their ambient concentrations, and complicated dose-response functions for assessing damages to human health and ecosystems.

The study employs a simplified top–down approach based on the estimates of Droste-Franke and Friedrich (2004) who applied the bottom-up Ecosence model to estimate annual mortality (in YOLL values) from NO_X, SO_X and PM_{10} pollutants in Ukraine. Mortality in terms of the annual number of deaths was estimated by Strukova et al. (2006) but only for $PM_{2.5}$ particles. These estimates were adjusted to the baseline growth trajectory. The changes in NO_X, SO_X, PM_{10} and $PM_{2.5}$ discharges due to post-2012 carbon reduction policies were linearly linked to the mortality values. Although no unique methodology exists to monetize health loses (Kuchler and Golan 1999), and the application of different methods would deliver very different results, mortality and morbidity values were not monetized in this study.

Since PM_{10} and $PM_{2.5}$ emissions are not monitored separately in Ukraine, and statistical data are only available for the TSP aggregate that includes PM_{10} and $PM_{2.5}$ emissions, following Droste-Franke and Friedrich (2004) and Strukova et al. (2006), an assumption was made that PM_{10} accounts for 50% of all TSP, and $PM_{2.5}$ accounts for 30% of PM_{10}.

5 Discussion of Results

Model results prove that the Ukrainian official pledge regarding its post-2012 CO_2 reduction policy reflected by the ET90 scenario does not imply any CO_2 abatement until 2028 (Fig. 2). For the 2008–2028 period the trajectory of the ET90 scenario coincides with the baseline trajectory (BAU scenario) and the latter does not foresee

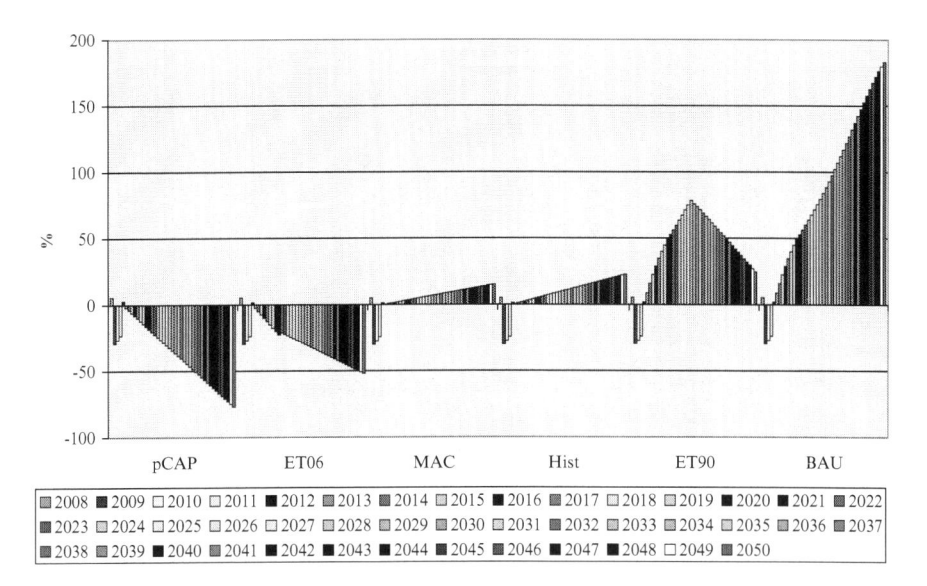

Fig. 2 Energy-related industry CO_2 emissions, as a percentage compared to 2007

any emissions reduction. Indeed, the ET90 target allows for an increase in industry energy-related CO_2 by 49% in 2020 and by 24% in 2050 from the level of 2007, generating "hot air" in 2013–2027. Although the scenario Hist only foresees a 2% lower emission target for Ukraine in 2050 compared to the scenario ET90, it does not generate "hot air" and allows for a smoother distribution of emission reduction effort over the model horizon thus leading to greater CO_2 reduction in absolute terms and less impact on the economy, as shown on the charts below.

Defining "hot air" as the difference between the allowed emissions according to the imposed constraint and the actual emissions, the EU90 scenario generates 1,777 Mt CO_2 of "hot air" over the period 2013–2027, as shown in Fig. 3. The annual amount of "hot air" gradually decreases from 268 Mt in 2013 to 12 Mt in 2027.

Results of model simulations indicate that post-2012 policies to some degree slow down production growth compared to the baseline trajectory, while at the same time promoting significant structural changes in favour of least energy-intensive sectors (Figs. 4–6). The extent of these structural changes is proportional to the stringency of the CO_2 abatement target. However, all scenarios show a similar pace of growth in cumulative production until 2020.

Although the scenarios pCap and ET06 require the steepest CO_2 reduction (of 77% and 50% respectively below the 2007 level in 2050), the cumulative output nearly doubles relative to the level of 2007 by 2050. As shown on the diagrams below, this growth occurs due to an expansion of the least energy intensive sectors.

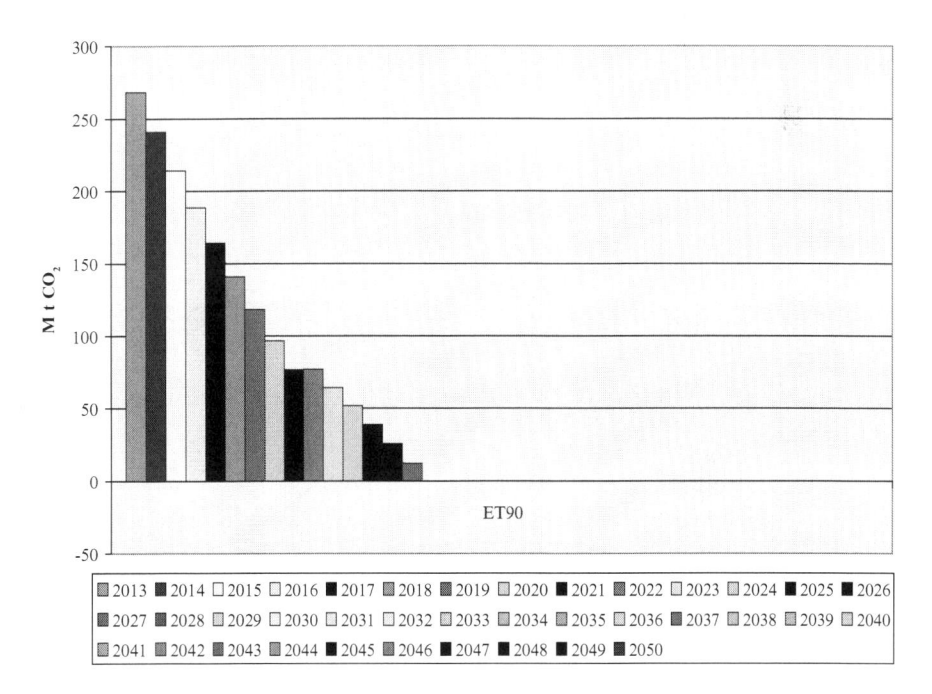

Fig. 3 Excess of the AAUs

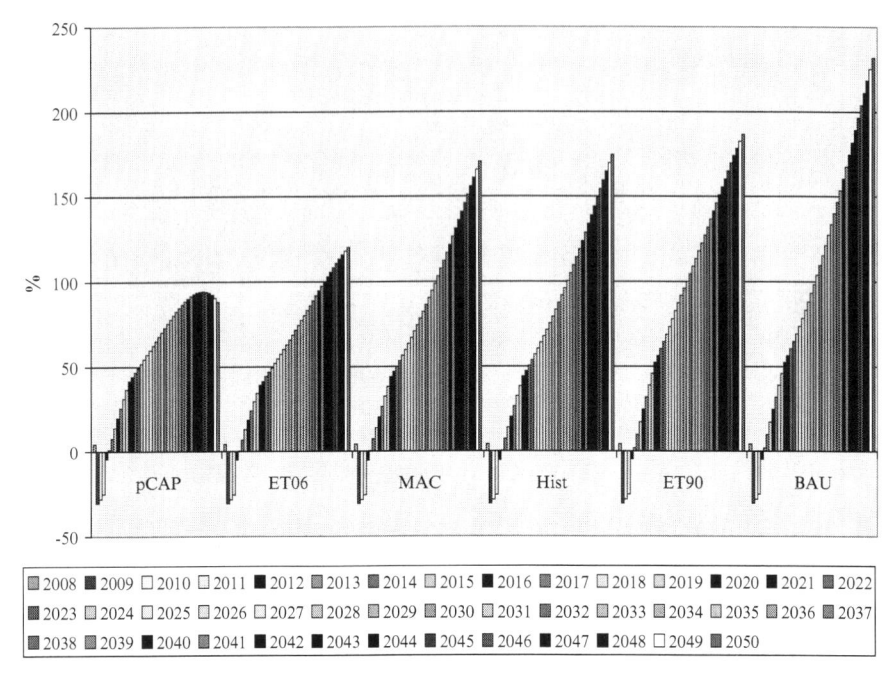

Fig. 4 The cumulative industry output, as a percentage compared to 2007

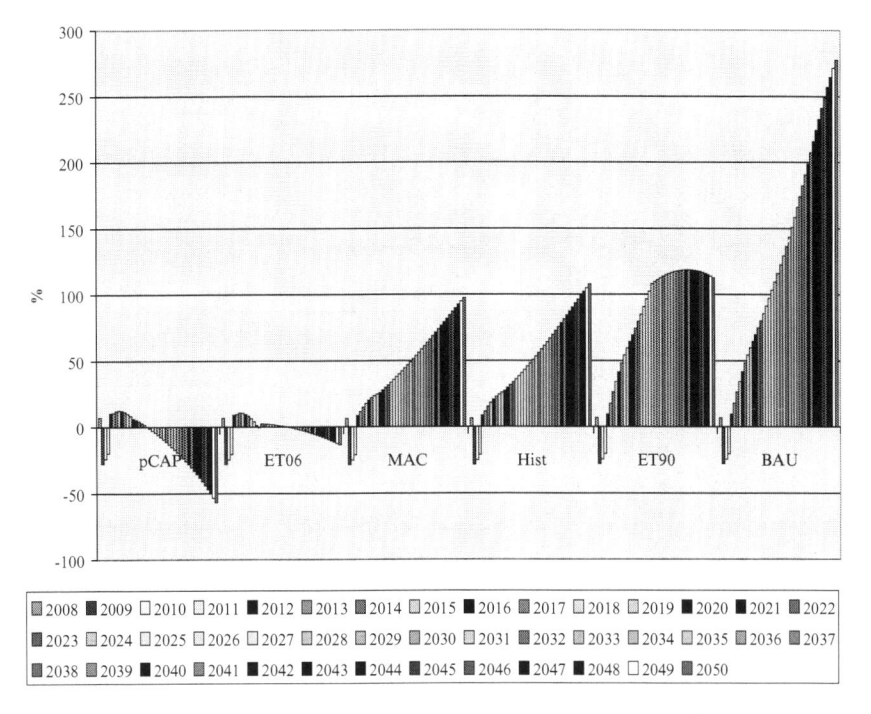

Fig. 5 Output of the most energy-intensive sectors, as a percentage compared to 2007

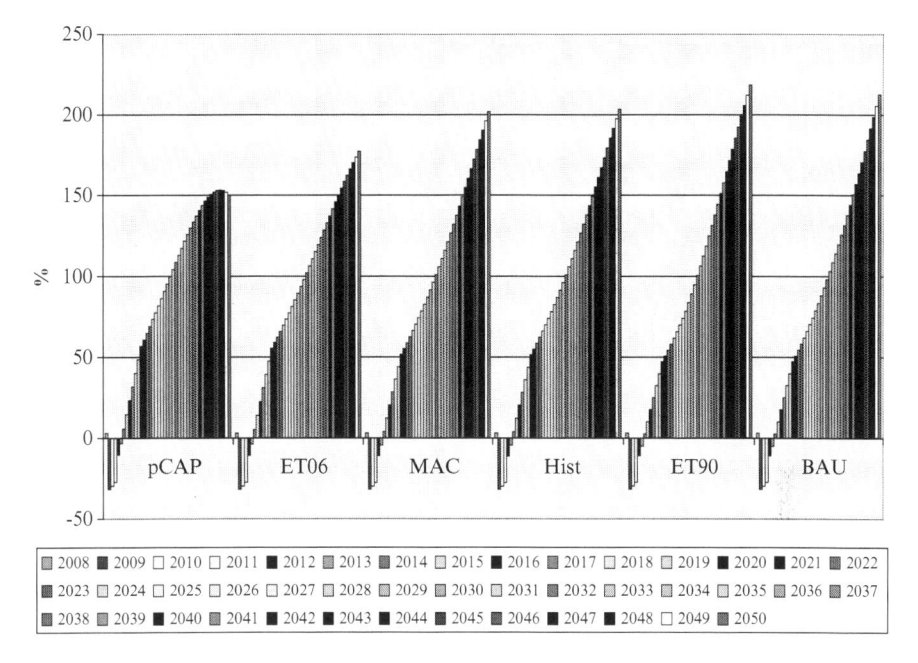

Fig. 6 Output of the least energy-intensive sectors, as a percentage compared to 2007

Despite the stricter abatement target, the scenario MAC ensures a similar growth in cumulative production to that of the scenarios Hist and ET90.

Output levels of the most energy-intensive sectors with a prevailing low technological mode such as coal, coke and metallurgical production, sharply decline compared to the baseline trajectory (BAU scenario) in the results of post-2012 policies reflected by the pCap, ET60, MAC and Hist scenarios (Figs. 7–9).

Among the absolute winners of post-2012 carbon reduction policies are the least energy-intensive sectors such as food processing, pulp and paper production, agriculture and the ROI aggregate of the least energy-intensive sectors (the light industry, trade and services, research and development, etc.) whose output generally increases in relation to the baseline (Figs. 10–13).

The cost of CO_2 reduction was calculated in terms of a marginal abatement cost (Fig. 14). The egalitarian principle reflected by the scenario pCAP is particularly unfavourable for Ukraine since its per capita CO_2 emissions are among the world's highest. Carbon dioxide abatement by 77% compared to the level of 2007 comes at a tremendously high marginal abatement cost of 667€/t CO_2 in 2050.

The country's welfare was measured both in terms of GDP and cumulative household consumption (Figs. 15 and 16). Model results show that all post-2012 CO_2 abatement policies allow continued GDP growth until 2020 as projected by the Ukrainian Ministry of Economy (2009a). Although strict environmental policies reflected by pCAP and ET60 scenarios require drastic CO_2 abatement below the level of 2007, they ensure an increase in national GDP above the 2007 level by

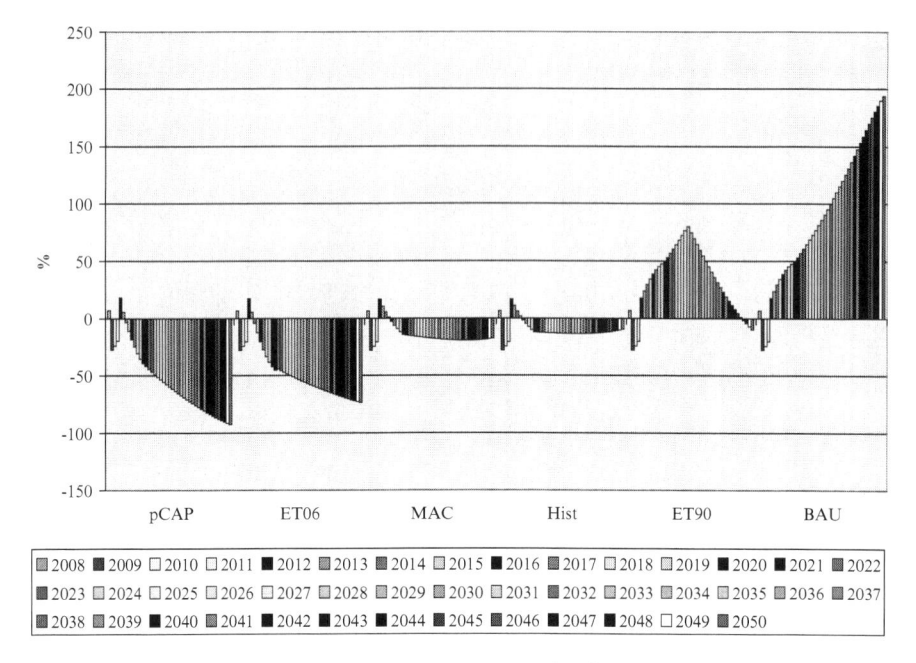

Fig. 7 Output of the coal sector, as a percentage compared to 2007

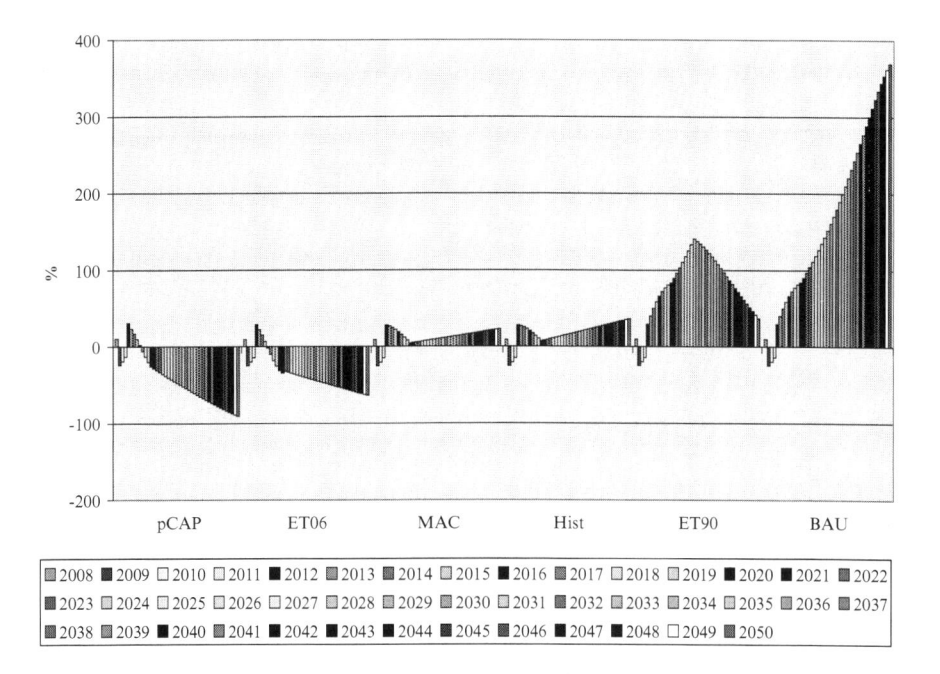

Fig. 8 Output of the coke sector, as a percentage compared to 2007

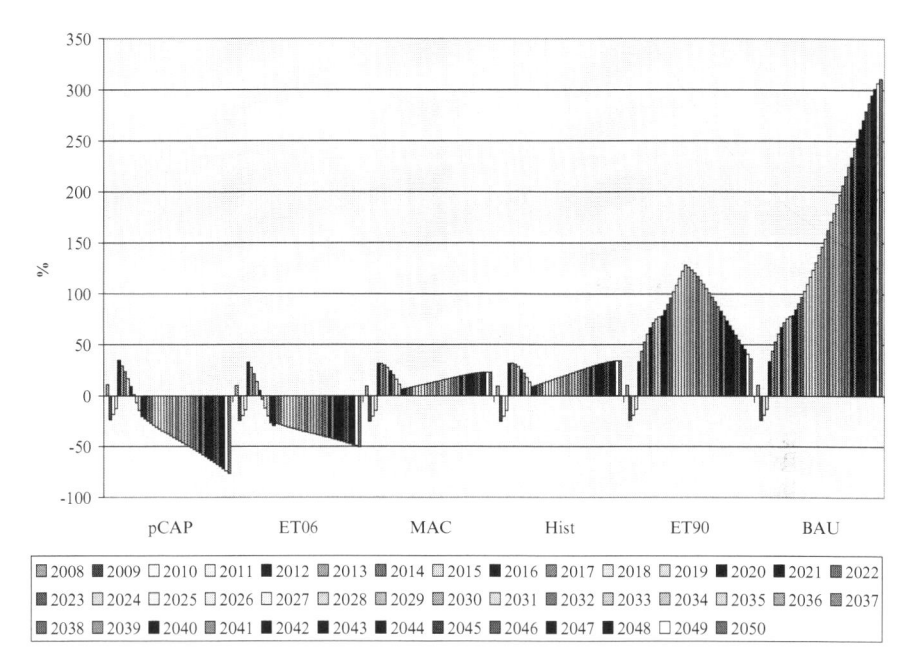

Comparative Analysis of Alternative Post-2012 Climate Policies

Fig. 9 Output of the metallurgical sector, as a percentage compared to 2007

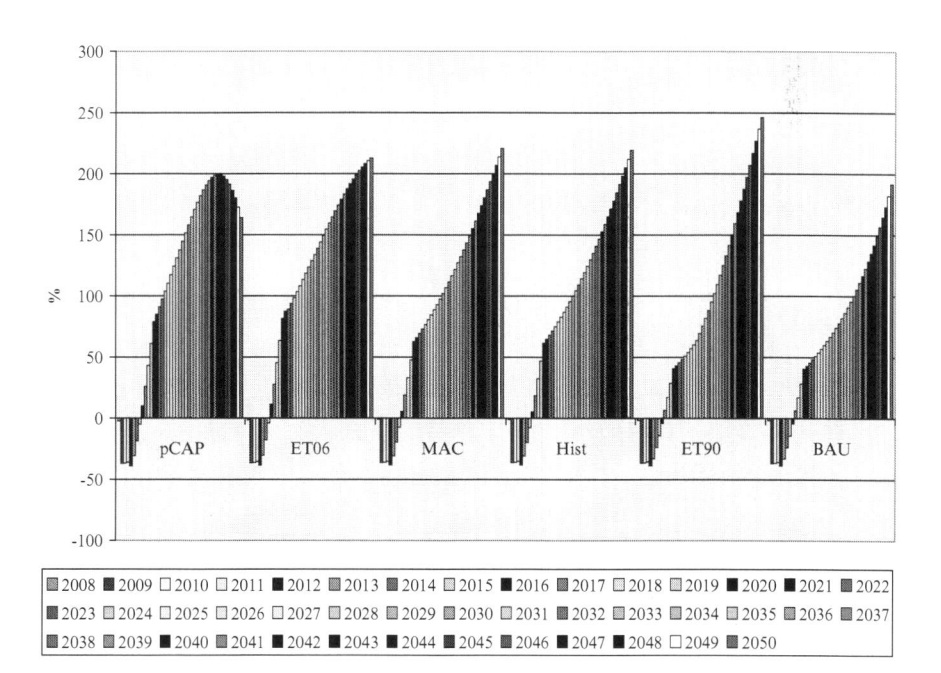

Fig. 10 Output of the food-processing sector, as a percentage compared to 2007

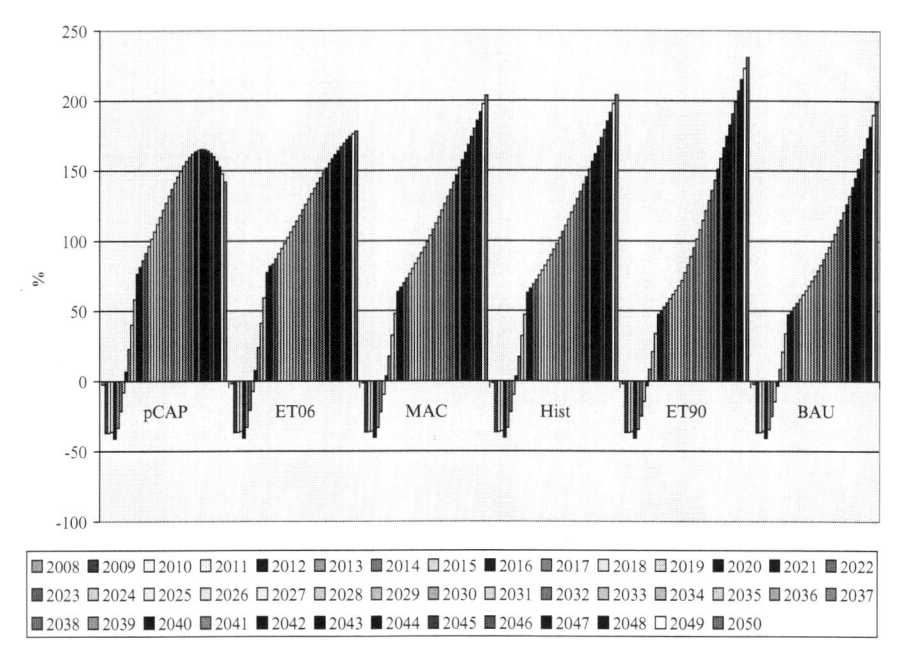

Fig. 11 Output of the agricultural sector, as a percentage compared to 2007

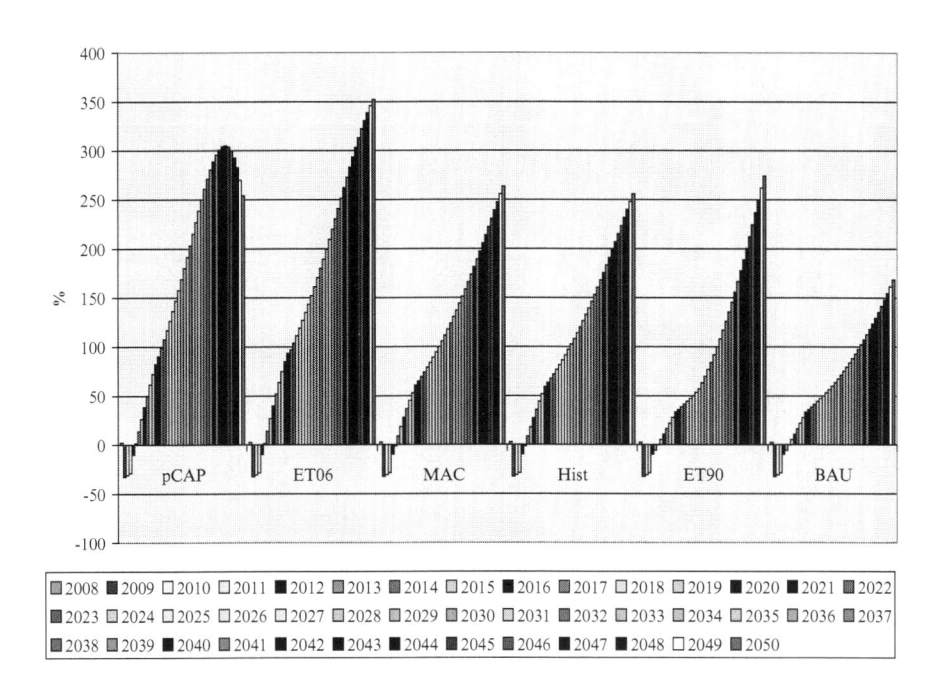

Fig. 12 Output of pulp and paper production, as a percentage compared to 2007

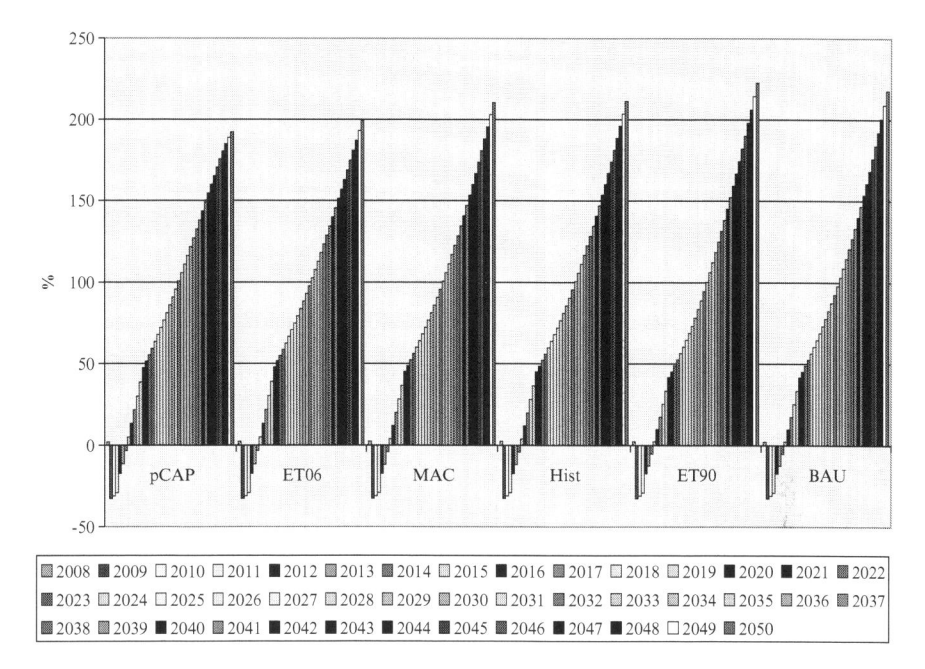

Fig. 13 Output of the ROI aggregate, as a percentage compared to 2007

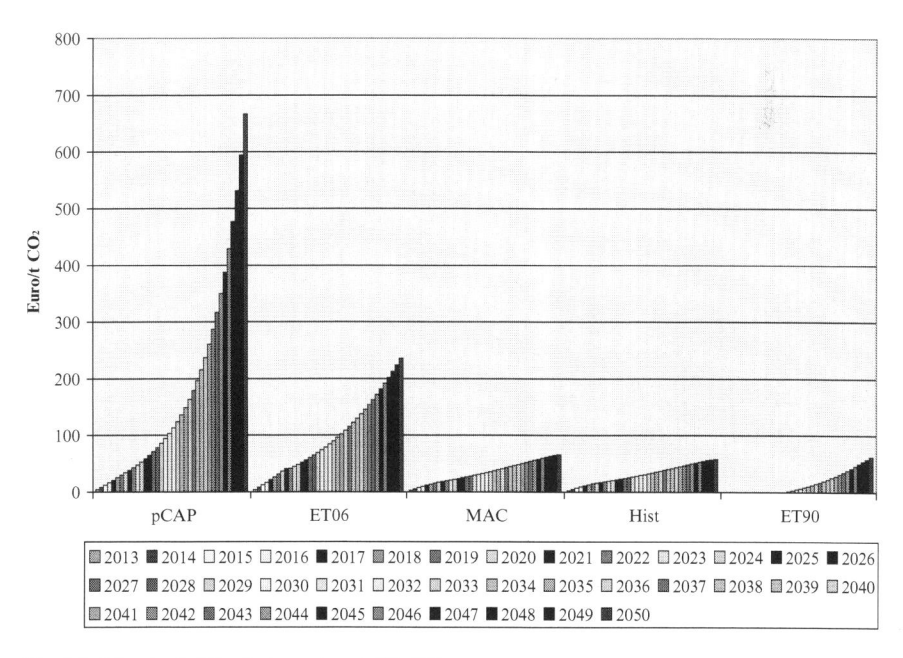

Fig. 14 Marginal CO_2 abatement cost, €/t CO_2

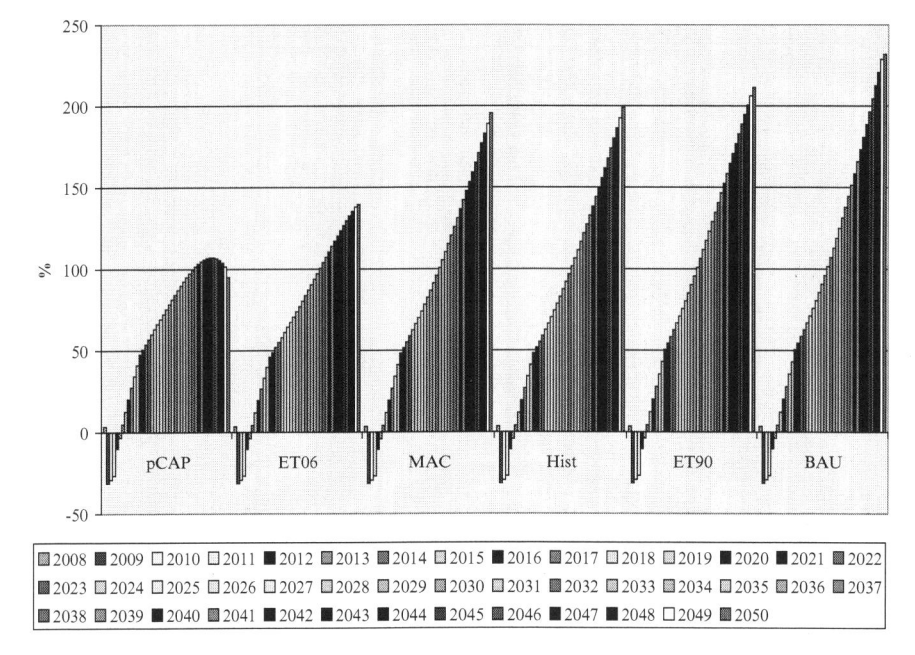

Fig. 15 GDP, as a percentage compared to 2007

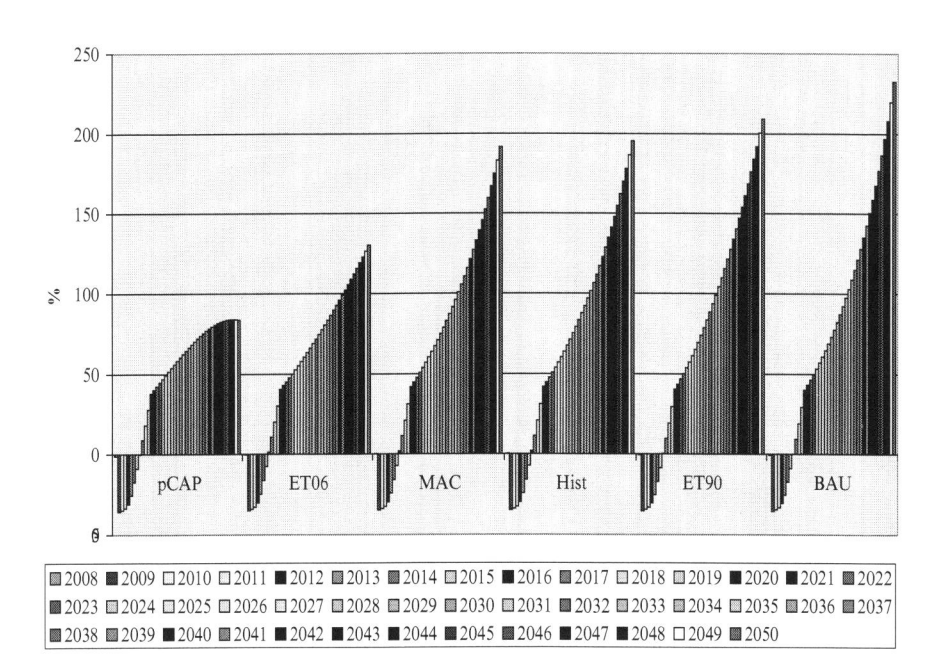

Fig. 16 Household consumption, as a percentage compared to 2007

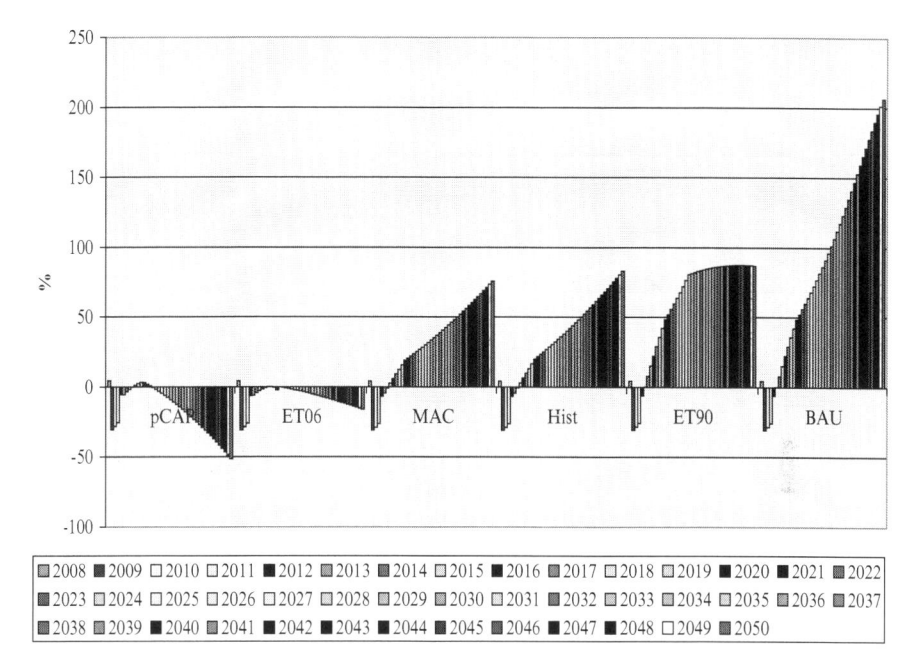

Comparative Analysis of Alternative Post-2012 Climate Policies 63

Fig. 17 Domestic energy consumption, as a percentage compared to 2007

100% and 140% respectively in 2050. Mild policies (MAC, Hist and ET90) allow for approx. a 200% increase in GDP by 2050 compared to the 2007 level.

Dynamics of cumulative household consumption follows similar trends to GDP.

Model results indicate significant energy saving reflected in terms of domestic energy consumption compared with the baseline trajectory (Fig. 17).

A decline in energy consumption and output of the most polluting industries induced by the post-2012 CO_2 abatement policies is accompanied by a simultaneous reduction in energy-related NO_X, TSP and SO_X emissions (Figs. 18–20). It results in a considerable reduction of human mortality and morbidity caused by these pollutants (Figs. 21 and 22). Although NO_X, TSP and SO_X cause substantial damage to ecosystems (acidification of soils, crops losses, eutrophication and acidification of surface and ground waters), these damages are likely to change at a similar rate. Once monetized, the adverse effects of air pollution would indicate significant losses to a national economy.

Without CO_2 reduction policies and end-of-pipe reduction of air pollution, mortality and morbidity in Ukraine would increase by 187% in 2050 relative to the level of 2007 (BAU scenario). Implementation of stringent CO_2 abatement targets represented by pCAP and ET06 scenarios would trigger a decrease in adverse health effects in 2050, by 51% and 31% respectively from the 2007 level. Moderate targets reflected by MAC, Hist and ET90 scenarios lead to growth in morbidity and mortality in 2050 by 36%, 43% and 47%, respectively, above the 2007 level (YOLL).

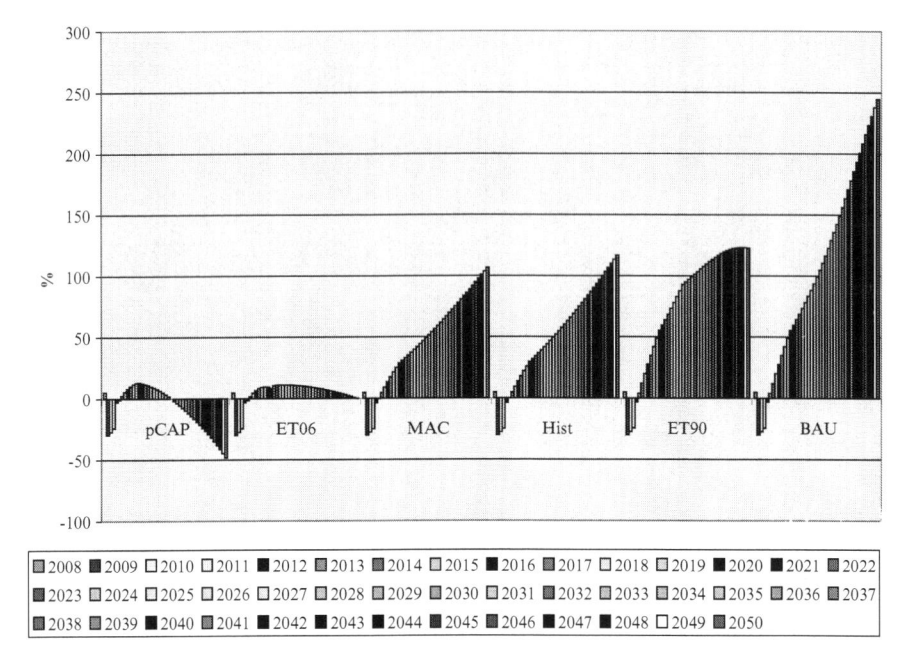

Fig. 18 NO$_X$ emissions in Ukraine (as a percentage compared to 2007)

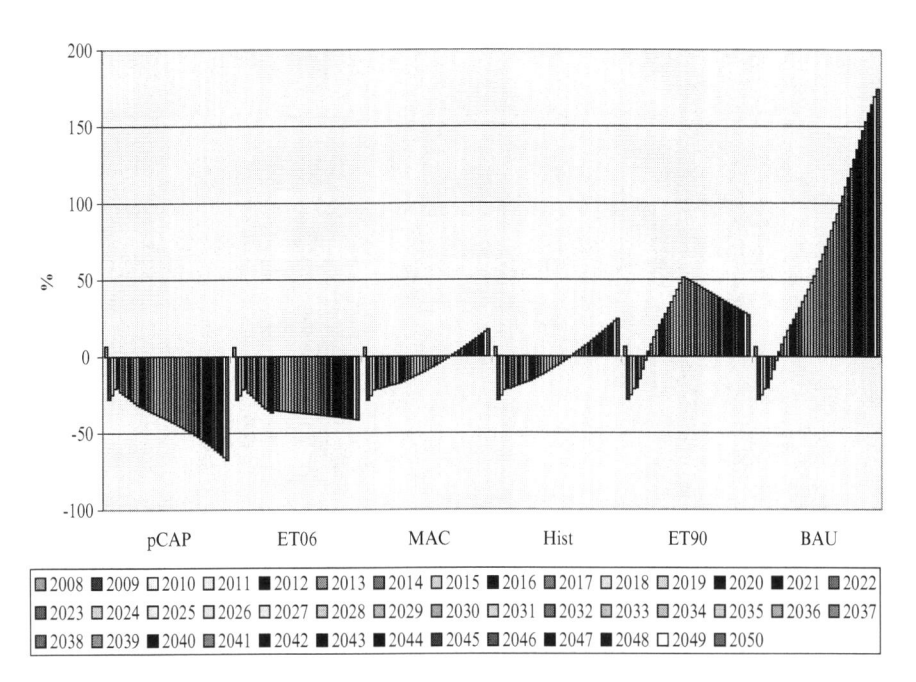

Fig. 19 SO$_X$ emissions in Ukraine (as a percentage compared to 2007)

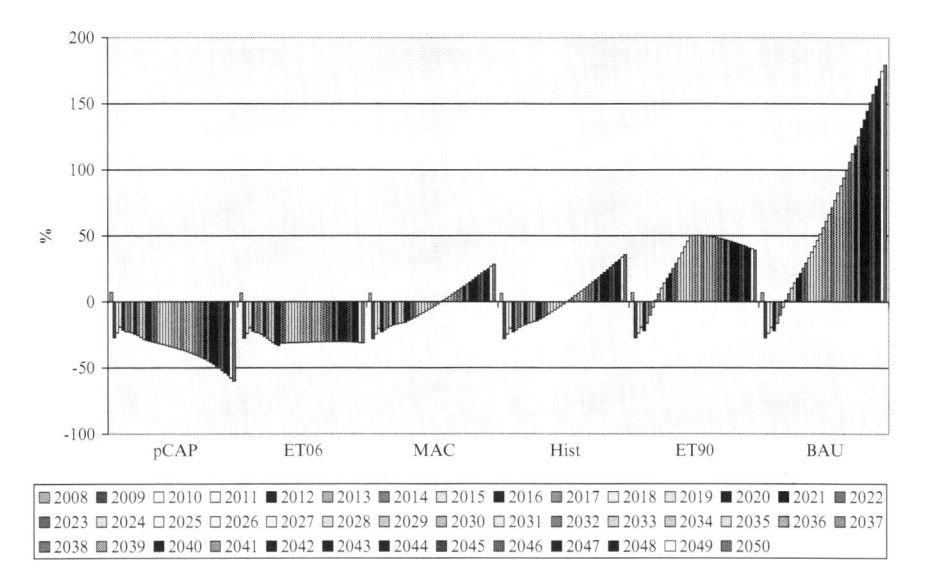

Fig. 20 TSP emissions in Ukraine (as a percentage compared to 2007)

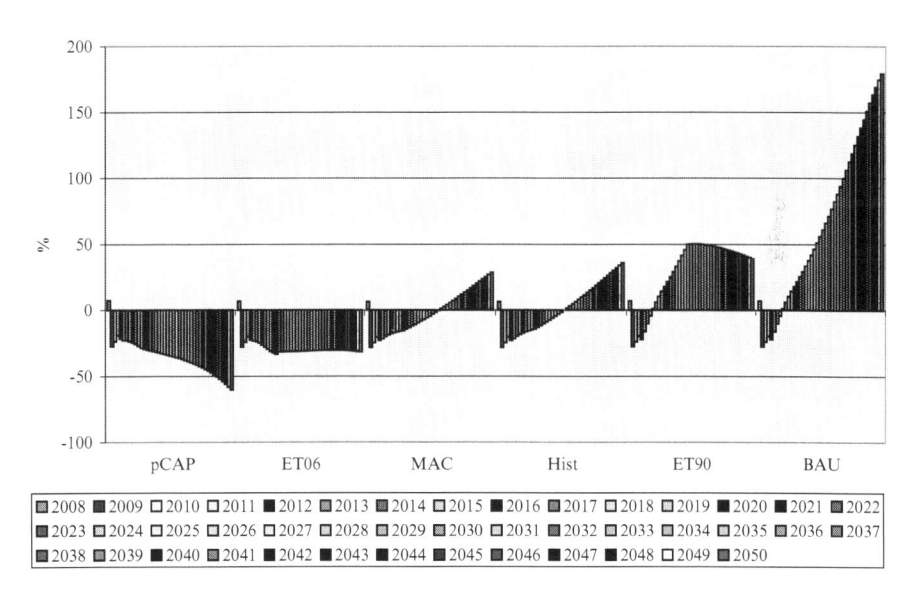

Fig. 21 Mortality and morbidity from NO_X, SO_X and TSP emissions (as a percentage compared to 2007)

Ukrainian economic growth without carbon reduction (BAU scenario) would result in 22,000 human deaths in 2020 and 52,000 deaths in 2050 from $PM_{2.5}$ discharges (low estimates) (Fig. 22).

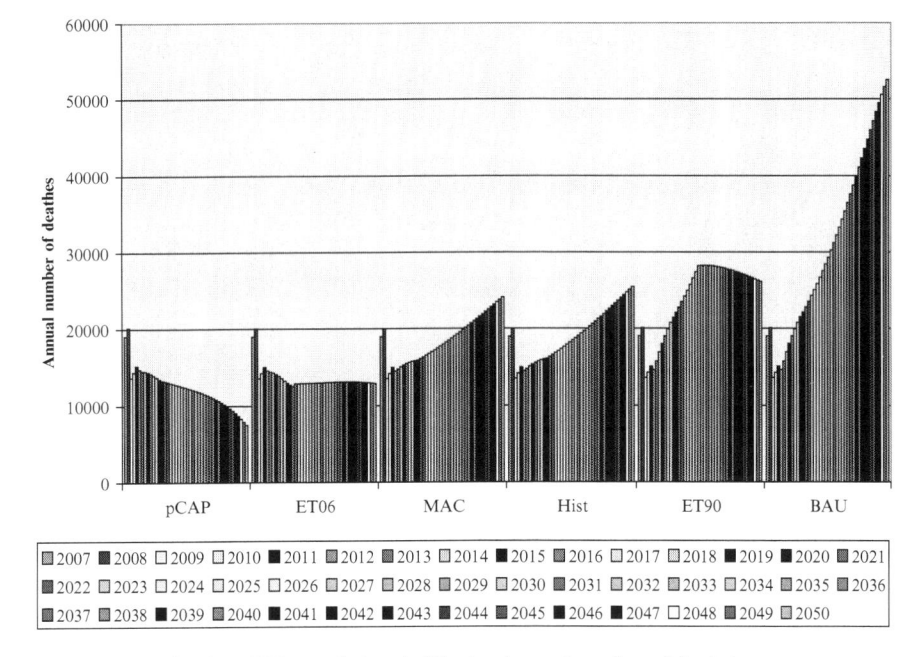

Fig. 22 Mortality from PM$_{2.5}$ emissions in Ukraine (annual number of deaths)

The implementation of low CO_2 reduction targets (MAC, Hist, and ET90 scenarios) would allow mortality in 2050 to be halved compared to the baseline values. Strict policies reflected by pCAP and ET06 scenarios decrease human mortality from PM$_{2.5}$ by 85% and 73% each relative to the baseline values in 2050. However, the net benefit on human health from CO_2 abatement is likely to be much higher, since the study does not link health effects to the emissions of other harmful energy-related substances such as CO, NMVOC and toxic metals due to the absence of country-level estimates of the health effects from these pollutants.

6 Conclusions

The application of a CGE framework to evaluate the alternative post-2012 CO_2 reduction targets for Ukraine allows the conclusion that the country could benefit from CO_2 reduction. CO_2 abatement brings structural changes towards the least energy-intensive industries with a high share of value added, a reduction in energy consumption and significant health improvements due to reduced air pollution. The magnitude of these effects depends on the stringency of the CO_2 abatement target.

Irrespective of the selected target, all scenarios show a similar pace of growth in cumulative output, GDP and household consumption until 2020. Therefore even the most stringent pCap and ET06 scenarios can be considered as policy measures over the 2013–2020 period. Such targets may be adopted over a longer term if significant technological improvements in energy savings are achieved in the country. Otherwise scenarios MAC and Hist that ensure both economic growth and CO_2 abatement can be selected.

The policy recommendations regarding the specific carbon reduction policy to be implemented in the country is beyond the scope of this study. Its ultimate objective is to assist Ukrainian delegation at the upcoming COP-16 negotiations by exposing the pros and cons of alternative post-2012 carbon reduction policies and the ancillary benefits that are associated with them.

References

Armington PS (1969) A theory of demand for producers distinguished by place of production. IMF S Pap 16:159–178

Bosello F, Roson R, Tol RSJ (2006) Economy-wide estimates of the implications of climate change: human health. J Ecol Econ 58:579–591

CAIT (2010) Climate analysis indicators tool (CAIT) version 7.0, World Resources Institute, Washington, DC. http://cait.wri.org. Accessed 10 July 2011

Chu Y-P, Lin S-M, Kuo C-W (2002) Analyzing Taiwan's air pollution: an application of the CGE model and the concept of green national product: https://www.gtap.agecon.purdue.edu/resources/res_display.asp?RecordID=1102. Accessed 10 July 2011

Copsey N, Shapovalova N (2008) Ukrainian environment policy and future SIDA assistance in the sector. SIPU report for the Swedish International Development Agency (SIDA) under contract 'Advisory Services for EU – Ukraine, Sida ref: 2007.002743. http://www.wider-europe.org/files/Ukrainian%20Environmental%20Policy.pdf. Accessed 10 July 2011

Criqui P, Kitous A, Berk MM et al. (2003) Greenhouse gas reduction pathways in the UNFCCC process up to 2025. Technical report. No. B4-3040/2001/325703/MAR/E.1 for the DG environment. CNRS-IEPE, Grenoble, France

Dessus S, O'Connor D (2003) Climate policy without tears: CGE-based ancillary benefits estimates for Chile. Environ Resour Econ 25:287–317

Droste-Franke B, Friedrich R (2004) Ukraine energy sector review: environmental issues, model air quality impacts of alternative energy scenarios – the EcoSense Ukraine Version, TTI/IER University of Stuttgart, Final report for the project Ukraine Energy Review funded by the World Bank Group Washington, Universität Stuttgart, Stuttgart

Ecofys (2006) Greenhouse gas stabilization targets: what are the near-term implications? Lee J, Center for Clean Air Policy, and Hoehne N, Ecofys. http://www.ccap.org/docs/resources/67/Lee_HoehneNearterm_Implications_of_Stabilization_Targets.pdf. Accessed 10 July 2011

Ecofys (2009) Climate action tracker. Detailed information on individual country pledges for greenhouse gas emission reduction. http://www.climateactiontracker.org/country.php?id=365. Accessed 10 July 2011

EMEP (2008) Centre on emission inventories and projections CLRTAP inventory submissions. http://www.ceip.at/emission-data-webdab/submissions-under-clrtap/2008-submissions. Accessed 10 July 2011

EMEP (2009) EMEP/CORINAIR emission inventory guidebook. Technical report No 6/2009. http://www.eea.europa.eu/publications/EMEPCORINAIR5/page002.html. Accessed 10 July 2011

Energy Information Administration (2009a) International energy statistics. CO_2 emissions. http://tonto.eia.doe.gov/cfapps/ipdbproject/iedindex3.cfm?tid=5&pid=5&aid=8&cid=&syid=1980&eyid=2008&unit=MMTCD&products=5. Accessed 10 July 2011

Energy Information Administration (2009b) International petroleum (oil) prices and crude oil import costs. http://www.eia.doe.gov/emeu/international/oilprice.html, International natural gas prices. http://www.eia.doe.gov/emeu/international/gasprice.html. Accessed 10 July 2011

Energy Research Centre (2009) Analysis of possible quantified emission reduction commitments by individual annex I parties, Winkler H, Marquardt A, Letete, T. http://www.erc.uct.ac.za/Research/publications/09Winkler-etal-possible-reduction-commitments.pdf. Accessed 10 July 2011

European Environment Agency (2009) EMEP/EEA air pollutant emission inventory guidebook. Technical report No 6/2009. http://www.eea.europa.eu/publications/emep-eea-emission-inventory-guidebook-2009. Accessed 10 July 2011

Ferris M C, Munson T S (2000) GAMS/PATH user guide. www.gams.com/docs/pdf/path.pdf. Accessed 10 July 2011

International Energy Agency (2009) Key world energy statistics 2009. http://www.iea.org/co2highlights/co2highlights.pdf. Accessed 10 July 2011

IIASA–the International Institute for Applied Systems Analysis (2008a) Comparison of GHG Mitigation Efforts for Annex 1 Parties. http://gains.iiasa.ac.at/gains/Annex1.html. Accessed 10 July 2011

IIASA–the International Institute for Applied Systems Analysis (2008b) Scenarios of SO_2, NO_x, and PM emissions in the non-EU countries up to 2020. www.iiasa.ac.at/rains/reports/CIAM%20report%201-2008v2.pdf. Accessed 10 July 2011

International Monetary Fund (2009) World economic outlook sustaining the recovery. www.imf.org/external/pubs/ft/weo/2009/02/pdf/text.pdf. Accessed 10 July 2011

IPCC (2007) Fourth assessment report. http://www1.ipcc.ch/ipccreports/assessments-reports.htm. Accessed 10 July 2011

Kuchler F, Golan E (1999) Assigning values to life: comparing methods for valuing health risks. Agricultural Economics Report No (AER784), USDA, Washington

McKinsey (2009) Reviving Ukraine's economic growth. http://www.mckinsey.com/aboutus/Ukraine_Economic_Growth_ENG.pdf. Accessed 10 July 2011

Ministry of Economy of Ukraine (2009a) Strategy of Ukraine's innovative development in 2010–2020 under the challenges of globalization. http://kno.rada.gov.ua/komosviti/control/uk/doccatalog/list?currDir=48718. Accessed 10 July 2011

Ministry of Economy of Ukraine (2009b) Main indicators of economic and social development in Ukraine (in Ukrainian)- 28.10.2009. http://www.me.gov.ua/control/uk/publish/category/main?cat_id=78198. Accessed 10 July 2011

Ministry of Environmental Protection of Ukraine (2006) Ukraine's report on demonstrable progress under the Kyoto protocol. http://unfccc.int/resource/docs/dpr/ukr1.pdf. Accessed 10 July 2011

Ministry of Environmental Protection of Ukraine (2008) National report on state of the environment in Ukraine in 2007. http://www.menr.gov.ua/cgi- bin/go?node=nac%20dop% 20p%20nps. Accessed 10 July 2011

Ministry of Environmental Protection of Ukraine (2009) National inventory of anthropogenic emissions in Ukraine for 1990–2007. http://unfccc.int/national_reports/annex_i_ghg_inventories/national_inventories_submissions/items/4771.php. Accessed 10 July 2011

Netherlands Environmental Assessment Agency (2009a) Exploring comparable post–2012 reduction efforts for annex I countries. http://www.pbl.nl/en/publications/2009/Exploring-comparable-post-2012-reduction-efforts-for-Annex-I-countries.html. Accessed 10 July 2011

Netherlands Environmental Assessment Agency (2009b) Pledges and actions –a scenario analysis of mitigation costs and carbon market impacts for developed and developing countries. http://www.rivm.nl/bibliotheek/rapporten/500102032.pdf. Accessed 10 July 2011

Nilsson C, Huhtala A (2000) Is CO_2 trading always beneficial? A CGE-model analysis on secondary environmental benefits. National Institute of Economic Research working paper, Stockholm, Sweden

Rutherford TF (1999) Applied general equilibrium modelling with MPSGE as a GAMS subsystem: an overview of the modelling framework and syntax. Comp Econ 14:1–2

State Statistics Committee of Ukraine (2009) Material and energy resources statistics. http://www.ukrstat.gov.ua/. Accessed 10 July 2011

State Statistics Committee of Ukraine (2010) Population in Ukraine. Available at http://www.ukrstat.gov.ua/. Accessed 10 July 2011

Strukova E, Golub A, Markandya A (2006) Air pollution costs in Ukraine. Fondazione Eni Enrico Mattei. Nota di lavoro 120.2006

UNFCCC (2009) Submission to the AWG-LCA and AWG-KP. Information relating to possible quantified emissions limitation and reduction objectives as submitted by parties. Joint submission by Australia, Belarus, Canada, Croatia, the European Community and its Member States, Iceland, Japan, Kazakhstan, Liechtenstein, Monaco, New Zealand, Norway, Russian Federation, Switzerland, Ukraine. http://unfccc.int/files/kyoto_protocol/application/pdf/awgkpjointqelrosubmission091009.pdf. Accessed 10 July 2011

UNFCCC (2010) Ukraine's pledge to the Copenhagen Accord. http://unfccc.int/resource/docs/2011/sb/eng/inf01.pdf. Accessed 10 July 2011

United Nations (1992) United Nations framework convention on climate change. UN document A: AC.237/18.2,3. United Nations

United Nations (2007) Environmental performance reviews: Ukraine – second review. www.unece.org/env/epr/epr_studies/Ukraine%20II.pdf. Accessed 10 July 2011

United Nations (2009) World Population Prospects: The 2008 Revision. Population Division of the Department of Economic and Social Affairs of the United Nations Secretariat. http://www.un.org/esa/population/publications/popnews/Newsltr_87.pdf. Accessed 10 July 2011

Van Vuuren DP, et al. (2006) Stabilising greenhouse gas concentrations at low levels: an assessment of options and costs Netherlands Environmental Assessment Agency. MNP Report 500114002/2006. http://www.rivm.nl/bibliotheek/rapporten/500114002.pdf. Accessed 10 July 2011

Wan Y (2006) Integrated assessment of China's air pollution-induced health effects and their impacts on national economy. http://www.soc.titech.ac.jp/publication/Theses2006/doctor/02D55113.pdf. Accessed 10 July 2011

World Bank (2003) The national strategy of Ukraine for joint implementation and emissions trading, National Strategy Studies (NSS). http://siteresources.worldbank.org/INTCC/1081874-1115369143359/20480440/Page182ToPage228NSSUkraineFinalReport2003.pdf. Accessed 10 July 2011

Design of Emission Allocation Plans and Their Effects on Production and Investment Planning in the Electricity Sector

Dominik Möst, Massimo Genoese, Anke Eßer-Frey, and Otto Rentz

Abstract The introduction of emissions trading and the design of allocation plans have far-reaching implications on the development of the power plant mix, on CO_2-emissions and the power plant investments of energy utilities. In particular CO_2- and electricity prices as well as the design of the allocation rules are becoming increasingly important for the investment strategies of energy utilities.

For this reason it is necessary to analyse the impacts of the EU Emission Trading Scheme on the future of power generation and investment decisions in the electrical power industry. For this purpose this paper presents some of the possibilities for analysing the impact of different allocation methods by using agent-based models and optimizing energy system models. Results show that the emissions allocation scheme has a significant influence on electricity generation planning and power plant investments and therefore also on the evolution of CO_2-emissions and the electricity market.

Keywords Agent-based model • emission allocation plans • emissions trading • energy and material flow model • investment planning

1 Introduction

Due to the possible effects on global warming, which is attributed to the man-made emissions of climate-relevant gases, climate protection has become a major topic within the environmental policy debate. To reduce the emissions of the greenhouse gas CO_2, a greenhouse gas allowance trading scheme (ETS) has been created across the enlarged European Union (EU) in accordance with the Emissions Trading

---

D. Möst (✉) • M. Genoese • A. Eßer-Frey • O. Rentz
Institute for Industrial Production, Universität Karlsruhe (TH), Hertzstraße 14, 76131 Karlsruhe, Germany
e-mail: Dominik.Moest@kit.edu

directive (ETD, 2003/87/EC). It was set up in January 2005 and was geared towards the energy industry and energy-intensive industries. Member states of the EU were obliged to provide so-called National Allocation Plans (NAPs), which fix CO_2-emissions reduction targets for different sectors of the national economy within a macro plan and which indicate how emission allowances are distributed to the relevant actors (a micro plan).

Due to the fact that within the ETS, the formerly free good "emission allowance" becomes scarce, companies are now forced to take this new production factor "emission allowance" into account (Fichtner 2007).

Since its introduction in 2005, the EU ETS has been characterised by increasing wholesale electric power prices across Europe as the price for emission allowances was integrated into spot prices of electricity. This price increase has led to a considerable public discussion on the legitimacy of the integration of CO_2 allowance prices into the market prices of electricity since emission rights themselves have mainly been allocated free of charge via NAPs.

To analyse the effects of emissions trading on investment and production planning decisions in the energy industry, so-called energy system models are widely being used. In the following, two modelling approaches for electricity markets will be presented, which show how emissions trading and NAPs can be incorporated into energy system models. First, the effect of CO_2-emissions trading on wholesale power prices and production planning will be presented. After that, results of a second model analysis concerning the effects of NAPs on investment decisions and the long-term development of emission allowance prices will be described. Before that however, in the following section important design options of NAPs will be illustrated.

2 Emissions Trading and National Allocations Plans

Emissions trading is an administrative approach used to control pollution by providing economic incentives for achieving reductions in the emissions of pollutants. A central authority (usually a government) sets a limit or cap on the amount of a pollutant that is allowed to be emitted. Any polluter is required to hold an equivalent number of credits or allowances representing the right to emit a specific amount. The total amount of credits cannot exceed the cap, limiting total emissions to that level. In general, the biggest advantage of emissions trading systems is seen in the exact target compliance, i.e. the emissions target is achieved without any information about emission reduction costs.

Assuming a given trading system and a reduction target, the crucial aspect is the initial allocation of emission rights. Basically, three general allocation methods are possible:

- Auctioning: the certificates are auctioned at the beginning of a trading period. In this case the expenditures for the certificates are cost and price relevant.
- A cost free allocation of emission allowances on the basis of former emissions (grandfathering).

- A cost free allocation of emission allowances on the basis of a reference unit, respectively a differentiated benchmark (benchmarking).

Furthermore, it has to be considered whether the emission allowances are allocated with a so-called ex-post adjustment. Unused emission rights have to be given back and thus cannot be sold on the market. In this case, the certificates are neither price nor cost relevant. The designated effect of the certificate trading systems is not achieved. Even if the emission allowances are allocated free of charge and thus will not affect the expenditures of a plant operator, the market price of the emission allowance will be integrated into the product price (electricity price), which leads to enormous additional profits (so-called "wind-fall profits") of energy utilities. The integration of these opportunity costs is inherent to the system (Fichtner 2007).

The dominant method for the initial allocation of emission rights in the EU: (within the period 2005 to 2007) is grandfathering without ex-post adjustment. In accordance with the European Burden Sharing agreement, every member state of the EU had to submit a National Allocation plan for the period 2005–2007, which is the first trading period and considered as a test period. Germany as the biggest emitter of CO_2 in the EU has chosen to provide allowances for the period 2005–2007 free of charge and most of the allowances for the second period 2008–2012 also free of charge. In total Germany has distributed 1,483 million emission allowances for the first trading period, thereof 21% to the emission intensive industries and 79% to the energy sector. About 15% of the emission allowances were allocated with the "option rule" with ex-post adjustment. 1,849 units participate in the emissions trading system. For units commissioned before 2002 the allocation is based on historical CO_2-emissions for a reference period. The quantity of the allowances is determined by multiplying the historical emissions data by a compliance factor ("grandfathering"). Allowances for installations commissioned between 1st January 2003 and 31st December 2004 are allocated based on announced CO_2-emissions data ("announced emissions"). If these announced emissions turn out to be too low or too high, an ex-post adjustment will be carried out. New installations (installed before 2007) are allocated with emission allowance free of charge for 14 years on the basis of a production forecast and a fuel-dependent benchmark, which is determined on the basis of the best-available technology. In general, as an alternative to the "grandfathering" rule, the option for announced emissions can be applied. If the "grandfathering" rule is applied, a plant is not allowed to run less than 60% compared to the base years; otherwise the allowances are reduced proportionally.

This implicates two things: The market price that an allowance is sold for, can be included as a cost component of generating electricity, irrespective of whether the allowances are distributed free of charge or not. The opportunity to sell the emission allowances is only provided if they have been allocated without ex-post adjustment; otherwise unused allowances have to be given back (see also Fichtner 2007). In consequence, the price for the emission allowance is not likely to be integrated completely into the pricing decision. Due to the choice of a fuel-dependent benchmark for new installations, the incentive to invest in low-emission-intensive generation technologies is reduced.

For the period from 2008 to 2012, the advantage of integrating the opportunity costs of emission allowances into electricity costs and thus generating "windfall profits" should be reduced with a significantly higher emission reduction factor for the electrical power industry in Germany. The new German allocation plan also contains less exceptional rules than the former one, e.g. the option rule has been eliminated. The allocation for new installations is based on a fuel-dependent benchmark (gas 365 g CO_2/kWh, coal 750 g CO_2/kWh) up to the year 2012 in combination with likewise fuel-dependent utilization hours (gas 7,500 h/a, coal 7,500 h/a and lignite 8,250 h/a) and a reduction factor due to the auctioning of certificates.

In addition to countries with a free allocation based on fuel-dependent benchmarks (e.g. Italy, Spain) there are also countries with a non-fuel-dependent benchmark (e.g. UK, Sweden).

In the following, a methodology is presented which was used to analyse the short-term effects of emissions trading on spot market prices. Thereafter, the impact of different allocation schemes on investments in the power industry is shown.

3 An Agent-Based Analysis of the Impact of CO_2-Emissions Trading on Spot Market Prices

The model used within this section can be categorized into the bottom-up energy system models. In general, the category of bottom-up approaches can be divided into optimisation models, equilibrium models, and simulation models (Ventosa et al. 2005). In the next section, an optimisation model integrating emissions trading will be presented. This subsection presents the agent-based approach PowerACE, which was developed to simulate the German electricity market and in particular to analyse the effect of emissions trading on wholesale electricity prices. The concept of agent-based simulation seeks to overcome some of the weaknesses of conventional modelling approaches by generating a simulation from a player's perspective which helps to integrate aspects such as player strategies, learning effects, or imperfect markets and information Bower (2001). The model approach that was used simulates the relevant players within the German electricity sector as one or more computational agents representing consumers, utilities, renewable agents, grid operators, government agents, and market operators. For a detailed description of the model see (Genoese et al. 2007).

The presented model incorporates a spot and a forward market for electricity, a market for balancing power and a market for CO_2-emissions. The aim of this paper is to analyse the impact of (exogenous) CO_2-emission allowance prices on spot market prices. The realistic simulation of the impact of certificate prices on spot market prices of electricity requires extensive data. Therefore, data has to be provided for electricity demand, renewable electricity generation, and the power plants in Germany as well as the prices for emission allowances.

The central basis for the analysis carried out in this section is the capability of the developed model to simulate spot-market prices in a realistic way. Previous papers have described the calibration of the model for the year 2001 (Genoese et al. 2007; Sensfuß et al. 2006). A comparison of model results and real world prices of the German spot market EEX shows that the model produces realistic results for the analysis of the German spot market. Every simulation is carried out as in the multi-run mode, to alleviate the effects of the random generated power plant outages. In order to provide a sound basis for the analysis of the impact of CO_2 allowance prices on spot market prices for electricity in the year 2005 a new calibration is carried out for the year 2004. 53 h with prices above 90 €/MWh are excluded from the analysis in order to exclude gaming effects and price outliers.

A comparison of the selected key indicators shows that the model provides a realistic picture of the main parameters for the electricity sector (see Genoese et al. 2007). Net electricity production and CO_2-emissions from the model are very close to real world data. The difference for both indicators is acceptable. It is less than 5% for CO_2-emissions and below 1% for the net electricity production. However, market prices from the model, which are based on fundamental data are below real world market prices, even if extreme market prices are excluded from the analysis. The simulation result is compared with the market price duration curve in Fig.1 in the upper left diagram. This result indicates that market prices in the year 2004 are not solely cost-driven. In a next step the simulation is run with a scarcity mark-up: this mark-up leads to a better correlation with real world market prices. Market prices and standard deviation are also closer to the real world time series. Therefore the application of scarcity mark-ups seems to improve the models capability of explaining the development of market prices in the year 2004. However, some differences remain, which may be caused by other factors that have not been integrated into the model. A detailed discussion about the German wholesale electric power prices of 2004 can be found in Rahn (2004). Possible effects are unexpected or unusual temperature development, load uncertainties and changing import/export flows. Considering all specific effects even a better correlation could be achieved, although this is not the key aspect of the analysis carried out in this section. Nevertheless, the model seems to be capable of providing a good basis for the analysis of the German electricity market.

Several scenarios have been defined to analyse the incorporation of CO_2-emission allowance prices into electricity prices. In the base scenarios the daily CO_2-emission allowance price has been incorporated into the variable costs of the supply side bidding taken in different proportions (0, 25, 50, 75, and 100%), irrespective of the power plant type.[1] Results are shown in Fig. 1 in the upper right diagram. Obviously the scenarios 0, 25 and 50% lead to electricity prices that are generally too low while the scenario of 100% leads to prices that are too high in the base-load period. The proportion of the CO_2-allowance price included in the variable

---

[1] In the following, we will use the term "allowance pricing" for the effect on variable costs.

Order market prices for the year 2004 and simulation results

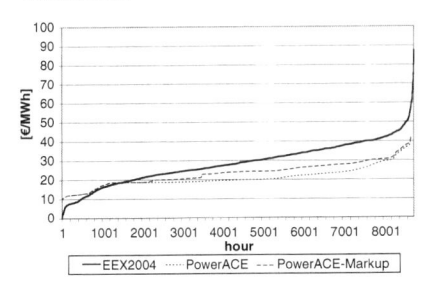

Pricing of allowance price into the electricity price in the base scenario for the year 2005

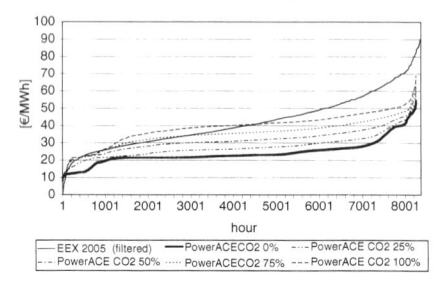

Variation of the "pricing" proportion depending on the technology; in 2005

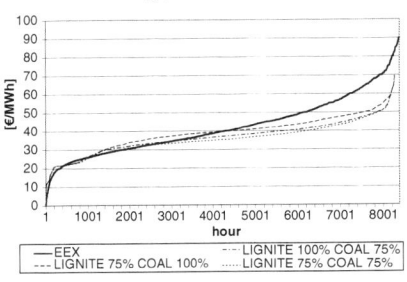

Mark-up factor and a pricing proportion for lignite with 70% and coal with 85%, in 2005

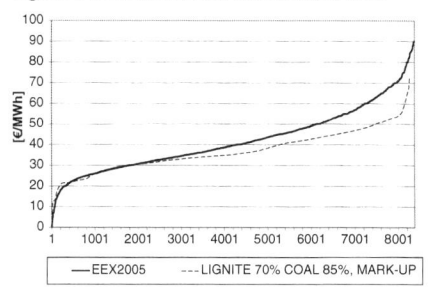

Fig. 1 Comparison of market prices and simulation results for different scenarios and years

costs seems to be about 75–100%. It can be seen from the model calculation, that emissions decline, the higher the proportion of the emission allowance price is that is included in the variable costs in the bid. This can be explained by a switch in the merit order from coal towards gas-fired and more efficient power plants.

The results lead to the assumption that the price for CO_2-emission allowance is likely to be priced between 75 and 100%. As mentioned in Sect. 2, about 15% of the emission allowances were distributed using the "option rule." It is not known exactly, which power plants were allocated using this rule. Thus, scenario variations were computed in this chapter, assuming that depending on the plant types the CO_2-allowance-price is included with different proportions in the variable costs of the power plant. The proportion for "allowance pricing" varies for lignite and coal-fired power plants. Results are shown in Fig.1 in the lower left diagram, where the scenario names refer to the fuel type and the proportion of the CO_2-allowance price used in the simulation (i.e. lignite 100% coal 100% means a full allowance pricing for both). Energy sources that are not mentioned have been priced at 100%. The results assume that coal and lignite-fired power plants in particular are not priced with the complete allowance price. The best fit seems to be in reducing both the proportion of lignite and coal-fired power plants.

In the next scenario, the scarcity mark-up factor presented is also included. The result is shown in Fig. 1 in the lower diagram on the right. A good fit is achieved for the scenario "LIGNITE: 70% COAL: 85%" in the price duration curve. The correlation coefficient reaches 0.68, the standard deviation 9.6, the average price 36.67, the minimum price 0, and the maximum price 72.75 €/MWh. It can be stated that the emission allowances are not priced completely, especially for lignite and coal-fired power plants. The reason for this might be the option rule and long-term contracts for the fuel supply (especially lignite), which both might partially avoid a switch in the merit order.

Based on the analysis of the results of the base load segment we can come to the conclusion, that about 75–100% of the CO_2-emission allowance price is included in the variable costs of the power plants. The reason for not completely pricing the emission allowances might be the allocation method. Fifteen percent of the emission allowances allocated free of charge in Germany have to be given back if they are not used and are therefore not price relevant for the bidding.

4 A Model to Analyse the Impact of Emissions Trading on Investment and Production Planning

The general objective of the energy system model PERSEUS-NAP[2] is to provide an analysis tool for the quantification of the economic and technological impacts that a CO_2-emissions trading system and the design of emission allocation plans may have on electricity prices, technology choices, CO_2-allowance prices and interregional power exchanges. PERSEUS-NAP is an energy and material flow model that applies a multi-periodic linear programming approach. The target function requires a minimisation of all decision-relevant expenditure within the entire energy supply system. This basically comprises fuel supply and transport costs, transmission fees, fixed and variable costs of the physical assets (operation, maintenance, load variation costs, etc.) and investment costs for new plants. The relevant techno-economic characteristics of the real supply system have been considered by implementing further equations covering technical, ecological and political restrictions. The most important technical restrictions are (a detailed description of the model can be found in Möst (2006):

- Physical energy and material balances: matching demand and supply taking into account storage options and the time structure of electricity and heat demand (load curves).
- Capacity restrictions: transmission capacities, availability of installed capacities, (de)commissioning restrictions, technical lifetimes of physical assets.
- Plant operation: maximum/minimum full load hours, fuel options, cogeneration options, load variation restrictions.

---

[2] *Program Package for Emission Reduction Strategies in Energy Use and Supply – National Allocation Plan.*

The PERSEUS-NAP model consists of 42 regions covering all Western, Central and Eastern European countries, in some cases even splitting one country into several regions. All power generators within one region compete on a free market for the regional electricity demand that has to be satisfied. However, at the same time there is also direct competition between the different regions given that neighbouring regions are connected by interconnection lines (represented as an interregional high voltage grid). The consideration of transmission capacities and losses as well as transmission fees ensures a realistic representation of the real power exchange characteristics within the model.

The interregional electricity market model – as it has been described until now – has already been successfully used for different analyses and studies (see e.g. Enzensberger 2003). However, the objective of analysing the impact of an emissions trading scheme on the physical electricity market requires the integration of a second market layer, namely the certificate market. Given the obviously strong interdependencies between both markets, the link has to be adequately reflected by the modelling approach that is selected. Every regional supply system is made up of a different set of physical power and heat generating facilities offering different operation options (availability, load variation possibilities, costs) and in particular different emission factors. However, emission rights, i.e. emission reduction targets, also vary between different countries and regional energy supply sectors. Therefore, any power exchange will directly affect emission balances and subsequently available emission rights. Furthermore, the direct links between power or heat generation and CO_2-emissions result in complex (price) interdependencies between the electricity and the certificate market.

NAPs of the emissions trading system are integrated into this linear programming model by a set of additional equations. Within the following model results, the allocation rules for new investments are of special interest. Within this model approach, new power plant technologies receive free emission allowances depending on the years of free allocation (e.g. 14 years compared to only up to 2012), the benchmark for fuel-type and full load hours (see Section 2), the capacity of the plant and the certificate price itself. As the certificate price is an endogenous result of the model calculations, the presetting of an endogenous parameter to calculate the investment grant could change the certificate price itself. Thus, an iteration process guarantees that the exogenously set investment grant (calculated with an exogenous certificate price from the former model calculation) will not vary from the certificate price calculated within the new model that is run.

Within the model it is assumed that the market prices of homogenous goods in an open and fully competitive market are set by marginal costs. We therefore use the marginal costs of the mathematical model to indicate both the resulting electricity prices as well as the certificate prices.

The model described above has been implemented as a PC version that can be run on most commercial PCs. However, due to its high complexity and the consequently large problem size, it requires state-of-the-art hardware components. The model is equipped with an MS Access-based data management system that enables easy data handling and a fully automated link to the mathematical module.

The model itself is programmed in GAMS (see Brooke et al. 1998). In order to solve the problem, commercial solvers such as CPLEX can be applied. The total model accounts for around three million variables. The calculation time ranges from 1 to 20 h and basically depends on the chosen time horizon.

5 Model Results: The Impact of the Design of Allocation Plans on Investment Planning

In the following some exemplary results of the PERSEUS-NAP model are highlighted. These results are based on three scenarios: A reference scenario (auctioning) with emission reduction obligations according to the allocation plans of 2005–2007 and 2008–2012 as well as a linear reduction from 2012 by 10% in total for the EU until 2030. It is assumed that new power plants are allocated with an auctioning of CO_2-allowances. In the second scenario (14 y allo.), an allocation scheme, which ensures 14 years of free allocation for new installations with fuel-dependent benchmarks and with adapted utilization hours is assumed. This scenario corresponds to the initial draft of the German NAP2. Within the third scenario (Curr. Nap) it is assumed that new installations receive a free allocation with fuel-dependent benchmark with adapted utilization hours until the end of the second emissions trading period (2012). This corresponds to the current version of the German NAP2.

Within the reference scenario, model results show that the future situation of the electricity sector in Germany is mainly affected by the nuclear phase out. Due to the emissions reduction obligations combined with an auctioning of certificates, new investments are mainly realized in gas and steam power plants. This has led to a steady increase in the share of gas in power production. Besides the replacement of nuclear power plants with gas and steam power plants in Germany, coal and lignite power plants, which have reached the end of their lifetime, are also mainly being replaced by less-carbon intensive technologies. Furthermore, the total electricity production in Germany remains at a relatively constant level, decreasing over some periods, however the total electricity demand is increasing. This has led to a significant increase in imports, especially from countries where new investments in nuclear power plants have been realized. Under an emissions trading system and the resulting market price for CO_2-emission allowances new nuclear power plants are an economically attractive option in European countries without a nuclear phase-out. The power exchange balance in Germany increases from a balanced level in the year 2005 up to an import of nearly 110 TW h/a by the year 2020. By contrast, the power exports in Switzerland increase up to 50 TW h/a by the year 2020 due to one new nuclear power plant and similarly the power export of France remains at a high level at nearly 80 TW h/a. The development of electricity production in Germany and France is shown in Fig. 2. Former model calculations using the PERSEUS model show (see e.g. Enzensberger 2003) that without emission reduction obligation, coal and lignite-fired power plants are the preferred investment for later periods, in particular to substitute the nuclear phase-out. Without emission reduction obligations, nuclear power plants are not an attractive option in other European countries. Thus the total share of electricity production from nuclear power plants decreases significantly within the power plant mix up to the year 2030.

In addition to the switch to less CO_2-intensive technologies under an emissions trading system, it has to be annotated that electricity prices will increase by more than 30% in the year 2010 compared to a scenario without emission reduction obligations. The development of marginal costs within the reference scenario is depicted for Germany, France, and Italy in Fig. 3. The marginal costs for CO_2-emission allowances start at a level of approx. 6 €/t CO_2 in the period 2005–2007, increase to over 14 €/t CO_2 in the second trading period and reach a value of up to 32 €/t CO_2 in the year 2030 (see Fig. 4). However, the marginal costs for CO_2-emission allowances have to be considered carefully and with regard to the model assumptions, as these can be strongly influenced by different factors and assumptions, like e.g. the amount of CO_2-allowances resulting from CDM projects.

Within the reference scenario Italy, Spain and the Netherlands are far from reaching their CO_2-emission reduction targets and thus are buyers of CO_2-emission

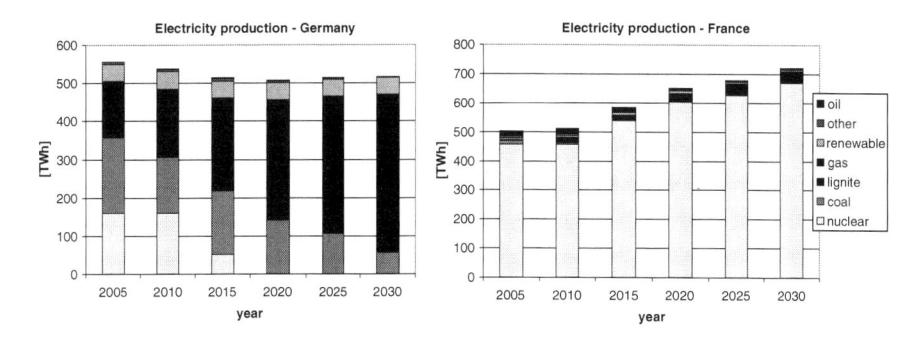

Fig. 2 Development of electricity production in Germany and France

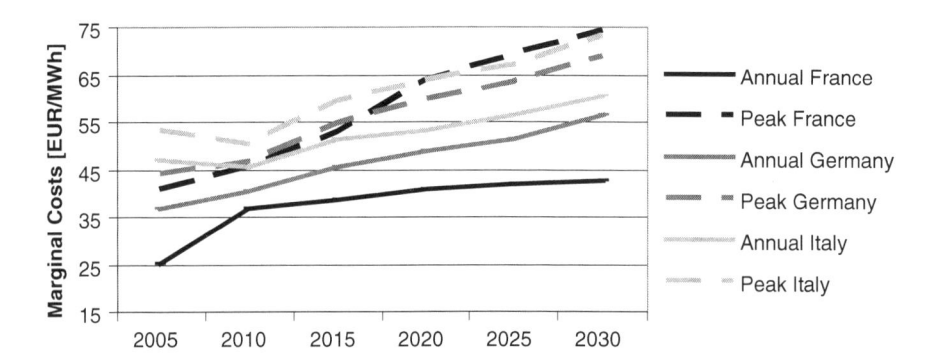

Fig. 3 Development of marginal costs of power production

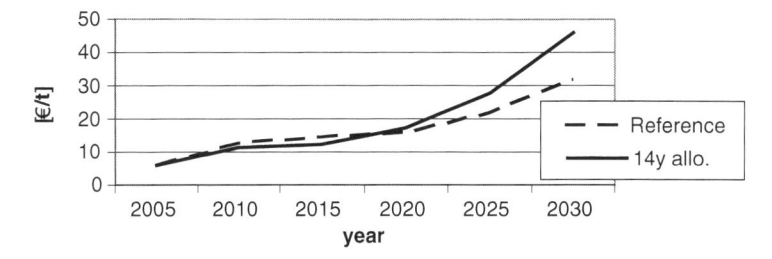

Fig. 4 Marginal costs for CO_2-emission allowances

allowances. Sellers of emission allowances are mainly Portugal, Germany, France, the UK and Greece.

Compared to the reference scenario, in the following scenarios, new investments receive free allocation based on a benchmark with adapted full load hours. This means, that lignite and coal power plants in particular receive a higher CO_2-emission allowance allocation than gas-fired power plants. In general, the free allocation of emission allowances can be seen as an investment grant. As this investment grant is lower for gas-fired power plants, lignite and coal-fired plants relatively speaking become more attractive. As expected, a significant increase in new investments can be seen in the model results for the second commitment period (2008–2012). In countries with nuclear power plants as an investment option, they are still the preferred option; however the total installed capacity is less than in the scenario with auctioning. Taking the investment grant into account, the share of coal power plants increases significantly in Germany. Besides coal-fired power plants, investments in gas and steam power plants are also realized in this second emission commitment period. The new capacities in the model run are consistent with announcements of energy utilities before the revision of NAP2, where approx. 17 GW of new coal and lignite power plants as well as approx. 13 GW of gas-fired power plants were announced (see e.g. VDEW 2007). Although lignite-fired power plants have not been chosen within the model calculation, a sensitivity analysis for the fuel price of lignite shows that these plants are an attractive option when a lower (but still realistic) fuel price than in the reference case is assumed. In general it could be stated that in comparison to the reference scenario the free allocation of CO_2-emission allowances on the basis of a fuel-dependent benchmark leads to higher investments in CO_2-intensive technologies. Due to the higher investment, which leads to a greater capacity and a higher electricity production in Germany, the power exchange balance is significantly influenced. Up to the year 2015, Germany will have a balanced power exchange. From 2015 onwards, energy imports will increase significantly from neighbouring countries and reach the same import level in the year 2030 compared to the reference scenario. The reason can be seen in the import of electricity from less CO_2-intensive nuclear power plants in neighbouring regions.

Due to the higher incentives to replace older plants earlier, the emission reduction target in the second emissions trading period (2008–2012) is achieved with lower marginal costs of CO_2-emission allowances than in the reference scenario.

However in later periods, marginal costs of CO_2-emission allowances increase significantly (atop the level of the reference scenario), as the effort to achieve the emission reduction target is higher, due to the investments in CO_2-intensive power plants (capital stock with a higher share of CO_2-intensive power plants) in former periods. The development of marginal costs of CO_2-emission allowances is depicted in Fig. 4.

The development of marginal costs of CO_2-emission allowances also has an impact on the development of marginal costs of electricity. The additional capacities in the first emissions trading period and the lower marginal costs of CO_2-emission allowances lead to lower marginal costs of electricity compared to the reference scenario. However, the marginal costs of electricity increase in most countries, but are less than in the reference scenario. In later periods, from 2015 onwards, marginal costs increase significantly and reach a higher level than in the reference scenario, which can be explained by the higher marginal costs of CO_2-emission allowances for these periods.

In a further scenario, the free allocation of allowances was reduced up to the year 2012, which corresponds to the current German NAP, as opposed to a free allocation for 14 years. After 2012, an auctioning of allowances is assumed. Model results show that the investment in gas-fired power plants increase compared to the scenario with 14 years of free allocation, whereas investments in coal and lignite-fired power plants decrease. The share of nuclear power plants is also slightly higher than in the scenario with a free allocation for 14 years. In Germany, less new plants are installed in the period from 2008 to 2012 compared to the scenario with 14 years of free allocation, however still more investments are realized than in the reference scenario. In total, 16 GW of new capacities are installed up to the year 2012. Marginal costs of emission allowances are quite similar to the development within the reference scenario and are approx. 1 €/t CO_2 less in the second emissions trading period compared to the reference scenario. This can be explained by the additional installed capacity compared to the reference scenario and the investment grant for the new capacities.

The former draft of the national allocation plan with 14 years of free allocation resulted in several declarations from the energy utilities (see e.g. VDEW 2007) to invest in coal and lignite-fired power plants. The model calculation shows the same tendency in the scenario with 14 years of free allocation, both in the amount and the type of power plants. As the model calculation under the scenario of the current NAP shows a significantly reduced investment in coal and lignite-fired power plants, the question arises as to whether the announcements of the energy utilities to invest in coal and lignite-fired power plants after the adaptation of the NAP2 will be realised to that extent in Germany.

6 Summary and Conclusions

Energy system analysis models have been widely and successfully used in the past supporting energy system development projections under different external circumstances. Within this paper it has been shown how such energy models can be amended in order to provide an analysis tool for certificate trading issues by taking into account different allocation schemes. The regionally differentiated representation of the energy supply system within the model and the integration of further energy-intense industry sectors are valuable steps in order to ensure the realistic consideration of existing technical or market-induced interdependencies between the two market layers, substitutional effects between different technologies and interregional effects such as electricity exchanges or certificate trading. This enables an analysis of the long-term development of the European energy systems focusing on the German one under different allocation schemes.

The analysis options shown within the scenario calculations cover the most relevant aspects that decision makers may need in order to get an indication of what are the most likely consequences are of introducing an emissions trading scheme in Europe: price information, energy system structures, technology choice and power exchange characteristics.

Based on the analysis of the short-term impact for the base load segment we come to the conclusion, that about 75–100% of the CO_2-emission allowance price is included in the variable costs of the power plants. The reason for not completely pricing the emission allowances might be the allocation method. Fifteen percent of the emission allowances allocated free of charge in Germany have to be given back if they are not used and therefore are not price relevant for the bidding. Another possible reason are long-term fuel contracts which might also partially avoid a switch in the merit order. By varying the share of the proportions of "allowance pricing" leads to the conclusion, that bids of lignite-fired power plants and coal-fired power plants are not endowed completely with the CO_2 allowance price. The analysis of shoulder and peak load segments shows that bids of gas-fired power plants are likely to include 100% of the price for emission allowances.

The agent-based model is mostly based on fundamental data, including scarcity mark-ups. The observed prices show that strategic behaviour might even have a higher influence as it can be explained by the modelled mark-ups. The results from running the model nevertheless show that with different emission allowance pricing, which is explicable with the allocation rules, this kind of electricity market model is purposeful. It is inherent to the system to include the price for the emission allowances in the bid of the power plants, if the allowances are liable to an ex-post adjustment, even if the emission certificates are distributed free of charge. To avoid windfall profits from the companies participating in the emissions trading, an auctioning of at least some of the emission allowances should be considered.

Within the scenario calculations for the long-term development with the second model, the impact of different allocation schemes on power plant investments and production planning was pointed out. Emission allocation schemes have a significant impact on the capital stock in the power industry. Within the scenario with an auctioning of emission allowances, gas-fired combined-cycle power plants are the preferred investment option. By contrast, a free allocation of emission allowances, especially with a long planning horizon of 14 years, leads to significantly higher investments in coal and lignite-fired power plants. The German national allocation scheme encourages pre-investments in the period 2008–2010, especially in coal- and lignite-fired power plants. In the short-term, emission reductions can be achieved due to the replacement of old capacities with this incentive. However, the involvement in relatively high CO_2-intensive technologies in the long-term capital stock necessitates intense efforts over later periods to achieve the emission reduction targets, which can also be recognized in the marginal costs of CO_2-emission allowance in the model results after the model period 2020. Thus in a nutshell, the effectivity of emissions trading strongly depends on the design of NAPs (see also Fichtner 2007), which means that emissions trading itself does not guarantee emission reduction measures with the lowest costs.

References

Bower D (2001) A model-based analysis of strategic consolidation in the German electricity industry. Energy Policy 29(12):987–1005

Brooke A, Kendrik D, Meeraus A, Raman R (1998) GAMS – A user's guide (Edition December 1998). GAMS Development Corporation, Washington, DC

Enzensberger N (2003) Entwicklung und Anwendung eines Strom- und Zertifikatmarktmodells für den europäischen Energiesektor. VDI Verlag, Düsseldorf

European Commission: Directive 2003/87/EC of the European Parliament and of the Council of 13 October 2003 establishing a scheme for greenhouse gas emmission allowance trading within the Community and amending Council Directive 96/61/EC. in: Official Journal of the European Union (2003a), S. 275/32–275/46

Fichtner W (2007) Der CO_2-Emissionsrechtehandel im Zentrum der umweltpolitischen Diskussion, in: Zeitschrift für Umweltpolitik und Umweltrecht (ZfU), Heft 2

Genoese M, Genoese F, Möst D, Fichtner W (2010) Price Spreads in Electricity Markets: what are the Fundamental drivers? Energy Market (EEM), 2010 7th International Conference on the European, pp. 1–6

Genoese M, Sensfuß F, Möst D, Rentz O (2007) Agent-based analysis of the impact of CO_2-emission trading on spot market prices for electricity in Germany. PJO Pac J Optim 3(3): 401–423

Möst D (2006) Zur Wettbewerbsfähigkeit der Wasserkraft in liberalisierten Elektrizitätsmärkten – Eine modellgestützte Analyse dargestellt am Beispiel des schweizerischen Energieversorgungssystems, Dissertation Universität Karlsruhe (TH). Peter Lang Verlag, Frankfurt

Rahn G (2004) Energie- und emissionshandel. BWK 58(4):50–54

Sensfuß F, Ragwitz M, Genoese M (2006) Assessing the impact of renewable electricity generation on spot market prices in Germany. Working paper. Submitted to Energy Economics

Sensfuß F, Ragwitz M, Genoese M (2008) The Merit-order effect: A detailed analysis of the Price effect of renewable ekectricity generation on spot opices in Germany. Energy Policy 36(8): 3076–3084

VDEW Verband der Elektrizitätswirtschaft e.V. (2007) Stromwirtschaft modernisiert Kraftwerkspark, Pressemeldung vom 12. Juli 2007

Ventosa M, Baillo A, Ramos A, Rivier M (2005) Electricity market modeling trends. Energy Policy 33(7):897–913

The Negotiation Process to Include International Aviation in a Post-2012 Climate Regime

Odette Deuber

Abstract In the past, negotiating climate policies to limit emissions from international aviation has proven to be exceedingly difficult. However, with the rapprochement of developing and industrialized countries in the face of a growing and evident need for adaptation and mitigation, positions are changing and new options to include aviation in a global climate regime are arguable. Against the background of the general political framework for a post-2012 climate regime, this article highlights the sector-specific challenges caused by the non-national nature of the sector and the current institutional setting. The paper presents possible options to include international aviation in a binding global climate regime and relates them to the negotiation positions of different actors. Special attention is paid to the global sectoral approach in international aviation coupled with the possibility of raising revenues for adaptation to climate change in developing countries. The paper comes to the conclusion that a global sectoral approach with climate financing could be the key to resolving the political deadlock between the need for effective global mitigation measures involving all global key operators and the need for a differentiated treatment of countries according to their capability and responsibility for climate change.

Keywords Adaptation funding • aviation • climate policy • common but differentiated responsibility • sectoral approach

Abbreviations

AGDG   Aviation Global Deal Group
AOSIS   Alliance of Small Island States

O. Deuber (✉)
Mathildenstr. 44, 72072 Tübingen
e-mail: odettedeuber@gmx.de

CBDR-principle	Principle of "Common but differentiated responsibilities and capabilities"
CO_2	Carbon dioxide
EU	European Union
EU ETS	European Emission Trading Scheme
GIACC	Group on International Aviation and Climate Change
IATA	International Air Transport Association
ICAO	International Civil Aviation Organization
IPCC	Intergovernmental Panel on Climate Change
LDC	Least Developed Countries
OPEC	Organization of Petroleum Exporting Countries
UNFCCC	United Nation Framework Convention on Climate Change

1 Introduction

The central challenge facing a post-2012 climate regime is to establish a commitment architecture that comprehensively takes into account the objective "to stabilize greenhouse gas concentrations in the atmosphere at a level that would prevent dangerous anthropogenic interference with the climate system" (Article 2 of the United Nations Framework Convention on Climate Change (UNFCCC)). Based on the scientific findings of the Third and Fourth Assessment Report of the Intergovernmental Panel on Climate Change (IPCC 2001, 2007), the European Union (EU), the Group of 20 and many other governments agreed on the target that the global annual mean surface temperature increase should be limited to a maximum of 2°C above pre-industrialized values (Council of the EU 2005; Point Carbon 2009a, b).

As an initial attempt to address risks posed by global climate change, the Kyoto Protocol's first 5-year commitment period officially began in January 2008. In December 2007, the international community came together in Bali to craft a 2-year roadmap to guide work in developing a post-2012 agreement. This roadmap, officially referred to as the Bali Action Plan, identifies a number of issues that negotiators will have to address to achieve a successful agreement at the 2009 Copenhagen climate change conference.

Emissions from bunker fuels, i.e. emissions from fuel used in international aviation and shipping, play a special role in international climate policies. These are currently excluded from the binding absolute emission targets in the Kyoto Protocol, although they are one of the fastest growing sources of greenhouse gas emissions. The sector's CO_2 emissions grew by 2.6% p.a. and 48% in total between 1990 and 2005, amounting to a CO_2 emissions level of around 960 Tg CO_2 in 2005 (WRI 2009). CO_2 emissions from bunker fuels are thus in the same order of magnitude as the emissions level of Germany, a large industrialized country (2007: 841 Tg CO_2 (EEA 2009)). International aviation is responsible for around half of CO_2 emissions from bunker fuels and its CO_2 emission growth rates are similar to the bunker fuel's average (IEA 2008).

While industrialized countries, i.e. Annex I countries, which have ratified the Kyoto Protocol, are obliged to reduce the total emissions from all other sectors by about 5%, the emission growth of bunker fuels can significantly impair global reduction efforts in other sectors. As a consequence, other sectors have to make even more significant reductions in emissions in order to achieve the 2 degree target (Anderson et al. 2006; Bows et al. 2009). In the EU, there is the risk that growth in the Community's share of aviation emissions could by 2012 offset more than a quarter of the environmental benefits of the reductions required by the EU target under the Kyoto Protocol (EC 2006).

Aircraft emissions released at high altitudes induce some significant non-CO_2 climate effects e.g. caused by the production of ozone, the reduction of methane and the formation of contrails and cirrus clouds (IPCC 1999). Current scientific evidence suggests that in aviation the sum of all radiative effects may exceed the radiative effect of CO_2 alone by a factor of 2–5 (Sausen et al. 2005; Lee et al. 2009b); however, considerable scientific uncertainties remain with regard to the non-CO_2 effects. Methodological difficulties in comparing short- and long-lived radiative effects and gases are particularly apparent in the aviation sector (Forster et al. 2006; Rypdal et al. 2005). In the negotiation process the focus is laid on limiting the global, long-lived greenhouse gas CO_2. At this point in time, considering non-CO_2 effects forms an additional hurdle with the potential to disrupt the whole negotiation process. A transitional arrangement from the initial inclusion of CO_2 only to covering climate impacts from all aviation emissions once there is a clear scientific basis seems to be the best way forward.

The objective of this article is to evaluate the current negotiation process on limiting emissions from international aviation and to identify a future policy framework which has both, the chance to be broadly supported and the potential to manage aviation emissions effectively. Against the background of the general political framework for a post-2012 climate regime, this article highlights the sector-specific challenges of international aviation. Possible options to include aviation in a post-2012 climate regime are outlined and evaluated in the context of past and current negotiation positions of different actors. The article provides a more detailed picture of a global sectoral policy framework in international aviation coupled with the possibility of climate financing. This approach is seen as a potential key to overcoming the political deadlock in the climate negotiation process in international aviation.

2 Political Framework for a Post-2012 Climate Regime

A fundamental requirement of any UNFCCC climate regime is to integrate countries in the commitment structure commensurate with their stage of development. This means that the "common but differentiated responsibilities and capabilities (CBDR)"-principle of developing and industrialized countries (Article 3 of UNFCCC) should be reflected in the type and degree of commitment. A future climate treaty to agree upon mitigation measures and to cope with adaptation will be negotiated on the basis of this principle.

In a post-2012 climate regime the commitment structures embedded in the Kyoto Protocol will probably be partly included; they are, however, discussed in a broader context. There is a move away from the historical division in "Annex I" and "Non-Annex I Countries," opening the floor for new combinations and degrees of commitment for developing countries (Watanabe et al. 2008). Diverse strategies for a post-2012 architecture have already been developed and discussed (e.g. Ecofys 2005; Den Elzen et al. 2007; Höhne 2005; Sterk et al. 2009; Members of the NGO Community 2009). At this stage it is still not conceivable as to how a post-2012 climate regime will finally be worked out. However, it can be assumed that the target for industrialized countries in 2020 will be in the range of 25–40% greenhouse gas reduction compared to 1990. For developing countries, a reduction of 15–30% compared to "business-as-usual" is then needed to cope with science-based postulations of the 2 degree target (Gupta et al. 2007, p. 776; Den Elzen and Höhne 2008; UNFCCC 2009). While it is certain that advanced developing countries and developing countries will be treated in a different manner, it is still unclear how the reduction in developing countries will be achieved (e.g. technology transfer, avoided deforestation) and, more importantly, who will finance this and with which institutional structures the transfers will be granted. Similar questions arise with regard to adaptation.

The UNFCCC and the Kyoto Protocol mandate Annex II Parties, OECD countries, to provide, among other things, financial resources to developing countries (Article 4.3 of the Convention, Article 11 of the Protocol). Negotiation practice in the climate protection process, however, has demonstrated that industrialized countries often showed great resistance to the granting of substantial financial transfers to developing countries as long as the developing countries are not willing to comprehensively monitor the investments and accept an appropriation of the funds for specified purposes.

The amount pledged or to be committed from Annex I Parties for climate financing remains far too low to meet the scale of the financing needs of developing countries in relation to climate adaptation and mitigation (Hepburn and Müller 2006; South Centre 2009). As an example, the operationalization of the Adaptation Fund which is to finance concrete adaptation projects had been caught up in a wrangle over its institutional arrangement for years (Watanabe et al. 2008, p. 150). In a post-2012 climate regime it is consensual that new, additional, also to existing Official Development Assistance flows, predictable and sustainable financial resources must be made available to support and finance various challenges of development. It is discussed how these financial resources can be raised and to what extent public or private investment is needed. It is apparent that innovative policy approaches are required as the need for adaptation funding by far exceeds the revenues which could be raised through domestic taxation (Müller 2006). The financial transfers from industrialized to developing countries, however, are crucial for the future South–North relationship.

In return, since the Bali Conference in 2007, the developing countries have been willing to participate more actively in a future climate regime, a long-standing postulation by some Annex I Countries, most prominently by the United States of America. According to the Bali Roadmap, all developed Parties have to reduce their emissions "quantitatively and in a comparable way" while developing countries have to make "their contribution to global emissions reduction with the support of developed countries in a measurable, reportable and verifiable manner" (UNFCCC 2008). Watanabe et al. (2008) see in the Bali Conference a significant shift in the battle lines and a rearrangement of positions and alliances that might well announce a decisive new era in global climate policy. They come to the conclusion that forging an alliance between North and South will be the key to successful negotiations on a post-2012 climate regime.

3 Specific Challenges for Including Aviation in a Binding Global Climate Regime

Emissions of international aviation are excluded from the binding absolute emission targets in the Kyoto Protocol. The transboundary nature of international aviation and the participation of international and domestic players cause several sector-specific challenges which make equal treatment with other sectors difficult.

3.1 Assignment to Parties

The question of emissions assignment to Parties was pivotal to the non-integration of the sector in the Kyoto Protocol. As at least two states are involved in international aviation, assignment could not be made according to the territoriality principle as in other sectors. Eight assignment options have been proposed by the Subsidiary Body for Scientific and Technological Advice. Later, however, only four of them – despite the status quo, i.e. no assignment at all – were considered to be feasible (UNFCCC 1996, 1997).[1] They have been evaluated comprehensively in research in recent years (e.g. Nielsen 2003; CE Delft et al. 2004, 2006). In spite of data-related uncertainties, these assignment options have been proven to be

---

[1]The five options are: assignment according to the country in which the bunker fuels are sold, assignment according to the nationality of the transporting company or to the country where an aircraft is registered or to the country of the operator, assignment according to the country of departure or arrival of the aircraft, alternatively: sharing of emissions between the country of departure and arrival and assignment according to the country of departure or destination of the passengers or cargo; alternatively, emissions related to the journey of passengers or cargo shared by the country of departure and the country of arrival.

feasible in practice, showing only slightly different distributional effects (Owen and Lee 2005; Lee et al. 2005). The Parties are in a position to appraise their implications both for themselves and for the commitment architecture of a future climate regime.

In theory, assignment to Parties is a reasonable solution. A prerequisite in practice, however, is that the international community agrees on a commitment structure that provides for assignment to Parties and goes hand in hand with a particular institutional setting. There are, however, sound arguments against allocating CO_2 emissions from international aviation to Parties and instead striving for a sectoral approach in international aviation, in which the assignment to Parties is superseded, see Sects. 4 and 5. To conclude, assignment to Parties represents more than a technical challenge; it is part of an institutional setting which could be agreed upon if political will prevails. The assignment itself should not be responsible for a political deadlock.

3.2 Institutional Setting and Principles

Article 2.2 of the Kyoto Protocol obliges Annex I countries to pursue the limitation of greenhouse gas emissions from international aviation by working through the International Civil Aviation Organization (ICAO).[2] In contrast to other sectors, there is a dual responsibility: UNFCCC discusses the issue of assignment whilst ICAO is responsible for the development of effective climate policies and measures.

In 2004, the ICAO General Assembly endorsed the concept of an open, voluntary emissions trading scheme in international aviation (ICAO 2004; ICAO/CAEP 2004; ICF Consulting 2004; Scheelhase and Grimme 2007). However, steps towards the implementation of an international emissions trading scheme have not, as yet, been taken. Dissatisfaction over this failure by ICAO has prompted the European Commission to develop an amendment to the European Emissions Trading Scheme (EU ETS) that includes all aircraft operators flying in and out of Europe from 2012 onwards in the trading scheme, see Sect. 4.3. The 2007 General Assembly of ICAO adopted a critical attitude towards this scheme and urged Member States not to apply an emissions trading system on another state's airlines "except on the basis of mutual agreement between those States." In response to this Assembly Resolution, all 42 European Member States of ICAO entered a formal reservation and stated that they did not intend to be bound by it (ICAO 2007).

In preparation for the climate summit in Copenhagen in 2009, the ICAO Assembly set up the Group on International Aviation and Climate Change (GIACC) in 2007. The Group, with an equal participation from developing and developed

---

[2]ICAO codifies the principles and techniques of international air transport. In order to ensure safe, secure and sustainable civil aviation, it fosters the planning and development of the international aviation market by setting standards. These standards, developed on a cooperative basis among its Member States, are uniform on a global level.

countries was entrusted with developing an action plan targeted at the reduction of aviation emissions. In the summer of 2009, the GIACC recommended non-binding fuel efficiency goals of 2% per annum. For many this represents little more than "business as usual" and would not deal with the emissions rise caused by a projected annual increase of 5% in air traffic. Longer-term targets of aviation carbon neutral growth by 2020 or of actual emission cuts were discussed without agreement. These few ambitious targets can be seen as a missed opportunity for ICAO to show leadership. The plan is not a credible basis for the Copenhagen Agreement as it lacks the essential elements of any climate strategy: a base year for measurement and a target for emissions reduction in absolute terms.

In sum, consensus at the global level through ICAO on the introduction or use of economic instruments has not been reached so far (Lee et al. 2009a). From the European perspective, the climate policy-making process in ICAO is rather slow and deficient. Over the past decade, work performed within the ICAO has not resulted in concrete actions to appropriately address the growth in emissions.

According to Oberthür (2003), the lack of action at ICAO has so far not been made up for by measures within the climate change regime. An important motivation for efforts of ICAO is the potential regulatory competition with the climate change regime. However, the UNFCCC process on limiting emissions from bunker fuels is also sluggish. In the past, OPEC countries and the United States of America blocked negotiations on bunker fuels much more than in any other sector. Moreover, developing countries did not urge developed countries to introduce effective mitigation policies in international aviation. Thus, given the lack of political will to limit emissions from bunker fuels within the UNFCCC, the motivation of potential regulatory competition has not been very forceful.

Furthermore, the choice of emission assignment regulation and the corresponding commitment architecture have immediate implications for the set-up of policies and measures, and vice versa.[3] Thus, for effective climate policy, these negotiation issues have to be treated together (CE Delft et al. 2006). A close co-ordination of UNFCCC and ICAO could contribute to a forward-looking policy process. However, in practice the two institutions are hardly linked. In theory, almost the same contracting states are represented in both organizations; the missing link is mainly due to inconsistent policies in countries with diverging positions of transport and environment ministries. Furthermore, co-operation is made difficult as the institutions have strongly diverging priorities and principles. One aspect exemplifying the different positions is the attitude towards unilateral action such as the inclusion of aviation in the EU ETS. Unilateral action turns out to be a strong driving force for an ambitious climate regime. It is generally in line with the principles and visions of UNFCCC. ICAO, however, strongly opposes it.

ICAO aims for a policy framework which treats all actors in the same way. The framework shall be uniform on a global level in order to avoid market distortion

---

[3] Some countries are Parties to the UNFCCC but not to ICAO and vice versa.

in the highly competitive air transport market. ICAO's institutional principle, however, appears to run counter to the CBDR principle of UNFCCC. In fact, the application of this fundamental principle of the UNFCCC process in the aviation sector represents a great challenge. The CBDR principle was set up to reflect differences in national circumstances of the countries and different historical responsibilities for climate change. The most relevant aspects influencing the responsibility for climate change and capability to cope with it are the economic structure of the country, which is closely related to the emissions reduction potential and its costs, the historical responsibility, the stage of development, the vulnerability to climate change and the dependency on the export of natural resources (Höhne 2005). International transport, however, differs from ground-based emission sources. It contributes to economic development by linking different economies and allowing economies to exploit comparative advantages. For example, in 2008, Emirates (Dubai), Singapore Airlines (Singapore) and Cathay Pacific Airways (Hong Kong) were the fourth, fifth and sixth largest airlines in the world with regard to international scheduled passenger-kilometers flown (IATA 2008). These airlines are highly competitive global players with considerable market shares. The economic benefit of the hubs in Dubai, Singapore and Hong Kong is facilitated by a favorable geographical location to interconnect different economic regions. The performance of the aviation industry is only limitedly related to the structure of the economy and historical responsibility. Due to the non-national nature of international air transport activities, it is not necessarily correlated with the economic performance of the nation state to which the transporting company belongs or in which fuel is sold.

In conclusion, the operationalization of the CBDR principle in the aviation sector plays an important role in the political debate and provides leeway within the negotiation process. A more subtle distinction of responsibility and capability could be a door opener to finding innovative negotiation solutions.

4 Negotiation Process for Including Aviation in a Post-2012 Climate Regime

While the first experiences with the implementation of binding abatement commitments under the Kyoto Protocol have been made in other sectors, the political process for limiting emissions in international aviation has developed only slightly in comparison. In view of sectoral particularities, the question arises as to how the sector can be integrated in a reasonable manner into a future climate regime. In order that institutional and methodological difficulties do not become a barrier to the introduction of binding absolute targets in international aviation, pragmatic and innovative approaches are required. In the following, different policy approaches for the aviation sector are outlined. Subsequently, positions of different country groups and regional initiatives which act as driving forces in the negotiation process are presented.

4.1 Possible Policy Approaches in the Aviation Sector

Realizable and feasible ways in which international aviation transport could be incorporated into a post-2012 climate regime are outlined comprehensively in CE Delft et al. (2006). In a multi-criteria analysis three approaches scored best: a global solution including the national level, a global sectoral approach and a regional start. They are described in the following.

4.1.1 Assignment to Parties and Stacked Policies and Measures

In this approach, emissions are allocated to the country of arrival or departure of the aircraft and are included in national emission totals. The route-based assignment option is chosen on the one hand as the market distortion and possibilities for evasion would be less compared with other options and on the other hand it reflects well the economic benefit of linking economies. In order to allow for differentiated commitments according to the CBDR principle, the targets as well as the policies and measures are stacked: all countries introduce, for instance, technology standards or agree to phase out "climate-unfriendly" subsidies. In addition, advanced developing and industrialized countries have to comply with intensity targets, i.e. by implementing performance standards and emission charges. In addition, industrialized countries commit themselves to absolute emission targets, preferably by establishing an emissions trading scheme. The policies address direct Kyoto-gases only while flanking measures are intended for indirect greenhouse gases. In this approach, UNFCCC as the central actor is responsible for setting the national targets and enforcing them. ICAO develops guidance on policies and measures while the countries coordinate and implement them.

4.1.2 Sectoral Approach

Various sectoral approaches are possible. All of these have one thing in common and that is that emissions are not allocated to countries but to the sector itself. In the sectoral approach favored in the analysis by CE Delft et al. (2006), the UNFCCC assigns responsibility for the sector emissions to the ICAO. ICAO implements an emissions trading scheme and sets a cap which agrees with UNFCCC policy targets in other sectors, providing the basis for an inter-sectoral linkage of trading schemes. The differentiation of responsibilities according to the CBDR principle should be route-based; however, how the final design works out is a matter of negotiation.[4]

---

[4]One way of implementing this differentiation would be to require operators to surrender allowances on specific routes only i.e. in and between industrialized and advanced developed countries. Another way would be to require operators to surrender allowances for all their

ICAO plays a key role in this institutional set-up while aircraft operators surrender allowances and nation states are responsible for the compliance of aircraft operators with the policies.

Alternatively to a global scheme harmonized with UNFCCC policy targets, a different sectoral commitment was discussed, consisting of pledges agreed under ICAO to contribute to mitigating climate change. This is in line with the current tasks and responsibilities of ICAO and could therefore build on the existing organizational capacities. Second, there would not be a direct need for differentiating commitments, since commitment could be made without reference to the UNFCCC's CBDR principle. However, the participation of developing countries is exceedingly doubtful if their specific interests are ignored. Furthermore, in view of the past, the question arises as to whether ICAO is capable of introducing stringent climate policy measures. The type of policies and measures most likely to be introduced by ICAO would be technical regulations, with potentially more stringent measures likely only on a voluntary basis, at best. Given the projected growth, a stabilization or absolute reduction of emissions seems unlikely for a sectoral commitment outside the UNFCCC. Against this background, CE Delft et al. (2006) consider this approach to be inferior to one which is harmonized with the UNFCCC policy framework.

4.1.3 Regional Start

In case international aviation is not incorporated into a global climate regime, groups of nations will implement political measures for limiting the climate impact of international transport. Using the example of the EU ETS and its possible expansion beyond European nations, CE Delft et al. (2006) evaluate the potential of such a regional start. The regional start is only second best as aspects of equity and a broad coverage are not guaranteed. It is not addressed in detail here since a regional start will only be considered a favorable option if a global solution fails to be achieved.

There are numerous criteria for assessing the different approaches: environmental effectiveness and economic efficiency aspects but also practical and political criteria addressing e.g. equity and the polluter-pays-principle. The global approaches are both effective and score best based on these criteria. They could minimize market distortion while at the same time maximizing the environmental effect by facilitating broad participation. Avoiding market distortion in the competitive international aviation market is one of the major key factors for political acceptance. In any case, a route-based system seems to be the best approach as effects on the competitive positions of airlines can be kept small, which is also a lesson learnt from the EU ETS (Wit et al. 2005). Furthermore, the link to the overall climate

---

emissions on routes in or between industrialized countries, for a part of their emissions on routes in or between advanced developing countries and no allowances for routes in or between least developed countries (CE Delft et al. 2006).

regime in terms of the international carbon market seems to be a prerequisite for binding ambitious targets in the aviation sector. As long as the environmental integrity of the overall climate regime is ensured, emission growth in aviation can be accepted. In both global approaches, the CBDR principle is taken into account on the level of policies and measures. However, looking at the overall global policy framework (see Sect. 2), it is questionable whether the proposed differentiation sufficiently meets the needs of developing countries. The two global approaches differ mainly with regard to the institutional set-up, namely the role of ICAO and UNFCCC, the coverage as well as the addressee of assignment; all of them critical matters for negotiation in the past (see Sect. 3).

In practice, many influential actors in the negotiation process, including the aviation industry, endorse the global sectoral approach. Section 4.2 provides a more detailed picture on positions of different actors in the negotiation process and Sect. 5 outlines how the global sectoral approach could be coupled with the need of developing countries for climate financing. The approach that will be short-listed in the future, however, depends not only on the benefits and drawbacks from an aviation perspective but also strongly on the overall negotiation process and principles and the overall commitment architecture in a post-2012 regime.

4.2 Nation States' Positions

The positions of all countries in the climate negotiation are continuously evolving over time. With changing governments after national elections, with new scientific findings and gradually advancing climate change, attitudes toward global climate policy are subject to change. Starting with the positions from the past Kyoto process, it will be shown how some Parties gradually shift their positions in the current negotiation process.

Several principal Annex I countries like e.g. the United States, Australia and Japan had been in favor of exemption of bunker fuels from the UNFCCC process. By supporting a global sectoral scheme under ICAO, the aspects of free competition and equal treatment of all states have been at the fore. However, looking at the ICAO policy-making process in the past, demanding an ICAO-based scheme that is uncoupled from the UNFCCC process goes hand in hand with a global policy of the "least common denominator," in which a strong climate regime does not have priority.

With new governments coming into power in Australia in 2007 and in the US in 2008, positions towards climate protection have changed radically. In June 2009, Congress adopted the US Waxman-Markey Climate Change Bill, which regulates the set-up of an ambitious national CO_2 cap and trade scheme (Climate Change Bill 2009; Greenair 2009). The upstream trading scheme, which should cut carbon emissions by 17% from 2005 levels by 2020 and 83% by 2050, indirectly also covers international bunker fuel sold in the US. However, the Climate Bill still has to be adopted by the Senate before it can be written into the law. In response to ICAO's failure to agree on a mechanism for dealing with international aviation greenhouse gas emissions, Australia has become the first country to formally propose that international aviation be controlled under a global sectoral agreement by the UNFCCC rather than by ICAO (Reuters 2009).

Developing countries formed, in the past, the direct counterpart to the advocacies in favor of a global scheme under ICAO. They firmly supported the application of the CBDR principle under UNFCCC in the form of non-inclusion of developing countries. However, in contrast to climate negotiations in other sectors under the Kyoto Protocol, the non-Annex I countries showed little initiative when it came to demanding absolute emissions reduction in air traffic by Annex I countries. This diffidence and partial blocking of negotiations can be traced back to the differing but mostly economic motives of individual groups of countries: the members of the Organization of Petroleum Exporting Countries (OPEC) fear a downturn in the demand for kerosene; the Alliance of Small Island States (AOSIS) and many other developing countries are themselves very much dependent on air traffic for tourism, the import and export of merchandise as well as the domestic transportation of merchandise. Moreover, there was little necessity to open air traffic to Clean Development Mechanism projects and thereby to financial transfers to developing and advanced developing countries since emission reduction potentials are very limited in their scope and rather cost-intensive compared to other sectors (e.g. energy production, waste treatment). Fundamentally, there is the fear that air transport will become more expensive as a result of the restriction on air traffic emissions and that demand for certain export goods such as tourism will fall, or that imported goods will experience significant price increases.

The positions of some developing countries, and especially of those developing countries which are most vulnerable to climate change like the AOSIS and the least developed countries (LDCs), are likely to change in the negotiation of a future climate regime. At the climate summit in Poznan in December 2008, the Maldives presented a proposal on behalf of 50 LDCs. As the LDCs have a strong interest in new and additional funding for adaptation, independent of bilateral replenishment, they launched a proposal suggesting an International Air Passenger Adaptation Levy (Group of LDCs 2008). As only those passengers are affected by the levy who have the capability of flying internationally, their defensive attitude towards a global scheme including flights from and to developing countries is gradually breaking down. They assessed the impact on tourism to be minimal. Furthermore, most of the governments are becoming increasingly aware of the findings by Stern (2007), that the costs of taking action to reduce greenhouse gas emissions now are smaller than the costs of economic and social disruption from unmitigated climate change. With advancing climate change, for some small island states the financial impacts of aviation mitigation policies on tourist mobility and trade appear to be minor compared with the costs of direct climatic impacts, the indirect environmental and societal change impacts (NEF and WDM 2008; UNWTO and UNEP 2008). Countries with emerging markets such as China, Brazil and Argentina, however, still oppose a global scheme and plead in favor of the CBDR principle on the mitigation side.

The political will among European decision-makers to address aviation emissions appears to be high as evidenced by the inclusion of aviation in the EU ETS (see Sect. 4.3). The EU is in favor of a global sectoral approach in which assignment to Parties is dispensable. Any action to reduce emissions should take into account the possible net negative impact on isolated regions, remote islands and LDCs. The European Council reiterates that Parties should commit themselves to working with ICAO in order to reach an agreement in 2010, which can be approved in 2011.

The European Commission and the Council of the EU are convinced that ICAO has the responsibility of facilitating the development and adoption of global measures by the end of 2011 (EC 2009; Council of the EU 2009). However, if by the end of 2011 ICAO fails to reach an agreement, the European Commission will endorse plans for emissions from international aviation to be allocated to Parties under the Copenhagen agreement, which will ensure comparable action by all developed countries (EC 2009). Whether the Member States and the European Council will advance the Commission's view, is questionable however.

The commitment architecture proposed by the EU (and Norway) is partially in line with the LDC proposal. Both the EU and the LDC proposal strive to adapt a scheme that includes all global emissions. According to the polluter pays principle, the responsibility should be assigned to air passengers on a personal level and not on a national country level. Different treatment of developed and developing countries should be accounted for in the form of financial compensation through revenues. In contrast to the LDCs' proposal on a levy, the EU, however, is in favor of an emissions trading scheme with auctioning. The aviation sector should be treated consistently with a global reduction path towards meeting the 2°C objective, notably with reduction targets of a 10% reduction below 2005 levels by 2020 (Council of the EU 2009, p. 7). The EU attaches importance to ensuring environmental effectiveness whereas the aviation levy can also be designed as a purely revenue-raising instrument without a (significant) impact on emissions.

4.3 *Role of the European Emissions Trading Scheme in Aviation*

For more than a decade the international community could not agree on concrete climate measures or targets for emissions from bunker fuels. Due to the political deadlock, the European Community finally decided to go ahead by including CO_2 emissions from all flights within, from and to the EU in the EU ETS from 2012 onwards. On the basis of a feasibility study (Wit et al. 2005), the European Commission put forward a draft proposal in December 2006. The final Directive of the European Commission and the European Parliament (Directive 2008/101/EC) was adopted in 2008.

Europe's advance strongly influences the global negotiation process. From 2012 onwards, roughly 50% of global CO_2 emissions from international aviation will be subject to a binding target, irrespective of a global consensus at the climate summit in Copenhagen. While the European Member States took decisions on the design of the scheme, the blocking attitude of non-EU countries has prevented them from joining the discussion on important design issues. As it is obvious that all countries have an interest in controlling aviation regulations concerning flights from their home destination, non-EU governments are under pressure to discuss mitigation options on a global level.

The EU ETS allows for the possibility of excluding flights departing from a third country to an EU airport if that country adopts measures for reducing the climate change impact of flights. The planned US cap-and-trade scheme could well qualify as such a measure, suggesting that flights departing from the US would be excluded from the EU ETS. However, the articulation between the US and EU scheme might not be so straightforward because the coverage applies to fuel purchase in the US rather than flights departing from a US airport. The implementation of different conflicting and potentially overlapping national and regional policies enhances the need for a uniform climate regime in aviation which could significantly reduce compliance costs (Greenair 2009).

Many of the active aviation market actors are basically in favor of a global homogenous regulation rather than a regional or national approach. They fear market distortion such as carbon leakage and want to ensure equal treatment of all actors in accordance with the Chicago Convention. Although the EU ETS is route-based to ensure the equal treatment of all airlines on the same route, there might be some market distortion between EU and non-EU airlines due to the fact that it is a regional approach (Scheelhase et al. 2008; CE Delft and MVA Consultancy 2007). With the European Directive having been adopted, airlines with a large share of flights falling under the EU ETS have incentives to stand up for the negotiation of a global climate deal at the UNFCCC summit in Copenhagen. In sum, including aviation in the EU ETS might have increased the political pressure on non-EU governments and on the airline industry to limit the so far unrestricted growth of international aviation emissions.

5 A Global Sectoral Approach in International Aviation Coupled with the Need for Adaptation Funding

There is a strongly growing and evident need to mitigate and adapt to climate change and a need for climate financing. The beginning of rapprochement between developed and developing countries represents a promising point of departure for the inclusion of aviation in a post-2012 regime (see Sect. 2). Given the highly competitive global aviation market in which advanced developing countries play a significant role, new options within the commitment architecture are arguable. One expression of a new era in climate negotiation in which negotiation principles are adapted to the changing environment and challenges is the idea of a global approach in which the need for funding for mitigation and adaptation measures is combined with a revenue-raising instrument to reduce aviation emissions.

Faced with a potential patchwork of different national and regional schemes, along with a proposal from LDCs for a levy on international aviation, the aviation industry has thrown its weight behind a global sectoral approach. In 2009, the International Air Transport Association (IATA) called for a global sectoral approach. IATA believes that with some political leadership and innovation solutions, equal treatment between airlines and differentiated responsibilities for States are completely consistent in the context of international aviation (IATA 2009). For the first time important business actors are boldly calling for the inclusion of international aviation in a post-2012 climate regime. An industry coalition, the "Aviation Global Deal Group" (AGDG) comprising key airlines from Europe and Asia was formed because ongoing efforts to address aviation emissions had been largely unsuccessful.[5] The Group's intention is to develop a practical, business-led solution that helps contribute to global efforts to address climate change. They argue in favor of a global scheme in which revenues are raised by auctioning. The Group suggests using auctioning revenues for climate change initiatives in the developing world and a proportion of the revenues to support low-carbon technology research and development programs in the aviation sector (AGDG 2009). The airlines' willingness-to-accept that revenue funds are spent predominantly outside the sector and do not inure to the benefits of either their customers or the airline's country of origin prove that the AGDG wants to take responsibility for the consequences of climate change, beyond their own financial interests. There is a real concern about tackling aviation emissions in a global sectoral scheme which includes all countries.

A global sectoral approach in international aviation designed to reduce or limit emissions and to raise revenues for adaptation at the same time creates differential treatment of countries through the allocation of revenues rather than by stacking commitments on the level of policies and measures. Müller (2006) and Agarwal (2000, p. 6) provide important arguments for such an approach. Agarwal (2000) introduces the distinction between "luxury" and "survival" emissions, referring to per capita emission figures of developing and developed countries. There is no generally accepted definition of "luxury" emissions. It is, however, difficult to argue that international air travel emissions are "survival" emissions, and indeed a large proportion would probably be legitimately classified as luxury emissions. Nef and WDM (2008) has assessed that the highest income group are disproportionately responsible for emissions from aviation. This is true for both, developing and developed countries. Müller (2006) argues in the context of "luxury" emissions that there are good reasons for personalizing or de-nationalizing the responsibility, so that individuals are associated with the responsibility for emissions, regardless of the sovereign territory on which they occur. Air passengers are responsible for

---

[5]In October 2009, the AGDP comprises several West-European airlines (Air France-KLM, British Airways, Finnair, Virgin Atlantic, the Virgin Blue Airline Groups), the airport operator BAA, one East-European Airline, LOT Polish Airlines and two key players from non-Annex I countries, Cathay Pacific and Qatar Airways.

emissions and reveal their economic capability by their ability to fly internationally. On ethical principles, it is therefore fair to ask all nations to address emissions from air travel in accordance with the CBDR principle. However, smaller developing island states, in which tourism constitutes a major industry and provider of local employment, might argue, that individual travel is a "luxury," but that tourism as such, which goes hand in hand with emissions, is "survival."

There are several surveys (Brouwer et al. 2008; Hooper et al. 2008) that evaluate air passengers' willingness to pay to offset the climate impacts of their flights. Brouwer et al. (2008) found in a survey at Schiphol airport that 75% of the air passengers are in principle willing to offset their greenhouse gas emissions, while differences are apparent depending on the home continent of the traveler. The motivation of air passengers who are willing to contribute stems from the recognition of responsibility and accountability of climate change as well as the genuine belief in the detrimental effects of climate change on future generations.

In practice, however, very few air travelers are currently offsetting their emissions. There is a large discrepancy between stated and revealed preferences. Brouwer et al. (2008) explain this gap between theory and practice due to the voluntary nature of offsetting programs. They argue that the willingness-to-pay increases if offsetting is mandatory which makes "free riding" impossible and if the effective use of revenues for climate change policy is guaranteed. According to Hooper et al. (2008) only a much smaller proportion of passengers is willing to offset. This proportion could, however, increase significantly if benefits of offsetting are reliably guaranteed. Furthermore, in the context of more robust and widespread climate change mitigation activity with standardized carbon markets as well as ambitious institutional responses to climate change, air passengers' willingness to pay would grow even more markedly (Hooper et al. 2008). The results of both surveys reveal that there are air travelers who are in principle supportive of measures that increase the cost of their travel based on the polluter pays principle. A prerequisite, however, is a robust, comprehensive and mandatory climate policy framework so that individual behavior contributes in real terms.

At the same time, there is an urgent need to provide adequate, predictable and sustainable financial resources to assist developing Parties that are particularly vulnerable to the adverse impacts of climate change in meeting the costs of adaptation. The cost of adaptation in the developing world will be in the tens to hundreds of billions of Euros annually (Stern 2007, p. 442). Since potential revenues from a fiscal instrument in air traffic might generate annual financial resources in the region of billions (Hepburn and Müller 2006; AGDG 2009), its implementation could contribute in real terms. Furthermore, these revenues could easily exceed the resources of the Special Climate Change Fund, the LDC Fund and the Adaptation Fund, which were established earlier on.

In principle, it is debatable whether two central challenges of the negotiation process can be addressed successfully by one single instrument, particularly as it has proved difficult in the past to effectively address each challenge individually. However, moral and pragmatic reasons demonstrate that there are chances to overcome the political deadlock of the past by addressing the subjects simultaneously.

Making funds available for adaptation is central to the North–South relationship and finally to the success of future climate regimes. Moreover, due to the genuinely international character of aviation, raising international funds is facilitated. Revenues are raised directly from responsible and capable individuals without touching on domestic regulations. Climate financing could be the key to resolving the political deadlock between the need for effective global mitigation measures involving all global key operators (reflecting the ICAO principle) and the need for a differentiated treatment of countries according to their capability and responsibility for climate change (CBDR principle).

6 Summary and Conclusions

In the past, limiting emissions from international air transport has proven to be politically exceedingly difficult, with sector-specific challenges hampering the negotiation process. The non-national nature of the emissions rendered the assignment to Parties difficult. The lack of political will and the institutional setting of the dual responsibility of UNFCCC and ICAO with strongly diverging principles adversely affected the political process. The operationalization of the moral obligation of CBDR under UNFCCC appeared to contradict the market principle of equal treatment of all actors under ICAO. This dilemma was clearly reflected in different negotiation positions of developing and developed countries in the Kyoto process.

Although the application of the CBDR principle is still one of the major challenges to be met, the situation does seem to have altered with regard to the post-2012 negotiations. UNFCCC, the EU, Australia, the Group of LDC, IATA and some leading airlines show a strong interest in including aviation emissions in a future climate regime. With the first steps taken in the Kyoto Protocol, with advancing climate change and with the growing need for adaptation and mitigation, negotiation positions change. A rapprochement between developed and developing countries can be observed, in the overall climate negotiations but also with regard to international aviation. If political will prevails, different policy approaches to include aviation in a future climate regime seem to be feasible, e.g. an assignment-based global scheme with stacked policies and measures, a global sectoral scheme in which assignment to Parties is indispensable or a regional approach. There are strong arguments in favor of a global sectoral scheme, but which approach is finally chosen depends largely on the overall negotiation process and commitment architecture.

A global sectoral approach in international aviation in which greenhouse gas emissions are limited while revenues for climate change purposes are raised, seems to be an attractive option. Such an approach may pave the way out of the past dilemma: it is generally in line with the CBDR principle under UNFCCC by providing the revenues predominantly to developing countries and it is consistent with the central postulation of ICAO – the equal treatment of all airlines. A global scheme in a highly competitive market is more likely to be accepted by industry than any regional approach. Revenues are raised from airlines which pass them on to their customers. This consistent implementation of the polluter-pays principle is, from an ethical and moral point of view, a very convincing and equitable strategy. However, raising revenues for developing countries might be part of the solution but it should not be at the expense of effective measures to tackle aviation's growing emissions. Absolute emission reduction targets are needed.

In order to implement a global fiscal scheme in international aviation there is definitely a need for stronger UNFCCC leadership and enhanced cooperation between UNFCCC and ICAO. In the Kyoto Protocol, Parties were charged to work through ICAO towards the development of policies and measures to limit the emissions of international aviation. Even though this UN organization seems to be predestined to implement policies in the international aviation market, the slow and non-committal policy-making process raises the question of the future role this institution will assume in a post-2012 climate regime. In sum, there is considerable leeway for negotiations on including aviation in a post-2012 regime: the targets themselves, the way in which the targets will be achieved, the institutional setting and the role of aviation in the overall commitment architecture.

References

Agarwal A (2000) Climate change: a challenge to India's economy. Centre for science and environment. Briefing paper for members of Parliament. http://www.cseindia.org/programme/geg/pdf/cse_briefing.pdf. Accessed 10 Oct 2009

Anderson K, Bows A, Upham P (2006) Growth scenarios for EU & UK aviation: contradictions with climate policy. Tyndall center for climate change research. Working paper 84. http://www.tyndall.ac.uk/sites/default/files/wp84.pdf. Accessed 22 April 2010

Aviation Global Deal Group (2009) A sectoral approach to addressing international aviation emissions. Discussion note 2.0, June 2009. http://www.agdgroup.org/pdfs/090609_AGD_Discussion_Note_2.0.pdf. Accessed 22 April 2010

Bows A, Anderson K, Mander S (2009) Aviation in turbulent times. Technol Anal Strateg 21:17–37. doi:10.1080/09537320802557228

Brouwer R, Brander L, Van Beukering P (2008) "A convenient truth": air travel passengers' willingness to pay to offset their CO_2 emissions. Clim Change 90:299–313. doi:10.1007/s10584-008-9414-0

CE Delft, Royal Netherlands Meteorological Institute, National Institute for Public Health and the Environment, Manchester Metropolitan University (2004) Climate impacts from international aviation and shipping. State-of-the-art on climatic impacts, allocation and mitigation options. Report for the Netherlands research programme on climate change. Scientific assessments and policy analysis, Delft, October 2004. http://www.rivm.nl/bibliotheek/rapporten/500036003.pdf. Accessed 22 April 2010

CE Delft, Netherlands Environmental Assessment Agency, Manchester Metropolitan University (2006) Aviation and maritime transport in a post 2012 climate policy regime. Commissioned by the Netherlands research programme for climate change, Delft, April 2007. http://www.rivm.nl/bibliotheek/rapporten/500102008.pdf. Accessed 22 April 2010

CE Delft, MVA Consultancy (2007) Implications of EU emission trading scheme for competition between EU and Non-EU airlines. Draft final report for directorate general for transport and civil aviation, November 2007. http://www.ce.nl/art/uploads/file/07_7520_56e.pdf. Accessed 22 April 2010

Climate Change Bill (2009) H.R.2454. An act. 111th Congress 1st session. http://www.gpo.gov/fdsys/pkg/BILLS-111hr2454eh/pdf/BILLS-111hr2454eh.pdf. Accessed 22 April 2010

Council of the European Union (2005) Presidency conclusions, Brussels, 22–23 March 2005. http://www.consilium.europa.eu/uedocs/cms_Data/docs/pressdata/en/ec/84335.pdf. Accessed 22 April 2010

Council of the European Union (2009) EU position for the Copenhagen climate conference (7–18 December 2009) council conclusions. 14790/09, Brussels, 21 October 2009. http://register.consilium.europa.eu/pdf/en/09/st14/st14790.en09.pdf. Accessed April 2010

Den Elzen M, Höhne N, Brouns B et al (2007) Differentiation of countries' future commitments in a post-2012 climate regime: an assessment of the "South-North Dialogue" proposal. Environ Sci Pol 10:185–203. doi:10.1016/j.envsci.2006.10.009

Den Elzen M, Höhne N (2008) Reduction of greenhouse gas emissions in Annex I and non-Annex I countries for meeting concentration stabilisation targets. Clim Change 91:249–274. doi:10.1007/s10584-008-9484-z

Directive 2008/101/EC (2008) Directive of the European Parliament and of the council of 19 November 2008 amending directive 2003/87/EC so as to include aviation activities in the scheme for greenhouse gas emission allowance trading within the community. Off J Eur Union. 13.0.2009 http://eur-lex.europa.eu/LexUriServ/LexUriServ.do?uri=OJ:L:2009:008:0003:0021:EN:PDF. Accessed 22 April 2010

Ecofys (2005) Options for the second commitment period of the Kyoto Protocol. Research report 203 41 148/01. UBA-FB 000771. http://www.umweltdaten.de/publikationen/fpdf-l/2847.pdf. Accessed 22 April 2010

European Commission (EC) (2006) Impact assessment. COM(2006) 818 final SEC(2006) 1685. Commission staff working document accompanying document to the proposal for a directive of the European Parliament and of the council amending directive 2003/87/EC so as to include air traffic activities in the scheme for greenhouse gas emission allowance trading within the community

European Commission (EC) (2009) Commission staff working document accompanying the communication from the commission to the European Parliament, the council, the European economic and social committee and the committee of the regions. Extensive background information and analysis. Part 2. {COM (2009) 39 final} {SEC (2009) 102}

European Environment Agency (EEA) (2009) EEA greenhouse gas data viewer. http://dataservice.eea.europa.eu/PivotApp/pivot.aspx?pivotid=475. Accessed 22 April 2010

Forster P, Shine K, Stuber N (2006) It is premature to include non-CO_2 effects of aviation in emission trading schemes. Atmos Environ 40:1117–1121. doi:10.1016/j.atmosenv.2005.11.005

Greenair (2009) A global scheme for aviation emissions provides a better deal than US and EU cap-and trade system. 19 August 2009. http://www.greenaironline.com/news.php?viewStory=573. Accessed 22 April 2010

Group of Least Developed Countries (2008) International air passenger adaptation levy. A proposal by the Maledives on behalf of the group of least developed countries (LDCs) within the framework of the Bali Action Plan, 12 December 2008. http://unfccc.int/files/kyoto_protocol/application/pdf/maldivesadaptation131208.pdf. Accessed 22 April 2010

Gupta S, Tirpak DA, Burger N et al (2007) Policies, instruments and co-operative arrangements. In Metz B, Davidson OR, Bosch PR et al (eds) Climate change 2007: mitigation. Contribution of working group III to the fourth assessment report of the intergovernmental panel on climate change. Cambridge University Press, Cambridge, UK

Hepburn C, Müller B (2006) IATAL – an outline proposal for an international air travel adaptation levy. Oxford Institute for Energy Studies. EV 36, October 2006. http://www.oxfordenergy.org/pdfs/EV36.pdf. Accessed 22 April 2010

Höhne N (2005) What is next after the Kyoto Protocol? assessment of policy options for international climate policy post 2012. ISBN 90-739-5893-8

Hooper P, Daley B, Preston H et al (2008) An assessment of the potential of carbon offset schemes to mitigate the climate change implications of future growth of UK aviation. Final OMEGA project report. Centre for air transport and the environment, Manchester. http://www.omega.mmu.ac.uk/using-carbon-off-setting-to-tackle-climate-change.htm. Accessed April 2010

ICF Consulting, CE Delft (2004) Designing a greenhouse gas emissions trading system for international aviation. Final report. Submitted to the International Civil Aviation Organization, May 2004

Intergovernmental Panel on Climate Change (1999) Aviation and the global atmosphere. Special report, Cambridge, UK

Intergovernmental Panel on Climate Change (2001) Climate change 2001: synthesis report. A contribution of working groups I, II, and III to the third assessment report of the intergovernmental panel on climate change. Cambridge University Press, Cambridge, UK

Intergovernmental Panel on Climate Change (2007) Climate change 2007: synthesis report. Contribution of working groups I, II and III of the fourth assessment report of the intergovernmental panel on climate change, Geneva

International Air Transport Association (2008) World air transport statistics, 53rd edn. Scheduled passenger-kilometer flown. http://www.iata.org/ps/publications/Pages/wats-passenger-km.aspx

International Air Transport Association (2009) A global approach to reducing aviation emissions. http://www.iata.org/SiteCollectionDocuments/Documents/Global_Approach_Reducing_Emissions_251109web.pdf. Accessed 22 April 2010

International Civil Aviation Organization (2004) Resolutions adopted by the assembly – 35th session, Montreal, 28 September–8 October 2004. Provisional Edition. http://www.icao.int/icao/en/assembl/a35/a35_res_prov_en.pdf. Accessed 22 April 2010

International Civil Aviation Organization/Committee on Aviation Environmental Protection (CAEP) (2004) Steering group meeting Bonn, 15–19 November 2004. Summary of discussions and decisions of the fourth meeting of the steering group. CAEP-SG/20042-SD/4. 25/11/04

International Civil Aviation Organization (2007) 36th assembly review. ICAO J 62. http://www.icao.int/icao/en/jr/2007/6205_en.pdf. Accessed 22 April 2010, 111 pages

International Energy Agency (IEA) (2008) CO_2 emission from fuel combustion, 528 pages

Lee DS, Owen B, Graham A et al (2005) Allocation of international aviation emissions from scheduled air traffic. present day and historical (report 2 of 3). Study on the allocation of emissions from international aviation to the UK inventory. CPEG 7. Final report to DEFRA global atmosphere division, December 2005. http://www.cate.mmu.ac.uk/documents/projects/mmuallocationsreport2currentdayv1_5.pdf. Accessed 22 April 2010

Lee DS, Fahey DW, Forster PM et al (2009a) Aviation and global climate change in the 21st century. Atmos Environ 43:3520–3537. doi:10.1016/j.atmosenv.2009.04.024

Lee DS, Pitari G, Grewe V et al (2009b) Transport impacts on atmosphere and climate: aviation. Atmos Environ 44:4678–4734. doi:10.1016/j.atmosenv.2009.06.005

Members of the Non-governmental Organization (NGO) Community (2009) A Copenhagen climate treaty. Version 1.0. A proposal for a Copenhagen agreement, June 2009. http://www.germanwatch.org/klima/treaty.htm. Accessed 22 April 2010

Müller B (2006) Montreal 2005: what happened and what it means. Oxford Institute for Energy Studies, Oxford, February 2006. http://www.oxfordenergy.org/pdfs/EV35.pdf. Accessed 22 April 2010

New Economics Foundation (NEF), World Development Movement (WDM) (2008) Plane truths. Do the economic argument for aviation growth really fly? http://www.wdm.org.uk/plane-truths-do-economic-arguments-aviation-growth-really-fly. Accessed 22 April 2010

Nielsen S (2003) Greenhouse gas emissions from international aviation and allocation options. ECOtransport consulting. Environmental Project No. 769 2003 on behalf of the Danish Environmental Protection Agency

Oberthür S (2003) Institutional interaction to address greenhouse gas emissions from international transport: ICAO, IMO and the Kyoto Protocol. Clim Pol 3:191–205. doi:10.1016/S1469-3062(03)00060-3

Owen B, Lee DS (2005) Allocation of international aviation emissions – allocation options 2 and 3 (report 1 of 3) study on the allocation of emissions from international aviation to the UK inventory – CPEG 7. Final report to DEFRA global atmosphere division, November 2005. http://www.cate.mmu.ac.uk/documents/projects/mmuallocationsreport1v14a.pdf. Accessed 22 April 2010

Point Carbon (2009a) G8 agree on 2°C Limit. 8 July 2009

Point Carbon (2009b) Poor nations back 2°C temperature target, 9 July 2009

Reuters (2009) Australia ups pressure against plane, ship emissions, 12 June 2009

Rypdal K, Berntsen T, Fuglestvedt J et al (2005) Tropospheric ozone and aerosols in climate agreements: scientific and political challenges. Environ Sci Pol 8:29–43. doi:10.1016/j.envsci.2004.09.003

Sausen R, Isaksen I, Grewe V et al (2005) Aviation radiative forcing in 2000: an update on IPCC (1999). Meteorol Ztg 14:555–561. doi:10.1127/0941-2948/2005/0049

Scheelhase J, Grimme W (2007) Emissions trading for international aviation – an estimation of economic impact on selected European airlines. J Air Transp Manag 13:253–263. doi:10.1016/j.jairtraman.2007.04.010

Scheelhase J, Grimme W, Schäfer M (2008) The inclusion of aviation into the EU emission trading scheme – impacts on competition between European and non-European network airlines. Trans Res D 15:14–25. doi:10.1016/j.trd.2009.07.003

South Centre (2009) Developed country climate financing initiatives Weaken the UNFCCC. Analytical note. SC/GGDP/AN/ENV/7, January 2009. http://www.southcentre.org/index.php?option=com_docman&Itemid=314&lang=en. Accessed 2010 April

Sterk W, Arens C, Beuermann C et al (2009) Towards an effective and equitable climate change agreement. A Wuppertal proposal for post-2012. First draft, May 2009. http://www.wupperinst.org/uploads/tx_wibeitrag/Wuppertal_Proposal_Post2012.pdf. Accessed 22 April 2010

Stern N (2007) The economics of climate change. The stern review. Cambridge University Press, Cambridge, UK

UNFCCC (1996) Communications from parties included in Annex I to the convention: guidelines, schedules, and process for consideration. Secretariat note FCCC/SBSTA/1996/9/Add. 1, UNFCCC, 8 July 1996, Geneva

UNFCCC (1997) Report of the subsidiary body for scientific and technological advice on the work of its fourth session, Geneva, Switzerland, 16–18 December 1996. FCCC/SBSTA/1996/20, 27 January 1997. United Nations Framework Convention on Climate Change

UNFCCC (2008) Report of the conference of the parties on its thirteenth session, held in Bali from 3 to 15 December 2007. Addendum. Part 2: action taken by the conference of the parties at its thirteenth session. FCCC/CP/1007/6/Add.1, 14 March 2008. http://unfccc.int/files/meetings/cop_13/application/pdf/cp_bali_action.pdf. Accessed 22 April 2010

UNFCCC (2009) Ad Hoc working group on long-term cooperative action under the convention. Sixth session. Bonn, 1–12 June 2009. FCCC/AWGLCA/2009/8, 19 May 2009

United Nation World Tourism Organization (UNWTO), United Nations Environmental Programme (UNEP) (2008) Climate change and tourism. Responding to global challenges. http://www.unwto.org/sustainable/doc/climate2008.pdf. Accessed 22 April 2010

Watanabe R, Arens C, Mersmann F et al (2008) The Bali roadmap for global climate policy – new horizons and old pitfalls. JEEPL 5:139–158. doi:10.1163/161372708X324169

Wit R, Boon B, van Velzen A et al (2005) Giving wings to emission trading. Inclusion of aviation under the European emission trading system (ETS): designs and impacts, Report for the European Commission, DG Environment No ENV.C.2/ETU/2004/0074r

World Resource Institute (WRI) (2009) Climate Analysis Indicator Tool (CAIT). Version 6.0, Washington, DC. http://cait.wri.org/. Accessed 22 April 2010

Part B
Greenhouse Gas Management, Emissions Trading and Business Strategies

Corporate Social Responsibility Programs for Emissions-Trading Risk Management in Canadian Banks

Brian Robertson

Abstract In the absence of a national emissions trading (ET) system, Canadian banks tackle ET risks largely through corporate social responsibility initiatives. Banks use the initiatives to screen investments based on alignment with social and environmental principles. While the banks' institutional adherence to normative criteria (set by CSR programs and initiatives) shows alignment with institutional norms, such adherence also leaves the banks vulnerable to emerging ET risks that such programs and initiatives do not address.

Keywords Banking • Canada • corporate social responsibility • emissions trading • institutional theory • investment • legitimacy • risk management

1 Introduction

Climate change drives global emissions-trading (ET) markets. The UN's major responses to climate change have come from (1) the UNFCCC Earth Summit in Rio de Janeiro (1992) and (2) The Kyoto Protocol (1997). In these, Annex-1 countries have agreed to reduce greenhouse gas (GHG) emissions, from 2008 to 2012, by 5.2% below 1990 levels. Under Kyoto, governments of Annex-1 nations delegate the responsibility of reducing GHG emissions to businesses and industries within their jurisdictions. Governments must implement policies to ensure that the culprits of climate change (certain industries) contribute sufficiently to national GHG-reduction plans. In Canada, these industries are called large-scale emitters (LSE), namely: power generation, mining, pulp and paper, chemical, iron and steel, smelting and refining, cement and lime, glass and glass container, and oil and gas.

B. Robertson (✉)
SolTerra Capital Corp., Toronto, Canada
e-mail: brianrobertson@solterracapital.com

Because of its initiative with the European Union Emissions-Trading Scheme (EU-ETS), the European Union shows the strongest adherence to the Kyoto Protocol. Many of the other (non-European) Kyoto signatories (USA, Japan, Canada, etc.) have undertaken voluntary Kyoto-compliance initiatives, some have legislated restrictions on certain industries; however, none have nation-wide mandated restrictions with specified sanctions and penalties for non-compliance.[1]

Governments do not face the challenges of adaptation to climate change alone. Banks, as the main supplier of financing to businesses, also play a critical role in determining the speed of the global economic reaction to target the worst impacts of climate change. Because investments in LSEs form a significant portion of banks' annual return on investment (ROI), banks must also track ET organizational changes in these industries.

Nicholas Stern asserts that the minimum damage caused by GHG emissions will range between 5 and 20% of annual global gross domestic product (GDP) (Stern 2009). Tackling climate change can cause risks of major socio-economic disruption, comparable to those created by the Great Depression and the subsequent World Wars that lead to, and to some extent, resulted from it (Sanger 2007).[2] Stern specifies that the costs of reducing GHG emissions can, in fact, be limited to around 1% of annual global GDP (Stern 2009). The variable that dictates the degree of economic disruption, or "market shock," that is, from the worrisome 5–20% range to the manageable 1%, is the speed at which the worst impacts are targeted (Stern 2009).

This paper examines the ET challenges faced by Canadian banks. Canada has been, hitherto, a resistant latecomer to address climate change on a national level. Canada was ranked 53 out of the 56 nations reviewed in 2008 for climate change adaptation/mitigation (Germanwatch 2008). In Canada, where no nation-wide legislation regulates ET allowances, banks manage ET risks in their investments through the internal implementation of organizational programs (i.e., corporate social responsibility [CSR] programs) and organizational adherence to standardized criteria (socially-responsible investment [SRI] initiatives). These normative efforts, with the common goal of sustainability management, currently form an institutionalized best-practice benchmark for Canadian banks. The question of this paper is whether these "normative" methods, such as the implementation of organizational programs and adherence to standardized criteria, actually address ET risks in investments, or simply measure a degree of alignment with institutional norms. The research sample used for this paper suggests that reliance on normative initiatives

---

[1]Examples of other schemes are: North America (Chicago Climate Exchange [CCX], Regional Greenhouse Gas Initiative [RGGI], California Global Warming Solutions Act & California Climate Exchange [CaCX], Mayors' Climate Protection Agreement, Western Regional Climate Action Initiative, Canadian Regulatory Framework for Air Emissions); Asia (Asia-Pacific Partnership on Clean Development and Climate, Japanese Kyoto Protocol Target Achievement Plan); Australia/New Zealand (Joint Australia/New Zealand Carbon Trading System, Australia Climate Exchange [ACX], New South Wales Greenhouse Plan) (European Management Journal, 2007).

[2]Noteworthy is that 4 years into the Great Depression, by 1933, one third of all banks in the United States failed (Richardson 2007b).

creates a risk divergence (i.e., banks are left vulnerable to ET risks that these normative practices do not address).

There is debate over the future role of banks in financing the activities of large businesses. An increasing number of the latter are turning to securities markets to meet their funding needs. Two main reasons, for the purposes of this paper, suggest that this debate has little to no bearing on the magnitude of the banks' role in influencing the environmental impacts of large businesses. Firstly, a study by Saidenberg and Strahen (1999) points out that the importance of banks, as suppliers of liquidity, rises during periods of economic stress and market shocks. Banks can provide a back-up source of liquidity on demand, whereas other financial institutions would have to maintain large amounts of cash and safe securities as assets (which would be costly because these assets provide lower rates of return) (Saidenberg and Strahen 1999). Moreover, during market shocks, banks tend to experience deposit inflows (of cash and safe securities) when elsewhere, liquidity dries up (Saidenberg and Strahen 1999). Secondly, while the securities market in Canada comprises 198 firms, the seven largest integrated firms generated over 70% of the industry's revenues (DoF 2009). Six of the seven largest integrated firms are in fact the investment arms, or securities dealer affiliates, of the six major Canadian banks (DoF 2009).

2 Institutional Theory

Broadly stated, institutional theory deals with the processes by which rules, norms, and structures become formal guidelines or principles that govern the behavior in a given activity (Scott 2008). Scott's definition applies not only to any regulatory, political, or economic environment, but also to market influences, their origins, and their effects. The Kyoto Protocol gave rise to three economic mechanisms (ET, Clean Development Mechanism [CDM], and Joint-Implementation [JI]) by which GHG emitters may simultaneously reduce emissions and comply with the protocol's rules. To what degree these economic mechanisms are implemented depends on the institutional arrangement of a given country.

Institutions need to take place somewhere; an institutional environment comprises the macro-level relationships (e.g. a constitution) that constrain the contractual arrangements of individuals (Davis et al. 1971). A symbiotic function is also at work with institutions – not only do institutions govern the activities of firms (as firms operate within the market and engage in transactions with others), but they also shape the very environment in which economic activity takes place (Williamson 2000; Frances 2004, pp. 3–4 in Garside 2007).

As mentioned, the responsibility of compliance and managing abatement costs under the Kyoto Protocol is passed down the chain, on to the businesses (the polluters) themselves. For banks, the institutional environment comprises three levels, each with its own challenges. Firstly, the sector has to manage its own emissions-reductions responsibility (which is straightforward and can be achieved through energy-efficiency planning and administrative changes). Secondly, the sector has to provide products and services that will help mitigate the economic risks of a carbon-constrained society (Labatt and White 2007). The third responsibility is to manage the risk implicit in clients' operations. While a tar-sand oil operation has to manage its own emissions obligations, the bank that invests in, or, provides financing to that project will need assurance of continued optimal performance with the added task of managing GHG emissions restrictions. Given the need to manage their own emissions affairs, those of their clients, and develop financial products to compete in the new emissions markets, banks in Annex-1 nations experience unique burdens and opportunities with ET.

3 Methodology

To understand the institutional environment in which the banks' ET initiatives take place, the first step is to identify the key industry regulators that set and enforce the institutional rules. The second step is developing a sample of Canadian banks and mapping out their initiatives, risks, and opportunities to address ET risks in their investments.

1. *Industry Structure and Regulators*

    - Government of Canada's Department of Finance;
    - Office of the Superintendent of Financial Institutions Canada (OSFIC);
    - Kyoto Protocol, Stern Report;
    - UNFCCC National communications (Annex 1);
    - UNFCCC Greenhouse gas inventories (Annex 1);
    - National environmental regulations/laws;
    - National Action Plan (or absence of) for GHG Mitigation/Reduction.

2. *Institutions (Norms, Standards, Rules)*

    - Industry reports, corporate social responsibility (CSR) reports, socially-responsible investment (SRI) publications, environmental footprint reports;
    - Industry standards (Global Reporting Initiative, World Reporting Institute, Equator Principles, World Bank, IFC, United Nations Environmental Programme Financial Initiative [UNEP FI]);
    - Industry Memberships (Jantzi Social Index, Dow Jones Sustainability Index, etc.)
    - Carbon Disclosure Project (CDP).

To enable current comparisons of the banks' ET initiatives, only their most recent (2007–2008) reports were reviewed. The banks used the Global Reporting Initiative (GRI) to compile their CSR reports, and this facilitated comparison in terms of content, quality, boundaries, disclosure principles, performance indicators, and sector supplements. Following this comparison, the assessment criteria behind each initiative were assessed in order to determine their effectiveness (scope and applicability) in addressing ET risks. Industry literature was also reviewed, and open-ended interviews were conducted with industry experts (the "big four" auditing firms, Canadian banking executives and portfolio managers, Canadian Standards Association [overseer of Canada's use of ISO 14064], university professors, and boutique ET firms [specializing in project finance]). The interviews were conducted to confirm/challenge/interpret the findings of the documentation review.

4 Canadian Banks

OSFIC divides its responsibilities over the 457 companies that constitute the Canadian financial system into (1) Deposit-Taking Institutions (150), and (2) Insurance Companies (299) (OSFIC 2009). Banks fall under the former category, and of the 72 banks in Canada, 22 are domestic and 50 are foreign (OSFIC 2009). The core of the banking system is the "Big Six" Canadian banks which control approximately 90% of all bank assets (DoF 2009). These banks exceed the Bank for International Settlements' norms by significant margins for capitalization and they have stable sources of funds from personal deposits, which account for two thirds of bank deposits (DoF 2009) (Table 1).

Table 1 The "big six" Canadian banks

Bank	Subsidiaries	Moody's/ standard and poor's	Notes
Bank of Montréal (BMO)	Harris Bankcorp (full-service U.S. subsidiary), Nesbitt Burns (securities), Trust Company of BMO	Aa3/AA	Purchased GKST Inc. (2008) Purchased AIG Life Insurance Canada (2009)
Bank of Nova Scotia (BNV)	ScotiaMcLeod Inc. (securities), Montreal Trust, operations in over 40 countries	Aa3/AA	Canada's most international bank Purchased E-Trade Canada for $444 million (2008)
Canadian Imperial Bank of Commerce (CIBC)	CIBC Wood Gundy (securities), CIBC Trust, Personal Insurance Company of Canada	Aa3/AA	Sold its corporate credit card business to US Bank Canada (2006)
National Bank	Lévesque Beaubien (securities), General Trust of Canada	A1/A	Largely focused on Québec
Royal Bank of Canada (RBC)	Royal Trust, RBC Dominion Securities, Voyageur Insurance	Aa2/AA	Canada's largest bank Sixth largest bank in North America
Toronto Dominion (TD)	TD Waterhouse (discount brokerage)	Aa2/AA	Canada's largest discount brokerage operation

5 Canadian Banks' ET Strategies

This section shows the initiatives contained in the banks' 2008 CSR reports and corporate websites in April 2009. The GRI guidelines, under which the reports were prepared, call for transparent, timely, and complete disclosure of a given organization's activities related to CSR. Since 2007, GRI and KPMG Sustainability have conducted research into climate change disclosure and found that "although most businesses report on climate change, the majority avoid reporting the risks to their business posed by this environmental threat. Rather, they extensively report on new business opportunities arising from it, such as establishing carbon funds" (GRI 2009).

All CSR reports contained sections on the banks' own emissions and the strategies taken to reduce their direct carbon footprints through minimizing the use of paper, better lighting, etc. The results below do not include these efforts, also known as operational footprints and include activities concerning:

1. Property management;
2. Procurement;
3. Waste reduction; and
4. Energy-use and GHG emissions.

The headings below show the variables (indexes/industry memberships and participation) and market activity that affect lending practices (concerning ET) of the "big six" banks (Table 2).

6 ET Risks

Categorizing ET risks is complex. Innovest Strategic Value Advisors (recently acquired by RiskMetrics Group) developed the world's first carbon-beta index for screening ET risks and exposure in given companies (McCabe 2007). The index focuses on four main areas related to each company under consideration:

1. Risk (carbon footprint);
2. Risk management (is the culture proactive or resistant to climate change?);
3. Market-driven upside opportunities (can management seize opportunities?);
4. Performance-improvement vector (performance trajectory – focus on tendencies, not a snapshot) (Kiernan 2007).

The index addresses each area by considering it against the following drivers, listed here in order of magnitude:

1. Industry-specific exposures and competitive dynamics;
2. Energy intensity, consumption patterns and electricity source mix;
3. Product mix – direct, indirect, and embedded carbon intensity (i.e. value chain emissions profile);

Table 2 Market activities of the "big six" banks

Bank	Indexes and industry membership	Equator principles and UNEP FI	CDP	Market activity
BMO	1. Jantzi[a] 2. DJSI[b] 3. FTSE4Good[c] 4. EBA[d]	Yes	Yes	BMO is contemplating integrating SRIs into standard portfolio offerings.
Organizational change?				In 2008, BMO grouped all environmental programs (operational footprint and lending practices) under an umbrella program "Clear Blue Skies Initiative (BMO Eco Strategy)." BMO is included in the Carbon Disclosure Leadership Index 2008. Lending guidelines were updated with due diligence questions related to climate change.
BNV	1. Jantzi 2. DJSI 3. FTSE4Good 4. Real Assets Social Impact Balanced Fund[e] 5. The Ethical Funds Company[f]	Yes	Yes	1. Lends to at least five renewable energy projects/ clients involved in hydro, wind and other renewable power opportunities. 2. Acts as the exclusive financial advisor to Enbridge Income Fund on its $42 million purchase of three wind power projects in Western Canada (altogether generating 71 MW of power). 3. Co-led, as syndications agent, a $300 million bank financing for construction of the two-phased Brookfield Power Prince wind project (126, 1.5 MW GE energy wind turbines).
Organizational change?				The Bank of Nova Scotia has maintained an environmental policy in place, since 1991, aimed at incorporating environmental risk into lending practices. The Scotia Global Climate Change Fund (launched Feb. 2008) provides Canadian mutual fund investors the opportunity to invest in environmentally responsible companies. A new language regarding environmental and social responsibility was introduced within the organization. BNV is also recognized as a Carbon Disclosure Leader. A Global Energy Solutions (GES) team addresses energy risk management by working with producers and consumers of energy to help mitigate their exposure to energy prices. GES assists with the trading of carbon emission credits or green energy credits and works with clients to structure programs that accomplish their desired carbon reduction goals. Lending practices follow an environmental lending policy, which seeks to identify and mitigate environmental risks in the bank's commercial and corporate lending activities.
CIBC	1. Jantzi 2. DJSI 3. FTSE4Good 4. CBA[g] 5. EBA 6. BCSD[h]	Yes	Yes	Led the IPO for GHG Emission Credit Participation Corp., which filed in June 2007 for an initial public offering on the Toronto Stock Exchange. The fund exposes investors to carbon emission credits. Natsource Asset Management LLC acted as sub-advisor.
Organizational change?				CIBC has an Environmental Risk Management (ERM) group that is responsible for overseeing environmental issues across the organization. The Environmental Management Committee comprises several business and functional units. The bank is developing carbon risk assessment tools to determine risks and opportunities associated with climate change and carbon markets. CIBC is recognized as a Climate Disclosure Leader. The Corporate Environmental Policy, completed in 2008, includes 10 environmental principles that frame the bank's Corporate Environmental Management Program.

(continued)

Table 2 (continued)

Bank	Indexes and industry membership	Equator principles and UNEP FI	CDP	Market activity
National	1. Jantzi 2. CBSR[i] Organizational change?	No	Yes	1. Portfolio of five companies (renewable energy sources) from the Energy Group in Calgary, AB. 2. The National Bank serves on investment dealer syndicates for the public offerings of various clean energy companies. Environmental criteria have been incorporated into credit policies and the bank has introduced controls to ensure that property taken as security conforms to environmental standards. Environmental site assessments are required for all financing applications submitted for commercial or industrial properties (or for residential properties with seven or more units). Assessments are performed by external environmental assessment firms. Also, in 2008 the bank launched its Cleantech Program, which provides environmentally-friendly companies with a range of financial services, including sales and trading, lending, and investment banking advisory services.
RBC	1. Jantzi 2. DJSI 3. FTSE4Good Organizational change?	Yes	Yes	1. RBC Jantzi Funds (three mutual funds). 2. RBC Alternative Energy Venture Fund. 3. Participating in the GEF Clean Technology Fund. 4. SRI Wealth Management team based out of RBC Dain Rauscher in San Francisco, managing ~USD$1 billion. 5. Energy and Utilities team through RBC Capital Markets in London (U.K.) that services the renewable energy sector (wind farms, small hydro and biomass projects). 6. Finances more than 25 wind farms in Canada, U.S., U.K., and Italy. 7. Runs a US $50 million Alternative Energy Investment fund. RBC's environmental policy is overseen by Corporate Environmental Affairs, which reports to the Conduct Review and Risk Policy Committee of the bank's Board of Directors. RBC releases both a CSR and an additional report "RBC Environmental Blueprint." The environmental policy subjects lending, debt, and equity underwriting services to environmental due diligence, and also incorporates environmental risk issues (including climate change, biodiversity and water) into relevant policies and decision-making processes. Also, the policy supports the development and integration of sector-specific guidelines for environmental risk assessment, including mitigation, management and escalation protocols. For portfolios, RBC tracks and reviews the GHG emission intensity of large industrial emitters in its lending portfolio to assess the potential risks and identify potential opportunities associated with forthcoming regulation of these emissions.
TD	1. Jantzi 2. CBA 3. EBA Organizational change?	Yes	Yes	SRI: September 4, 2007 TD Asset Management launched: 1. TD Global Sustainability Fund; 2. TD Canadian Core Plus Bond Fund (fixed income fund); 3. New series extensions for three existing mutual funds. In 2007 TD set its "Green Road Map," consisting of its Environmental Policy and Environmental Management Framework. This supports the bank's commitment to making its Canadian operations carbon-neutral, with

(continued)

Table 2 (continued)

Bank	Indexes and industry membership	Equator principles and UNEP FI	CDP	Market activity
		2010 as the target. The bank has also hired a Chief Environment Officer, joined the Montreal Climate Exchange, and signed the United Nations Principles for Responsible Investing. TD Business Banking incorporates environmental due diligence as an essential component of the overall lending process. Risk ratings are assigned to each account. Clients' environmental policies and track records are periodically reviewed, along with site visits, and industry sector due diligence. TD developed a Risk Management Decision Tree (RMDT) that specifies the conditions to be applied to all lending transactions. Also, the bank's Industry Risk Rating Review process will be upgraded in 2009 to reflect broad-based environmental and social issues.		

[a]Jantzi: The Jantzi Social Index is a market capitalization-weighted common stock index consisting of 60 Canadian companies that pass a set of social and environmental screens

[b]DJSI: The Dow Jones Sustainability North America Index comprises the top companies in terms of economic, environmental, and social criteria for the North American region and provides a benchmark for sustainability-driven North American equity portfolios

[c]FTSE4Good: A financial index series designed by the Financial Times Stock Exchange to identify and facilitate investment in companies that meet globally-recognized corporate responsibility standards

[d]EBA: Environmental Banker's Association: A not-for-profit trade association that meets formally twice a year to promote the exchange of environmental risk management and sustainable development lending information, and, for members to network

[e]Real Assets Social Impact Balanced Fund: A fund that assesses companies according to seven environmental and social performance measures in addition to financial criteria

[f]The Ethical Funds Company: Offers a family of socially-responsible mutual funds with approximately $2 billion in assets under management

[g]CBA: Canadian Banker's Association: provides feedback on proposed new and revised environmental statutes that may affect the business activities of the Canadian banks and their clients (public policy influence)

[h]BCSD: Business Charter for Sustainable Development: adheres to 16 principles for sound environmental management in the realms of health, safety, and product stewardship

[i]CBSR: Canadian Business for Social Responsibility: A non-profit organization of Canadian business leaders that seek to operate in a socially, environmentally, and financially-responsible manner

4. Geographic distribution of production assets relative to specific regulatory and tax-related considerations;
5. Technology trajectory – level of progress achieved towards adapting and replacing production technologies (some companies can reduce emissions at much lower costs than others);
6. Strategic governance (the extent to which companies integrate climate change factors into their business planning impact overall risk);
7. Performance improvement vector;
8. Ability to identify and monetize revenue opportunities on the upside (manufacturing cost efficiencies, new product/service opportunities, emissions trading, and clean technology) (Kiernan 2007).

These drivers seek to assess and expose the types of risks below. Table 3 is a general overview.

On the other hand, the highest possibility of earning profits is found in the following financial opportunities:

Table 3 General overview (Labatt and White 2007; Kiernan 2007; Richardson 2007a)

Risk	Generic examples
Regulatory risk	Emissions from the company's own operations
	Indirect emissions from the company's supply chain, especially energy (especially as the scope of responsibility within the energy supply chain remains undefined in Canada)
	Emissions linked to the use of a company's goods and services[a]
	Policy changes, e.g., termination of subsidies for renewable energy[b]
	Investments in energy companies that may or may meet their national renewables proportion targets
Physical risks	Negative weather developments, especially in carbon-regulated industries such as electric power, oil, and gas producers
	Additional costs due to change in weather patterns, especially in the utilities sector
	Loss of property assets
	Loss from investments in agriculture, fisheries, forestry, health care, tourism, water, real estate, and insurance
Legal risks	Litigation against companies that contribute to climate change
	Litigation against companies that failed to address climate change risks[c]
Reputational risks	Investments in controversial energy projects
Competitive risks	Investments in immature technologies[d]
	Business disruption coverage
	Price volatility in carbon markets
	Higher energy costs
	Increased credit risks by affected clients
Project risks	Local legitimacy of a chosen standard of validation/verification used for attaining emissions credits (ISO, Gold Standard, CCX, etc.)
	DOE not available (e.g. credit default by DOE)
	Host country letter of approval revoked
	Incorrect/insufficient baseline or monitoring methodology used
	Validation risk
	Verification risk
	International transaction log risk

[a]S&P warns on car sector emissions targets as "real risk" (Nicholls 2007) [b]In May 2007, BP abandoned plans to build a green power plant, blaming a lack of government support via subsidies [c]The mining firm, Xstrata, issued an IPO through an American investment bank in 2003 and, of the resulting 360-page document, one line was devoted to climate change. Xstrata's core line of business was shipping high-sulfur coal. In 2004 the Japanese government began publicly ruminating about imposing carbon-taxes on high-sulfur imported coal and within 48 h Xstrata lost ~10% of its capital to the marketplace. In this case the bank was not sued, but such cases involving corporate negligence will not likely be overlooked in the future (Kiernan 2007) [d]CCS raises unique liability exposures (Elkinton 2007)

Table 4 Opportunity costs (Labatt and White 2007; Kiernan 2007)

Opportunity cost	Generic examples
ET profit	Loss through arbitrage-negligence
	Alternative risk transfer and new insurance products
	Carbon neutral insurance coverage
	Carbon-delivery guarantee for CDM credits[a]
	ET insurance
	Insurable carbon
Insurance products	Weather derivatives[b]
	New climate mitigation products
	Microfinance for climate-friendly activities
Retail banking	Advisory service for small renewable energy project loans
	Clean-tech/energy investments[c]
Corporate banking and project finance	Counterparty credit for carbon trading
	Climate change-related products[d]
	Carbon funds trading services
Investment banking	Green technology

[a]Swiss Re (via European international insurance) developed an insurance product for CDM projects (2006) [b]Allianz closed the first catastrophe bond for river flood losses ("In Brief," Env. Finance, May 2007) [c]Swiss Re closed €329 million clean energy fund w/10-year term (Nicholls 2007) [d]Ecomagination, GE's green products arm, has sales rising faster (12%) than GE's (9%) (The economist, June 2, 2007)

1. Global long-only equities;
2. Long/short equities;
3. Fixed income;
4. Real estate; and
5. Clean tech private equity (Kiernan 2007).

The examples of opportunity costs below represent the likely forgone opportunities due to the banks' limited understanding and development of ET strategies. Banks can reverse this situation by traditional due-diligence methods of competitive benchmarking and market research to assess opportunities, plan, develop niches, and involve the appropriate stakeholders (Table 4).

7 CSR Reporting and ET Risks

The "big six" Canadian banks are managing the ET risks implicit in their corporate banking/financing and investment arms through adherence to CSR initiatives. Three of the six major Canadian banks acknowledge, through policy initiatives or revisions in progress, the need to develop more comprehensive management tools and procedures to address ET risks.

There are several advantages to organizations that issue CSR reports. These organizations usually have CSR programs and initiatives. Such programs improve recruitment by attracting better employment candidates, and likewise, improve retention by increasing morale. The CSR initiatives can be delegated to a CSR department, or to an existing department such as public relations, human resources, or business development. This delegation can range from the involvement of a single employee for a month-long project, to a permanent team of specialists.

CSR initiatives help to develop a reputation-sensitive corporate culture – one that is weary of scandals or practices involving environmental, social, or labour issues. This corporate culture manages risk better than one without such initiatives (Harris 2007).

With a price on carbon emissions, the effectiveness of these initiatives on environmental risks (ET) remains limited. CSR procedures tend to approach these issues as intangible and non-quantifiable (Bansal 2006). CSR aggregates – and where possible – unites social and environmental issues into decision-making and reporting procedures. The price on emissions not only multiplies the number of environmental issues, but removes them from the CSR paradigm of hierarchical coordination. Instead, market-coordination is required. In the words of Innovest's CEO, "It is a very, very subtle set of relationships, one that's changing all the time" (Kiernan 2007).

Banks in Canada (and any federally regulated trust and insurance firms with over CAN$1 billion in equity) are required, by legislation, to issue CSR reports (CCA 2007). Since 2002 the GRI has issued guidelines on how to report on social and environmental responsibility; for the "big-six" Canadian banks it is the de facto standard for issuing such reports. The problem lies on the reliance, by the "big-six" banks, on those very reporting requirements to address ET risks.

Scott and Meyer show that a characteristic of institutional environments is the elaboration of rules and requirements to which individual organizations must conform if they are to receive support and legitimacy (1983). The negative aspect is that an organization receives support and legitimacy for conformity, even if the institutional arrangement itself does not best address the problem in the institutional environment. The CSR initiatives rely on pre-determined criteria to encourage/discourage the banks to invest in firms based on the latter's degree of business alignment with social and environmental principles. This makes the banks vulnerable to the overabundance of ET risks that those normative principles do not address.

Several other problems emerge from this reliance on CSR reports to address ET risks. One is that CSR reports are, by their nature, mouthpieces and PR tools for organizations to market their brands. Therefore, an implicit interest exists to tone down, re-word, or even omit negative reporting. Shareholders and stakeholders experience an asymmetry of information in major organizations, and individuals naturally have few objective standards by which to monitor and judge organizational performance to begin with (Hinings and Kondra 1998).

Another issue is the isomorphism implicit in institutional environments and a natural inclination to avoid "leaving the pack." Any one of the big-six banks will look to the other five and match the average degree of conformity. There is no tangible advantage (especially in doing so alone) in addressing a national institutional paralysis in dealing with climate change and ET issues. This would simply expose vulnerability.

Another conflict is that organizations that merely comply with institutional arrangements are prone to paradigm stasis. Furthermore, "paradigm stasis may render decision-makers unable to perceive the need for change, even in the face of impending threats" (Berger and Luckman 1967, Drucker 1993, all in Hinings and Kondra 1998). The "threats" are ET risks that remain un-assessed in the current CSR initiatives, or, competitive pressure from foreign banks that have stronger and more practical institutional arrangements to address ET in their investments, and, offer financial products to help clients address ET.

Lastly, by restricting the CSR reports to the GRI Guidelines, the banks all benefit from a network externality by using the same guidelines. Furubotn and Richter define a network externality as the utility of a commodity – one that is part of a network – which depends on the number of potential connections the commodity can achieve (2005). Therefore, from a reputational perspective, strictly adhering to GRI guidelines for issuing CSR reports reinforces the banks' collective legitimacy.

8 Industry Memberships and ET Risks: Equator Principles

The Equator Principles categorize project proposals based on criteria that assess project risks and potential impacts. The criteria provide a framework for determining, assessing, and managing risk in projects in which environmental and social issues play a role. Eligible projects are green-field/expansions/upgrades and have expected capital costs of US $10 million or more. They can be in any industry sector, including project finance advisory activities (Equator). The principles themselves are based on the policies of the World Bank and its private sector arm, the International Finance Corporation (IFC).

A bank's interest in adopting the principles stems from the assurance they imply. Borrowers have to demonstrate compliance with detailed processes that constitute inclusive best-practice management of social and environmental issues in the activities for which the borrowers receive financing. Once a bank adopts the principles, the bank is deemed an "Equator Principles Financial Institution" (EPFI) and can use this title in its marketing efforts, such as press releases, websites, and CSR reports.

The process behind the Equator Principles involves three steps. Firstly, the financier categorizes the project according to its level of environmental and social impacts, i.e. the project would be classified as A, B, or C. Secondly, the financier determines which criteria, from 19 categories, apply to the project in question. The categories cover issues such as the protection of cultural property and heritage, fire prevention, waste minimization, baseline environmental conditions, and feasible alternative courses of action. The third and final step is to incorporate the IFC industry-specific performance standards and environmental, health, and safety guidelines into the chosen criteria.

An example would be the financing of a new open-pit gold mine. Under the first step, the project would be classified under Category A: "Projects with potential significant adverse social or environmental impacts that are diverse, irreversible or unprecedented" (The Equator Principles, 2009). For step 2, the following criteria would apply:

1. Assessment of the baseline social and environmental conditions;
2. Consideration of feasible environmentally and socially preferable alternatives;
3. Requirements under host country laws and regulations, applicable international treaties and agreements (The Equator Principles, 2009).

The third step, to incorporate the IFC industry-specific performance standards and environmental, health, and safety guidelines into criteria A, B, and C, could be the IFC's Guidelines for Environmental Air Emissions and Ambient Air Quality. It states:

"Where possible, facilities and projects should avoid, minimize, and control adverse impacts to human health, safety, and the environment from emissions to air. Where this is not possible, the generation and release of emissions of any type should be managed through a combination of energy use efficiency, process modification, selection of fuels or other materials, the processing of which may result in less polluting emissions, application of emissions control techniques" (IFC Guidelines 1 2009). The definition for "Application of emissions control techniques" states:

"Defined as the exercise of professional skill, diligence, prudence and foresight that would be reasonably expected from skilled and experienced professionals engaged in the same type of undertaking under the same or similar circumstances globally. The circumstances that skilled and experienced professionals may find when evaluating the range of pollution prevention and control techniques available to a project may include, but are not limited to, varying levels of environmental degradation and environmental assimilative capacity as well as varying levels of financial and technical feasibility" (IFC Guidelines 2 2009).

The vagueness involved with applying the criteria explains why The Equator Principles have received criticism for a lack of pervasiveness in reviewing GHG emissions-related issues. A Dutch NGO, Milieudefensie, researched the indirect GHG emissions from companies financed by Dutch banks. Ironically, ABN AMRO had the lowest environmental performance, despite adherence to the Equator Principles (Nielsen and Pols 2007). The bank had annual indirect GHG emissions of ~250 million tons (in 2005) from industries to which it provided financial services (Nielsen and Pols 2007). This figure is higher than the annual GHG emissions of the Netherlands and comprises nearly 1% of the total annual global GHG emissions (Nielsen and Pols 2007). Ironically, Triodos was the best performer of the Dutch banks, and at the time of study did not adhere to the Equator Principles.

9 Industry Memberships and ET Risks: Carbon Disclosure Project

The CDP is an independent, not-for-profit organization that asks the world's largest corporations to disclose their plans for tackling climate change. Responses are made publicly available; companies that don't respond are "named and shamed" (Labatt and White 2007). In 2008, 3700 of the world's largest corporations submitted their greenhouse gas emissions data to the project (CDP 2009). In addition, the project provides a coordinating secretariat for institutional investors with a combined $41 trillion of assets under management (CDP 2009).

The questionnaire itself aims to cover five areas of investment-relevant information concerning their greenhouse gas emissions:

1. Analysis of the commercial risks and opportunities from climate change including: regulation, physical risks from extreme weather events, changes in technology and shifts in consumer attitude and demand;
2. Strategy to respond to the risks and opportunities that climate change presents;
3. GHG emissions accounting;
4. GHG emissions management, reduction and cost implications; and
5. Climate change governance (CDP 2009).

Up to 2008, Innovest conducted the global research for the CDP since the survey's inception in 2002. The founder and CEO of Innovest states quite clearly that "as a risk-assessment exercise, disclosure means positive little" (Kiernan 2007).

10 Industry Memberships and ET Risks: UNEP Finance Initiative

UNEP FI is a global partnership between UNEP and the financial sector involving over 160 organizations. The goal is to understand the impacts of environmental and social considerations on financial performance.

The UNEP FI's activities range from arranging networking forums, teaching members about best-practice policy, sustainability management and reporting, investment and lending practices, and professional development (UNEP 1 2009). The UNEP FI also provides consulting services for regional and global institutions when finance accords and trade agreements are being developed (UNEP 1 2009).

Members are required to pay annual contribution fees, attending one annual general meeting once every 2 years, and submit a brief report annually, detailing the policy and practice steps the member organization has taken in the previous year to advance its commitment to the UNEP FI Statements (UNEP 2 2009). In order to become a member, an organization must sign a statement that is an aspirational, voluntary declaration of intent (UNEP 3 2009). The statements are unilateral, non-binding commitments and, therefore non-contractual in nature (UNEP 3 2009). The intent is to "endorse the principles set forth... and ... ensure that policies and business actions promote the consideration of the environment and sustainable development" (UNEP 3 2009).

11 Conclusion

The "big-six" Canadian banks control ~90% of the domestic banking market and are obliged, by legislation, to issue annual CSR reports. These reports are prepared in accordance with the GRI guidelines, which stress timely, transparent, and complete disclosure of the banks' operations.

ET risks stem from climate change, and these risks make banks vulnerable in three ways: (1) responsibility to address each bank's own carbon-footprint, (2) the need for each bank to seize market share in the emerging ET markets, and (3) the responsibility to address GHG-emissions issues in the bank's clients' operations. The risk implicit in assessing the vulnerability in clients' operations is highly complicated and involves an implicit asymmetry of information.

The banks are approaching the oncoming risks associated with ET through their adherence to CSR initiatives that are marketable in CSR reports. Several problems arise by limiting ET-risk assessment initiatives to the criteria shown (Equator Principles, CDP, UNEP FI, etc.) in these reports. The predominant conflict is the banks' continued vulnerability to the emerging risks associated with ET and the institutional transfer to a carbon-strained economy, despite the reach of the CSR initiatives' criteria.

References

Bansal T (2006) Ivey On... Best practices in corporate social responsibility. Ivey Bus J, http://www.old.iveybusinessjournal.com/view_article.asp?intArticle_ID=627. Accessed 11 July 2011

Berger PL, Luckmann T (1967) The Social Construction of Reality: A Treatise in the Sociology of Knowledge. Anchor Publishing, New York

CCA (2007) Measuring and reporting corporate social responsibility. Canadian Co-operative Association, Guelph

CDP (2009) Carbon Disclosure Project. http://www.cdproject.net. Accessed April 2009

Davis LE, North DC, Smorodin C (1971) Institutional change and American economic growth. Cambridge University Press, London

DoF (2009) Securities market: in "Canada through the banks" and "The Canadian Financial System". Department of Finance Canada. http://www.fin.gc.ca/toce/2002/cansec_e.html. Accessed April 2009

Drucker PF (1993) Innovation and Entrepreneurship. Collins, New York

Elkinton M (2007) Taking the long view. Environ Financ 8(9)

European Management Journal (2007) List of main emissions trading policy schemes and initiatives, per region, pp. 1–2, Volume 1 - Issue 1/2

The equator principles. (2009) http://www.equator-principles.com/index.php/about-the-equator-principles Accessed 11 July 2011

Furubotn EG, Richter R (2005) Institutions and economic theory: the contribution of the new institutional economics, 2nd edn. University of Michigan Press, Ann Arbor

Garside WR (2007) Economic growth and development – an institutional perspective. Institutions and market economies. Palgrave Macmillan, New York

Germanwatch (2008) Climate change performance index 2008. www.germanwatch.org/klima/ccpi2008.pdf. Accessed April 2009

GRI (2009) Current priorities with climate change. global reporting initiative. http://www.globalreporting.org/CurrentPriorities/ClimateChange/. Accessed April 2009

Harris M (2007) PricewaterhouseCoopers Canada LLP

Hinings CR, Kondra AZ (1998) Organizational diversity and change in institutional theory. Organ Stud 19(5):743

IFC Guidelines 1 (2009) IFC's environmental, health, and safety guidelines for environmental air emissions and ambient air quality. International Finance Corporation. http://www.ifc.org/ifcext/enviro.nsf/AttachmentsByTitle/gui_EHSGuidelines2007_GeneralEHS_1-1/$FILE/1-1+Air+Emissions+and+Ambient+Air+Quality.pdf. Accessed April 2009

IFC Guidelines 2 (2009) FC's environmental guidelines – mining projects. International Finance Corporation. http://www.ifc.org/ifcext/enviro.nsf/Content/EnvironmentalGuidelines and www.ifc.org/ifcext/policyreview.nsf/AttachmentsByTitle/EHS_Draft_Mining/$FILE/Clean+Draft+Mining+July+9.pdf. Accessed April 2009

Kiernan M (2007) Carbon trading: yesterday, today and tomorrow: discussion on the evolution of the carbon trading. Carbon trading seminar. Toronto CFA Society

Labatt S, White R (2007) Carbon finance: the financial implications of climate change. Wiley Publications, Hoboken

McCabe J (2007) First 'green' bond index launched. Environ Financ 8(6)

Nicholls M (2007) S&P warns on car sector emissions targets. Environ Financ 8(6)

Nicholls M (2007) Swiss Re closes €329 million clean energy fund. Environ Financ 8(7), http://www.environmental-finance.com/news/view/311. Accessed 11 July 2011

Nielsen JB, Pols D (2007) Investing in climate change 2007, Milieudefensie. http://www.milieudefensie.nl/klimaat/publicaties/rapporten/bankenklimaatrapport. Accessed April 2009

OSFIC (2009) Office of the Superintendent of Financial Institutions Canada. http://www.osfi-bsif.gc.ca/osfi/index_e.aspx?DetailID=568. Accessed April 2009

Richardson J (2007a) Putting a premium on emissions. Environ Financ 8(5)

Richardson G (2007b) The Collapse of the United States banking system during the great depression, 1929 to 1933. New archival evidence. Australas Acc Bus Financ J 1(1):12

Saidenberg MR, Strahen PE (1999) Are Banks Still Important for Financing Large Businesses? Economics and Finance, Journal of the Federal Reserve Bank of New York 5(12). http://www.ny.frb.org/research/current_issues/ci5-12.pdf. Accessed Sept 2007

Sanger T (2007) Lessons from the depression: political leadership needed to forge environmental new deal. Canadian Center for Policy Alternatives. http://www.policyalternatives.ca/MonitorIssues/2007/09/MonitorIssue1725/. Accessed Oct 2008

Scott WR (2008) Institutions and organizations: ideas and interests. Sage Publications, Thousand Oaks

Scott WR, Meyer JW (1983) Organizational environments: ritual and rationality. Sage Publications, Beverly Hills

Stern (2009) The stern review: the Economics of climate change. http://www.hm-treasury.gov.uk/independent_reviews/stern_review_economics_climate_change/sternreview_index.cfm. Accessed April 2009

The Economist (2007) Fairfield v the valley. Special report on business and climate change

UNEP 1, 2, and 3 (2009) UNEP FI. http://www.unepfi.org/. Accessed April 2009

How Does Emissions Trading Influence Corporate Risk Management?

Case Study of a Multinational Energy Company

Edeltraud Günther, Martin Nowack, and Gabriel Weber

Abstract The purpose of this chapter is to investigate regulatory climate change risks related to emissions trading. We propose that a deeper integration of climate change risks in risk management is necessary. Therefore we derive a six-step risk management process according to Draft International Standard for ISO 31000. We argue that this formalized risk management standard is a useful tool to integrate climate change risks in risk management. Following this approach we examine the interconnections between emissions trading and corporate risk management based on a case study conducted in the multinational energy company Vattenfall. We apply a content analysis of Vattenfall's publicly available risk reports as part of the annual reporting. In this chapter we find that Vattenfall's exposure to climate change risks is high. Major climate change related risks are the electricity price risk, political risk, investment risk, and environmental risk. This work adds to existing literature dealing with carbon disclosure. By focusing on physical climate change risks as well as risks related to emissions trading we propose to reduce the existing gaps in the literature.

Keywords Carbon disclosure • Climate change risks • Emissions trading • Mitigation • Risk reporting

---

E. Günther (✉)
Technische Universität Dresden, 01062 Dresden, Germany

University of Virginia, McIntire School of Commerce
e-mail: bu@mailbox.tu-dresden.de

M. Nowack • G. Weber
Technische Universität Dresden, 01062 Dresden, Germany

1 Introduction

With respect to climate change, there are many features that influence a company's risk management. At the macroeconomic level, there are influencing factors, which are directly linked to climate change. Oil and energy prices can be influenced by extreme weather conditions. Oil price shocks often accompany the hurricane season and the number and severity of hurricanes is expected to grow due to climate change (Vecchi and Soden 2007). Furthermore, there is a link between energy prices and weather conditions, particularly in the Nordic countries, where the energy price varies primarily with precipitation and the associated supply of hydro-power (Bye et al. 2008). The increase of extreme weather events and their variability due to climate change will presumably increase energy price volatility. On the macroeconomic level, corporate risk management should be aware of the price of CO_2 allowances as well.

Five sector-specific indicators are related to climate change and emissions trading and are therefore to be addressed by corporate risk management: The own-price elasticity of demand for the products, the average variable cost of production, the tonnes of CO_2 emitted per marginal unit output, the electricity consumed per marginal unit output and the market share of non-EU suppliers (Oxera 2004). Companies from the same industry often take similar positions towards policy developments on climate change for economic and political reasons. First, members of the same industry share many economic and technological characteristics, because they produce and sell similar products or services. This resemblance can lead to identical risk strategies because all members of an industry are affected in the same way by new regulation. Corporate risk management should also be aware of physical climate risks. These risks such as extreme weather events, rising sea levels and their financial impacts pose a significant challenge for companies. Very often this involves higher costs such as increasing insurance fees for factories that are near a coast if there is a danger of rising sea levels. However, business can also benefit from the physical impacts of climate change, as many European winegrowers expect (Battaglini et al. 2007). Regulatory risks and opportunities are an important issue for corporate strategic CO_2-management as there are uncertainties about the emissions trading regulations and other climate change policies. Figure 1 shows that the aforementioned risks are all affecting entire industry sectors, as opposed to individual companies.

Figure 1 shows company-specific climate change risks (Wellington and Sauer 2005). Litigation risks are an important issue although these may prove to be more relevant in the United States as different lawsuits against several utilities for greenhouse gas emissions and a lawsuit against carmakers corroborate. Businesses such as large emitting utility companies also face reputation risk as a consequence of global warming. On the contrary, firms leading with climate-friendly strategic management gain a reputational advantage. Risks and opportunities also arise from competition concerning climate change issues (Gardiner et al. 2007). Corporate risk management should make sure that a company gains value by

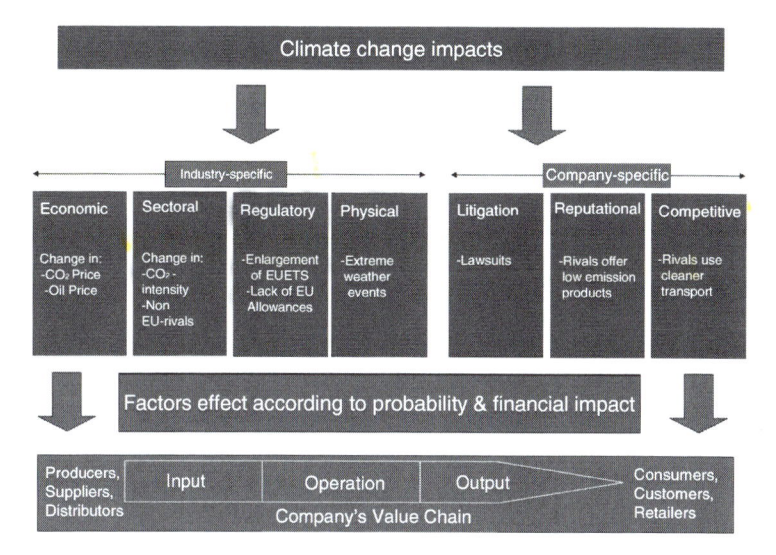

Fig. 1 Climate change risks and opportunities (derived from Busch and Hoffmann 2007)

delivering products or services that use lower energy and cause lower emissions than rival products or services.

2 Literature Review

There is a growing body of literature assessing the impacts of Emissions Trading Schemes to the energy sector such as Ahman and Holmgren (2007), Denny and O'Malley (2009), Laurikka and Koljonen (2006), Neuhoff et al. (2006), and Zachmann and von Hirschhausen (2008). However, few authors scrutinize the carbon disclosure of electricity companies taking into account Emissions Trading Risks. GRI and KPMG (2007) investigated sustainability reports of 50 companies from different sectors and found that companies reported little on the business risks of climate change compared to its opportunities. Few companies reported on the risk of legal action, and almost no companies reported on risks or business disruptions caused by extreme weather events such as floods, storms and droughts (GRI and KPMG 2007). More than one fifth of the companies reported on the risks of future regulations or legislation related to climate change. Many of these examples were concentrated in Europe. The most anticipated future regulation or legislation related to climate change was emissions trading, consistent with emissions trading being the most commonly reported business opportunity. About half of the companies reporting on potential future regulations or legislation were from the energy sector. The survey shows that when it comes to the reporting of climate risks in particular, the European energy sector is leading.

Okereke (2007) as well as Pinkse and Kolk (2007) assess responses to the Carbon Disclosure Project from a cross-sectoral perspective. As implicit in cross-sectoral studies, this work has no particular focus on electric utility companies.

Sullivan and Kozak (2006) investigate electric utility companies' carbon disclosure in sustainability reports, annual reports, responses to the Carbon Disclosure Project, and company websites. The authors found that the majority of the companies do not provide sufficient information. For most of the analyzed companies, it was not possible to fully understand the risks and opportunities presented by climate change to their business, nor was it possible to assess the implications of climate change for their longer-term strategies (Sullivan and Kozak 2006). This paper underlines that the quantity and quality of carbon disclosure still shows evident shortcomings. The existing empirical work focuses on carbon disclosure in corporate responses to the CDP, or sustainability reports. An in-depth analysis of carbon disclosure in annual reporting over time is still missing. Furthermore, existing literature investigates carbon disclosure in a broader scope taking into account climate change policies, governance and management, operations, emissions inventories, as well as allocations and emissions management strategies (Sullivan and Kozak 2006). This work focuses on the carbon disclosure of physical climate change risks as well as risks related to emissions trading. We propose to reduce the existing gaps in the literature by conducting a case study in a large energy company.

3 Background on Climate Change Risks and Opportunities in the Electricity Industry

The energy industry is of great relevance to the climate as it is responsible for 24% of global greenhouse gas emissions (Stern 2007). The electricity industry is undertaking large efforts to assure a more climate friendly power generation. Technology options include electricity production from wind, nuclear, or hydro power, as well as equipping fossil fuel plants with carbon capture and storage (CCS), and replacing conventional transportation fuel with biofuels (Naucler and Enkvist 2009). Energy companies can gain competitive advantages if they create innovations and establish them in the markets. Innovations can generate both an increase of market shares and possible cost reductions. Power generation leads to opportunity costs, which occur, resulting from the unconsidered possibility of selling CO_2 allowances. Thereby companies can benefit from windfall profits (Sijm et al. 2006). Hitherto, a price increase of EU allowances affected stock returns from the most important electricity corporations covered by the EU ETS (Oberndorfer 2008). Climate policy can have a positive impact on the electricity industry. For example the German Renewable Energy Source Act (EEG) led to a boom, especially in wind power generation (Hoffmann 2007). Through Kyoto Mechanisms i.e. Joint Implementation and Clean Development Mechanism some energy companies generate carbon certificates for

Table 1 Opportunities and risks due to climate change in the energy sector

Opportunities	Risks
Increased market share through clean technologies	Physical risks
Cost reduction through innovations	Availability of resources
Revenues from selling emission allowances	Regulatory risks
Windfall profits through free allocation of emission allowances	Financial risks
Competitive advantages through subsidies for climate-friendly technology options	Insurance risks
Use of Kyoto-mechanisms (joint implementation and clean development mechanism)	Reputational and competitive risks

example by energy efficiency projects in other countries (Oleschak and Springer 2007, Schneider et al. 2008). Table 1 gives an overview of the opportunities and risks due to climate change.

As Table 1 shows climate change causes significant risks for the energy sector. Higher ambient temperatures can reduce the efficiency of conventional power stations and lead to losses in power grids. Increasing cloud cover reduces the efficiency of solar power. Decreasing precipitation and higher evaporation lead to lower water levels and therefore to less electricity from hydropower. Increasing extreme weather events can lead to increased storm damages to offshore and onshore wind power plants (IPCC 2007).

The electric utility sector also faces regulatory risks. Climate policy often addresses the energy sector as a large emitter (Neuhoff et al. 2006). In detail, climate policy outcomes can be the implementation of Emission Trading Schemes (ETS) or the support of climate-friendly technologies. Moreover, climate change induces increasing uncertainties caused by the broad spectrum of possible impacts and the huge forecast uncertainties. Investment analysts need comprehensive supervision to assess climate change risks (Sullivan and Kozak 2006). If companies do not provide such information they face the risk of having their financial rating downgraded (Venkataraman and Kernan 2007). Furthermore, insurance costs will also rise as insurance companies take into account climate change risks (Dlugolecki and Keykhah 2002). In addition, reputational and competitive risks may affect energy companies that lag behind their peers in understanding and managing the impacts of this issue (Gardiner et al. 2007).

4 Research Method and Data Sample

This paper examines the interconnections between emissions trading and corporate risk management. We propose that a deeper integration of climate change risks in risk management is necessary. Thus we derive a six-step risk management process according to the Draft International Standard for ISO 31000. We argue that this formalized risk management standard is a useful tool to integrate climate change risks in risk management.

Our investigation is based on a case study conducted in a multinational electric utility company. In this paper we apply a content analysis of publicly available risk reports as part of the annual reporting of the electric utility company within the period from 2005 to 2007. Our approach is to derive a six-step risk management approach and to apply it to the management of emissions trading. Then we investigate how the case study company integrates emissions trading in their risk management. Thereby we conduct a qualitative content analysis (Krippendorff 2004). By applying this method, messages can be investigated in an objective-intersubjective, generalizable and replicable matter (Neuendorf 2002).

5 Risk Management Approach

5.1 Definition of Risk and Risk Management

Corporate activities such as investment decisions are characterized by uncertainty. Risk denotes the potential variation (negative or positive) that may arise from the uncertainty regarding future developments. The ISO/IES Guide 73 defines risk as "the combination of the probability of an event and its consequences." The process whereby organizations methodologically address the risks attached to their decisions is defined as risk management. Risk management determines the possible influencing factors of decisions. The aim of risk management is to create and ensure the maximum sustainable value to all the activities of an organization (Dallas 2006). It should minimize negative impacts and highlight the positive ones. Therefore, risk management is increasingly recognized as being concerned with both positive and negative aspects of risk[1] (IRM et al. 2002). The risk management process we derive is constituted by the following six iterative steps: risk strategy, risk identification, risk assessment, risk treatment, risk monitoring and risk reporting.

5.2 Steps of the Risk Management Process

5.2.1 Risk Strategy

Every entrepreneurial activity is associated with a certain level of risk. Nevertheless, in a risk strategy the corporation has to decide how much risk it is willing to

---

[1] Also in the ISO risk management standard which is still under development (ISO/CD 31000 – General guidelines for principles and implementation of risk management).

accept and able to take. Derived from the overall strategy, a risk strategy and its resources and responsibilities are assigned to the different levels of the corporation from the chief executive to the department manager. Moreover, the risk strategy has to be integrated into the general business strategy.

5.2.2 Risk Identification

In the risk identification phase, the corporation sets up an inventory of all relevant risks. A risk is relevant for a corporation when the achievement of its objectives could be affected. Risks, which are not under the control of the corporation, are to be identified, as well as risks that can be influenced by the corporation. Only risks, which are identified at this stage could be analyzed in depth in the subsequent stages of the risk management process. It is imperative that an unidentified risk is an incalculable risk. To have complete risk identification, it is essential that the employees and the responsible managers deal with relevant and actual information and that they are sensitized to identify risks. A structured and standardized approach is helpful but should be adapted to the requirements of the corporation.

5.2.3 Risk Assessment

Risk assessment is defined by the ISO/IEC Guide 73 (2002) as the overall process of risk analysis and risk evaluation. The risk analysis identifies the level of exposure to uncertainty while in the risk evaluation the decision is made on how to handle a risk. The range of potential consequences could be expressed in quantitative terms or in qualitative terms as negligible, minor, moderate, major, critical or catastrophic. The probability can also be expressed in quantitative probabilities or in qualitative terms as certain, likely, possible, unlikely, and rare. In a risk matrix, both risk attributes are integrated in one chart. The consequences of the damage are plotted on the abscissa and the ordinate is assigned to the probability of occurrence. Further risk analysis methods and techniques can be found (IRM et al. 2002). After the risk analysis, the risks have to be compared and evaluated against risk criteria. Risk criteria such as associated costs and benefits or legal requirements are used to make decisions about the significance of risks.

5.2.4 Risk Treatment

A corporation has different ways of treating its risks. The major elements of risk treatment are avoidance (if not possible, mitigation), transfer or acceptance of risk. As illustrated in Fig. 2 the aim of risk treatment is to reduce the impacts and avoid risks with high occurrence probabilities in order to minimize the expectation value. Compliance with laws and regulations is obligatory. An organization must understand the applicable laws and must implement a system of controls to achieve compliance.

Fig. 2 Risk treatment

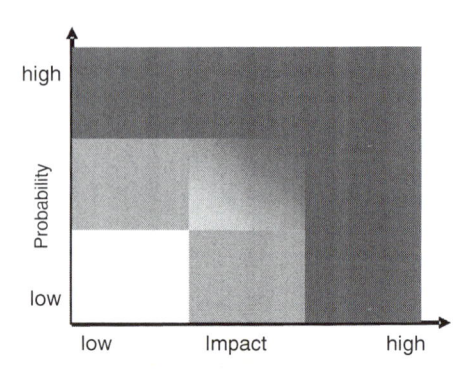

5.2.5 Risk Monitoring and Reporting

The risk management process requires a review and reporting structure. The review process has to ensure that the risk management process and its measures are effective and efficient and has to adapt the process to the dynamic development of the corporation. Besides internal reporting, the corporation can be obliged to report to external stakeholders.

In Germany the corporate MD&A report according to § 315 of the German Commercial Code (HGB) that specifies the reporting commitments of German corporations. This explicitly requires an illustration and assessment of the expected development of the corporation and its opportunities and risks. The underlying assumptions are to be specified. In paragraph (2)2.a) it asks for an explanation of the aims and methods of the risk management.

In the following section, a case study of a multinational utility company will be presented. As the case study is explanatory, it is conducted to gain consolidated findings for the industry sector. Therefore it focuses on industry-specific risks such as regulatory and physical risks. From regulatory risks the risks related to emissions trading will be illuminated.

6 Findings

The case study of the utility company includes a content analysis. We present our findings following the risk management approach presented above.

6.1 *Risk Strategy of the Utility Company*

When assessing Vattenfall's risk strategy we found that the Board of Directors hold the responsibility for internal control and risk management in the company as Fig. 3 shows.

How Does Emissions Trading Influence Corporate Risk Management? 135

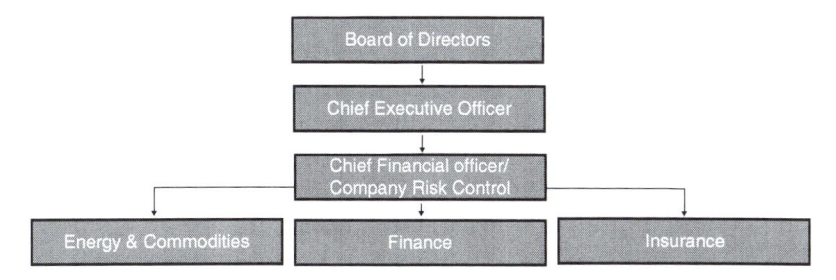

Fig. 3 Strategic risk organization, adapted from Vattenfall (2007)

However the board has given the company's management and in particular the chief executive officer and the chief financial officer a risk mandate. The management further allocates this mandate to the business unit level. The strategy is that each unit manages its own risks and has some room to maneuver within its respective mandate. An independent risk control function – the company's risk control oversees the risks and reports them on a continuous basis to the chief executive officer (Vattenfall 2007). Our findings go along with Porter (2004), who argues that internal risk control has been raised from its lowly and private organization position to become the basis for enterprise-wide risk management thinking, for risk-based regulation, and for accountability and governance.

6.2 Risk Identification in the Utility Company

Vattenfalls's risk control identifies risks and for develops models and measurement methods for risk management (Vattenfall 2007, p. 66). Figure 4 shows the probability and impact of risks identified by Vattenfall's risk management.

Figure 4 shows the different risks in the company's operations. From 2004 to 2006 the potential financial impact of some risks, such as volume risk, electricity price risk, political risk, and fuel risk rose. With the exception of volume risk, the probability of these risks also increased.

6.3 Risk Treatment in the Utility Company

In this section, we assess Vattenfall's treatment of the different risk types. We find that many of Vattenfall's risks are impacted by physical and regulatory risks of climate change as Fig. 5 demonstrates.

Figure 5 shows that those risks having a large financial impact are in particular connected with emissions trading and the physical impacts of climate change. These risks are electricity price risk, political risk, investment risk, and environmental risk.

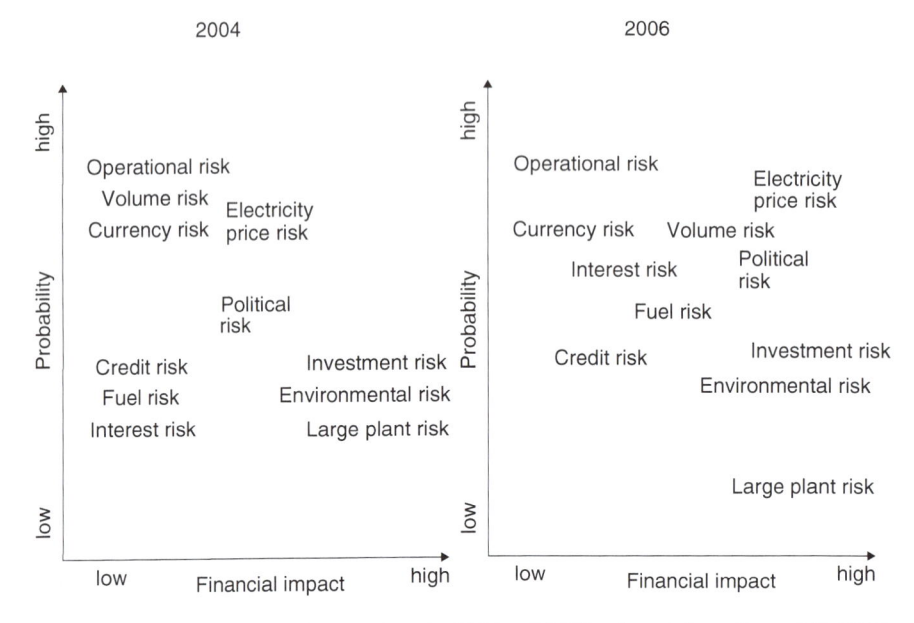

Fig. 4 Risks of the company's operations in 2004 and 2006, adapted from Vattenfall (2005, 2007)

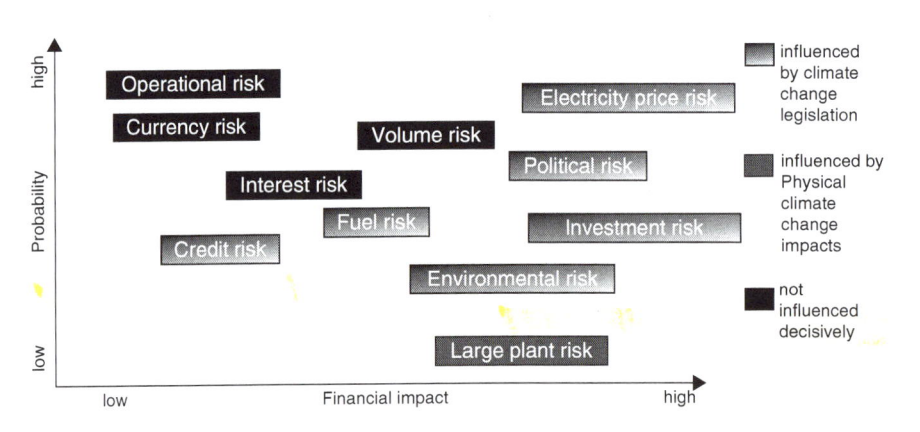

Fig. 5 Risks of Vattenfall's operations in relation to climate change legislation and physical climate change impacts in 2006, adapted from Vattenfall (2007)

Electricity price risk has the greatest effect on Vattenfall's earnings (Vattenfall 2007, p. 66). Electricity prices are determined by supply and demand. An important factor for demand is temperature; for example, in the Nordic countries, cold weather leads to greater demand due to greater heating needs, while in continental Europe, hot weather leads to higher demand due to rising use of air conditioning. Therefore climate change will definitely have an impact on electricity prices as relatively speaking,

European warming will be higher than that of global warming and according to more realistic moderate scenarios the temperature increase will be highest in Northern Europe (Ciscar 2009, p. 33). Furthermore, supply varies inter alia because of an uneven feed-in of wind power (Vattenfall 2007). Climate change impact on wind energy resources in Europe, however, is relatively uncertain (Pryor et al. 2005).

Production costs of electricity is a reflection of the price of CO_2 emission allowances and the market prices of oil, natural gas and coal (Vattenfall 2007, p. 66). Vattenfall's electricity price risk is thus also a risk based on the weather (temperature and precipitation), and the prices of oil, natural gas, coal and CO_2 emission allowances and consequently very sensitive of direct and indirect climate change impacts.

Although most of Vattenfall's coal-fired plants use lignite from the company's own mines, the company is exposed to fuel price risk (Vattenfall 2007, p. 66). As hurricane Katrina showed climate change-related extreme weather events can have an effect on the oil supply and therefore can increase fuel price risk.

Vattenfall uses external rating information to manage and limit its credit risk (Vattenfall 2007, p. 67). The company's credit risks are linked to regulatory climate change impacts as rating agencies take into account a company's allocation of CO_2 emission allowances (Venkataraman and Kernan 2007).

As a capital-intensive company Vattenfall faces investment risk (Vattenfall 2007). Prior to every investment, e.g. in power plants decisions, a risk analysis referring to fuel price forecasts, electricity price forecasts and the prices of CO_2 emission allowances, amongst others, is performed. Prices of CO_2 emission allowances reflect climate change policy outcomes such as the stringency of caps (Vielle and Viguier 2007), and therefore climate change regulation has an effect on investment risk. Investment risk can also arise due to the repair and maintenance of plants such as hydro-power facilities. Repair and maintenance can be necessary due to climate change-related extreme weather events and also due to changed precipitation matters.

Vattenfall also faces risks linked to the operation of power generation and heat production plants (plant risks). The plants can be damaged as a result of incidents and breakdowns, which, generally, give rise to substantial costs due to shutdowns (Vattenfall 2007, p. 68). Plant risks could increase due to climate change-related extreme weather events. For example, in summer 2007 a nuclear power plant partly owned by the company had to be de-rated because the nearby river was too warm to be used for cooling in the power plant.

Vattenfall is also exposed to political risk, which it defines as the commercial risk that can arise as a result of political decisions (Vattenfall 2007, p. 68). To identify risks, the company differentiates between changes in policies, for example policies in finance or regulation, and a change in the rules (Vattenfall 2007, p. 68). An example for a change in the policies is the shortage of emission allowances in the second trading period of the EU Emissions Trading Scheme. A change in the rules is for example a shift from one policy instrument to another such as from carbon taxes to emissions trading schemes. To mitigate this risk of changing rules, the company conducts active business intelligence activities and maintains contacts with decision-makers in relevant markets (Vattenfall 2007, p. 69). The political risk is also linked to the physical impacts of climate change as policy windows for more stringent climate change legislation can open due to extreme weather events or other climate change-related phenomena.

When assessing environmental risks, Vattenfall distinguishes inter alia between environmental liabilities and environmental risks (Vattenfall 2007, p. 69). Environmental liabilities refer to environmental problems that occurred in production plants, installations or operations and where requirements have been extended to take action as a result of more stringent legislation, authorized restrictions or new conditions in the company's environmental policy (Vattenfall 2007, p. 69). Environmental risks refer to the probability of accidents and defects in operations, combined with their impact on the environment (Vattenfall 2007, p. 69). As a consequence environmental risk can increase due to both more stringent climate change policy (environmental liabilities) as well physical climate change events, which can cause defects in operations (environmental risks).

7 Conclusion

In this chapter we proposed to investigate the influence of emissions trading on corporate risk management. We argued that energy companies face significant risks with regard to climate change policy as well as physical climate change risks. By conducting a content analysis we found that the case study company's exposure to climate change risks is high. Especially with regards to electricity price risk, political risk, investment risk, and environmental risk, physical climate change impact and climate change legislation play a major role. Consequently risk management in the energy sector should be aware of those risks and improve its integration into the operational risk management routine. Also, for the external assessment of climate risk exposure, these risks should be predominantly evaluated. Hence, further research is necessary to discern to what extent emissions trading and climate change risk should be integrated into an overall risk management framework and what this could look like in detail. Also, further research about the strength of emissions trading and climate change influence on the different risks, e.g. electricity price risk or political risk, is essential. In addition researchers should assess the influence of company-specific climate risks in connection to litigation, reputation and competition on corporate risk management.

References

Ahman M, Holmgren K (2007) New entrant allocation in the Nordic energy sectors: incentives and options in the EU ETS. Clim Policy 6:423–440

Battaglini A, Barbeau G, Bindi M, Badeck F-W (2007) European winegrowers' perceptions of climate change impacts and options for adaptation. Reg Environ Change. doi:10.1007/s10113-008-0053-9

Busch T, Hoffmann V (2007) Emerging carbon constraints for corporate risk management. Ecol Econ 62:518–528

Bye T, Bruvoll A, Aune FR (2008) Inflow shortages in deregulated power markets – reasons for concern? Energy Econ 30:1693–1711

Ciscar J-C (ed) (2009) Climate change impacts in Europe, Seville

Dallas MF (2006) Value & risk management: a guide to best practice. Blackwell, Oxford

Denny E, O'Malley M (2009) The impact of carbon prices on generation-cycling costs. Energy Policy 37:1204–1212

Dlugolecki A, Keykhah M (2002) Climate change and the insurance sector – its role in adaptation and mitigation. Greener Manage Int 39:83–98

Gardiner D, Anderson M, Schlesinger R (2007) Climate risk disclosure by the S&P 500. Ceres, Boston

GRI & KPMG (2007) Reporting the business implications of climate change in sustainability reports. GRI & KPMG, Amsterdam

Hoffmann VH (2007) EU ETS and investment decisions: the case of the German electricity industry. Eur Manage J 25:464–474

Institute of Risk Management (IRM), The Association of Insurance and Risk Managers (AIRMIC), ALARM The National Forum for Risk Management in the Public Sector (2002) A risk management standard, London

Intergovernmental Panel on climate change (IPCC) (2007) IPCC forth assessment report, Geneva

ISO/IEC Guide 73 (2002) Risk management – vocabulary – guidelines for use in standards

Krippendorff K (2004) Content analysis: an introduction to its methodology, 2nd edn. Sage, Thousand Oaks

Laurikka H, Koljonen T (2006) Emissions trading and investment decisions in the power sector – a case study in Finland. Energy Policy 34(9):1063–1074

Naucler T, Enkvist PA (2009) Pathways to a low-carbon economy – version 2 of the global greenhouse gas abatement cost curve. McKinsey & Company, Stockholm

Neuendorf KA (2002) The content analysis guidebook. Sage, Thousand Oaks

Neuhoff K, Martinez KK, Sato M (2006) Allocation, incentives and distortions: the impact of EU ETS emissions allowance allocations to the electricity sector. Clim Policy 6(1):73–91

Oberndorfer U (2008) EU emission allowances and the stock market: evidence from the electricity industry. ZEW Discussion Paper No. 059 2008, Mannheim

Okereke C (2007) An exploration of motivations, drivers and barriers to carbon management: the UK FTSE 100. Eur Manage J 25(6):475–486

Oleschak R, Springer U (2007) Measuring host country risk in CDM and JI projects: a composite indicator. Clim Policy 7:470–487

Oxera (2004) CO_2 emissions trading: how will it affect UK industry? Report prepared for the carbon trust, Oxford

Pinkse J, Kolk A (2007) Multinational corporations and emissions trading: strategic responses to new institutional constraints. Eur Manage J 25(6):441–452

Porter M (2004) The Risk Management of Everything: Rethinking the Politics of Uncertainty. Demos, London

Pryor SC, Barthelmie RJ, Kjellström E (2005) Potential climate change impact on wind energy resources in northern Europe: analyses using a regional climate model. Clim Dyn 25:815–835

Schneider M, Holzer A, Hoffmann VH (2008) Understanding the CDM's contribution to technology transfer. Energy Policy 36:2930–2938

Sijm J, Neuhoff K, Chen Y (2006) CO_2 cost passthrough and windfall profits in the power sector. Clim Policy 6(1):49–72

Stern N (2007) The economics of climate change: the stern review. Cambridge University Press, Cambridge

Sullivan R, Kozak J (2006) The climate change disclosure of European electric utilities. Insight Investment, London, UK

Vattenfall (2005) Annual report 2004, Stockholm

Vattenfall (2007) Annual report 2006, Stockholm
Vecchi GA, Soden BJ (2007) Increased tropical Atlantic wind shear in model projections of global warming. Geophys Res Lett 34:L08702
Venkataraman S, Kernan P (2007) Climate change and its effects on credit quality – the perspective of standard & poor's. In: Bassen A (ed) Carbon disclosure project report 2007. BVI, Frankfurt am Main.
Vielle M, Viguier L (2007) On the climate change effects of high oil prices. Energy Policy 35: 844–849
Wellington F, Sauer A (2005) Framing climate risk in portfolio management. World Resources Institute, Washington, DC
Zachmann G, von Hirschhausen C (2008) First evidence of asymmetric cost pass-through of EU emissions allowances: examining wholesale electricity prices in Germany. Econ Lett 99(3): 465–469

A Model for the Valuation of Carbon Price Risk

Henry Dannenberg and Wilfried Ehrenfeld

Abstract Modeling the price risk of CO_2 emission allowances is an important aspect of integral corporate risk management related to emissions trading. In this paper, a pricing model is developed which may be the basis for evaluating the risk of emission certificate prices. We assume that the certificate price is determined by the expected marginal CO_2 abatement costs in the current trade period as well as by the long-term marginal abatement costs. The price risk is modeled on the basis of a mean reversion process.

Due to uncertainties about the future state of the environment, we suppose that within one trade period erratic changes in the expected marginal abatement costs may occur leading to shifts in the price level. In addition to the parameter estimation, it is also an objective of this work to modify the mean reversion process so that such abrupt changes in the expected reversion level can be displayed. Because of the possibility of transferring spare allowances to a subsequent period we take into account the fact that the expected long run marginal abatement costs act as a lower limit for the price in the trading period.

Keywords CO_2 • emissions trading • EU ETS • EUA • mean reversion process • risk

JEL D81, G32, L59, Q54, Q56, Q58

We gratefully acknowledge funding of the project behind this article from the German Federal Ministry for Education and Research (BMBF). The responsibility for the content of this publication rests with the authors.

H. Dannenberg (✉) • W. Ehrenfeld
Halle Institute for Economic Research (IWH), Kleine Märkerstr. 8, 06108 Halle, Germany
e-mail: wilfried.ehrenfeld@iwh-halle.de

1 Introduction

In 1997, an international agreement was resolved with the goal of reducing global greenhouse gas (GHG) emissions – the Kyoto Protocol. To achieve this goal, the emission caps of six GHGs were defined for developed countries and economies in transition to comply with. The mean reduction is about 5% compared to the base year of 1990 and to be achieved within the Kyoto Period from 2008 to 2012. Within this framework, the European Union has committed itself to a reduction target of 8%. To facilitate this reduction, three flexible mechanisms are included in the protocol: the "Clean Development Mechanism" (CDM), the "Joint implementation" (JI), and the "International Emissions Trading" (IET). While JI allows industrialized countries to undertake emission reduction projects in other industrialized countries and receive "Emission Reduction Units" (ERUs) in return, CDM enables reduction projects in developing countries to be accomplished and "Certified Emission Reductions" (CERs) received. ERUs and CERs can be used by countries to meet their emission caps to a certain degree, while IET permits international emissions trading between countries.

As IET takes place on a country level, the European Emissions Trading System (EU ETS) arranges emissions trading on a corporate level. The EU ETS was introduced at the beginning of 2005 by the European Union. Directive 2003/87/EC sets up a framework for emissions trading in Europe between 2005 and 2012 and specifies the details such as allocation and sanctions. The aim of the EU ETS is a cost effective reduction of CO_2 emissions in the energy sector and other emission-intensive industries such as the cement industry. It is mainly combustion units with more than 20 MW that are affected. For each unit, a certain amount of certificates of European Allowances (EUA) are assigned. Each certificate allows for the emission of one metric ton of CO_2. At the end of each year in the compliance period, companies running a respective unit must submit allowances that match the amount of their emissions.

To comply with the cap, emission reduction measures are to be taken by companies. The surplus of certificates can be sold on the market and the endowment of allowances is insufficient the companies can buy EUAs on the market. Hence, the right to emit a certain amount of CO_2 becomes a tradable good whose price is determined by supply and demand. EUAs are traded at certain spot and future markets. The largest of these are: Nordpool in Scandinavia, the European Climate Exchange (ECX) in the Netherlands, and the European Energy Exchange (EEX) in Germany. Currently, three periods are planned in the EU ETS: one trial phase from 2005 to 2007, the so-called "Kyoto-Phase" from 2008 to 2012, and the third phase from 2013 to 2020. During these phases EUAs can be traded not only by firms which are committed to the EU ETS but by any natural or juristic person as well. Within the phases, certificates may be transferred between years (so-called "banking and borrowing"), between the phases this is not allowed. In the future the transfer of spare allowances to the next transfer period will probably also be allowed ("banking"), whereas "borrowing" will remain prohibited.

For companies that take part in the emissions trading system the price of these certificates is an important factor for decisions on investments in carbon-avoiding technologies. The profitability of such an investment depends largely on the development of the allowance price. Because this development is uncertain, investment risk for business arises. Hence, the question is raised for the company as to whether it can bear the risk associated with a specific investment decision, if there is sufficient equity. The determination of the CO_2 certificate price risk is therefore a necessary prerequisite to make concrete decisions regarding investment alternatives that can be taken.

In this chapter, a model is developed to value CO_2 certificate price risk. It is not the aim of the work to receive a forecast for the expected price on a specific date and time but for its probability distribution. The chapter is structured as follows: Sect. 2 provides an overview of the existing literature on the subject of carbon license price. Section 3 delineates the theoretical price formation. Section 4 presents the design of our model and the chapter concludes with a short summary.

2 Literature

The literature dealing with the price of carbon can be classified into three groups. The first one estimates the expected price of carbon or the price of GHG emission certificates in general. To obtain estimates for a certain point or period of time, preferably macro models or models for the energy market are used. Springer (2003) delivers an overview of 25 models and their results. The bandwidth of estimated GHG prices lies between 3 and 74 USD/t, which is remarkable. Matthes et al. (2003) summarize the results from other models and assume a price spread between 5 and 30 EUR per tonne CO_2 equivalent. For further consideration an estimated price of 10 euros per tonne of CO_2 is selected.

The second group concentrates on the determination of factors which influence the price of carbon. Wirsching (2004) distinguishes between long-term and short-term factors. Among the long-term factors one can find the design of the national allocation plans (NAPs), abatement costs and abatement potential, the share of renewables in the energy production, and the conditions under which CERs and ERUs are accepted for compliance in the EU ETS (the so-called "linking directive"). Short-term factors include the price ratio between coal and gas, the dependence of renewables from weather influences and economic growth. Uhrig-Homburg and Wagner (2006) conduct an expert survey of various market participants and name regulatory and political factors as important factors besides the fundamentals already listed. Sijm et al. (2005) distinguish supply and demand factors and those related to market structure, regulation, and intervention. The most important factor for market structure is the number of active market participants and their power to influence market prices through strategic action. Furthermore, the market sentiments are recognized as relevant because of the immaturity of the market.

The papers mentioned above only treated factors qualitatively. Mansanet-Bataller et al. (2007) undertake a first empirical analysis. They estimate a multivariate, linear regression model for the carbon price and receive significant positive coefficients both for the current and lagged price of electricity and for the lagged price of oil. The ratio between the gas price and the electricity price also has a significant positive influence on the price of carbon. One possible interpretation of this connection may be that – because of an increase in gas prices – more coal is used for energy production. Burning coal releases much more carbon dioxide than gas, although it only delivers the same amount of energy. Consequently, the demand for carbon allowances is rising as are the prices. Coefficients for mean temperature and total precipitation are not significant but extreme temperatures have a highly significant positive influence. The correlation between EUA price, fuel price, and weather is also estimated by Point Carbon (2007). Prices for coal or gas are used for the fuel prices dependent on usage in energy production due to their price difference. In 2006, the correlations of the EUA price to fuel prices and weather were 0.46 (0.89 in 2005) and 0.35 (0.48 in 2005). Point Carbon calls changes in fundamentals the main driver for trading.

The third group examines whether the carbon market can be described by stochastic processes or uses stochastic processes to create technically oriented models for the carbon market. Seifert et al. (2008) present a stochastic equilibrium model for the spot market which can be solved analytically (in a special case). Benz and Trück (2009) examine the stylized facts of emissions trading and suggest that the spot market for EUAs should be modeled using regime switching models because of the different phases in volatility and prices. Daskalakis et al. (2009) study spot and futures prices from the EEX in Germany. Their results suggest that carbon spot prices follow a random walk with discontinuous shifts. They estimate parameters for some stochastic processes and find that the behaviour of spot prices should be approximated by a jump diffusion model which goes back to Merton (1976). Paolella and Taschini (2008) investigate the tail thickness of an unconditional distribution as a measure of risk and develop a GARCH model for a conditional distribution.

Uhrig-Homburg and Wagner (2007) concentrate on the relation between spot and future markets. After comparing the historical evolution of spot and future prices, they find that prices are connected by the cost-of-carry approach. Fehr and Hinz (2007) find that the market reacts mainly to changes of fundamentals like the coal-to-gas price ratio, temperature and precipitation and present a stochastic equilibrium model which includes these factors. They also present a first approach how to use their results in risk management using fuel switching. In their investment risk model for the energy sector, Yang and Blyth (2007) model the carbon price development as a random walk. To integrate uncertainty into future climate policy the long term simulation is completed by a price shock following a policy change. IEA (2007) exposes the results from a simulation using this model.

In this paper, we also develop a stochastic price model to assess the emissions allowance price risk based on the mean reversion process. From the approach of the other papers mentioned above like Benz and Trück (2009), we differ in that we concentrate on the long-term behavior of the price process rather than on the short-term behavior. Further, we focus on the risk associated with emissions allowances rather than on the explanation or prediction of the price development itself. The objective of this article is therefore as in Yang and Blyth (2007) the derivation of a risk distribution for the CO_2 price. A major difference to the paper by Yang and Blyth lies in the underlying stochastic process and in the modeling of price jumps, which seems more appropriate to the current institutional framework.

3 Theoretical Pricing of Emissions Allowances

Within a period of trade, there are certain amounts of certificates available which allow the emission of a politically-desired quantity of CO_2. Companies which are involved in the emissions trading system have the opportunity to consume the assigned certificates for their own emissions and to sell the surplus or to purchase missing certificates on the market. It may be profitable for companies to invest in CO_2-avoiding technologies if the unused emission rights can be sold at a high price on the respective markets. If the costs of emission avoidance in own businesses (or alternative investment in the context of JI or CDM) are higher than the prices of adequate emissions certificates, a positive pay-off for a company results when no investment is made. Instead of investing, companies will purchase certificates on the market. As all market participants face the same decision, the prices for certificates of a trade period reflects the "make or buy"-decision of all market participants. The price of certificates for one period of trade shall therefore be defined by the last and consequently most expensive entity of CO_2-emissions to be reduced. These costs are termed as marginal abatement costs. The current market price should be equal to the (possibly discounted) marginal avoidance cost for the period.[1]

The marginal abatement costs of CO_2-emissions of one trade period can only be accurately determined at the end of this period, since only at that time it is known how much CO_2 was effectively avoided and at what cost. Before that point in time there is uncertainty about how high the marginal abatement costs will actually be. However, expectations about these can be formed (also by models). The variety of expectations regarding the marginal abatement cost over a certain period is reflected by the current market price. It processes all available information and projections and thus represents the currently best estimate of the marginal abatement cost of a period. For the certificate price it would therefore be expected that it varies stochastically around the marginal abatement costs expected by the market.

Within a trading period, however, additional information can be provided leading to a fundamental reassessment of the expected marginal abatement costs

---

[1]Discounting is neglected here for reasons of better illustration.

by the market. These information shocks can arise from information regarding policy and regulatory issues. Another cause is information about market fundamentals that directly affect the emissions of CO_2 and therefore the supply and demand for CO_2 allowances. Especially information about unexpected environmental events, like e.g. strong weather events can lead to realignment. Therefore, for example, assuming that until a certain date less CO_2 was emitted than it was supposed up until then, expectations about the amount of CO_2 emissions over the entire period would change. Thus, over this period less CO_2 has to be avoided than was previously assumed. The market then forms new expectations about the marginal abatement costs for the entire period based on the new information. For this reason, sudden shifts in the price can be imagined which do not simply lead back to stochastic fluctuations.

In addition, according to the current state of policy planning, certificates that were not used over a specific period can be transferred to the subsequent period from 2013 on for all the following trading periods, while the transfer of allowances from the subsequent period into the current period is not likely to be allowed. In contrast, it was not possible to transfer allowances from the first trading period (2005–2007) to the second (2008–2012). This change to the institutional framework ensures that an oversupply as was observed in the first period does not lead to total price deterioration anymore because the allowances gain a certain minimum value due to their transferability. This minimum value is determined by the marginal abatement costs expected in the long run. Due to a period length of 5 years it can be assumed that the long-term marginal abatement costs are reflected in the futures prices for the subsequent period. Therefore, it can be expected that these long-term marginal abatement costs form a lower price limit for a period. Since – in contrast to banking – borrowing is not allowed, the marginal abatement costs of one period can increase significantly above the long-term marginal abatement costs. If, for example, in the long run, 1 tonne of CO_2 can be avoided by the construction of modern power plants for 15 EUR in the short term this is not possible. Hence, in the short term other measures must be taken to reduce CO_2 emissions with which higher costs might be associated.

For better illustration and for simplicity we assume in the following that the storage of certificates is free of charge. There are no fees or deposit interest rates considered here, but in principle these costs can be included in the model. Under this assumption, the difference between short-and long-term marginal abatement costs reflect the risk that the certificates in the current period are scarce. If there is certainty about oversupply in a period, the price of certificates will largely match[2] the future prices for the subsequent period, as excess allowances can be sold in the subsequent period at this price. If there is a possibility that certificates in the current period are scarce, then the cost of the certificates in the current period will rise over the following term price. The extent of the difference is defined by both the

---

[2]Taking interest rates into account, the spot market price would be equal to the discounted future price.

probability that there is a shortage as well as by the costs of emissions reduction that are necessary in the event of shortages. Therefore, if the probability that a certain amount has to be spent on emission avoidance in the current trading period is very low, the price difference between the future price and the current price is lower than when its probability is very high. This means that by comparing prices of the current trading period with the prices of future periods, conclusions can be drawn about the risk of shortage can be drawn. Below it is demonstrated how, based on a certain stochastic process, the CO_2 certificate price risk can be modeled taking into account information made available by the market.

4 Carbon Price Modeling

4.1 The Mean Reversion Process

As Fichtner (2005, p. 65) points out, it is appropriate to consider CO_2 emissions allowances as a "normal" factor of production. The scarcity of the good CO_2 caused by the emissions trading system leads to the emergence of a new production factor. Emissions rights are now necessary for production and are "used up" in the production process and therefore have to be managed under economic aspects. Hence, for modeling the price of CO_2 allowances it seems more adequate to use models known from commodity price modeling rather than to use e.g. equity share price models.

Basically, there are different stochastic processes available in order to describe potential future prices of commodities. These are, for instance, the geometric Brownian Motion (e.g. Brennan and Schwartz 1985) with or without jumps and the mean reversion process used later on including or excluding jumps e.g. Blanco et al. (2001) and Blanco and Soronow (2001a, b). The mean reversion process can be traced back to the Dutch mathematicians George Uhlenbeck and Leonard Ornstein[3] and can be considered as a modification of a random walk where price alterations do not occur entirely independently. The process displayed here is a discretized form of the standard Vasicek (1977) version and is defined by

$$\Delta S_{t+1} = \alpha(S^* - S_t) + u_{t+1}, \text{ with } u_{t+1} \overset{i.i.d.}{\sim} N(0, \sigma^2). \quad (1)$$

In this model the spot market price in t is denoted by S_t, the expected price change by $\Delta S_{t+1} = S_{t+1} - S_t$ and the equilibrium price level of the process by S^*. After a stochastic shock occurring between t and $t + 1$ (u_{t+1}), the spot market price S_{t+1} is "pulled back" towards the mean level S^* by the first summand of the mean

---

[3]Uhlenbeck and Ornstein (1930, p. 823ff.).

reversion formula $\alpha(S^* - S_t)$. The mean reversion rate α stands for the strength with which the price is drawn back to the mean. The volatility of the process is σ.

For commodities such as energy or gas, the mean is determined by the marginal cost of production and the extent of demand. In the short run there are deviations from this arithmetic mean, but in the long run the price converges towards the marginal costs of production as a result of competition among the producers. The modeling of energy or gas prices using the mean reversion process is quite common.[4] Applications include early contributions from Schwartz (1997), Schwartz and Smith (2000) and Clewlow et al. (2000), to recent papers from Andersson (2007) and Bernard et al. (2008).

As outlined in Sect. 3, a stochastic process which can map the expected marginal abatement costs as a defined mean for the price is required. Because the mean reversion process shows the needed characteristics, we suggest this process as a modeling basis to render CO_2 prices.[5] In the literature, mean reversion processes with jumps are also applied.[6] These short term jumps (spikes) appear as a result of demand shocks or production downtimes in non-storable goods.[7] If the short term demand elasticity is low, large price jumps can arise. This kind of mean reversion process is called a mean reversion jump diffusion (MRJD). It is particularly used in electricity market modeling. For modeling emission allowances it appears less applicable, because EUAs are storable within the trading periods. Therefore, for modeling the CO_2 allowance price, a mean reversion process without jump-diffusion is used here.

4.2 Modification of the Mean Reversion Process

What happens when new information becomes known which fundamentally changes the expectations of the marginal abatement costs? The change of expectations can be quite abrupt in this case. Therefore, it is assumed that expectations for the average marginal abatement costs can be altered by new information entering the market.[8] Hence, the mean of the process S^* is shifted by this new information. To reproduce the abrupt price shifts due to fundamental changes in expectation, the mean reversion process (1) has to be modified, which leads to the following model:

$$\Delta S_{t+1} = \alpha(S^*_{t+1} - S_t) + u_{t+1} \qquad (2)$$

---

[4]Blanco et al. (2001, p. 74).
[5]Spangardt and Meyer (2005) also represents this view.
[6]See for example Straja (2001, p. 1ff.).
[7]Blanco and Soronow (2001b, p. 83).
[8]See e.g. Spangardt and Meyer (2005, p. 226).

with

$$S^*_{t+1} = \begin{cases} S^*_t & \text{if } J(p) = 0, \\ H & \text{if } J(p) = 1. \end{cases}$$

This model reveals no classic mean reversion process but an interlinking chain of multiple mean reversion processes which feature different characteristics of parameters, mainly the mean reversion level. S^*_t denotes the mean reversion level at time t, S^*_{t+1} the reversion level at time $t+1$. J is the "jump" variable and acts like a switch: either a shift of the mean reversion levels occurs from t to $t+1$ ($J = 1$) or not ($J = 0$). J follows a Bernoulli process with parameter p, whereas p refers to the probability of a shift causing information to emerge. If no shift of the mean reversion level occurs from t to $t+1$, then $S^*_{t+1} = S^*_t$. If the level is shifted, the new reversion level S^*_{t+1} is H, whereby this level can neither exceed a certain upper price limit S_{max} nor drop below a certain lower price limit S_{min}.

As long as banking is allowed, the reversion level of the current trading period will not fall below the long-term marginal abatement costs, because the allowances do not necessarily have to be used in the actual trading period but can rather be transferred to the next. The future price of the next trading period can serve as a proxy for the long term marginal abatement costs. The maximum price in a trading period is determined by the threatened penalty for non-submission of the necessary certificates plus the price of a replacement certificate from a future period. If all certificates of a period are used up, then only certificates for the next trading period can be submitted. Thus, borrowing over the term border can be done indirectly to the price of the penalty. Therefore, the upper price limit to be expected equals the long-term marginal abatement costs plus this penalty. Here, for the modeling of the new reversion level H a PERT distribution is chosen: $H \sim \text{PERT}(H_{min}, H_{mod}, H_{max})$ while H_{min} is the minimum, H_{mod} the modal and H_{max} the maximum value of the PERT distribution. The PERT distribution is a version of the beta distribution. The distribution is defined by[9]

$$\text{PERT}(H_{min}, H_{mod}, H_{max}) = \text{Beta}(a, b) \cdot (H_{max} - H_{min}) + H_{min}$$

with

$$a = \frac{(\mu - H_{min}) \cdot (2H_{mod} - H_{min} - H_{max})}{(H_{mod} - \mu) \cdot (H_{max} - H_{min})}, \quad b = \frac{a \cdot (H_{max} - \mu)}{(\mu - H_{min})} \quad \text{and}$$

$$\mu = \frac{H_{min} + 4H_{mod} + H_{max}}{6}.$$

---

[9] See e.g. Vose (2008, p. 405).

The modeling of the jump height based on the PERT distribution is chosen to achieve an (approximately) unbiased price modeling. As described in the previous sections, it is assumed that all available information are processed by the market and are reflected in the allowance prices of the current period and future prices of periods to come. A risk model, which expects a different price than the market without processing any additional information is therefore inappropriate. A process, which models the distribution of certificate prices for a future date must therefore exhibit the current reversion level as the expected value. This kind of distribution may be generated by using symmetric distributions like the normal distribution for risk modeling.

One thing against the use of a symmetrical distribution in modeling the jump height H is that price limits exist. If the jump height is modeled with a normal distribution or a uniform distribution,[10] under- or overruns of this price level are possible at any time. In particular, if the modeled price of the current period is only slightly above the future price, then the probability of receiving an improper reversion level is very high in the case of a leap. This could be dealt with by modifying the price leap. If the price in the model is shifted below a lower price limit it could be corrected to this lower price limit. This correction, however, means that the leaps are not unbiased anymore. The jump distribution is no longer symmetrical. Therefore, the jump height should be modeled with a distribution, whose expected value equals the last available reversion level, but is not necessarily symmetric.

An appropriate distribution for modeling the jump height can be the PERT distribution. Given the current reversion level this distribution can be constructed in such a way that its expected value equals the original reversion level. An exception is the case in which the short-term and long-term marginal abatement costs barely differ. In this case, no PERT distribution can be constructed. In practical terms this means that the market assesses the risk of a shortage as extremely low or zero. Thus, available information suggest that in fact an oversupply is certain and that no jumps would occur until the end of the period. Accordingly, in this case no distribution of the jump height can be constructed.

4.3 Evaluation of the Historical Price Development of CO_2 Allowances

Having specified a model to describe the price characteristics of emission allowance prices, we will now investigate whether a mean reversion process with level shifts could have been the case in the first trading period. For this purpose an empirical study of the EEX spot market allowance price series for the period between 04/08/05 and 28/12/07 is carried out (Fig. 1). For this period, 607

---

[10] See e.g. Yang and Blyth (2007, p. 11).

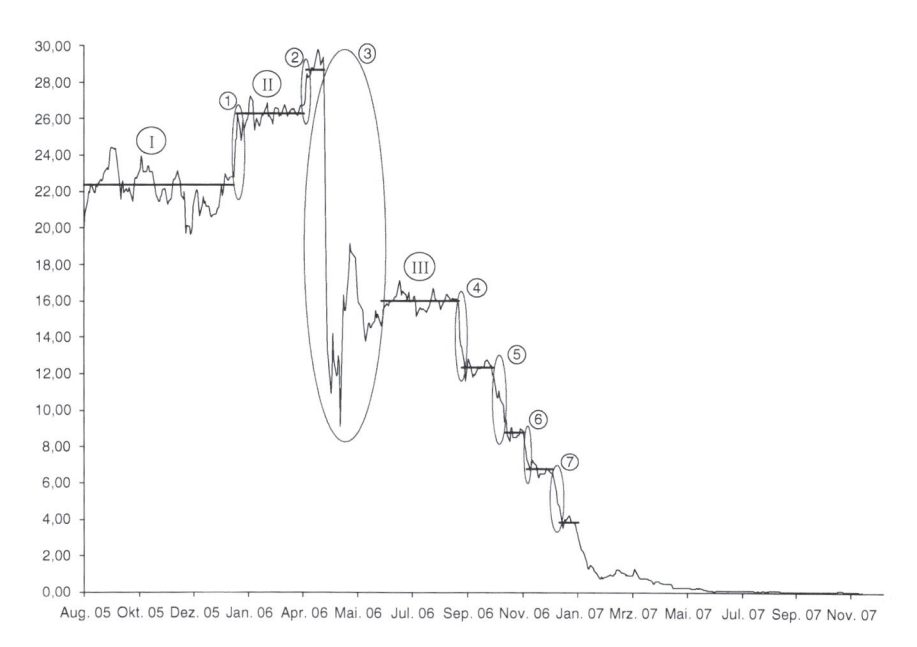

A Model for the Valuation of Carbon Price Risk 151

Fig. 1 CO$_2$ certificate price 04/08/05–28/12/07

settlement prices are available. Similarly, an estimation of the values for the current state of the second trading period is done (Fig. 2). For the period from 10/04/08 until 30/01/09, there were 204 settlement prices available.

Throughout the first months (from 04/08/05 to 16/01/06), the time series reveals certificate prices around the level of 22 EUR. The week from 13/01/06 to 19/01/06 is characterized by extremely cold weather in large parts of Europe, a rapid increase in the oil price, and very high energy prices. Since gas and oil can be substituted by coal and energy production from coal discharges significantly more CO$_2$, one could have observed expectations of increasing marginal abatement costs throughout these times. From 19/01/06 to 04/04/06 the price remained at around 26 EUR. Within the following 3 weeks until 24/04/06, the price increased to almost 30 EUR due to an oil price level of record height as well as increases in energy price on the German energy market. Hence, market participants foremost consolidated energy concerns may have adjusted their expectations on the marginal abatement costs of the respective business period upwards.

Throughout the week from 21/04/06 to 27/04/06 certificate prices were cut almost by half. At this time the individual reports on emissions were published by the Netherlands, Belgium, France, Spain, and the Czech Republic revealing that national corporations have emitted far less than expected. Consequently, the expected marginal abatement costs of the section decreased to a level well below the initial one. After the actual number of emissions was included in the prices until the end of June 2006, the new price level accumulated at around 16 EUR until the week from 15/09/06 to 21/09/06. Subsequently, the price dropped several times

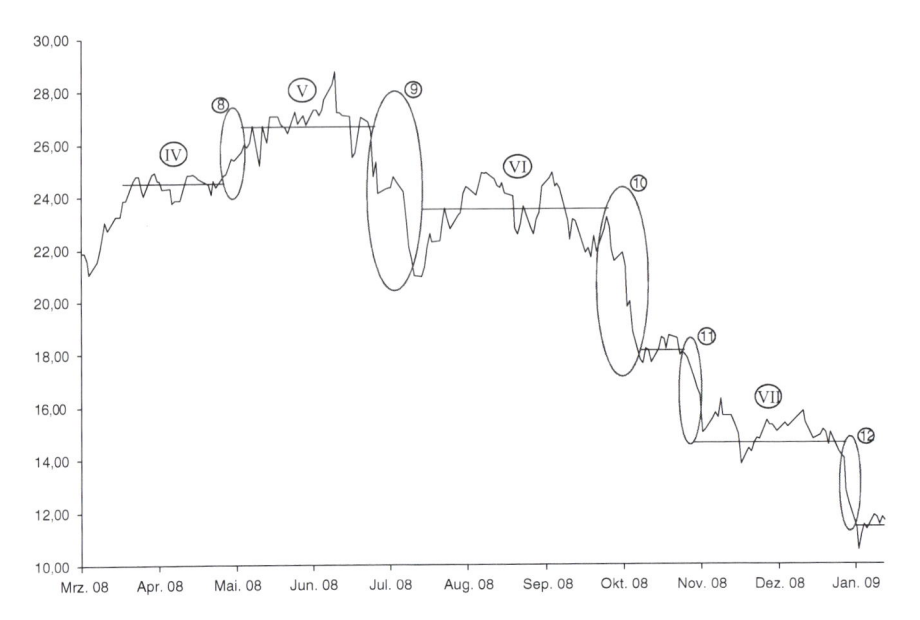

Fig. 2 CO_2 certificate price 10/04/08–30/01/09

until hitting the one Euro mark on 19/02/07. The time series principally reveals no typical mean reverting behavior from September 2006 to February 2007 due to the continuous downfall. During this period, various types of information became known indicating that less CO_2 will be emitted in the trading period than expected initially. Oil and gas prices were declining and extraordinary high temperatures throughout the winter could be observed. Additionally, the market realized the prevalent excessive supply with certificates. However, a detailed review supports the hypothesis of erratic shifts in the reversion level. Between 18/09/06 and 26/09/06, the price level decreased from 16 to 12 EUR remaining there until 26/10/06 but falling again until 10/11/06 to 8.50 EUR. Around this level, the price fluctuated until 28/11/06 before declining to 6.50 EUR in early December 2006 where it stayed until the end of the year. Following that, there were two further jumps until 19/02/07. The expected marginal abatement costs then approached a level close to zero (about two Cents) which persisted until the end of the first trading period.

For the second period, similar trends can be observed. First, the price moved from early April until mid-May 2008 around a level of 24.50 Euro, then rising to a level of about 26.70 Euro by the end of May. During this period sharply rising oil prices could be observed. At this price level the certificate price remained until mid-July and then dropped until early August to approximately 23.50 Euro. This time period was ruled by falling oil and electricity prices. The certificate price remained at this level until mid October. From autumn 2008 onwards, the macroeconomic outlook worsened. The economic forecasts were revised downwards at short intervals, which is also shown by various downward leaps in CO_2 prices.

4.4 Parameter Estimations for Single Sections

In the following, we use logarithmic price data to obtain relative price changes instead of absolute price changes in the model calibration. Below, several sections of the certificate price will be examined in detail. In the first trading period (see Fig. 1) the sections are from 04/08/05 until 16/01/06 (period 1), 19/01/06 to 04/04/06 (period 2), 26/06/06 to 19/09/06 (period 3) and 19/02/07 to 28/12/07 (period 4). These periods seem to follow a mean reversion process, but the reversion level is different. The periods were first tested on stationarity. For the periods 1, 2 and 3, the hypothesis that a unit root exists can be discarded, but not for period 4 (see Table 1). It is quite probable that the price in period 4 is no longer or hardly determined by marginal abatement costs, but rather the case that the prices here seem to be primarily controlled by speculation. Therefore, this period will not be investigated further.

Now the parameters of the individual mean reversion processes are estimated. A mean reversion process is characterized by the level of the process (mean), the mean reversion rate and the volatility. These parameters are estimated by setting the absolute price change of the current period in relation to the prices of the previous period.[11] Accordingly, a simple linear regression is applied. Figure 3 demonstrates the procedure for period 1. The mean reversion rate is calculated as the negative of the slope. The equilibrium level of the process is represented by the intersection of the regression line with the abscissa. The volatility of the process is the standard error of the error term. Table 2 lists the estimated parameters for various periods.

The mean reversion speed moves here in a range between 0.11 and 0.38. The volatility of the individual periods varies from 0.0142 to 0.0195. Throughout the observed period, seven level shifts are identified. The respective heights in relation to the initial level are shown in Table 3.

For the second trading period, the parameter estimation is done analogous to the procedure for the first trading period. There were four periods examined (see Fig. 3). These are the sections from 10/04/08 to 19/05/08 (period 5), 26/05/08 to 17/07/08 (period 6), 04/08/08 to 15/10/08 (period 7) and 17/11/08 to 15/01/09 (period 8). As shown in Table 4, the relevant periods can be taken as stationary.

Table 1 Test on stationarity of the four observed periods of the first trading period[a]

Period	Beginning	End		t-statistics	p-value
1	04/08/05	16/01/06	Augmented Dickey–Fuller test	−3.017174	0.0363
2	19/01/06	04/04/06	Augmented Dickey–Fuller test	−2.778447	0.0683
3	26/06/06	19/09/06	Augmented Dickey–Fuller test	−3.465997	0.0123
4	19/02/07	28/12/07	Augmented Dickey–Fuller test	−0.450509	0.8967

[a]The unit root test was carried out with a constant. In addition to the investigated spot market prices, the future prices for the year 2008 in the first trading period 2005–2007 were also examined. These prices can also be taken as stationary

---

[11]See Blanco and Soronow (2001a, p. 71).

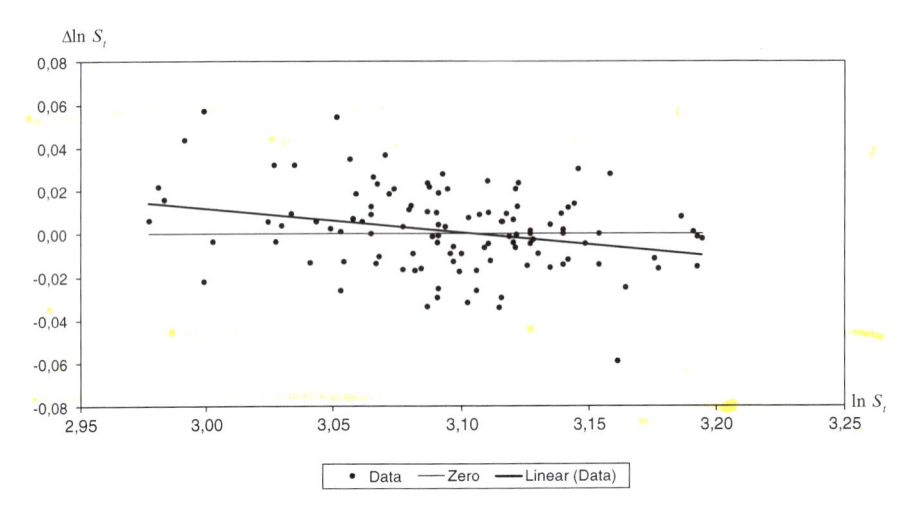

Fig. 3 Estimation of the mean reversion speed period 1 of the first trading period

Table 2 Estimated parameters of three mean reversion processes in the first trading period

Period	Beginning	End	Mean reversion speed	Observations	Volatility	Level of the process
1	04/08/05	16/01/06	0.11	116	0.0195	3.1
2	19/01/06	04/04/06	0.38	54	0.0142	3.3
3	26/06/06	19/09/06	0.24	62	0.0151	2.8

Table 3 Level shifts in the first trading period

Time period	16/01/06–19/01/06	04/04/06–05/04/06	25/04/06–26/06/06	19/09/06–22/09/06	27/10/06–08/11/06	28/11/06–01/12/06	29/12/06–05/01/07
Height	5.2%	2.7%	−17.3%	−9.4%	−13.4%	−12.3%	−29.8%

Table 4 Test on stationarity of the four periods observed in the second trading period

Period	Beginning	End		t-statistics	p-value
5	10/04/08	19/05/08	Augmented Dickey–Fuller test	−3.080943	0.0411
6	26/05/08	17/07/08	Augmented Dickey–Fuller test	−2.807491	0.0667
7	04/08/08	15/10/08	Augmented Dickey–Fuller test	−2.773381	0.0692
8	17/11/08	14/01/09	Augmented Dickey–Fuller test	−2.742357	0.0767

For the sections of the second trading period, the parameters of the mean reversion processes are also determined (Table 5). The same estimation procedure was used as for the data of the first trading period.

Here, the mean reversion speed moves between 0.19 and 0.56. The volatility was in the range of 0.0137–0.0278. During the period, five level shifts were observed (Table 6).

A Model for the Valuation of Carbon Price Risk   155

Table 5 Estimated parameters of four mean reversion processes in the second trading period

Period	Beginning	End	Mean reversion speed	Observations	Volatility	Level of the process
5	10/04/08	19/05/08	0.56	26	0.0137	3.2
6	26/05/08	17/07/08	0.38	39	0.0239	3.3
7	04/08/08	15/10/08	0.19	52	0.0220	3.2
8	17/11/08	14/01/09	0.29	38	0.0278	2.7

Table 6 Level shifts in the second trading period

Time period	19/05/08–26/05/08	17/07/08–04/08/08	15/10/08–27/10/08	14/11/08–17/11/08	14/01/09–19/01/09
Height	2.7%	−3.8%	−8.2%	−6.7%	−9.8%

Over the period, a total of 12 level shifts were observed within 612 trading days.[12] Thus, the jump probability was $12/612 \approx 2\%$. In principle, it is conceivable that within a certain period, contrasting information could emerge with a short time lag (e.g. 1 day), which would neutralize each other. Although, our event analysis shows no evidence that mutually contradictory information have been neutralized. In addition, certain leaps of the reversion level could be too small to be identified in the historical data. Hence, the actual jump probability tends to be higher than calculated.

One solution to this problem could be a correction of the jump probability derived from historical observations. Assuming that jumps under a certain size cannot be identified in historical data, the jump probability has to be corrected by the area under the PERT distribution in the related interval. For example, if it is defined that jumps in the order of +/− 1 EUR cannot be identified, the related area under the PERT distribution has to be determined for correction. If this area equals e.g. 0.2, 20% of the modeled jumps will lie in a range where they could not be observed in historical data if they happen. Therefore, starting from a calculated jump probability of 2%, in the model a probability of $2/(1–0.2) \approx 2.5\%$ should be adopted. However, in the following example we waive such a correction.

Generally, we expect that in the future, new information will lead to level shifts with a similar probability as until now.[13] Further, it cannot be excluded that similar strong level shifts of up to 30% will appear again in the future. Of course, it is possible that under the current institutional framework different jump probabilities and jump heights respectively are realistic. Above all, at the end of a trading period, the jump probability could increase significantly if scarcity subsists. Such observations have hitherto not yet been made and therefore current experiences are used here for calibration.

---

[12] The period between 19/02/07 and 28/12/07 will not be examined, because here the oversupply of the first trading period led to a collapse of the market.

[13] The relevant price history is still quite short. As in every model calibration based on historical data, the past holds the best information available. The more empirical data that is available, the more reliable the parameter estimations will be.

4.5 Simulation of the Certificate Price

Having developed and parameterized a model, which could form the basis for evaluating the price risk of certificates, the subsequent paragraph presents an exemplary simulation of the price risk using the Monte-Carlo technique.[14] Initially, it is assumed that the marginal abatement costs to be expected at the beginning of the period are 25 Euros. Likewise, the spot price S_1 is also assumed to be 25 Euros. In the following, a time series is simulated over 250 trading days which is the equivalent of one normal trading year. The volatility σ is set to 0.0194 which equals the average value of the entire distance of the first and second trading period. In addition, based on the values of the periods examined the jump probability is set to $p = 0.02$. For the mean reversion speed an average value is adopted with $\alpha = 0.3071$. Regarding the PERT distribution we assume that a maximum price shift of 30% is possible, as it was over the first two trading periods.[15] Therefore, the minimum reversion level after a level shift results as the maximum of the lower price limit and 70% of the reversion level of the previous trading day. The maximum reversion level after a jump is the minimum of the upper price limit and a 30% increase on the last trading reversion level. It is therefore:

$$H_{\min} = \max(S_{\min}; 0, 7S_t^*) \quad \text{and} \quad H_{\max} = \min(S_{\max}; 1, 3S_t^*).$$

The expected value of the PERT distribution equals the reversion level on the last trading day. Therefore the modal value of the distribution is determined by $H_{\mathrm{mod}} = \frac{6S_t^* - H_{\max} - H_{\min}}{4}$. Then, after the price has reached the lower price limit, a secure oversupply is expected, so that in this case the reversion level does not change anymore after that. If the upper price limit is reached, it is assumed that the certificates in the current period are certainly not sufficient and so the short-term marginal abatement costs cannot underrun the maximal possible value. Figures 4 and 5 serve to illustrate the modeling of a jump and a possible price development. For the example shown here it is assumed that the future price of the subsequent period and thus the minimum price $S_{\min}$ of the modeled period is 15 EUR.[16] As the

---

[14] Monte Carlo methods are a class of computational algorithms used when it is unfeasible to compute an exact result using a deterministic algorithm. As opposed to deterministic simulation methods (such as molecular dynamics) Monte Carlo techniques are stochastic. This means that the computation of the results relies on repeated random sampling using random or pseudo-random numbers. Because of the necessity of numerous repeated calculations and (pseudo-)random numbers, these methods are most suited to calculation by computers. In the simulation of physical or mathematical systems with a large number of coupled degrees of freedom such as fluids or cellular structures or with serious uncertainty in inputs such as the quantitative risk evaluation in business, Monte Carlo methods are widely used. For technical details and application see e.g. Vose (2008, p. 56ff.).

[15] Basically, for price increases and decreases different maximum change rates can be specified.

[16] The current price history suggests that the actual price is even lower.

A Model for the Valuation of Carbon Price Risk

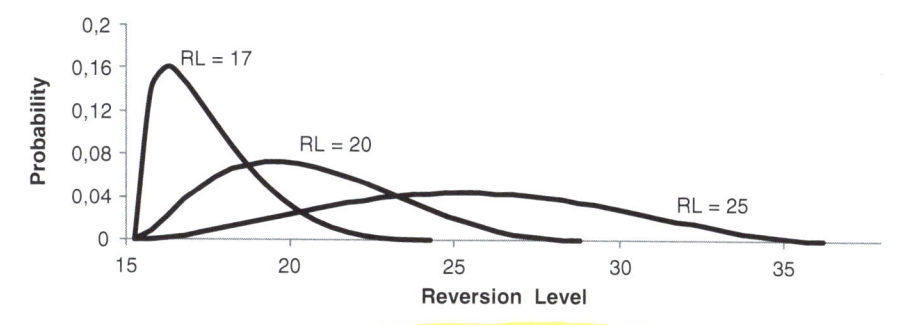

Fig. 4 Illustration of the PERT distribution depending on the reversion level

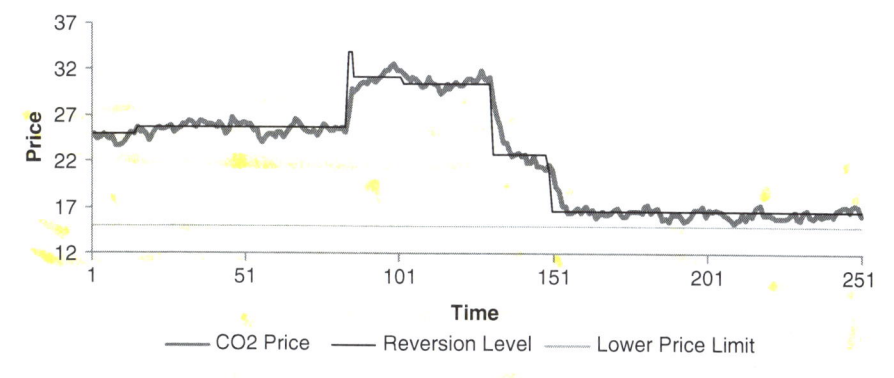

Fig. 5 Potential CO$_2$ price development ($T = 250$)

penalty for non-submission of allowances is 100 EUR for the period 2008–2012 for the maximum price $S_{max} = 115$ EUR results.

Figure 4 presents three different jump distributions as a function of the reversion level of the previous day. If the process is already very close to the lower price limit, the risk of undersupplying allowances in this period is very low and consequently the probability of a sharp price change is low. The greater the distance between the current reversion level and the lower price limit, the more likely high jumps according to the amount will be.

Figure 5 presents a potential price development over a period of 250 trading days. Simulated daily prices, the reversion level and the lower price limit are shown. By the repeated simulation of such a price process, a probability distribution for any point of time in the trading period can be determined. For Fig. 6 we simulated 5,000 time series to derive the probability distribution of the allowance price on the last trading day of the period. On average a price of 24.90 EUR can be expected, which mainly relates to the expected marginal abatement costs at time $t = 1$. Only with a residual probability of 1% was a price higher than 54.33 EUR observed. The skewness of the distribution is due to the modeling of the jump height.

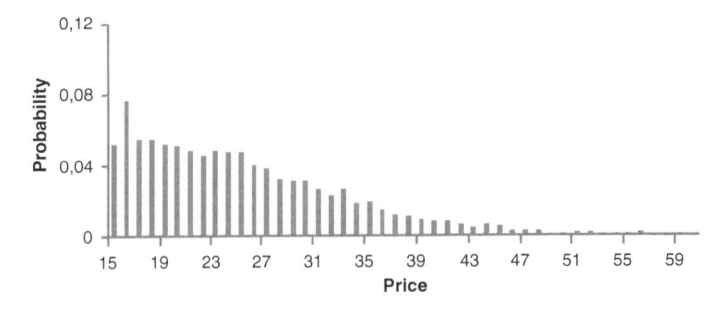

Fig. 6 Distribution for the CO_2 price on the last trading day ($T = 250$ trading days)

Based on this distribution, an assessment of the certificate price risk can be carried out, because conclusions on possible cost and expenditure loads can be drawn from the distribution providing information about the necessary risk reserve. A company which faces, for example, the alternatives of buying certificates immediately and storing them or waiting to buy the certificates later can assess whether sufficient liquidity and equity is available to bear such a risk on the basis of the distribution. If the company waits, there is the risk that the price will rise, making the certificates to be bought later so expensive that the company will realize a loss. If the certificate price declines, certificates saved could not be sold at the price expected, making an investment unprofitable hindsight. These losses must be compensated by sufficiently high equity and cash reserves. With this strategy, there is also the chance that prices will fall and hence, the revenue of the company can be increased. Furthermore, by investing in CO_2-avoiding technologies the certificate price risk can be altered. This risk can also be assessed on the basis of the model presented here.

5 Summary and Conclusion

This chapter shows how the CO_2 certificate price can be modeled for use in a risk management context. The mean reversion process is modified to include multiple level shifts in the mean arising from information shocks related to the expected marginal abatement costs. Because unspent allowances can be transferred to a subsequent period, we incorporate the fact that the expected long run marginal abatement cost acts as a lower limit for the price in the trading period. In the related period, the upper price limit is set by the allowance price in the subsequent period plus a penalty for non-submission of the necessary certificates. The model is calibrated with empirical data from the EEX emission allowance time series. Exemplarily, with this set of parameters, we simulate numerous time series to derive the probability distribution of the allowance price on a certain day of trade providing information on the related price risk.

In contrast to our approach, Benz and Trück (2009) suggest the combination of Markov switching and AR(1)-GARCH models for the stochastic modeling of emissions allowances. Our method differs from their analysis in that they concentrate on the short-term spot price behavior, whereas we focus on the long term perspective which is of particular interest for the evaluation of corporate investment risk. Therefore, we focus on the modeling of equilibrium-level shifts of the process rather than on the short-term behavior of the variance. In principle, a combination of the short-term approach proposed by Benz and Trück and our long-term risk assessment method seems conceivable.

Yang and Blyth (2007) also present a model for the valuation of carbon price risk. Contrary to their work we use a chain of mean reversion processes rather than the Geometric Brownian Motion as a basis for our work. Because of the theoretical considerations delineated in Sect. 3 and the empirical observations shown in Sect. 4, the usage of the mean reversion process seems more appropriate for the modeling of carbon price risk. As an extension to their approach we include multiple stochastic shocks with a determined probability for the mean of the carbon price deviant to one deterministic shock event in their work. Compared to Yang and Blyth we do not assume symmetrical uniform distributed jumps but consider the existence of price limits in the actual institutional framework. Therefore an asymmetric distribution as possible is chosen. Additionally, we use a distribution whose expected value equals the reversion level before the jump to obtain a nearly undistorted distribution for the carbon price risk.

Further research is still suggested in the modeling of the shifts of the reversion level. Here, the question arises as to whether these should be modeled related to the development of other economic variables (e.g. GDP). It could also be investigated, as to whether a correlation between maturity and jump height exists. Therefore, no large jumps should be observed at the end of the period because conditions differing from the expectations should have only a minor effect on the marginal abatement costs. On the other hand, the probability for a jump to happen could increase at the end of a period. The modeling considered both an upper and a lower price limit. The parameters of the model have been determined on the basis of historical price patterns. In principle, also individual perceptions and expectations could be introduced. Furthermore, variable mean reversion speeds and volatilities could be taken into account. Thus, in times of high uncertainty, greater price fluctuations are imaginable. In the model, there were no interest rates or holding costs of allowances included. A consideration of these variables makes an adjustment to the price limits and reversion levels necessary. The availability of additional data may improve the parameter estimation of the PERT distribution. Therefore, a modification of this distribution in terms of the kurtosis is conceivable. Furthermore, the long-term marginal abatement costs can be subject to transformations. Here, mainly regulatory risks, but also innovations are to be named which lead to a reassessment of the long-term marginal abatement costs.

References

Andersson H (2007) Are commodity prices mean reverting? Appl Financ Econ 17:769–783
Benz E, Trück S (2009) Modeling the price dynamics of CO_2 emission allowances. Energy Econ 31:4–15
Bernard J-T, Khalaf L, Kichian M, Mcmahon S (2008) Forecasting commodity prices: GARCH, jumps, and mean reversion. J Forecast 27:279–291
Blanco C, Soronow D (2001a) Mean reverting processes – energy price processes used for derivatives pricing & risk management. Commodities Now, June 2001, 68–72
Blanco C, Soronow D (2001b) Jump diffusion processes – energy price processes used for derivatives pricing & risk management. Commodities Now, September 2001, 83–87
Blanco C, Choi S, Soronow D (2001) Energy Price Processes Used for derivatives pricing & risk management. Commodities 1:74–80
Brennan MJ, Schwartz ES (1985) Evaluating natural resources investments. J Bus 58(2):135–157
Clewlow L, Strickland C, Kaminski V (2000) Making the Most of Mean Reversion. Energy Power Risk Management. Risk Waters Group 5(8)
Daskalakis G, Psychoyios D, Markellos RN (2009) Modeling CO_2 emission allowance prices and derivatives: evidence from the European trading scheme. J Bank Finance 33:1230–1241
Fehr M, Hinz J (2007) A quantitative approach to carbon price risk modeling. Working paper. Institute for Operations Research, ETH Zentrum, Zürich
Fichtner W (2005) Emissionsrechte, Energie und Produktion, Schmidt, Berlin
IEA (2007) Climate policy uncertainty and investment risk. IEA Publications, Paris
Mansanet-Bataller M, Pardo A, Valor E (2007) CO_2 prices, energy and weather. Energy J 28:73–92
Matthes FC, Cames M, Deuber O, Repenning J, Koch M, Kohlhaas M, Schumacher K, Ziesing H-J (2003) Auswirkungen des europäischen Emissionshandelssystems auf die deutsche Industrie. Endbericht. http://www.bmu.de/emissionshandel/doc/4773.php. Accessed 23 July 2009
Merton RC (1976) Option pricing when underlying stock returns are discontinuous. J Financ Econ 3:125–144
Paolella MS, Taschini L (2008) An econometric analysis of emission-allowance prices. J Bank Finance 32:2022–2032
Point Carbon (2007) Carbon 2007 – a new climate for carbon trading. http://www.pointcarbon.com/polopoly_fs/1.189!Carbon_2007_final.pdf. Accessed 23 July 2009
Schwartz ES (1997) The stochastic behavior of commodity prices: Implications for valuation and hedging. The Journal of Finance 52:923–973
Schwartz ES, Smith JE (2000) Short-term variations and long-term dynamics in commodity prices. Manage Sci 46:893–911
Seifert J, Uhrig-Homburg M, Wagner MW (2008) Dynamic behavior of CO_2 spot prices. J Environ Econ Manage 56(2):180–194
Sijm JPM, Bakker SJA, Harmsen HW, Lise W, Chen Y (2005) CO_2 price dynamics: the implications of EU emissions trading for the price of electricity. ECN report ECN-C-05-081, ECN publication
Spangardt G, Meyer J (2005) Risikomanagement im Emissionshandel. In: Licht M, Spangardt G (eds) Emissionshandel – ökonomische Prinzipien, rechtliche Regelungen und technische Lösungen für den Klimaschutz. Springer Verlag, Berlin, Heidelberg
Springer U (2003) The market for tradable GHG permits under the Kyoto Protocol: a survey of model studies. Energy Econ 25:527–551
Straja S (2001) Mean-reversion jump diffusion. Montgomery Investment Technology, Inc., Radnor
Uhlenbeck GE, Ornstein LS (1930) On the theory of Brownian motion. Phys Rev 36:823–841
Uhrig-Homburg M, Wagner M (2006) Market dynamics and derivative instruments in the EU emissions trading scheme – an early market perspective. Energy Environ 19(5):635–655

Uhrig-Homburg M, Wagner M (2007) Forward price dynamics of CO_2 emission certificates – an empirical analysis. SSRN Working Paper 941167. http://ssrn.com/abstract=941167. Accessed 23 July 2009

Vasicek O (1977) An equilibrium characterization of the term structure. J Financ Econ 5:177–188

Vose D (2008) Risk analysis – a quantitative guide, 3rd edn. Wiley, Chichester

Wirsching M (2004) Determinanten der Preisbildung fütyr Emissionsrechte (EU-Allowances) im Rahmen des Europäischen Emissionshandelssystems. Sonderpublikation KfW Bankengruppe, Frankfurt/Main

Yang M, Blyth W (2007) Modeling investment risks and uncertainties with real options approach. IEA Working paper LTO/2007/WP 01. IEA, Paris

Integration of a New Emission-Efficiency Ratio into Industrial Decision-Making Processes – A Case Study on the Textile Chain

Grit Walther, Britta Engel, and Thomas Spengler

Abstract Because of increasing CO_2-emissions and resulting climate change, ratios for emission accounting (and thus reduction) have gained importance both in research and practice. Indicators such as the Cumulative Emission Intensity (CEI) are able to account for all emissions along a supply chain. However, in order to improve such ratios over time, it is not sufficient for stakeholders to calculate and publish them once a year. Instead, these ratios have to be implemented into the decision-making processes of companies and entire supply chains.

Against this background, a concept for implementing emission accounting indicators into decision-making processes within supply chains has been developed. On the one hand, the aggregated indicator is applied top-down for the benchmarking of sites or suppliers using efficiency analysis methods. On the other hand, the ratio is calculated bottom-up based on production planning models. Thereby, no weighting of environmental and economic criteria is applied, but all Pareto efficient solutions are calculated. The decision-making levels are connected using the Pareto optimal solutions. Thus, the decision maker is free to make decisions about trade-offs between the economic and environmental criteria. The concept has been applied to the textile supply chain.

Keywords CEI • corporate decision-making • emission efficiency • supply chain • trade-offs

G. Walther (✉)
Schumpeter School of Business and Economics, Bergische Universität Wuppertal, Rainer-Gruenter-Str. 21, 42119 Wuppertal, Germany
e-mail: walther@wiwi.uni-wuppertal.de

B. Engel • T. Spengler
Braunschweig University of Technology, Katharinenstr. 3, 38106 Braunschweig, Germany
e-mail: aip-pl@tu-braunschweig.de

1 Introduction

Because of increasing information on Climate Change, as provided by the Intergovernmental Panel on Climate Change (IPCC 2007), emissions reduction is becoming a major topic for consumer behavior, governmental legislation and corporate decision-making. Thereby, the focus often lies on the reduction of carbon dioxide (CO_2) emissions, since CO_2 contributes considerably to Climate Change. In Germany, CO_2-emissions from companies account for 20% of the total CO_2-emissions as can be seen in Fig. 1 (Umweltbundesamt 2007). Hence, companies are forced to control and reduce their emissions of Global Warming Gases in general, and CO_2-emissions in particular.

Companies are therefore looking for adequate indicators to measure their emission efficiency. Ratios for emissions accounting such as Sustainable Value (SV), Sustainable Value Added (SVA), Climate Leadership Initiative (CLI), Sustainable Asset Management (SAM), or CEI have gained importance both in research and practice. However, in order to improve such ratios over time, it is not sufficient for stakeholders to calculate and publish them once a year as it is current practice for the SV, SVA, and CLI. Instead, the ratios have to be implemented into the decision-making processes of the whole supply chain.

Against this background, a concept for implementing emission accounting indicators into decision-making processes within supply chains is explored in this chapter. On the one hand, an aggregated emission accounting indicator is applied top-down for rating companies and benchmarking sites or suppliers applying methods of efficiency analysis. On the other hand, the ratio is calculated bottom-up based on production planning models. The levels are connected based on Pareto optimal decisions. Thus, the decision maker can decide based on trade-offs between the economic and environmental results. The concept has been applied to the textile supply chain.

First, the general idea of implementing methods for measuring environmental performance into decision-making processes is described (Sect. 2). Following that, the hierarchical concept for the implementation of an efficiency ratio into

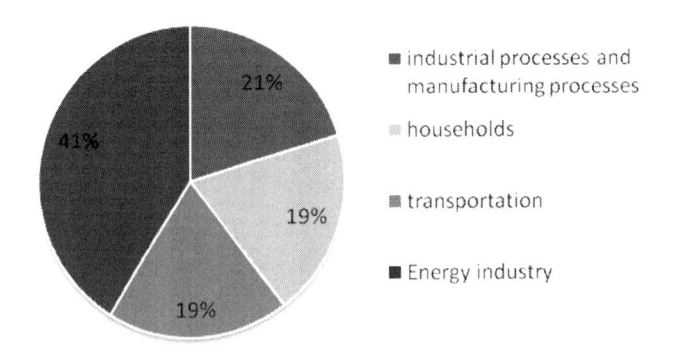

Fig. 1 Sources of anthropogenic CO_2-emissions in 2004 [Umweltbundesamt (2007)]

decision-making processes within supply chains is specified combining aggregated top-down and disaggregated bottom-up approaches using the trade-offs between economic and environmental results. The approach is then applied to the example of a textile supply chain (Sect. 3) and finally the chapter closes with a summary and future perspectives (Sect. 4).

2 Implementation of Environmental Performance into Corporate Decision-Making

Companies are rated and benchmarked according to their environmental performance, e.g. with regard to CO_2-emissions. The indicators for such ratings are often calculated by stakeholders such as non-governmental organizations. Methods such as SV, CLI and CEI are frequently used, but are calculated separately from other indicators such as turnover, return on investment or value added. However, in order to allow for improvements over time, it is not sufficient for stakeholders to only calculate and publish such indicators once a year. Instead, the indicators need to be calculated by the companies themselves and an assessment of environmental performance has to be implemented into corporate planning procedures (Angell and Klassen 1999). Letmathe and Balakrishnan (2005) state that companies often try to comply with environmental regulations without having a systematic plan, therefore operating in a reactive manner. This often leads to high costs. Letmathe/Balakrishnan assume that this is caused by a lack of planning methods, which explicitly account for emissions.

Against this background, the following section presents a concept for implementing environmental performance indicators into decision-making processes within supply chains. As can be seen in Fig. 2, the concept is based on a hierarchical system.

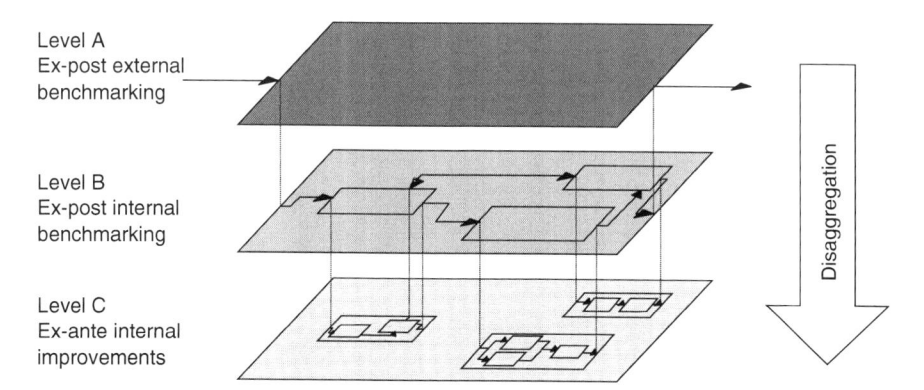

Fig. 2 Levels of decision-making and the integration of indicators for environmental performance measures

On level A, an indicator for measuring environmental performance is used for external rankings and the benchmarking of enterprises. On this level, analyses are conducted ex-post. The middle and the bottom level constitute the internal levels of decision-making within a company. On level B, the internal benchmarking of suppliers within a supply chain or sites of a company is aimed at applying efficiency measures. The analyses at this level are also ex-post, and the indicator is applied as an aggregated ratio. Thus, a company or a site can only determine its distance to efficient competitors. Improvement options cannot be detected immediately. Therefore, planning models are applied in order to improve the indicator on the disaggregated level C. For this reason, no weighting of environmental and economic criteria is applied, but all Pareto efficient solutions are calculated. Connections between the internal decision-making levels are established based on trade-offs between economic results and environmental performance. In the following, the concept is described in detail.

2.1 External Benchmarking: Calculation of Efficiency Measures

Since increasing attention has turned towards the environment, a huge number of approaches have been developed to measure the environmental performance of companies. These approaches attempt to report a company's internal and overall environmental impacts, and compare them with the impacts from other companies. Examples are the SV, the SVA, the CLI, the SAM, and the CEI.

Some ratios for benchmarking companies with regard to their environmental performance like the SV (Figge et al. 2006, Figge and Hahn 2005) and the SVA (Figge and Hahn 2004) neglect the preceding and subsequent processes of companies and thus only account for internal emissions. Such ratios can lead to the outsourcing of processes with high environmental impact but low value added (Clift 2003).

The CLI comprises of the "best in class" of companies by a score that is distinguished by sectors. The aim is to assess the potential risks and opportunities related to climate change. The calculation is based on the results of a questionnaire, which companies fill in voluntarily. The data requested include emissions along the entire supply chain (CLI 2007). However, results seem arbitrary, since data is only voluntarily provided by the companies, and therefore no consistent and audited procedures are required for data gathering, and data on the emissions of the suppliers is often estimated by the companies.

A study by SAM and WRI (World Resource Institute) focused on the usage phase within the life cycle and evaluated the ten biggest OEMs in the automotive industry. This report is explicitly forward-looking, focusing on the main factors affecting OEMs' exposure to carbon constraints, and drawing on the latest available information. Supplier emissions are also accounted for (Austin et al. 2004). However, the procedure requires a lot of data and information, and is therefore only applicable for selected sectors and supply chains.

The CEI is able to account for all emissions along the supply chain, i.e. all emissions of a company caused by own and any preliminary production steps as well as any succeeding emissions from recycling activities (Schmidt and Schwegler 2005, 2008). Based on the CEI, a rating of companies (regarding all preliminary emissions from the supply chain), the benchmarking of a company's different sites (even if these sites have varying vertical integration), as well as an evaluation of suppliers (based on total emissions of the supplier instead of the supplied parts) becomes possible. In order to calculate the CEI, a company has to know the prices and the amount of products that are bought and sold, the total turnover, as well as any direct emissions that occur. However, the CEI of all suppliers is also required, which means that all suppliers have to take part in the CEI accounting system, and therefore this kind of system should be initiated from the onset.

Analyses show that the presented approaches arrive at different results; e.g. Daimler Chrysler has a very high SV (Figge and Hahn 2005), but only a CLI score of 75, thus being awarded the last position for CLI in its sector (CLI 2007). The SAM-report stated that BMW is the company with the worst score (Austin et al. 2004), while BMW achieved a very high CLI between 2004 and 2006 (CLI 2007).

These contradictory results demonstrate that there is still need for standardization in the field of evaluation and benchmarking of companies and supply chains with respect to environmental performance respective emissions. Existing approaches either neglect the preliminary chain, or are too complex and therefore costly to apply, or not transparent in data gathering, or request the participation of all companies as well as an initiation.

Nevertheless, the ratios are already used for the benchmarking and rating of companies and supply chains. However, an aggregated indicator does not deliver the information that is necessary for improvement measures. Therefore, the indicators need to be applied on the internal benchmarking and planning level.

2.2 Internal Benchmarking: Integrated Supply Chain Management Through Efficiency Analysis

While efficiency measures can be applied by stakeholders for external benchmarking at level A, they should also be used on an aggregated base for internal benchmarking of sites or for an evaluation of the efficiency of suppliers on level B as described in the following. In doing so, it becomes possible to establish an integrated supply chain management with regard to a company's emission impact.

The performance measurement of sites as well as suppliers is a multi-criteria problem, comprising of qualitative and quantitative site-related factors. Approaches that can be used for this kind of assessment are the benefit-analysis (Zangemeister 1976), or the more sophisticated methods of multi-attribute decision making (MADM) or multi-objective decision making (MODM) (Zimmermann and

Gutsche 1991), as well as the Data Envelopment Analysis (DEA) (Charnes et al. 1978). The MADM and MODM require weights to determine the optimal solution. On the contrary, no external weights are necessary for DEA (Charnes et al. 1978). Instead, the weights are determined by an endogenous calculation. Another difference lies in the results of the calculations. The MODM and MADM deliver the best in class or a relative rank. The DEA defines the relative efficiency and does not specify a certain solution. Thus, DEA can be used for benchmarking by determining the strengths and weaknesses of evaluated sites. An important application is the use of DEA to identify shortcomings, e.g. identifying inefficient processes (Klein and Scholl 2004). The efficiency of a decision making unit (DMU) is obtained as the maximum of a ratio of weighted outputs to weighted inputs subject to the condition that the ratios for every DMU are less than or equal to unity (Charnes et al. 1978).

For the bi-objective case, the principals of the DEA efficiency measurements can also be used. However, non-dominated solutions can also be mapped in a diagram in this case and efficient DMUs can be determined. Depending on the conditions and assumptions, several efficiency measures can be applied (e.g. see Cooper et al. 1999). One of these efficiency measures is the radial projection, which delivers the distance to the efficient frontier. In Fig. 3, this measure is used as an example and applied for minimizing costs and emissions simultaneously.

It is now possible for the decision maker to compare their own situation relative to others. Depending on the distance to the efficient frontier, the decision maker can then determine if a change in one's own position is necessary e.g. by reducing costs or emissions at the process level. Other input- and output-oriented efficiency measures are described by Allen (2002).

However, in order to improve the efficiency measure, it must be implemented into the corporate decision-making processes. A concept for implementation at the disaggregated level is presented in the following section.

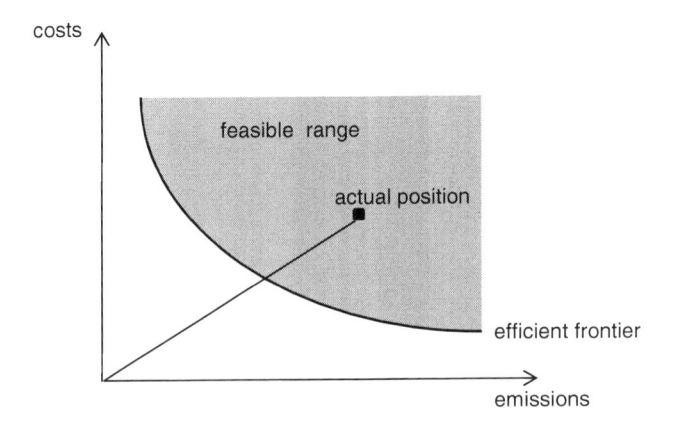

Fig. 3 Radial efficiency measure

2.3 Internal Improvement: Planning Models for Emission Efficiency

So far, external as well as internal evaluations and benchmarking are based on the ex-post data of companies, suppliers, and sites. Thus, the performance is only known in retrospect and improvements are no longer possible. Therefore, it is the aim at the disaggregated level C to plan ex-ante and to implement efficient alternatives.

As a prerequisite, processes as well as material flows and emission reduction measures need to be analyzed in detail. Based on this information, planning models can be implemented that are able to consider not only economic, but also environmental objectives. In the following, it is assumed that coherences exist between environmental and economic objectives, and that it is possible to develop linear (LP) or mixed-integer linear programming (MILP) production planning models taking into account both aspects simultaneously.

Different methods can be applied if two or more objectives are to be regarded simultaneously. First, all objectives can be expressed in monetary terms. In our case, this would mean that emissions have to be monetarized, e.g. applying the current or expected price for emission certificates. Such a procedure leads to one-objective LP or MILP models that can be solved using standard solvers (for an example see Letmathe and Balakrishnan 2005). However, emission prices are very volatile (CO_2-Handel 2007), and there are still numerous companies that are not participating in emissions trading. A second method is to apply weights to every objective aiming at a balance between conflicting objectives (for an example see Krikke et al. 2003). However, defining these weights is a very subjective procedure. Additionally, information and transparency is lost with ex-ante weighting, and weights might also change depending on the planning situation. Therefore, no monetization or weighting procedures are applied in the following, but the Pareto optimal frontier is determined as denoted by Steuer and Piercy (2005):

$$\max\{c^1 x = z_1\}$$
$$...$$
$$\max\{c^k x = z_k\}$$

$$\text{s.t.} \{x \in IR^n | Ax \leq b,\ b \in IR^m,\ x \geq 0\}$$

where k is the number of objectives. A *solution* $x' \in S \subset IR^n$ is *efficient* if and only if there is no $x \in S$ such that $c^i x \geq c^i x'$ for all i and there is at least one $c^i x < c^i x'$ (Steuer and Piercy 2005). The Pareto efficient frontier consists of the image of the set of all efficient solutions. Since the determination of all efficient solutions in an MOP is extremely CPU time-consuming, methods for an approximation of the efficient frontier can be applied. For details on the bi- and three-objective linear and continuous case see Quariguasi et al. (2006, 2007), for a generalized method for bi-objective combinatorial problems see Ehrgott and Gandibleux (2007).

Fig. 4 Approximation of the efficient frontier

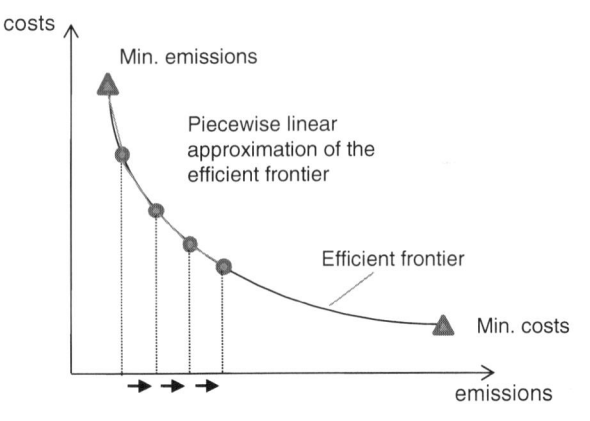

A piecewise linear approximation of the efficient frontier for the bi-objective case, which is the case we focus on in this contribution, is presented in Fig. 4.

As a result of this calculation, the decision-maker is aware of all efficient solutions, i.e. solutions for which there are no improvements in one objective possible without associated deterioration for another objective. Hence, the decision-maker can now freely decide based on his own trade-offs. However, the choices regarding the trade-offs are complex, since they not only depend on internal corporate decisions, but also on the situation of competitors as well as on normative trade-offs for society (Huppes and Ishikawa 2005). If stakeholders are increasingly aware of greenhouse gas emissions for example and consequently there is increasing pressure on companies to reduce emissions, companies might be willing to pay more for reducing a certain amount of emissions to fulfill increasing social requirements. Additionally, a company might be willing to pay more if the risk of a negative image exists, i.e. if competitors have a far better efficiency ratio. Therefore, a connection to the upper levels of implementation of the CEI ratio into corporate decision-making processes is necessary as is presented in the following.

2.4 Connecting the Levels: Decision-Making Based on Trade-Offs

Looking at the hierarchical concept presented within this chapter, the ex-post efficiency of one's own site/company is first determined compared to other sites/companies for the current situation (see Sects. 3.1 and 3.2). Following that, possible emission reduction alternatives are calculated ex-ante based on planning models (Sect. 3.3). As a final step, the decision-making levels described are then connected. This step allows the decision-maker to determine how changes at the disaggregated planning level affect the internal and/or external rating and benchmarking at the higher levels.

For connecting the planning levels, we use common characteristics shared by MODM and DEA efficiency measurement. Thus, the efficient frontier is plotted on the benchmarking level(s). Thereby, the efficiency of the current situation can be compared to the future (potential) efficiency after implementing the emission reduction options. For measuring this potential efficiency ex-ante, the same efficiency measures as on the upper efficiency levels can be applied (for efficiency measures see Sect. 3.2 and Cooper et al. (1999), for an example see Quariguasi et al. (2006)).

As a result, changes in the efficiency measures can be determined ex-ante, and the company/site can check, if and with which measures the efficiency ratios of competitors can be achieved. Thereby, the trade-offs calculated at the disaggregated level obtain a managerial relevance when analyzing the resulting difference in the performance ratios on the upper levels of the presented concept. Since the impact of internal improvement options on the performance measure at the aggregated level is now known to the decision-maker, he can more easily decide, which trade-offs to accept and thus, which measures to apply.

3 Case Study: Emission Intensities Within the Textile Chain

In this chapter, the presented concept is applied to the textile supply chain and it is shown how the environmental and economic performance can be optimized at the three levels of decision-making. Thereby, we focus on the textile chain of a specific textile retailer.

This retailer is ambitious in terms of sustainable objectives and intends to develop a climate protection strategy. Therefore, the aim is to adopt measures to achieve CO_2 savings in production processes and transportation. To achieve this, the whole supply chain is audited with regard to economic and environmental aspects. In the following, this business case is taken as a background for applying the presented concept. However, the special case and data presented have been modified in order to keep the confidentiality of the retailer and its suppliers.

3.1 External Benchmarking

First, the retailer calculates its own CEI aiming to reduce total CO_2-emissions along the supply chain. Data on direct emissions, turnover, prices and amounts of the supplies, as well as the CEI of suppliers must be collected. Based on this calculation, the retailer can carry out ex-post analyses. These analyses can be conducted by comparing its own CEI with an external benchmark, e.g. the average CEI of the sector, or by conducting time series analyses with regard to changes of the indicator over time. In the following, we assume that the retailer discovered a need for improvement of the CEI. This improvement can only be achieved at the lower levels of the presented concept.

3.2 Internal Benchmarking

In order to locate the potential for improvement, the retailer examines its own textile supply chain in more detail. As presented in Fig. 5, this chain consists of seven basic steps. In the textile chain, there is a non-homogeneous energy demand resulting in varying emission rates along the chain. As can be seen, the dyeing process demands the highest amount of energy. Thus, improving the CEI indicator for the dyeing process could be an important start.

In the following, it is assumed that the retailer decided to benchmark several dyeing suppliers in search of a potential improvement. This benchmarking is conducted based on price and CEI as presented in Table 1. As can be seen, there is a trade-off between price and CEI.

Depending on the criteria by which the suppliers are evaluated, a suitable method for benchmarking and evaluation of the different suppliers is to be chosen. For the multicriteria case, the DEA is applicable. In our case, the suppliers only need to be assessed in terms of price and CEI. Since this is a two-dimensional evaluation, both criteria can be visualized in a diagram (Fig. 6). Every supplier represents one dot in the diagram. The non-dominated suppliers are mapped as efficient DMUs. As shown in Fig. 6, suppliers *J*, *I*, *H*, *E* and *F* are dominated by

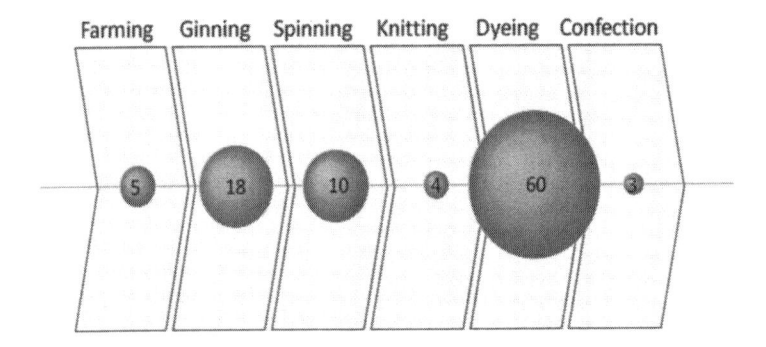

Fig. 5 Relative energy demand (%) along the textile chain [Systain Consulting GmbH (2007)]

Table 1 CEI and price for 170,000 T-Shirts of potential and current dyeing suppliers

	Price × quantity (US $)	CEI (kg CO_2/US $)
Supplier *A*	45,013	14.10
Supplier *B*	45,748	14.00
Supplier *C*	47,018	13.90
Supplier *D*	49,560	13.80
Supplier *E*	50,830	13.80
Supplier *F*	51,131	13.85
Supplier *G*	50,100	13.75
Supplier *H*	49,800	14.10
Supplier *I*	48,000	14.00
Supplier *J*	46,000	14.20

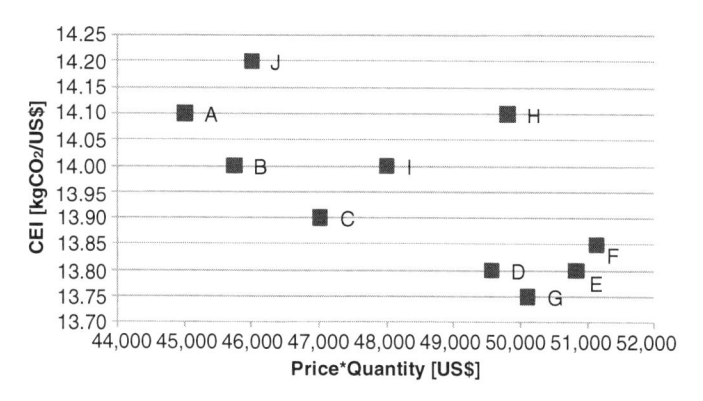

Integration of a New Emission-Efficiency Ratio into Industrial Decision-Making 173

Fig. 6 Benchmarking of suppliers

suppliers A, B, C, D and G. Thus, suppliers A, B, C, D and G form the efficient frontier.

In the following, we focus on the dominated supplier I. If I is a supplier from which the retailer currently procures T-Shirts, the retailer could use the results to either change to a more efficient supplier or – if the relationship is a good one – to help supplier I to improve its performance. In the following, it is assumed that the retailer provides the benchmarking results to supplier I in order to motivate improvement.

3.3 Internal Improvements

Assuming that dyer I is a current supplier of the retailer, he can easily see that he has to improve price and/or CEI. If the CEI of the remaining textile chain is disregarded in the following (thus focusing on the direct emissions of dyer I), I has three options. Since the CEI is determined as follows:

$$\mu_I = \frac{E_I}{AV_I} = \frac{E_I}{T_I - S_I}$$

Variables

μ_I: CEI of supplier I
E_I: direct emissions of supplier I
AV_I: value added of supplier I
S_I: supplies purchased by supplier I
T_I: turnover of supplier I

the supplier could either decrease its internal (direct) emissions, or decrease the costs of its supplies, or increase its turnover. Assuming that constant quantities are ordered by the retailer, an increase in turnover is only possible by increasing the prices. Since the dyer needs to be competitive in terms of the price, this option is neglected in the following. Furthermore, the assumption is that the dyer does not want to take into account a decrease in its added value. Therefore, the aim is on minimizing internal emissions E_I as well as supplies S_I (respectively costs) by optimizing its own processes.

To dye textiles, a huge amount of thermal energy is needed, since the chemicals need to be heated to a high temperature in order to be absorbed by the textiles. In developing countries, it is common to use diesel for the heating process. After technical retooling, it is possible to substitute diesel by LPG or gas. Thereby, each fuel has a specific emission factor and specific costs. However, cheaper fossil fuels usually have a higher emission rate than the more expensive fuels.

In the following, a simplified mathematical model with two objectives is presented. On the one hand, the aim is on minimizing total costs and on the other hand on minimizing total emissions. The only constraint is that the energy demand of the heating process is to be satisfied. Thereby, the total energy demand can be fulfilled by diesel, LPG, natural gas or linear combinations of all three fuel types. Other constraints like capacity requirements, energy demand of various products etc. could be added to the model. In the following, it is also assumed that no additional investment is necessary. Therefore, costs arise for fossil fuels only and all other costs are not relevant for this decision.

3.3.1 Variables

Decision variables	
Amount of diesel used (L)	x_{diesel}
Amount of LPG used (L)	x_{lpg}
Amount of gas used (m^3)	x_{gas}
Other parameters and variables	
Costs (US $)	C
Total emissions (t CO$_2$)	E
Amount of T-Shirts sold (pc)	$t_{T\text{-}Shirt}$
Amount of energy needed per T-Shirt (TJ/pc)	$d_{T\text{-}Shirt}$
Emission factor diesel (t CO$_2$/TJ)	e_{diesel}
Emission factor LPG (t CO$_2$/TJ)	e_{lpg}
Emission factor gas (t CO$_2$/TJ)	e_{gas}
Energy density diesel (TJ/L)	ED_{diesel}
Energy density LPG (TJ/L)	ED_{lpg}
Energy density natural gas (TJ/m^3)	ED_{gas}
Total energy demand (TJ)	D
Costs of diesel (US $/L)	c_{diesel}
Costs of LPG (US $/L)	c_{lpg}
Costs of natural gas (US $/m^3)	c_{gas}

Mathematical model

$$\min C = x_{diesel} \cdot c_{diesel} + x_{lpg} \cdot c_{lpg} + x_{gas} \cdot c_{gas}$$

$$\min E = e_{diesel} \cdot ED_{diesel} \cdot x_{diesel} + e_{lpg} \cdot ED_{lpg} \cdot x_{lpg} + e_{gas} \cdot ED_{gas} \cdot x_{gas}$$

Subject to

$$ED_{diesel} \cdot x_{diesel} + ED_{lpg} \cdot x_{lpg} + ED_{gas} \cdot x_{gas} \geq D$$

$$D = t_{T-Shirt} \cdot d_{T-Shirt}$$

Currently, the supplier *I* dyes 170,000 T-Shirts and uses 124,000 L diesel for heating. It is assumed that the costs for diesel, LPG and natural gas are 0.56 US \$/L, 0.33 US \$/L and 0.20 US \$/m^3 respectively.[1] Diesel has the highest emission factor with 74 t CO_2/TJ, followed by gas with 64.1 t CO_2/TJ, and LPG with 63 t CO_2/TJ [Umwelt-Online (2007)]. Each T-Shirt has an energy demand of 2.57×10^{-5} TJ ($d_{T-Shirt}$). The energy density is 4.64×10^{-5} TJ/L for LPG, 3.50×10^{-5} TJ/m^3 for gas and 3.58×10^{-5} TJ/L for diesel.

The lowest costs can be achieved using natural gas. However, LPG has a lower emission rate, although it is more expensive. Between these extreme points, there is an infinite number of other combinations of energy mixes, each with a certain rate of total emissions and costs. The Pareto efficient solutions of the linear production planning model are illustrated in Table 2. As can be seen, trade-offs occur between costs and emissions. The lowest costs of 25,013 US \$ accompany the highest emission rate of 281 t CO_2. In this particular case, only gas is used. Contrary to that, the lowest emission level of 276 t CO_2 accompanies the use of LPG, but results in total costs of 31,131 US \$.

In Fig. 7, the linear approximation of the efficient frontier for the energy consumption of the dyer is shown. To reach the efficient frontier, the supplier can

Table 2 Selective Pareto efficient solutions for fuel substitution

Costs (US \$)	Emissions (t CO_2)	LPG (L)	Diesel (L)	Gas (m^3)
25,013	281	0	0	125,063
25,748	280	11,334	0	110,036
27,018	279	30,927	0	84,062
28,289	278	50,520	0	58,088
29,560	277	70,112	0	32,114
30,830	276	89,705	0	6,140
31,131	276	94,336	0	0

---

[1]The prices are converted from Indian rupee to US dollars using an exchange rate of 0.02525 US \$/Rs. (exchange rate from 24.10.2007).

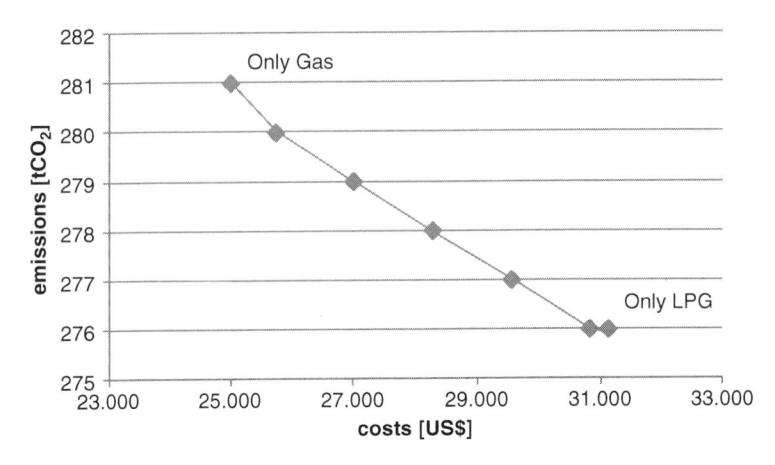

Fig. 7 Linear approximation of the efficient frontier of costs and emissions of different fuels

now choose between the trade-offs that are presented. If he prefers low costs, he would choose a position on the left hand side of the frontier and use gas for the heating processes. If he prefers to reduce emissions, he would choose a point more on the right hand side of the frontier and therefore opt to use more LPG. The position or point on the frontier that should be chosen depends on the current situation with regard to the benchmarking results of competitors.

3.4 Connection Between the Levels

After supplier *I* has calculated the efficient solutions with their corresponding trade-offs between costs and emissions, he can transform these figures into prices and CEI. The price is calculated in a simplified way by adding the constant added value (see explanation for this assumption in Sect. 3.3) of 20,000 US $ to the costs. The results are presented in Table 3.

Since the supplier received the information from the benchmarking analysis, he is aware of his position compared to his competitors. Therefore, the supplier can combine this information with the trade-offs between costs and total emissions, and work out how its position to competitors would change when using other fuels. In Fig. 8, the potential changes in the position of the supplier to its competitors are shown. From the current position, supplier *I* can become efficient if he chooses a position on the efficient frontier. On the left hand side of the frontier, the same costs but a lower CEI can be achieved compared to competitor A with the exclusive use of gas.

As can be seen in Fig. 8, the supplier can choose between a lower price and therefore higher CEI, and a higher price and therefore a lower CEI. To reach the efficient frontier, the use of gas for the heating process would be the optimal

Table 3 Transformed trade-offs of price and CEI

Price × quantity (US $)	CEI (kg CO$_2$/US $)
45,013	14.05
45,748	14.00
47,018	13.95
48,289	13.90
49,560	13.85
50,830	13.81
51,131	13.80

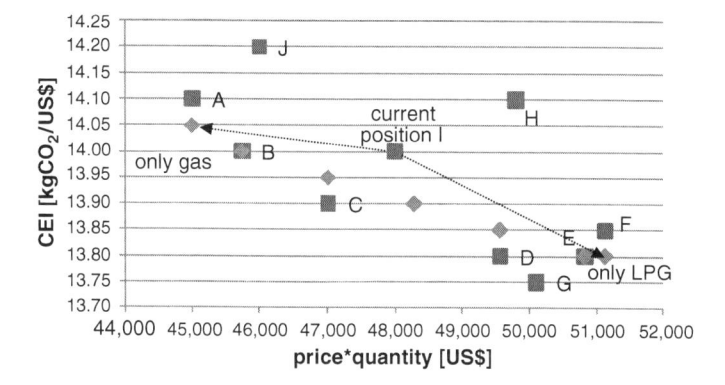

Fig. 8 Plotting the efficient frontier of the disaggregated level on the internal benchmarking level

strategy, because the use of LPG is inefficient compared to competitors. Since the use of gas lies on the efficient frontier, but accompanies a relatively high CEI, the retailer could offer to accept a higher price and receive a lower CEI instead.

4 Summary

An integrated concept for implementing environmental performance measures into corporate decision-making was presented within this chapter. Economic and environmental aspects were considered on different decision-making levels. On the upper levels, an external and internal ex-post benchmarking of companies, suppliers and sites was carried out. On the lower disaggregated level, ex-ante planning and at the same time a consideration of economic and environmental aspects was carried out by applying bi-objective models. Thereby, no weighting of the objectives was carried out, but the efficient frontier was calculated allowing the decision-maker to make decisions about trade-offs between economic and environmental results. Plotting these trade-offs on the aggregated levels shows changes in the benchmarking results of one's own company compared to competitors. The decision-maker could therefore choose trade-offs that coincide with the requirements set by efficient competitors.

The concept was exemplarily applied to a simple case in the textile chain. One textile retailer analyzed its supply chain and identified a high energy demand in the dyeing process. He benchmarked all potential and current dyeing suppliers and determined the efficient ones. Subsequently, he provided this information to a supplier, which was not on the efficient frontier and therefore expected to have the potential for improvement. To improve its position, the dyer analyzed its own processes. It was observed that the diesel used for the dyeing process could be substituted by other fossil fuels e.g. natural gas and LPG. The efficient frontier of the costs and the total emissions was calculated. On this frontier, the decision maker then chose the optimal trade-off as a result of the information he received at the aggregated level.

Acknowledgements The authors would like to thank the German BMBF (Ministry of Education and Research) for supporting the research project "Cumulative Emission Intensities for Assessment of Climate Protection Measures along Supply Chains – EINBLIK" (Promotional Reference 01LS05083). We would also like to thank our project partners: Institute of Applied Sciences at the University of Applied Sciences Pforzheim, Systain Consulting GmbH (Hamburg), Volkswagen AG (Wolfsburg) for their cooperation, conjoint discussions, and the provision of information and data.

References

Allen K (2002) Messung ökologischer Effizienz mittels Data Envelopment Analysis. DVU, Wiesbaden

Angell LC, Klassen RD (1999) Integrating environmental issues into the mainstream: an agenda for research in operations management. J Oper Manage 17:575–598

Austin D, Rosinski N, Sauer A, le Duc C (2004) Changing Drivers: The Impact of Climate Change on Competitiveness and Value Creation in the Automotive Industry. Washington, DC: World Resources Institute and Sustainable Asset Management

Charnes A, Cooper WW, Rhodes E (1978) Measuring the efficiency of decision making units. Eur J Oper Res 2:429–444

CLI (2007) Carbon disclosure project report 2007, Global FT500. http://www.cdproject.net/reports.asp. Accessed 10 Oct 2007

Clift R (2003) Metrics for supply chain sustainability. Clean Technol Environ Policy 3/4:240–247

CO_2-Handel (2007) Homepage of emissions trading and climate protection. http://co2-handel.de/article102_0.html. Accessed 10 Oct 2007

Cooper WW, Park KS, Pastor JST (1999) RAM: a range adjusted measure of inefficiency for use with additive models, and relations to other models and measures in DEA. J Prod Anal 11:5–42

Ehrgott M, Gandibleux X (2007) Bound sets for biobjective combinatorial optimization problems. Comput Oper Res 34:2674–2694

Figge F, Hahn T (2004) Sustainable value added: Ein neues Maß des Nachhaltigkeitsbeitrags von Unternehmen am Beispiel der Henkel KGaA. Vierteljahreshefte zur Wirtschaftsforschung 73:126–141

Figge F, Hahn T (2005) The cost of sustainable capital and the creation of sustainable value by companies. J Ind Ecol 9(4):47–58

Figge F, Hahn T, Daverio C, Persson M, Brunczel B, Wilhelm A, Mauritz C (2006) Sustainable Value of European Industry – A Value-Based Analysis of the Enviromental Performance of European Manufacturing Companies, ADVANCE-Project: Forres/Berlin, www.advance-project.org

Huppes G, Ishikawa M (2005) A framework for quantified eco-efficiency. J Ind Ecol 9(4):25–41
IPCC (2007) Climate change 2007: summary of policymakers. IPCC Secretariat, Geneva
Klein R, Scholl A (2004) Planung und Entscheidung. München, Vahlen
Krikke H, Bloemhof-Ruwaard J, van Wassenhove LN (2003) Concurrent product and closed-loop supply chain design with an application to refrigerators. Int J Prod Res 41(16):3689–3719
Letmathe P, Balakrishnan N (2005) Environmental considerations on the optimal product mix. Eur J Oper Res 167(2):398–412
Quariguasi JFN, Bloemhof-Ruwaard JM, van Numen JAEE, van Heck HWGM (2006) Designing and evaluating sustainable logistics networks. Int J Prod Econ 111(2):195–208
Quariguasi JFN, Walther G, Bloemhof-Ruwaard JM, van Numen JAEE, Spengler T (2007) A methodology for assessing eco-efficiency in logistics networks. Eur J Oper Res 193(3): 670–682
Schmidt M, Schwegler R (2005) Wertschöpfungsbasierte Erfolgsmessung unternehmensbezogener Klimaschutz-Aktivitäten. Institute for Applied Sciences, University of Applied Sciences Pforzheim (ed) Pforzheimer Forschungsberichte
Schmidt M, Schwegler R (2008) A recursive ecological indicator system for the supply chain of a company. J Cleaner Prod 16(15):1658–1664
Steuer RE, Piercy CA (2005) A regression study of the number of efficient extreme points in multiple objective linear programming. Eur J Oper Res 162(2):484–496
Systain Consulting GmbH (2007) Personal information about the textile supply chain
Umweltbundesamt (2007) Nationale Trendtabellen für die deutsche Berichterstattung atmosphärischer Emissionen seit 1990. http://www.umweltbundesamt.de/emissionen/publikationen.htm. Accessed 27 Oct 2007
Umwelt-Online (2007) Decision 2007/589/EG of the EG Commission by 18.07.2007. http://www.umwelt-online.de/regelwerk/eu/05_09/07_0589b.htm. Accessed 23 Oct 2007
Zangemeister C (1976) Nutzwertanalyse in der Systemtechnik – Eine Methodik zur multidimensionalen Bewertung und Auswahl von Projektalternativen, Dissertation Technische Universität Berlin 1970, 4th edn. Wittemann, München
Zimmermann H-J, Gutsche L (1991) Multi-Criteria Analyse, Einführung die Theorie der Entscheidungen bei Mehrfachzielsetzungen. Springer, Berlin

Offensive GHG Management and Small and Medium-Sized Enterprises

Charlotte Hesselbarth and Barbara Castrellon Gutierrez

Abstract The implementation of the EU Emissions Trading Scheme (EU ETS) on 01.01.2005 highly affects corporations of various sectors, industries, and dimensions. Among the businesses that are involved there are a significant number of Small and Medium Sized Enterprises (SME). While all participants have to cope with additional administrative burden and expenses, SMEs seem to be particularly affected because of above-average transaction costs, expenses for implementing missing IT-systems or the costs of human resource training.

The chapter analyses the characteristics and resource availability that enable SMEs to cope with the challenges of the EU ETS successfully. A typology of Greenhouse Gas management strategies is introduced pointing out that an offensive GHG management is indeed demanding and resource-intensive in the short term, but advantageous, cost-efficient, and less risky from a longer-term perspective. Although these considerations generally concern corporations of any size and sector, the special focus is on SMEs. In this chapter, we discuss the particular resources and advantages that enable SMEs to pursue such an offensive, sustainable-oriented GHG management strategy successfully.

Keywords GHG management strategies • internal resources • offensive GHG management • small and medium-sized enterprises

---

C. Hesselbarth (✉)
Centre for Sustainability Management, Leuphana University Lueneburg, Scharnhorststraße 1, 21335, Lueneburg
e-mail: hesselbarth@uni.leuphana.de

B.C. Gutierrez
Centre for Emissions Trading, Martin-Luther-University Halle-Wittenberg, Große Steinstraße 73, 06099 Halle, Germany
e-mail: barbara.castrellon-gutierrez@wiwi.uni-halle.de

1 Introduction

The implementation of the EU Emissions Trading Scheme (EU ETS) in 2005 marks a far-reaching turning-point in European environmental policy. For the first time, the market-based approach of tradable permits was put into force in a cross-national dimension. All over Europe, energy-generating and energy-intensive corporations are not only confronted with various new legal obligations and administrative requirements, but also with a modified business environment and the necessity to develop greenhouse gas (GHG) management strategies.

While all participants in the EU ETS have to cope with additional administrative burdens and expenses, SMEs – representing a good share of the total number of participants – seem to be particularly affected. On the one hand, ET and GHG management prove highly significant for them, on the other hand, SMEs feel overburdened with ET because of special characteristics that seem to put this category of corporations at a disadvantage compared to large enterprises.

Based on a typology of GHG management strategies (Sect. 2), the chapter analyses the situation of SMEs in the EU ETS and their resource availability for GHG management (Sect. 3).

The research focuses on the question whether SMEs have certain resources and advantages that enable them to pursue an offensive, sustainable-oriented GHG management strategy successfully (Sect. 4).

2 Characteristics and Relevance of SMEs in the EU ETS

2.1 SMEs in the German Economy – Definition and Significance

The industrial landscape in most European countries is shaped by SMEs. In Germany they form the backbone of the economy. Often referred to as "the engine of the business world," SMEs are an essential source of jobs, create entrepreneurial spirit and innovation and are thus crucial for fostering competitiveness and employment.

There are differing definitions concerning SME classification: the well-known definition of the European Commission (2006) defines the category of SMEs as enterprises which employ less than 250 persons and which have annual revenues not exceeding 50 million Euros, and/or a balance sheet total of 43 million Euros at the utmost. In addition, SMEs have to be largely independent, i.e., no other corporation is allowed to hold more than 25% shares in the company.

The criteria of the recently adjusted definition of SMEs according to the European Commission are summarized in Fig. 1.

This definition seems appropriate for the considerations of this chapter because it is based on a Europe-wide definition of SMEs. Furthermore, most public funding activities typically refer to the threshold explained in the definition mentioned above.

Offensive GHG Management and Small and Medium-Sized Enterprises 183

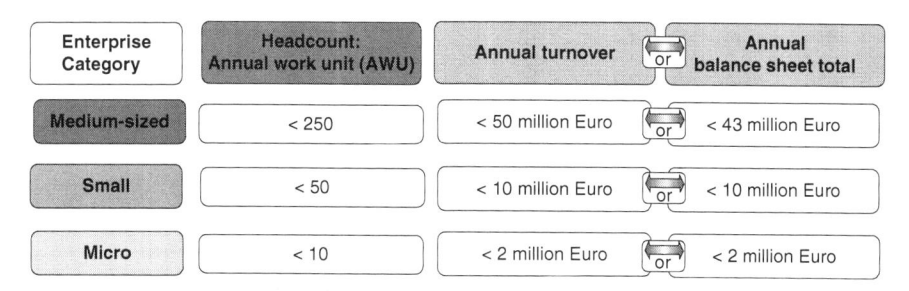

Enterprise Category	Headcount: Annual work unit (AWU)	Annual turnover	or	Annual balance sheet total
Medium-sized	< 250	< 50 million Euro	or	< 43 million Euro
Small	< 50	< 10 million Euro	or	< 10 million Euro
Micro	< 10	< 2 million Euro	or	< 2 million Euro

Fig. 1 The new SME definition according to the European Commission (European Commission 2006, p. 14)

Success potentials	Disadvantages for success
Flexibility	concentration of power in large-scale enterprises
personal communication and networking	Bureaucracy
proximity to the market	lack of succession planning and continuity
clear and simple structure	difficult integration of new employees
intensive personal contacts	limited financial resources
long-lasting cooperations of high quality	problems in establishing research cooperations
high level of participation	missing economic know-how (e.g. marketing)
motivation and creativity	high financial uncertainty
innovative orientation	
adaptability	
local/regional/national marketing	
not listed on stock exchange	

Fig. 2 Success potentials and disadvantages of SMEs (Ergenzinger and Krulis-Randa 2006, p. 79)

The significance of SMEs for the German economy is illustrated by the fact that in 2006 about 99.7% of the German enterprises fell into the category of SMEs (measured by the size of turnover). Note that the definition of SMEs in Germany is based on modified thresholds (<500 employees, <500 million euro annual revenues, IfM Bonn 2008???, p. 1). German SMEs generate 47.2% of net value added. With respect to the number of persons employed, 70.6% of the employees and 83.0% of the trainees were working in SMEs (IfM Bonn 2008).

2.2 General Characteristics of SMEs

In comparison to large-scale enterprises, SMEs possess a wide range of structural particularities and special features. These characteristics are either conducive or inhibiting for business success. Figure 2 below lists a number of success potentials and disadvantages discussed in the SME literature (see Ergenzinger and Krulis-Randa 2006, p. 79):

In many cases SMEs are confronted with restricted resources and market imperfections to a great extent. Very often it is difficult for them to obtain capital or credit, to cope with bureaucracy and the requirements of the regulatory framework, or to withstand increasing competitive pressure. Most of these external challenges are similar to large enterprises, but overcoming the disadvantages is much more difficult for SMEs due to a lack of infrastructure, financial resources, and workforce. Their limited resources may also reduce access to new technologies or emerging markets. Often it proves difficult to integrate new employees due to a strong und unique corporate culture. Occasionally regarded as an inhibiting aspect, a strong corporate culture may turn out to be an advantage for offensive GHG management.

In spite of the deficits mentioned above, SMEs also show some characteristics that prove essential for competitiveness and business success in general and with respect to the EU ETS. Flexibility, proximity to the market, strategies for niche markets, and a distinct innovative orientation all have to be considered as key elements for companies' success. Besides, SMEs are characterized by a high level of participation: Commitment, motivation and creativity of employees turn out to be the main source of innovative products, technologies, or business ideas in dynamic markets.

Generally operating in local and regional networks, SMEs enjoy high public awareness in the regional context that can be helpful for marketing and structural policy. With respect to sustainable management, absence from the stock exchange releases SMEs from the short-term pressure of publishing quarterly results and enables longer-term strategies.

2.3 Impact upon SMEs due to Emissions Trading (ET)

The above-mentioned characteristics of SMEs highly affect companies' capabilities to participate in ET. In January 2005, the EU ETS was implemented in Germany as well as in the other European member states (Hesselbarth 2009, p. 67). According to the "Greenhouse Gas Emission Allowance Trading Law" (Treibhausgasemissionshandelsgesetz [TEHG]), facilities of energy-generating and energy-intensive industries are obliged to participate in the EU ETS (Annex I TEHG).

Results of an empirical study dated from 2006 show that a good share of facilities in the German state of Saxony-Anhalt impacted by ET may be categorised as SMEs (32 out of 77 facilities). Since substantial similarities to the respective situation in Germany have been proven, it can be assumed that a relatively high share of enterprises affected by ET in Germany are SMEs (Castrellon Gutierrez 2011).

In the second trading period (2008–2012) of the EU-ETS, the "de-minimis-rule" for small-volume emitters was implemented besides other changes and system simplifications. According to this rule, facilities that emit no more than 25,000 million tons CO_2 per year (small facilities) obtain allowances according to § 6 (9) and § 7 (4) ZuG 2012 on the basis of historical emissions, and without applying a fulfilment factor. The de-minimis-rule was explicitly introduced in order to provide reliefs from administrative burdens for small emitters. SMEs were also expected to benefit from this rule.

This only occurs to a minor degree however: Indeed, in the second trading period allowances were allocated to almost half the affected German facilities (792 total) according to the de-minimis-rule (547 power supply facilities and 245 industrial facilities). However, small facilities are not necessarily operated by SMEs. Since the size of the facility does not correlate with the size of the enterprise (Castrellon Gutierrez 2011), SMEs operate both small and large facilities and, therefore only benefit from the de-minimis-rule to a small degree. Even in the case of an allocation according to the de-minimis-rule, this is insufficient to overcome the deficits of SMEs related to ET (such as lack of experience with volume-based instruments, lack of know-how, limited human and financial resources, etc.). Most frequently, disadvantages such as above-average transaction costs for market activities, expenses for implementing IT-systems for allowance trading and risk management, or lacking financial and hedging know-how are considered as reasons for insufficient strategic orientation and inactive market behaviour (Hesselbarth 2009, p. 439). As a result, SMEs miss business opportunities by not fully exploiting internal and external success potentials generated by proactive and offensive GHG management. In Sect. 3 analyzes strategic aspects that are relevant for SMEs to profit from ET.

3 Strategic GHG Management Under the EU ETS

3.1 Strategic GHG Management – Necessity and Definition

The launch of the EU ETS does not only imply new legal requirements such as emission permits (allowances), monitoring systems, or emission reports, but represents a paradigm shift from long-time dominating command-and-control policies towards a market-based regulation. This completely changes the relationship between both the regulatory authority and a firm as well as the entire framework for corporate decisions and procurement, production, and investment strategies depending on CO_2 intensity. Instead of observing fixed standards, corporations in the EU ETS are confronted with a flexible obligation to provide sufficient allowances based on the emissions of the previous year. Various options such as internal emission abatement, allowance trading, banking allowances, or participating in JI/CDM projects are available and can be chosen freely depending on the company's respective costs and benefits (Hesselbarth 2009, p. 449).

As the market for emission allowances and associated emerging markets (e.g. for energy-efficient or monitoring technologies, consultant and financial services, etc.) is related to various new risks (e.g. cost, risks of applying new technologies), innovative and proactive companies can also generate competitive advantage due to cost structure, image effects, reduced risk exposure, or improved terms of financing.

Due to the fact that ET typically turns out to be of substantial strategic relevance to SMEs (see Sect. 4.1 in more detail), strategic considerations and the systematic integration of carbon risks and carbon potentials prove to be essential for competitiveness and the corporate value of SMEs. Strategic GHG management includes all corporate decisions relevant to the generation, development, and maintenance of success potential that refer to carbon dioxide emissions, emission allowances as a new production factor, and all operations within the EU ETS and related emerging markets (Hesselbarth 2009, p. 438).

3.2 Typology of Basic Strategies for GHG Management

In the following, GHG management strategies are characterized for analytical purposes by some attributes initially used by Meffert and Kirchgeorg (1998) to classify environmental corporate strategies. The resulting typology contains three types of management strategies: compliance, risk-averse strategies, and offensive GHG management (see Fig. 3).

	Compliance management	Risk-averse GHG management strategy	Offensive GHG management
Dominating motive for strategy choice	• minimization of workload and direct/additional expenses	• minimization of (market) risks; • transfer of so far successful strategy patterns	• mid- and long-term optimization of compliance costs and corporate risks • sustainable orientation
Main focus	• compliance with essential legal requirements • if necessary/possible: purchase or selling of emission allowances on the market	• compliance • far-reaching risk hedging • avoidance of additional risks	• compliance • active portfolio management (internal emission reduction, purchase, JI/CDM projects, carbon funds, etc.) • integrated strategy development (procurement, production, investment, communication, etc.)
Level of adaptation and activity	• adaptive	• adaptive but active (using historical experiences as well as established patterns and structures)	• innovative and anticipating
Time of strategy development	• reactive	• reactive	• proactive
Reference level	• internal, supplemented by anonymous market transactions	• internal and external • market-focused	• internal and external • stakeholder orientation
Type of strategy development	• isolated	• partially integrated (production, controlling, procurement, risk management)	• integrated and holistic
Communication and marketing	• defensive • generally low communication intensity	• main focus on risk aspects • emphasizing possibilities of the EU ETS for active risk management and hedging	• intensive internal and external stakeholder dialogues • offensive climate protection and sustainable marketing • transparent and balanced GHG reporting • climate strategy disclosure
Strategy enforcement	• individual (anonymous market transactions)	• individual and cooperative (market-based cooperations and already established relations)	• individual and cooperative (all stakeholders)

Fig. 3 Typology of basic GHG management strategies (Following Hesselbarth 2009, p. 450)

Compliance management focuses on the fulfilment of legal requirements with a minimal workload and low additional expenses in the short term. First market observations lead to the conclusion that most SMEs choose the compliance strategy (Knoll and Huth 2008, p. 84; Baumann 2006, pp. 154–155). While this strategy primarily proves to be reactive, adaptive and dominated by an isolated and individual approach, offensive GHG management represents an anticipative, proactive and sustainability-oriented strategy. Besides legal compliance, offensive GHG management takes advantage of the flexibility by applying different instruments and methods, e.g. investing in abatement technologies, partnering in CDM projects, and the active trading of allowances, with a long-term perspective. The strategy is characterized by an integrated perspective, intensive stakeholder dialogues, cooperative behaviour, and the use of sustainability-oriented structural policy in public, policy, and market arenas (Schneidewind 1998; Hesselbarth 2009, p. 279). Risk-averse GHG management concentrates on risk management aspects by using the wide portfolio of existing hedging instruments. This strategy seems rational for enterprises that are extremely exposed to risks and experienced in trading and risk management, but only have restricted limited resources available for an offensive GHG management.

3.3 Strategy Choice – Relevant Determinants and Portfolio for GHG Management Strategies

In order to analyse the choice of strategy by SMEs participating in the EU ETS, a portfolio for GHG management strategies is presented in the following. The portfolio is based on two dimensions:

1. Strategic relevance of the EU ETS
2. Relative strength of internal resources for GHG management

These dimensions are operationalized as listed below.

1. Strategic Relevance of the EU ETS

   - Direct financial impact of allowance allocation on the corporate financial position and the results of operation
   - Cost reduction potential (no-regret potentials, profitable project-based credits)
   - Attainable revenue: selling of surplus allowances, windfall profits, increase in revenues due to low-carbon fuel mixture and modified merit order, JI/CDM projects (technology export, credits, product sales), sales opportunities on emerging markets (environmental technologies, consulting and financial services, etc.)
   - Effects on innovative abilities and productivity
   - Extent of carbon risks exposure (price risks, volume risks, regulatory risks, etc.)

Economic resources	Know-how	Motivation	Social-psychological aspects	Institutional framework
• access to financial resources/venture capital • manpower for GHG management • low transaction costs (I&K infrastructure, trading systems) • low abatement costs, high abatements potentials • moderate profitability expectations • CO_2-efficient technologies and products • flexible production systems • procurement and market networking	• know-how concerning energy and process engineering • knowledge of information channels and technlogy providers • know-how and experiences concerning trade arrangements and hedging instruments • legal knowledge (EU ETS, project mechanism)	• low abatement costs, high abatements potentials • high energy costs • high financial importance of GHG management for companys profit • foreseeable shortage of EUA • image as sustainable champion • low transaction costs • sustainability orientation • high stakeholder orientation, intensive stakeholder dialogues • high commitment for GHG management	• social appreciation of carbon responsibility • optimistic perspective concerning functionality and efficiency of the EU ETS • climate-friendly corporate culture • economic thinking, innovation orientation • curiosity and willingness to learn • acceptance of increasing importance of climate change and sustainibillity	• advanced emission controlling, risk management, and sustainable management systems • integrated strategy planning • market screening and trading systems • organizational structures for GHG management (departments, integration of GHG management tasks)

Fig. 4 Strength of internal resources for GHG management – relevant determinants (Based on Hesselbarth 2009, p. 457)

- Potential for profiling as a climate-friendly and responsible corporation; image effects
- Impact on the company's position on the financial markets (reduction of carbon risks, access to carbon funds and sustainability indices)
- Extent of stakeholder demands (investors, NGOs, regulatory authorities, etc.) and foreseeable changes of societal norms and values

The strategic relevance accrues from opportunities and threats related to the EU ETS. This dimension is parameterized by

2. Relative Strength of Internal Resources for GHG Management

The ability to implement a GHG management strategy is based on a set of not only economic but also knowledge-based, motivational, socio-psychological, and institutional resources as detailed in Fig. 4.

Assuming that both dimensions (strategic relevance of the EU ETS, and relative strength of internal resources) possess a low, medium, and high value, this results in a matrix with nine fields, enabling SMEs to position their GHG management situation as a strategic business unit and to deduce a (rough) strategy recommendation.

4 Suitability of an Offensive GHG Management for SMEs

According to the matrix presented in the previous section, offensive GHG management seems appropriate if SMEs are highly impacted by ET and certain internal resources for GHG management are available. These preconditions – high strategic relevance and available resources for offensive GHG management, are analysed in the following section in more detail.

Fig. 5 GHG management strategies (Based on Hesselbarth 2009, p. 458)

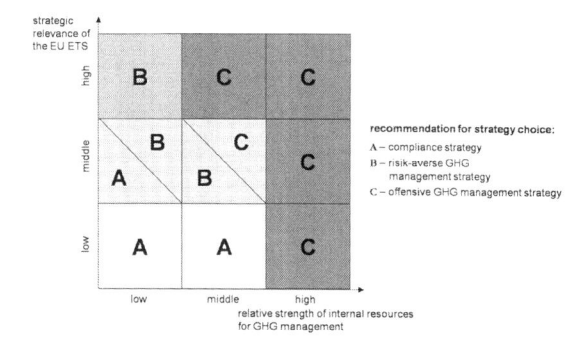

recommendation for strategy choice:
A – compliance strategy
B – risk-averse GHG management strategy
C – offensive GHG management strategy

4.1 Strategic Relevance of ET for SMEs

In many cases ET proves strategically relevant for SMEs to a large extent. This fact generally results in the recommendation to choose an offensive GHG management strategy (Fig. 5). The following arguments substantiate this strategic significance (see also Sect. 3 for general parameters):

- There is a high financial impact of allowance allocation on the financial positions of SMEs.
- Considerable cost reduction potentials can be generated due to high abatement volume and low abatement costs in most energy-intensive industries operated by SMEs.
- ET stimulates innovation processes that are essential for SMEs productivity, efficiency, and competitiveness.
- Emerging markets in the context of the EU ETS offer various opportunities for SMEs to find a niche in a market for carbon-friendly products, technologies, or business ideas. Because of market proximity and flexibility, SMEs are particularly qualified to seize market opportunities.
- Company's climate risk exposure and GHG management strategy is enormously relevant for SMEs' access to capital markets in the future.
- SMEs attract local/regional interest and, therefore, possess high potential for image effects and profiling as climate-friendly and responsible corporations.
- Anticipating foreseeable changes of societal norms and values (climate friendly lifestyle, etc.) SMEs are able to reduce the costs of adjustment and ensure their competitiveness by offensive and proactive GHG management.

4.2 Internal Resources and Approaches for Successful Offensive GHG Management in SMEs

As pointed out in Sect. 3.2, offensive GHG management does indeed prove demanding and resource-intensive in the short-term, but advantageous, cost-efficient, and less risky in a longer perspective. Furthermore, this proactive, anticipating, and holistic offensive strategy has to be considered essential on the way towards sustainable development. Although there are some arguments for pure compliance management, future-oriented SMEs with certain internal resources are recommended to implement an offensive GHG management that is able to fulfil the requirements for a profitable, responsible, and sustainable corporate orientation.

Naturally, the strategic deficits and disadvantages discussed in Sect. 2.2 (such as restricted financial and human resources, missing know-how, over-average transaction costs, etc.) impact SMEs' capacities to participate actively in ET and pursue an offensive GHG management strategy. Nevertheless, SMEs possess some strength and internal resources that can balance the disadvantages.

1. The high strategic relevance and financial impact of ET stimulates the innovative ability in SMEs. High shares of energy costs, substantial abatement potentials, and flexible production systems promote innovation and the reduction of carbon intensity.
2. SMEs are often particularly motivated for sustainable and climate-friendly management. This can be justified either by ethical reasons or by image effects and reputation.
3. SMEs are typically characterized by market proximity and customer intimacy. Intensive stakeholder dialogues enable SMEs to anticipate changes of societal norms and values with respect to climate change and develop climate-friendly products and services at an early stage.
4. Due to the fact that SMEs are not listed at stock exchange, they are not so extremely exposed to short-term pressure of quarterly results. Thus long-term optimization of compliance costs and corporate risks in the EU ETS, moderate payback periods, and long-term planning in general are facilitated. This perspective turns out to be essential for offensive GHG management and sustainable management on the whole.
5. Flexibility, qualification, creativity and motivation of the employees are considered as most important competitive factors and fundamental resources for offensive GHG management. Employees in SMEs are typically highly qualified and used to fulfilling several functions simultaneously. Sometimes this causes staff shortages and lack of time (Reiner 2004, p. 9; Mugler 1999, p. 78), nevertheless, motivation, job satisfaction, and commitment (for climate-friendly management, energy-efficient innovation, etc.) prove to be high in SMEs due to both interdisciplinary and challenging tasks as well as social networks.
6. Restricted human resources and the multi-functionality of employees in SMEs tend to result in integrated organizational structures for GHG management. Integration of GHG management is far-reaching: Carbon intensity is included as a vital criterion in every research, investment, procurement, and production decision and GHG management tasks extend to all hierarchy levels.
7. Most frequently, SMEs are embedded into regional networks with suppliers, cooperation partners, stakeholders, local authorities, etc. Thus opportunities for bundling know-how, economies of scale, or joint research activities emerge.

This enumeration points out that SMEs – in spite of commonly affirmed strategic deficits – definitely have certain economic, knowledge-based, motivational, socio-psychological, or institutional resources available for offensive GHG management.

Effective offensive GHG management demands on the one hand, a strengthening of existing success potentials, and on the other hand, a minimising of disadvantages and shortcomings. Some crucial starting points to reduce constraints for offensive GHG management in SMEs are listed in the following:

- Facilitated access to capital and credits improves the financial situation and promotes building up financial, trading, and hedging know-how.
- Knowledge transfer by the Chamber of Commerce and Industry (Industrie- und Handelskammer [IHK]) and advisory offices provides up-to-date knowledge (legal requirements, technical support, strategic advice, etc.).
- Cooperation with SME-specialized consultancies, advisory services, experienced traders, or scientific institutions supports knowledge transfer.
- Utilization of internet-based trading floors/exchange platforms allow small-volume allowance trading with minimal transaction costs and no charges (such as "Carbon Pool Europe" or the platform of CO_2ncept [2009]).
- Intensified cooperation (with competitors, local universities, Chamber of Commerce and Industry, etc.) in the field of human resource training promotes the acquisition of ET-specific knowledge and improves the manpower situation in SMEs.
- Measures such as the harmonization of reporting systems, automation, and the building up of electronic communication reduce transaction costs.
- Participation in research cooperation and domestic offset projects together with local partners (allowed from 2013 onwards) induce learning processes and enable low-cost emission allowances to be generated.

5 Conclusion

The implementation of the EU ETS and increasing stakeholders' awareness concerning climate-friendly corporate behaviour does not only have an impact on large corporations but also a considerable proportion of SMEs to a great extent. This turns out to be doubly challenging: On the one hand, ET proves to be of particular strategic relevance for these SMEs – this category of firms seems to be at a disadvantage due to various structural deficits and sometimes developing an active GHG management poses great burdens on SMEs.

In contrast to pure compliance management, offensive GHG management is considered not only as a demanding, but as a sustainable, future-oriented, and long-term economically advantageous strategy, too. After analysing the characteristics of SMEs, the chapter at hand points out that SMEs indeed possess certain internal resources as well as approaches to reduce constraints in order to establish an offensive GHG management successfully. Moreover, the great importance of SMEs for sustainable development demands to empower them for the challenges of offensive GHG management. Although the chapter concentrates on Small and Medium Sized Companies, a generalization can be made that offensive GHG management proves to be essential for corporations of any size and sector in order to ensure competitiveness and corporate success in a longer-term perspective.

References

Baumann S (2006) Die Markteinführung des Emissionshandels in Deutschland – Die emissionshandelspflichtigen Unternehmen im Spannungsfeld zwischen Theorie und Praxis, Tübingen

Castrellon Gutierrez B (2011) Emissions trading and Small and Medium-sized Enterprises in Germany, Martin-Luther-University Halle-Wittenberg (forthcoming 2011)

CO_2ncept (2009) Der Kleinmengenhandel. http://www.co2ncept-plus.de/klein-mengenhandel.0.html. Accessed 25 Nov 2009

Ergenzinger R, Krulis-Randa JS (2006) Unternehmer als Erfolgsfaktor von KMU – Was kann das Management davon lernen?. In: Berndt R (ed) Managementkonzepte für kleine und mittlere Unternehmen, Berlin

European Commission (2006) The new SME definition – User guide and model declaration. http://ec.europa.eu/enterprise/enterprise_policy/sme_definition/sme_user_guide.pdf. Accessed 2 Dec 2009

Hesselbarth C (2009) Wirkungen des EU-Emissionshandels als ökonomisches Instrument der Umweltpolitik auf das betriebliche Nachhaltigkeitsmanagement, Aachen

Institut für Mittelstandsforschung (IfM) Bonn (2008) KMU-Anteile in Deutschland 2007, nach Berechnungen des IfM Bonn 2008. http://www.ifm-bonn.org/index.php?id=540. Accessed 25 Nov 2009

Lisa K, Huth M (2008) Emissionshandel aus soziologischer Sicht – Wer handelt eigentlich wie mit Emissionsrechten? Umweltwirtschaftsforum UWF 2008(2):81–88

Meffert H, Kirchgeorg M (1998) Marktorientiertes Umweltmanagement – Konzeption, Strategie, Implementierung mit Praxisfällen, 3rd edn, Stuttgart

Mugler J (1999) Betriebswirtschaftslehre der Klein- und Mittelbetriebe, Springers Kurzlehrbücher der Wirtschaftswissenschaften, Vol. 2, 3rd edn, Wien, New York: Springer

Reiner D (2004) Strategisches Wissensmanagement in der Produktentwicklung – Methoden und Prozesse für kleine und mittlere Unternehmen, Wiesbaden

Schneidewind U (1998) Die Unternehmung als strukturpolitischer Akteur, Marburg

Part C
New Technologies and Instruments in the Field of Emissions Trading

The Potential of Ocean Iron Fertilization as an Option for Mitigating Climate Change

Christine Bertram

Abstract Ocean iron fertilization is currently being discussed as one measure that could contribute to climate change mitigation by stimulating the growth of phytoplankton in certain parts of the ocean and enhancing oceanic CO_2 uptake. Its implementation is greatly debated however and its mitigation potential has not yet been explored well. At present, it is still not possible to use carbon offsets generated through iron fertilization projects for complying with the Kyoto Protocol as trading these offsets is currently only possible on voluntary carbon markets. Company interests in such a commercial use of ocean iron fertilization do however already exist.

Consequently, there is a need to explore the potential of ocean iron fertilization as a climate change mitigation option as well as regulatory issues connected with its implementation. This article combines these two aims by first examining the scientific background, quantitative potential, side effects and costs of ocean iron fertilization. In a second step, regulatory aspects such as its legal status and open access issues are reviewed. Moreover, the chapter analyses how the regulations for afforestation and reforestation activities within the framework of the Kyoto Clean Development Mechanism (CDM) could be applied to ocean iron fertilization.

The main findings of this chapter are that the quantitative potential of ocean iron fertilization is limited, that potential adverse side effects are severe, and that its costs are higher than it was initially hoped. Moreover, the legal status of ocean iron fertilization is currently not well defined, open access might cause inefficiencies, and the CDM regulations could not be easily applied to ocean iron fertilization.

Keywords CDM • Kyoto protocol • Ocean iron fertilization

C. Bertram (✉)
Kiel Institute for the World Economy, Duesternbrooker Weg 120, 24105 Kiel, Germany
e-mail: christine.bertram@ifw-kiel.de

1 Introduction

The world is very likely to experience a range of adverse climate change impacts in the coming decades, emphasizing the need to investigate measures to mitigate these impacts (Forster et al. 2007; Barker et al. 2007). Ocean iron fertilization is currently being discussed as one measure that could contribute to climate change mitigation (see e.g. Denman 2008 or Buesseler et al. 2008). It aims at stimulating phytoplankton growth in certain parts of the ocean by artificially adding iron to the water, thereby enhancing the uptake of oceanic CO_2 and reducing atmospheric CO_2 concentrations.

The utilization of ocean iron fertilization is however highly debated, due to the fact that its effects – both intended and unintended, are still not yet fully understood (Buesseler et al. 2008; Powell 2008a). Nevertheless, there are still vital commercial interests that favour this method in order to sequester CO_2, generate carbon offsets, and sell these offsets on carbon markets (Leinen et al. 2008). At present, selling carbon offsets generated through iron fertilization projects is only possible on voluntary carbon markets and these carbon offsets cannot be used to comply with the Kyoto Protocol (Powell 2008a). However, continually increasing CO_2 emissions into the atmosphere could put further pressure on the inclusion of more sinks into a Post-Kyoto agreement (Rehdanz et al. 2005; Michaelowa et al. 2005). Therefore, given the commercial interests that support the implementation of ocean iron fertilization on larger scales, it is necessary to investigate its potential as a climate change mitigation option as well as the regulatory issues that would be connected with its implementation.

This chapter starts off with a description of ocean iron fertilization including its scientific background, quantitative potential, side effects and costs. The chapter then goes on to explore some regulatory issues that are connected with the utilization of ocean iron fertilization. This includes analyzing general aspects, such as the legal status of ocean iron fertilization or its open access resource character. Moreover, specific aspects arising from the Kyoto regulatory framework for afforestation and reforestation projects within the Clean Development Mechanism (CDM) are investigated.

2 Sequestration From Ocean Iron Fertilization

2.1 Scientific Background

The idea of fertilizing the ocean with iron in order to stimulate phytoplankton growth dates back to John Martin, who published his so-called Iron Hypothesis in 1990 (Martin 1990). Martin suggested that iron could be the limiting factor for photosynthesis in some parts of the ocean, where the concentration of macronutrients is high but the concentration of chlorophyll is low. These parts of the ocean are called high-nitrogen, low-chlorophyll (HNLC) regions and are located in the sub-arctic North Pacific, the eastern equatorial Pacific, and, most importantly, the Southern (Antarctic) Ocean. The idea of ocean iron fertilization is to stimulate the growth of phytoplankton by artificially adding iron to the surface of the ocean in these HNLC regions in order to increase the amount of CO_2 being used for photosynthesis and stored in the resulting biomass.

To understand how this fertilization process could help in sequestering CO_2, it is necessary to explore the marine carbon cycle in greater detail (see e.g. Raven and Falkowski 1999 or Denman 2008). Phytoplankton will carry out photosynthesis by taking up CO_2 that is dissolved in seawater and by converting this dissolved inorganic carbon (DIC) to particulate organic carbon (POC). Some of this POC will then sink from the surface of the ocean to the deep ocean or even to the ocean floor, which leads to increasing CO_2 concentrations in the ocean's interior and decreasing CO_2 concentrations in the ocean's upper layer. This process is referred to as the biological pump. Eventually, the carbon exported to the deep ocean will reach the surface ocean again due to ocean circulation. Nevertheless, the carbon has the potential to circulate in the deep ocean for decades or even centuries, which could qualify as sequestering CO_2. Indeed, not all of the carbon that has been taken up by phytoplankton will be transported to or sequestered in the deep ocean. Instead, a large proportion of this carbon will return to the atmosphere within short time scales due to remineralisation or the respiration and excretion from higher animals that eat phytoplankton (Fig. 1).

In this context, it is necessary to distinguish between carbon export, sequestration and CO_2 drawdown from the atmosphere. While carbon export refers to the amount of carbon removed from the surface layer of the ocean, carbon sequestration refers to the amount of carbon actually stored in the interior of the ocean for a long time horizon, e.g. for a hundred years.[1] This differentiation is important because more than 50% of the POC is already remineralized within the first 100 m of sinking. Further on, only about 2–25% of the carbon reaches a depth between 100 and 500 m and only 1–15% of the carbon sinks below 500 m (Powell 2008b). Consequently, the amount of carbon sequestration depends on the depth that is deep enough to keep the carbon away from the surface ocean for a hundred years. However, this depth varies and depends on several factors, including the chosen location and the initial conditions at the selected ocean site, ocean currents, temperature, weather conditions, the depth of the wind mixed layer, lateral patch dilution and grazing activity (see De Baar et al. 2005 or Powell 2008b for further information).

Another interaction of special interest is the one between carbon export, carbon sequestration and carbon drawdown from the atmosphere into the ocean. When enriching surface HNLC waters with iron, phytoplankton growth will use the CO_2

---

[1] A hundred years is the time horizon, which the Kyoto Protocol (UNFCCC 1997) adopted for the calculation of global warming potentials, so that this time horizon could be considered to be equivalent to permanent carbon sequestration.

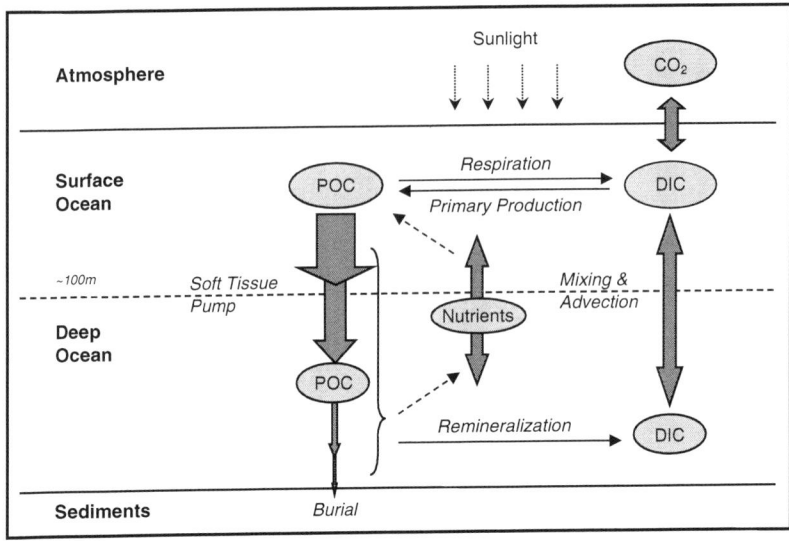

Presentation based on *Denman* (2008) and *Powell* (2008b).

Fig. 1 Schematic Representation of the Soft Tissue Pump and Part of the Marine Carbon Cycle.

that is already present in the surface ocean to carry out photosynthesis. The resulting decrease in the CO_2 concentration in the upper layer of the ocean is expected to lead to a drawdown of CO_2 from the atmosphere into the ocean. Consequently, it should be of interest to assess the potential of ocean iron fertilization with respect to mitigating atmospheric CO_2 concentrations, in particular the amount of CO_2 drawn down from the atmosphere and subsequently sequestered in the deep sea (Gnanadesikan et al. 2003).

2.2 Quantitative Potential

So far, only a dozen ship-based experiments have been carried out, in which relatively small patches of water were fertilized and the resulting effects studied. In addition to these, modelling studies have been carried out to analyze the effects of ocean iron fertilization on broader temporary and spatial scales, and natural ocean iron fertilization events have also been studied. All of these various studies made it unequivocally clear that iron addition leads to enhanced photosynthetic activity. The extent of carbon export and sequestration still remain hard to measure however and the observed results vary greatly (Powell 2008d).

During the patch fertilization experiments, observed carbon export ranged from 0 to 27% of primary production. The CO_2 gas flux from the air into the sea was on average reported to be 3% of primary production. Because the overall CO_2 concentrations between the air and sea only balance out slowly however, the uptake of CO_2 by the ocean could have continued after the short experimental observation time, which was only several weeks (see De Baar et al. 2005 and Boyd et al. 2007 for synthesis reports about the ship-based experiments).

The export efficiency of ocean iron fertilization can also be expressed as the ratio of exported carbon (C) to the amount of added iron (Fe). A wide range of these efficiency ratios was observed during the patch fertilization experiments. According to De Baar et al. (2008), export efficiencies to a depth of 100 m ranged from 0 to 650 mol C per mol Fe up to 6,648 mol C per mol Fe. Converted to masses, this would imply that 1 t of iron added to the surface ocean could induce a carbon export of between zero and 1,400 t of carbon from the surface ocean to a depth of 100 m. Extrapolation would result in an export efficiency down to a depth of 250 m that would be half of these amounts and even less for depths below 500 m. Model simulations suggest that the cumulative sequestration potential of patch fertilization for a time horizon of a hundred years could be at most some ten million tons of carbon (Denman 2008).

In addition to patch fertilization, large-scale ocean iron fertilization is another possible option, whereby all macronutrients in all HNLC regions of the global ocean would be depleted. Recent model simulations suggest that the potential of such large-scale ocean iron fertilization could be 26–70 gigatons of carbon (Gt C) over a hundred years, which could be broken down to 260–700 million tons of carbon per year (see Denman 2008 for a summary of these simulation results).

To assess the potential of ocean iron fertilization, one should reflect on the scope of anthropogenic CO_2 emissions, which amounted to 7.8 Gt C in 2005 and could reach up to 37 Gt C by the year 2100. Cumulated CO_2 emissions by the year 2100 might well be in the range of 770–2,540 Gt C (Forster et al. 2007). Consequently, no single mitigation strategy alone has the potential to guarantee a stabilization of atmospheric CO_2 concentrations. Large-scale ocean iron fertilization could on the one hand contribute to a substantial share of the portfolio of mitigation options aiming to achieve stringent stabilization targets. Patch fertilization on the other hand, which is probably more realistic and feasible, would only have a relatively small impact. Still, future research may explore ways of enhancing sequestration efficiency and thus the quantitative potential of ocean iron fertilization (De Baar et al. 2008). What is more, compared to existing climate targets laid down in the Kyoto Protocol, which sum up to a joint reduction effort of 0.25 Gt C at the most (UNFCCC 2008), the potential of ocean iron fertilization would be considerable.

2.3 Side Effects

In spite of its positive potential to sequester CO_2, ocean iron fertilization might also bring about a number of adverse and unintended side effects. For example, ocean iron fertilization could influence food web dynamics because phytoplankton is at the bottom of the food chain. While this could cause positive effects, e.g. on overfished fish stocks, it could also have negative effects, e.g. on the development of toxic algal blooms. Moreover, the remineralization of sinking organic matter could lead to anoxia in the subsurface ocean following large-scale ocean iron fertilization. More indirect side effects of ocean iron fertilization could also include nutrient depletion and lower primary production downstream of the fertilization site, an enhanced production of the forceful greenhouse gases nitrous oxide (N_2O) and methane (CH_4), increased ocean acidity, and altered physical properties of the ocean (see e.g. Denman 2008; Powell 2008c or Gnanadesikan et al. 2003).

When considering the possible adverse side effects of ocean iron fertilization, one should also bear in mind that these effects are both scale and time dependent. No harmful negative effects have been observed during patch fertilization experiments. Nevertheless, such effects may occur if iron fertilization experiments are scaled up with respect to the amount of iron added to the water, the size of the fertilized ocean site, and the time horizon of the iron fertilization experiment (Powell 2008c).

2.4 Cost Estimates

Early estimates for the costs of ocean iron fertilization were very low so that it appeared to be quite a cheap method to reduce atmospheric CO_2 concentrations. For example, Markels and Barber (2001) estimated a cost of 1.1–2.2 USD per t CO_2 sequestered. With less optimistic and more realistic assumptions regarding the sequestration efficiency of ocean iron fertilization, costs are more likely to range from 8 to 80 USD per t CO_2 sequestered (Boyd 2008). Still, these cost estimates are based on the sequestration efficiency ratios that were observed during the patch fertilization experiments, which in turn are quite uncertain and will vary over one order of magnitude. Consequently, Barker et al. (2007) also points out that there are no reliable cost estimates available for ocean iron fertilization as a mitigation option.

Moreover, the few cost estimates that are available only include the direct costs of the fertilization activity (Boyd 2008). This ignores further costs such as those for potential negative downstream effects, e.g. on fisheries. In addition, the costs for monitoring and verification as well as the costs for unintended side effects would also have to be included. This could lead to deductions from carbon offsets that are to be generated. These deductions would occur if there was an outgassing of other greenhouse gases such as N_2O or CH_4, which would offset the initial CO_2 sequestration. All these additional cost factors imply that any cost estimate, which is only based on export or sequestration efficiency ratios, will probably underestimate the true costs. Moreover, due to the fact that potential side effects are hard to predict and measure, costs will be even more difficult to estimate.

A comparative assessment of iron fertilization with other mitigation strategies would also need to include the ratio of estimated costs to occurring risks. Boyd (2008) classifies ocean iron fertilization as a medium-risk, medium-cost mitigation strategy and states that other strategies with lower risks may have lower costs as well. However, CO_2 emissions continue to rise with an increasing momentum and the impacts of anthropogenic climate change are expected to be severe. What is more, company interests remain strong with the deliberate aim of selling carbon offsets from ocean iron fertilization activities. On the other hand, there are scientists that strictly oppose a commercialization of iron fertilization (Chisholm et al. 2001).

Consequently, a strict regulatory framework would be needed if carbon offsets generated through ocean iron fertilization were to be integrated into a Post-Kyoto agreement or carbon offset markets – whether these be those markets regulated under a successor agreement to the Kyoto Protocol or voluntary ones. The next section of this chapter therefore reviews certain criteria which would have to be considered when setting up a regulatory framework for ocean iron fertilization, taking into account the findings of this section that cover its scientific background as well as the regulatory framework for afforestation and reforestation activities within the CDM of the Kyoto Protocol.

3 Regulatory Aspects of Ocean Iron Fertilization

3.1 Ocean Iron Fertilization and International Law

One of the most crucial factors influencing the regulation of ocean iron fertilization is that iron fertilization activities would predominantly take place on the high seas, where no national jurisdiction applies. Consequently, ocean iron fertilization would fall under the jurisdiction of international law. At present, ocean iron fertilization falls into a "legal grey area" and is neither bindingly prohibited nor regulated. However, dumping activities that are contrary to the aims of the United Nations Convention on the Law of the Seas (UNCLOS), the Convention on the Prevention of Marine Pollution by Dumping of Wastes and Other Matter (London Convention or LC) or the London Protocol (LP) and that could harm the marine environment or marine living resources are banned under international maritime law. This could also apply to iron fertilization, taking into account its potential harmful side effects (Freestone and Rayfuse 2008).

The same reasoning was adopted by the Parties to the LC/LP, who consider ocean iron fertilization to be dumping because it is contrary to the aims of the Conventions. In a non-binding resolution put forward under the umbrella of the International Maritime Organization (IMO) in October 2008, they therefore state that ocean iron fertilization should not be carried out unless it is for the purpose of careful scientific research, which in turn should be subject to the permission of member states (IMO 2008). This emphasizes the fact that there is an urgent need to establish an internationally agreed legal framework, including permit requirements and liability regulations for ocean iron fertilization. Moreover, it will have to be made clear as to how to link international agreements such as the Kyoto Protocol or a successor agreement, the LC/LP and the UNCLOS (Freestone and Rayfuse 2008).

3.2 Ocean Iron Fertilization and Open Access

Another consequence of the fact that iron fertilization activities would take place on high seas and the fact that such activities are currently not bindingly prohibited or regulated by international law is that ocean iron fertilization could in principle be carried out by anybody and to an arbitrary extent. Put differently, no private property rights have currently been assigned for the implementation of ocean iron fertilization on the high seas.

Thus, the possibility of generating carbon offsets through iron fertilization activities could be considered to represent an open access resource, meeting the criteria of non-excludability and rivalry. The implementation of ocean iron fertilization can be considered to be non-excludable as long as there are no effective ways of preventing somebody from carrying out these activities. Moreover, the implementation of ocean iron fertilization can be considered to be rivalrous because once that somebody has added iron to the water in order to enhance photosynthesis and phytoplankton growth, macronutrients will be extracted from the water and these macronutrients will no longer be available for other ocean iron fertilization projects.

Assuming that the resulting carbon offsets could be sold on large carbon markets, a profit incentive would be available for companies engaging in iron fertilization activities. However these companies would not have to bear all the resulting social costs in an open access setting, which could lead to a non-efficient overuse of ocean iron fertilization and welfare losses. This effect would be enhanced if there were further negative externalities resulting from adverse side effects of the fertilization activity, e.g. decreasing fish stocks due to nutrient depletion. Consequently, a strict regulation of iron fertilization activities, employing taxes or volume restrictions, would be desirable, not only from an ecological but also from an economic point of view.

3.3 Ocean Iron Fertilization and the Kyoto Clean Development Mechanism

So far, carbon offsets generated through iron fertilization activities could only be sold in the relatively small segment of voluntary carbon markets. Still, as long as the legal status of ocean iron fertilization is not clearly defined and CO_2 emissions continue to rise with increasing momentum, company interests in selling carbon offsets generated through iron fertilization projects are likely to remain strong.

Consequently, strict regulations would be needed if these offsets were to be integrated into a Post-Kyoto agreement or regulated carbon markets in the future. It is therefore briefly discussed in the following how the Kyoto regulations for afforestation and reforestation within the CDM framework,[2] which play a major role on regulated but also on voluntary carbon markets, could be applied to iron fertilization activities.

Basic requirements within the CDM framework stipulate that projects have to bring about a benefit for the host country's sustainable development and that they have to be approved by the host party. Neither would be possible for iron fertilization activities because they would take place on the high seas far away from any country (Freestone and Rayfuse 2008). Another basic issue applying to afforestation and reforestation projects under the CDM is the definition of a project site boundary, which is central to calculating the net anthropogenic greenhouse gas removals by sinks attributable to a project. However it would be very difficult to determine the boundaries of a project area in advance of an iron fertilization project due to the rapid dilution and dispersion of the fertilized ocean patch, which moreover depends on local ocean currents.

The demonstration of additionality, showing that a project would not have happened without the CDM, is another important concept within the CDM framework. This is not likely to be problematic however in connection with iron fertilization activities, provided that there are no competing usages for the selected ocean sites. This is because ocean iron fertilization would only be profitable given the possibility to create and sell carbon offsets (Leinen 2008). Moreover, ocean iron fertilization does not represent a common practice and if the only alternative to fertilizing the ocean with iron was not to use a specific ocean site at all, then iron fertilization activities could be considered to be additional per se.

The most problematic issue in connection with creating carbon offsets through iron fertilization projects is likely to be the difficulties involved in measuring, monitoring, and verification. Greenhouse gases, which would have to be considered for monitoring an iron fertilization project, are CO_2, N_2O and CH_4. Moreover, the data to be measured and monitored would at least have to include CO_2 drawdown from the atmosphere and carbon export to the deep ocean but also oxygen or nutrient depletion in the deep sea or in upwelling regions downstream of the project site as well as downstream environmental impacts on food web dynamics or potentially occurring unpredictable side effects (Cullen and Boyd 2008).

There are some techniques, which may be used for measuring these aspects, but, nevertheless, the measurement of air sea gas exchange and carbon export remains difficult. Measurement, monitoring, and verification are further complicated by the fact that side effects that have to be taken into account could affect the ocean on a

---

[2]The CDM within the Kyoto framework allows Annex 1 countries to carry out emission reduction or removal projects in Non-Annex 1 countries for compliance with their own emission reduction targets. For detailed information on the regulation of afforestation and reforestation activities within the CDM framework see UNFCCC (2005).

global scale and might only be apparent in a few decades. A combined approach, using models in addition to experimental observations, could help in this respect, but there is still a considerable amount of uncertainty connected to the adequacy and use of such models (Watson et al. 2008). In order to create transparency with regard to iron fertilization, reporting would therefore also be necessary, not only in terms of monitoring and verification but also regarding possible environmental impacts.

Another issue, which has to be kept in mind, is that the carbon storage induced by ocean iron fertilization might not be permanent. A reversal of greenhouse gas removals would be possible due to an outgassing of CO_2 or an enhanced production of N_2O and CH_4. This non-permanent storage could be accounted for by issuing temporary or long-term credits as under the CDM (UNFCCC 2005). This approach will only be appropriate however if net greenhouse gas removals attributable to the iron fertilization project always remain positive. Otherwise, nobody would be held responsible for the emissions occurring after the end of the project's crediting period.

A final aspect arising from the CDM framework for afforestation and reforestation is the possibility of leakage. In this context, leakage refers to increasing greenhouse gas emissions, which occur outside of a project site's boundaries but can be attributed to a certain project activity. Leakage that occurs will have to be taken into account when calculating the amount of carbon offsets to be issued for a project activity by subtracting the respective amounts from actual net greenhouse gas removals (UNFCCC 2005). In the context of iron fertilization activities, CO_2 emissions generated by the use of vessels and aircrafts in connection with a certain project activity would have to be taken into account. Moreover, the upwelling of CO_2 that is remote from the project site, decreased carbon export downstream from the project site due to nutrient depletion, and an increased production of N_2O and CH_4 that are remote from the project site would have to be considered (Leinen 2008). Market leakage effects with regard to iron ore markets would also have to be taken into account. Although these are not very relevant for patch fertilization they might become of relevance should ocean iron fertilization be carried out on larger scales.

4 Conclusion and Future Outlook

It has been made unequivocally clear by the Fourth Assessment Report of the IPCC that human-induced greenhouse gas emissions are contributing to a warming of the global atmosphere, thus causing climatic changes, which are very likely to bring about negative effects for humankind. For this reason the search continues for new methods to mitigate climate change impacts. Ocean iron fertilization has been suggested as one such method.

However, as indicated in this chapter it is in particular the quantitative potential of ocean iron fertilization that is rather limited. Estimates for the cumulative quantitative potential of patch fertilization amount to some ten million tons of carbon for a hundred years. In contrast, large-scale iron fertilization could reach a cumulative potential of 26–70 Gt C for the same time horizon and could therefore significantly contribute to achieving stringent global climate targets. However, large-scale ocean iron fertilization does not seem realistic at present, e.g. due to certain logistic constraints.

Furthermore, there is a great deal of uncertainty connected to the potential negative side effects of ocean iron fertilization, including unforeseeable changes to food webs and ecosystems, impacts on fisheries, an increased production of nitrous oxide or methane as well as oxygen depletion and ocean acidification. In addition to this, iron fertilization seems to be more costly than it was initially hoped, and the uncertainty about its costs remains high due to the uncertainty that is also connected to its sequestration efficiency. Consequently, it might well be the case that other options for mitigating climate change are cheaper and/or connected to fewer risks.

The substantial uncertainties connected with ocean iron fertilization and its effectiveness have given rise to a great deal of public resistance against its use, with the scientific community also convinced that it would currently be premature to carry out iron fertilization commercially (Buesseler et al. 2008). Contrarily, there are a few companies that hope to be able to sell carbon offsets generated through iron fertilization projects, although they do still admit the need for further research (Leinen 2008). Consequently, the future has to show if iron fertilization will one day be better understood and work more efficiently, so that it could be used as a real mitigation option. However, this still requires more scientific research, which might be slowly scaled up.

If ocean iron fertilization is used one day to mitigate climate change by enhancing oceanic CO_2 uptake, then carbon offsets generated by these projects might be sold on global carbon markets. There are however several regulatory issues which would have to be addressed before this could be made possible. The current legal status of ocean iron fertilization and the open access issue highlight the fact that international permit requirements and liability regulations for these activities are necessary. Furthermore, CDM regulations could not be easily applied to ocean iron fertilization due to the particularities of the latter.

Even if a regulatory framework for ocean iron fertilization was put in place, one should not regard ocean iron fertilization as the royal road for mitigating climate change, which should have become apparent in this chapter. In the short run in particular, it does not seem probable that iron fertilization could contribute significantly to climate change mitigation. This is an important issue because greenhouse gas emissions will have to be reduced soon and to a great extent if a dangerous level of climate change is to be avoided. Consequently, it would seem more promising at the moment to invest in mitigation strategies, which already exist and are already better understood or which promise a higher mitigation potential and connected to fewer risks and uncertainties.

In this context, it also has to be kept in mind that iron fertilization does not constitute a technology, which will be easily controlled. It takes place in the changing surroundings of marine ecosystems, and its effects crucially depend on biogeochemical, physical and ecological interactions, which are not easy to understand and beyond human control. Interference with these ecosystems might bring about unintended effects that have not yet been considered, which would also speak in favour of other mitigation or sequestration options.

Acknowledgements Updated and slightly revised from *Energy Policy*, 38 (2): 1130–1139. I thank Katrin Rehdanz for helpful comments and discussion. The DFG through the Excellence Initiative "The Future Ocean" provided welcome financial support. All errors and opinions are mine.

References

Barker T, Bashmakov I, Alharthi A, Amann M, Cifuentes L, Drexhage J, Duan M, Edenhofer O, Flannery B, Grubb M, Hoogwijk M, Ibitoye FI, Jepma CJ, Pizer WA, Yamaji K (2007) Mitigation from a cross-sectoral perspective. In: Metz B, Davidson OR, Bosch PR, Dave R, Meyer LA (eds), Climate Change 2007: Mitigation. Contribution of Working Group III to the Fourth Assessment Report of the Intergovernmental Panel on Climate Change, Cambridge University Press, Cambridge, United Kingdom and New York, NY, USA

Boyd PW (2008) Implications of large-scale iron fertilization of the oceans. Introduction and synthesis. Mar Ecol Prog Ser 364:213–218

Boyd PW, Jickells T, Law CS et al (2007) Mesoscale iron enrichment experiments 1993–2005: synthesis and future directions. Science 315:612–617

Buesseler KO, Doney SC, Karl DM et al (2008) Ocean iron fertilization – moving forward in a sea of uncertainty. Science 319:162

Chisholm SW (2000) Stirring times in the southern ocean. Nature 407:685–687

Chisholm SW, Falkowski PG, Cullen JJ (2001) Dis-crediting ocean fertilization. Science 294:309–310

Cullen JJ, Boyd PW (2008) Predicting and verifying the intended and unintended consequences of large-scale ocean iron fertilization. Mar Ecol Prog Ser 364:295–301

De Baar HJW et al (2005) Synthesis of iron fertilization experiments: from the iron age in the age of enlightenment. J Geophys Res 110:24, C09S16

De Baar HJW, Gerringa LJA, Laan P et al (2008) Efficiency of carbon removal per added iron in ocean iron fertilization. Mar Ecol Prog Ser 364:269–282

Denman KL (2008) Climate change, ocean processes and ocean iron fertilization. Mar Ecol Prog Ser 364:219–225

Forster P, Ramaswamy V, Artaxo P, Berntsen T, Betts R, Fahey DW, Haywood J, Lean J, Lowe DC, Myhre G, Nganga J, Prinn R, Raga G, Schulz M, Van Dorland R (2007) Changes in Atmospheric Constituents and in Radiative Forcing. In: Solomon S, Qin D, Manning M, Chen Z, Marquis M, Averyt KB, Tignor M, Miller HL (eds), Climate Change 2007: The Physical Science Basis. Contribution of Working Group I to the Fourth Assessment Report of the Intergovernmental Panel on Climate Change, Cambridge University Press, Cambridge, United Kingdom and New York, NY, USA

Freestone D, Rayfuse R (2008) Ocean iron fertilization and international law. Mar Ecol Prog Ser 364:227–233

Gnanadesikan A, Sarmiento JL, Slater RD (2003) Effects of patchy ocean fertilization on atmospheric carbon dioxide and biological production. Glob Biogeochem Cycles 17(2):17, 19/1-19/17

IMO (2008) Ocean fertilization operations should be allowed only for research, say parties to international treaties. Press Briefing 51 of 11 November 2008, London. www.imo.org

Leinen M (2008) Building relationships between scientists and business in ocean iron fertilization. Mar Ecol Prog Ser 364:251–256

Leinen M, Whaley D, Whilden K (2008) Are carbon offsets appropriate for ocean iron fertilization? response to science policy forum on January 11, 2008, San Francisco

Markels M Jr, Barber RT (2001) Sequestration of carbon dioxide by ocean fertilization. In: Maroto-Valer MM, Song C, Soong Y (eds) Environmental challenges and greenhouse gas control for fossil fuel utilization in the 21st century. Kluwer, New York, pp 119–132

Martin JH (1990) Glacial-interglacial CO_2 change: the iron hypothesis. Paleoceanography 5(1):1–13

Michaelowa A, Tangen K, Hasselknippe H (2005) Issues and options for the post-2012 climate architecture. An overview. Int Environ Agreements 5:5–24

Powell H (2008a) Fertilizing the ocean with iron. Oceanus Mag 46(1):4–9

Powell H (2008b) Will ocean iron fertilization work? Oceanus Mag 46(1):10–13

Powell H (2008c) What are the possible side effects? Oceanus Mag 46(1):14–17

Powell H (2008d) Lessons from nature, models, and the past. Oceanus Mag 46(1):18–21

Raven JA, Falkowski PG (1999) Oceanic sinks for atmospheric CO_2. Plant Cell Environ 22:741–755

Rehdanz K, Tol RSJ, Wetzel P (2005) Ocean carbon sinks and international climate policy. Energ Policy 34(2006):3516–3526

UNFCCC (1997) Report of the conference of the parties on its third session, FCCC/CP/1997/7/Add.1, Kyoto, 1–11 December 1997

UNFCCC (2005) Report of the conference of the parties serving as the meeting of the parties to the Kyoto protocol on its first session, decisions 1-8/CMP.1, FCCC/KP/CMP/2005/8/Add.1. Montreal, 28 November to 10 December 2005

UNFCCC (2008) National greenhouse gas inventory data for the period 1990–2006, FCCC/SBI/2008/12, 17 November 2008

Watson AJ, Boyd PW, Turner SM et al (2008) Designing the next generation of ocean iron fertilization experiments. Mar Ecol Prog Ser 364:303–309

A New Sector Mechanism for Clean Coal Technologies in a Carbon Constrained World

John Kessels

Abstract Coal is inexpensive, plentiful and will continue to play a major role in the global energy system for the foreseeable future with currently 40% of the world's electricity generated by coal. Climate change mitigation policies and measures will also continue to place stricter caps on emission of greenhouse gases. This paper is based on two IEA Clean Coal Centre reports that analyze what role clean coal technologies (CCTs) can play in a world where carbon emissions are constrained. The paper analyses economic instruments that could accelerate the implementation of CCTs. The paper's technical focus is on carbon capture and storage (CCS) technologies. From a scenario analysis involving major world regions it appears that CCT technologies have a significant potential for climate change mitigation. The paper puts forward the premise that for CCTs the Kyoto Protocol and emissions trading has failed to fulfil this potential. The role and design of emission trading schemes is critical in encouraging CCTs implementation. The current post-2012 climate policy regime proposals involving CCS are unlikely to encourage rapid deployment of CCTs. A separate technology agreement specifically targeting CCTs is also put forward in this paper as another option to accelerate the implementation of CCTs and in particular CCS.

1 Introduction

The collapse of the financial markets in 2008 resulted in many governments injecting billions of dollars into banks to stabilize and prevent the further collapse of the financial markets in Europe and the USA. Part of this funding has been earmarked for energy investment with CCS one of several technologies set to benefit from additional funding. The urgency is highlighted by the Intergovernmental Panel

---

J. Kessels (✉)
IEA Clean Coal Centre, SW15 6AA London, United Kingdom
e-mail: john.kessels@iea-coal.org.uk

on Climate Change (IPCC) Fourth Assessment Report that warned of the potential consequences of failing to stabilize CO_2 emissions. Governments made little progress negotiating new climate change mitigation treaty at the climate conference in Copenhagen in December 2009.

The negotiations on the design of a post-2012 international climate policy are set to culminate with a decision on the new framework. A key technology as yet unrecognized at the UNFCCC level is CCS. The current international context on CCS has widely diverging views on this issue with a multitude of different options being put forward. Unless there is a new mechanism it is highly unlikely that CCS will be included in the clean development mechanism (CDM), due to opposition from several parties. There is a need for more international consensus and integration on CCS as a mitigation option.

The IPCC (2007) Fourth Assessment report states that it is clear that the growing world energy demand will require major energy supply investments in all countries with upgrades of energy infrastructure. This growing energy demand coupled with climate change mitigation and security of supply policies, will create opportunities to achieve greenhouse gas (GHG) emission reductions. The Fourth Assessment states that "without the near-term introduction of supportive and effective policy actions by governments, energy-related emissions, from fossil fuel combustion, are projected to rise by over 50% from 26.1 $GtCO_2$-e (7.1 GtC) in 2004 to 37–40 $GtCO_2$ (10.1–10.9 GtC) by 2030." Therefore, it is important that effective policies are put in place to allow for the development and commercialization of CCS with new and existing coal plants. This view is also supported by the IEA, which highlights the importance of building CCS demonstration projects as soon as possible.

In a previous IEA Clean Coal Centre, "Clean Coal Technologies for a Carbon Constrained World" report it was identified that there is a large abatement potential in the coming decades, notably through the application of CCS. If 50% of the power plants to be built or replaced in nine important world regions (China, India, Indonesia, the USA and Canada, Japan and Korea, Australia, and the EU) after 2020 are equipped with CCS, the GHG reduction may amount up to more than 4,500 $MtCO_2$/yr in 2030 compared to the baseline of conventional coal-based power production.

The reduction of emissions will require the use of several technological approaches as there is no one single solution. It is important that action takes place as early as possible as consumption of coal is growing internationally with projections that there will be a growth to 1,400 GWe of coal-fired plants globally by 2030 (IEA 2007). A key clean coal technology (CCT) is CCS and it could play a critical role. Depending on the capture technology and the concentration of CO_2 when it is captured, the estimated costs of generating electricity using CCS on a coal-fired power plant range from US$20–70/t of avoided CO_2 (IPCC 2005). One option to encourage mitigation technologies such as CCS is the use of economic instruments that are currently being considered or used in several countries to reduce CO_2 emissions, such as Australia, Canada, USA and Europe (Kessels 2008).

The analysis is based to a large extent on existing literature and the current developments with the European Union Emission Trading System (EU ETS) involving CCS. A preliminary qualitative analysis on the impact of measures to encourage CCS deployment are examined including the United Kingdom CCS competition, allocation of 300 million European Union Allowances (EUAs) from the EU ETS and the recent announcement of €1.050 billion to fund CCS projects. In addition, alternative financial incentives are examined.

The purpose of this paper is to argue that current measures to encourage the implementation of CCS projects partially using emissions trading allowances is the wrong incentive to use in the short to medium term. Ultimately, the use of emissions trading to drive CCS technology albeit partially is likely to fail and delay the uptake of CCS technologies. However, in the long term once CCS is a near commercial technology it should be integrated into emissions trading systems. At the international level a new sectoral mechanism is needed to encourage the uptake of CCTs and CCS in particular from the power sector.

It is clear that CCTs must play a role in meeting future emission reduction and climate change challenges. In order for CCTs to play a role it is important that there is a viable framework to encourage technology transfer and diffusion. The current Kyoto Protocol (KP) mechanisms fail to provide an adequate framework for incentivizing CCS projects. As well as reducing emissions, CCS technology transfer would provide energy security. However, to accelerate the process of implementing CCTs will require a redesign of the KP mechanisms or an alternative option.

The KP has developed to the stage where it has been ratified with 1,450 registered projects with expected annual reductions of around 270 Mt CO_2 equivalent. The projects are spread around 50 countries in the developing world. However, few of these projects are using CCTs and none use CCS. Yet, according to the IEA, fossil fuels will account for almost 85% of the growth in energy demand between now and 2030. Coal-fired generation currently generates 39% of the world's total electricity production (IEA 2005).

According to the IEA, world energy demand will increase by 45% between now and 2030 – an average rate of increase of 1.6% per year. Coal is expected to make up more than a third of the overall rise (IEA 2008). Therefore, it is clear that coal will continue to remain a key and important global energy resource during the entire twenty-first century, especially with the growing consumption of coal in developing countries, in particular, China and India.

It is important that governments and signatories to the UNFCCC take the lead in promoting a strategy that would allow the acceleration of CCTs globally. This paper discusses a possible new sectoral mechanism to encourage the uptake of CCS and other CCTs. First, the current situation with coal, the UNFCCC and the KP is discussed (Fig. 1).

Second, the hypothesis is put forward that a new mechanism is urgently needed for CCTs under the UNFCCC with a target that avoids the complexity, bureaucracy and limitations of the KP mechanism. The hypothesis is that a new sectoral mechanism covering the power sector is needed within a post-2012 UNFCCC agreement. This would encourage the acceleration of CCTs in the key coal using countries. The main basis for measuring emission reductions from the CCTs will be based on increasing the efficiency of power plants, research and development on

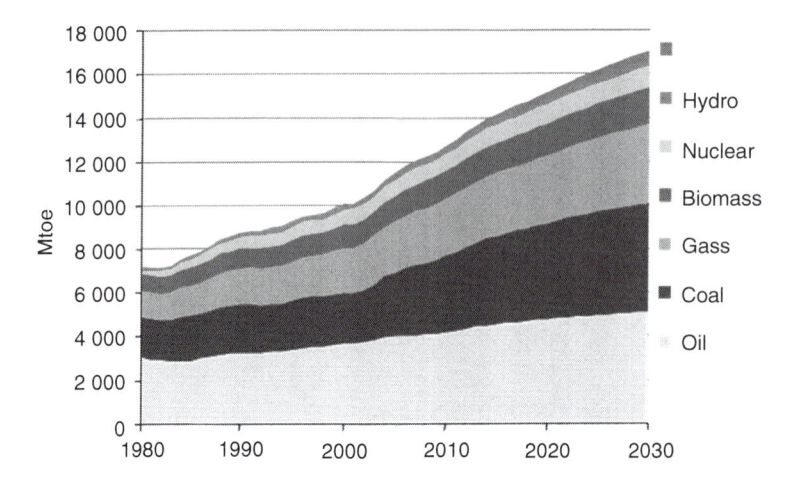

Fig. 1 Energy mix 1980–2030

zero emissions technology linked with technology transfer and diffusion. This system could be based on benchmarking efficiency structured around a country's average thermal efficiency for their plants using best available technology.

Third, the procedures for adding an additional protocol to the UNFCCC are discussed as well as a section on emissions trading and its role with CCTs. The existing technologies and advanced technologies that could be included in the protocol are also outlined. Finally, it is discussed how to further develop this proposal.

2 The Use and Future of Coal

The demand for all types of energy throughout the world continues to grow with the increasing world population and consequently economic growth. Coal's main use is electricity generation. Steam coal is also used for process heat in industry and in many residential and commercial sectors. While internationally many industries are switching to natural gas in the long run coal will be the dominant energy source. There is currently little incentive for many countries to switch to CCTs. Yet, there is both currently and projected major investment in the use of coal.

There are also several international collaborations aiming at and encouraging the use of CCTs through various programmes. These include the Carbon Sequestration Leadership Forum (CSLF), Global Carbon Capture and Storage Institute (GCCSI) and five IEA Implementing Agreements that involve coal. It is clear that coal will continue to play a major role in the global energy mix and with high CO_2 emissions it is important to encourage and accelerate the use of CCTs.

A New Sector Mechanism for Clean Coal Technologies 213

Coal is the world's most abundant fossil fuel. China, India, USA, Canada, Russia, South Africa and many countries in Europe have large quantities of coal reserves. It is important to distinguish between reserves and resources. Resources are the world's total of a fossil fuel estimated by geologists. In terms of reserves there are three types, "proved" reserves, which are defined as the quantity of coal that can be economically recovered using existing technology. The other types of reserves are "probable" and "possible" reserves. It should also be noted that if the cost of coal increases then some reserves can be recovered economically. A further important caveat regarding reserves is the different interpretations that countries have in estimating their reserves.

The main sources of data are the IEA; the BP Statistical Review; The Energy Information Administration (EIA); the US Department of Energy (US DOE) and the World Energy Council (WEC). The global overview in Fig. 2 above is based on the 2006 annual BP Statistical Review outlining the worldwide fossil fuel reserves up until the end of 2005. To put the figures in context there is approximately 160 years of coal, 65 years of gas and 45 years of oil at current usage rates.

If government policies remain unchanged the total world energy demand, according to the IEA Reference Scenario, will increase by 55% between 2005 and 2030. Oil will continue to remain the single largest fuel at 32% with coal at 28%, natural gas 22%, nuclear at 5% and the remainder made up of renewables. Globally, in the electricity sector coal produces 40% of the electricity. Fig. 3 illustrates the increase in world primary energy demand by fuel between 2005 and 2030 (IEA 2007).

To put this in context, fossil fuel related CO_2 emissions would increase by 57% between 2005 and 2030. According to the IEA and IPCC scenarios, it is highly

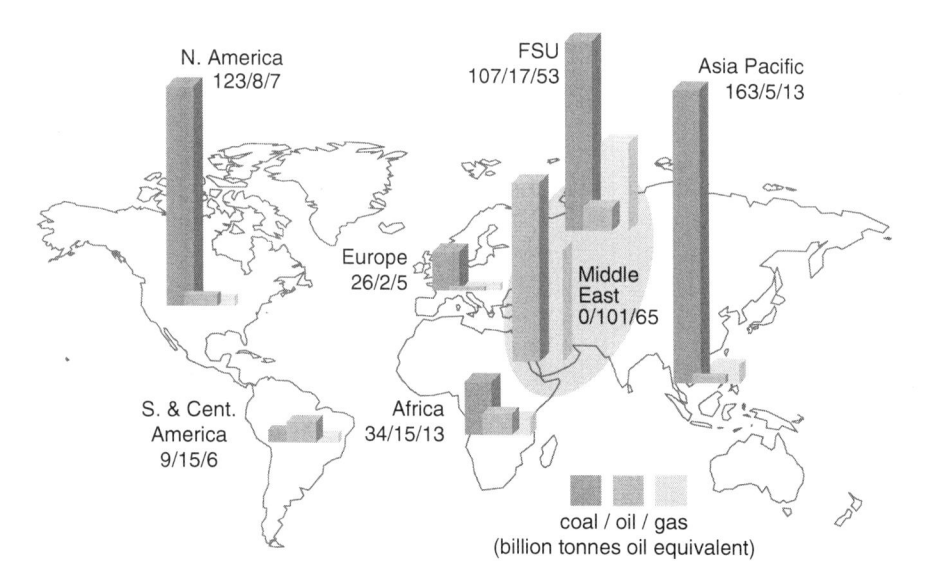

Fig. 2 Worldwide fossil fuel reserves

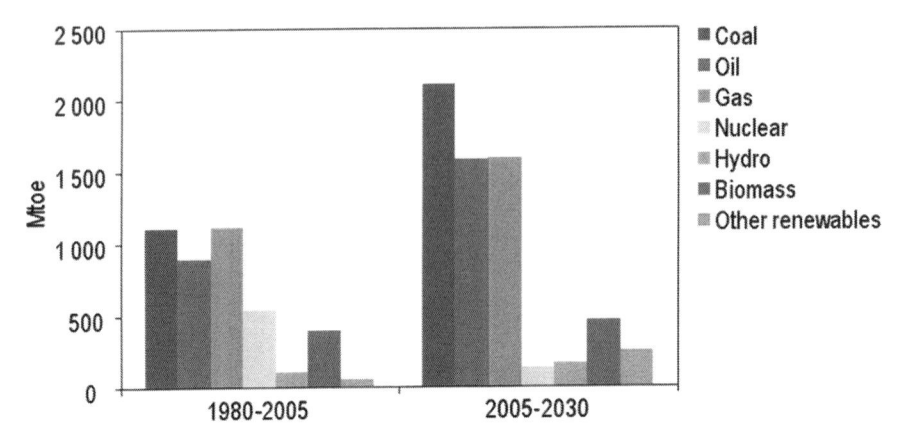

Fig. 3 Increase in world primary energy demand (IEA 2007)

likely that coal will remain a key global energy resource during the entire twenty-first century, especially given the growing need for coal-based electricity in emerging economies such as China, India and in Southeast Asia. It is urgent that plants using CCTs, in particular CCS, are built using the best available technology. In some countries where supercritical power stations with higher efficiency could be built, subcritical power stations are still the preferred option. Due to loans from banks linked to performance guarantees that do not recognize supercritical technologies as being reliable or consistent enough.

Over 1,000 GW of coal-fired power plants operate worldwide. Almost two thirds of these plants are over 20 years old with an average efficiency of 29%. They annually emit around 4 $GtCO_2$. Measures to encourage the replacement of plants at the end of their technical life with modern plants of 45% efficiency would result in total annual GHG emission reductions of around 1.4 $GtCO_2$ (IEA 2005a). There is an expectation that by 2025, internationally installed coal-fired generation capacity will increase by more than 40% and exceed 1,400 GW. In the USA alone, 250 GW of new generation capacity will need to be built by 2025 (Bohm et al. 2007). The US Energy Information Agency (EIA) annual energy overview of 2008 estimates that the USA will have an additional coal-fired generating capacity of 104 GW, compared to 156 GW in their review of 2007. This includes 4 GW of coal-to-liquids and 29 GW of integrated gasification combined cycle (IGCC) plants (EIA 2007).

It is important to better understand and assess the role that coal will play in providing energy security of supply. Governments want to ensure that their citizens have a secure and reliable energy supply that is not vulnerable to disruptions. This objective could supersede climate change policy. It is difficult to ensure stability with key energy resources located in a few countries, as is the case with crude oil and natural gas where up to 40% are located in the Middle East and Russia. This is also the case with coal with 80% of known coal reserves located in six countries.

A combination of energy supply options and a balanced approach is needed that takes into account coal, renewables, gas, oil and nuclear. However, coal can play a key role in contributing to energy security recognising that a combination of providing energy security as well as climate change mitigation measures to limit GHG emissions requires a balanced policy. China, India and many other countries where the economy is growing rapidly have abundant coal supplies with low prices. To ensure the use of coal in contributing to energy security requires the deployment of CCTs. Supercritical coal combustion (SPCC), IGCC with CO_2 capture and storage, are likely to be among the most important CCTs. In addition, the increasing use of low-rank coals with high ash will make the implementation of circulating fluidised bed combustion (CFBC) more attractive. However, CFBC currently makes up only 2% of the world's coal fleet so it will play a limited role (Kessels et al. 2007).

2.1 United Nations Framework Convention on Climate Change

The First Assessment Report of the IPCC, published in 1990, induced international consensus on the dangers of climate change. During the World Summit on Sustainable Development, in 1992 in Rio de Janeiro, agreement was reached on the United Nations Framework Convention on Climate Change (UNFCCC). The key article in the UNFCCC is Article 2, stating the need for:

> stabilisation of GHG concentrations in the atmosphere at a level that would prevent dangerous anthropogenic interference with the climate system.

The UNFCCC distinguishes its Parties in Annex I and non-Annex I parties. Annex I countries are the industrialized countries – normally high-income, and a high level of industrialization and technological development. The Annex I countries are responsible for the majority of the historical GHG emissions. The non-Annex I countries are developing countries; in general responsible for a small share (<15%) of climate change to this date. It was also acknowledged that the non-Annex I countries are most vulnerable and are likely to suffer the most from the climate change.

The UNFCCC was the first international initiative in response to scientific concern about the increasing atmospheric concentrations of GHG and the possibility of climate change. Since the 1992 UNFCCC (UNFCCC 1992), there has been ten Conference of Parties and ongoing work by the two Convention Subsidiary Bodies. The third conference (COP-3) held in Kyoto, in 1997 produced the KP.

2.2 Kyoto Protocol

The KP calls for 38 industrialized countries to make legally binding commitments to reduce their GHGs by the period of 2008–2012. The KP also outlined flexible mechanisms, which countries could use to reduce their emissions with JI, CDM and emissions trading. In order for the KP to become legally binding at least 55 Parties must ratify it and they must account for at least 55% of total Annex 1 parties CO_2 emissions in 1990.

The KP to date has been unsuccessful in accelerating the use of more sustainable energy technologies. Capture and storage of CO_2 is not explicitly recognised as something that can be supported by the Kyoto mechanisms. A possible reason is that Kyoto was too early for these new technologies to be included. However, CO_2 capture and disposal is a new field that offers the opportunity to explore linking the introduction of the technology with carbon credits. In addition, other CCTs offer large emission reductions but the structure of the KP and its process restrict the likelihood of CCT JI or CDM projects. Many Governments are in the process of developing policies and measures to respond to their KP commitments. There is no specific policy regarding CO_2 capture and disposal or CCTs that recognize the benefits of emission reductions from utilizing these technologies. In addition, the high cost makes it unlikely in the short term of introduction of these technologies on a large scale in either developed or developing countries.

Given the problem of the KP not including the US and developing countries not required to meet any mitigation targets it is not an ideal protocol to encourage the use of CCTs. Therefore it is proposed to put forward a new protocol or sector-based mechanism based solely on recognizing CCTs and accelerating their use by rewarding countries that implement state of the art CCT instead of conventional coal technology.

There are currently several sets of post-2012 frameworks proposed for international climate policy. Many of the frameworks focus on Kyoto-type GHG targets and timetables for parties. Others are oriented towards implementation or stimulation of climate-friendly technology without the focus on emission targets.

3 What is the Process for a New Amendment or Protocol to be Added?

There are possibly two options for putting forward a proposal to the UNFCCC on recognizing and acting on the important role that CCTs will have on the global scale. First is as an amendment to the UNFCCC as outlined in the text of the UNFCCC under Article 15 (1)

> Any Party may propose amendments to the Convention.

For an amendment to be agreed upon it will need as stated in Article 15 (3)

> The Parties shall make every effort to reach agreement on any proposed amendment to the Convention by consensus. If all efforts at consensus have been exhausted, and no agreement reached, the amendment shall as a last resort be adopted by a three-fourths majority vote of the Parties present and voting at the meeting. The adopted amendment shall be communicated by the secretariat to the Depositary, who shall circulate it to all Parties for their acceptance.

Once this is done the amendment must be accepted by three fourths of the Parties to the Convention. If this is agreed then the amendment enters into force on the 90th day after the date on which the Party submits the amendment to the Depositary.

The other option open is under Article 17 of the UNFCCC, which states what is needed to adopt a protocol to the UNFCCC and they are:

1. The Conference of the Parties may, at any ordinary session, adopt protocols to the Convention.
2. The text of any proposed protocol shall be communicated to the Parties by the secretariat at least six months before such a session.
3. The requirements for the entry into force of any protocol shall be established by that instrument.
4. Only Parties to the Convention may be Parties to a protocol.
5. Decisions under any protocol shall be taken only by the Parties to the protocol concerned.

Several countries have put forward new proposals to include CCTs in the post-2012 treaty to be negotiated in Copenhagen. One option is to present a protocol to be adopted by the COP in Copenhagen. Recently, the EC proposed a new sector-based mechanism, which could also include CCTs.

4 Emissions Trading

Emissions trading is based on the concept of tradeable allowances or permits with environmental quotas or ceilings, based on restricted use of a resource. The rationale behind emissions trading is to encourage efficient emissions reduction by establishing property rights for the emission of GHGs. For instance, the creation of property rights for CO_2 emissions will give them monetary value and encourage efficiencies through trading those rights.

In the case of emissions trading, property rights for CO_2 emissions are calculated and established by the regulatory authority. Consequently, this gives CO_2 emissions a monetary value and combined with a limited amount of allowances encourages efficient use with the creation of a market. The largest example of this type of market is the EU ETS established in 2005. Pigouvian taxes and cap and trading systems such as the EU ETS are not specifically designed to encourage deployment of cleaner energy technology. Both these economic instruments increase the value of using a commodity and thus create an externality if the resource is not used efficiently.

There are advantages and disadvantages of using tradeable permits to reduce CO_2 emissions. The advantages include:

- government establishes a level of emissions it wants to achieve then sets a limit or cap. This is difficult to do with a tax in setting the tax at a level to limit emissions;
- creation of a market allows participants to trade and theoretically maximize their net comparative advantage benefits;

- encourages technology innovation, and
- minimizes economic costs.

The disadvantages include:

- difficulties in designing a CO_2 tradeable permit scheme;
- difficulties in the appropriate allocation of permits, and
- information requirements.

An emissions trading system, based on the performance of existing programmes, should contain the following features:

- total emissions for the whole trading system will be limited in stages (say 3–5 years each) that participants will perceive as achievable at a reasonable cost;
- trading will produce cost savings if participants face a range of abatement costs through improved process efficiencies and development of lower emission technologies;
- banking, borrowing, trading periods, provisions for new entrants and closures;
- actual emissions will be verified (and potentially audited) for each participant, and
- an efficient compliance regime will check that each participant holds sufficient allowances for the actual emissions and enforce penalties where appropriate.

There are interesting comparisons that can be made between a CO_2 and sulphur dioxide (SO_2) trading market, such as the one in the USA. On the environmental side the SO_2 acidic effects are localized, measurable and can be visibly tangible unlike CO_2 effects which are global and long term and not as tangible as the effects of SO_2. With less evidence of damage this can make it less understood or accepted by the public. SO_2 in the USA is produced by one industry making it relatively simple to manage. In contrast, CO_2 covers a wide range of sectors making it difficult to manage and also opens it to criticism when sectors, particularly transport that produce CO_2 are exempt. SO_2 is normally produced at one point in the production process, which makes it simpler to monitor, control and verify reductions. In comparison, CO_2 is produced from a multitude of different processes and stages, which results in it being difficult to comprehensively manage. Lastly, the US SO_2 programme involves only a few thousand units as opposed to the CO_2 EU ETS programme, which has nearly 11,000 installations. This can make it difficult to manage especially when the trading programme crosses national boundaries as is the case with the EU ETS, where in the USA the SO_2 programme is managed by the federal government.

4.1 Is the EU ETS Working?

The EU ETS had resulted in emission reductions and has led to a new industry created around the trading of carbon credits. Table 1 illustrates the size and value of carbon market transactions in 2006 and 2007. It is clear that the EU ETS has been

A New Sector Mechanism for Clean Coal Technologies 219

Table 1 Carbon market volumes and values in 2006–2007 (World Bank 2008)

	Volume (MtCO$_2$e)	2006 Value (US$ million)	Volume (MtCO$_2$e)	2007 Value (US$ million)
Allowances AS				
EU ETS	1,104	24,436	2,061	50,097
New South Wales	20	225	25	224
Chicago climate exchange	10	38	23	72
UK ETS	Na	Na		
Sub-total	1,134	24,699	2,109	50,394
Project-based transactions				
Primary CDM[a]	537	5,804	551	7,426
Secondary CDM	25	445	240	5,451
Joint implementation	16	141	41	499
Other compliance and voluntary transactions	33	146	42	265
Sub-total	611	6,536	874	13,641
Total	1,745	31,235	2,983	64,035

[a] Clean development mechanism

successful in generating the highest volume of trade and value compared with other carbon markets, including the clean development mechanism (CDM).

4.2 Does the EU ETS Act as an Incentive for CCS?

The establishment of the EU ETS created a market in "carbon certificates," therefore putting a value or price on carbon emissions. The underlying premise is that a high carbon price will encourage and drive the development, adoption and deployment of the most appropriate and cost-effective CCT technologies using market forces to drive innovation and achieve environmental goals. Case studies with other emission trading markets such as the USA sulphur dioxide permit trading programme have shown this to be a useful strategy. However, these markets illustrate the unexpected consequences and significant differences between the CO$_2$ market and the SO$_2$ market that include:

- scale of the total impact with CO$_2$ emissions being global and SO$_2$ being more local or regional;
- economic impact on the adopters versus the non-adopters (nations/regions);
- community reaction to increased prices for electricity where measures have been implemented as in the case of the EU ETS.

In theory, emissions trading systems should deliver emission reductions by creating incentives to participants in the system, which allows reductions to occur wherever they are least-cost. The key being that there are feasible options to implement least-cost measures, which is not the case at this stage with CCS technologies.

5 Conventional Coal Technologies

Several different technologies for coal power production exist, among which pulverized coal (PC), IGCC, pressurized fluidized bed combustion (PFBC), and CFBC. For the purposes of this proposal we assume that conventional coal technologies are PC only without any CCT added such as desulphurization and flue gas desulphurization (FGD) and selective catalytic reduction (SCD) (reduction of NO_x). The first two are probably the main options for coal power production for the decades to come.

Total investment costs in the US for a 550 MWe plant is about 1,300$/kWe for PC and 1,600$/kWe (Rosenberg et al. 2004). While the corresponding investment costs for a natural gas combined cycle (NGCC) plant may be as low as 500$/kWe, PC competes well with NGCC plants: the estimated costs of electricity are today about 4.3 cent/kW h for PC and 5.1 cent/kW h for NGCC. The relatively high value for the latter (while associated with low investment costs) is explained by high costs for fuel (natural gas).

Today, PC is by far the most widely employed coal power generation technology. Despite the worldwide commercial use and acceptance of gasification processes and combined cycle power systems. While today coal power plants operate on average at 36% efficiency, the state-of-the-art PC power plant has a generating efficiency of typically 45% (for hard coal or lignite).

5.1 What Clean Coal Technologies Should the Protocol Include?

CCTs are rapidly developing. In Europe, agreements on energy use and air pollution reduction have induced deployment of increasingly efficient coal technologies, improving efficiency by a net 10% and reducing CO_2 emission factors by 15% over the last 25 years (Lako 2004). There are several different types of CCT that have been successfully developed and are being used on a commercial scale. Whether a technology is a CCT depends, apart from the technology itself, on the following: coal handling, coal pre-treatment, coal transformation and handling, coal combustion, flue gas treatment, and coal ash utilization.

This proposal suggests initially focusing on examining the following CCTs and their suitability for inclusion in a protocol based on their efficiency:

- Supercritical Pulverized Coal Combustion (PCC)
- Integrated Gasification Combined Cycle (IGCC)

The following section is taken from an IEA CCC upcoming report, which gives an overview of the main characteristics of the two CCT put forward as part of the Protocol and their suitability.

5.1.1 Supercritical Pulverized Coal Combustion (PCC)

Pulverized coal-based sub-critical steam cycle technology is well established and supercritical plants are operating on a commercial basis in several countries. Several pulverized coal-fired supercritical steam cycle plants, using steam pressure of around 240 bar and a temperature of around 540°C, and unit sizes in the range 400–900 MWe, have been developed and are operating in Europe and the USA. These plants can achieve generation efficiencies (LHV basis) of up to around 42% (ATLAS Website 2004).

The high efficiency of supercritical PCC clearly reduces GHG emissions compared to normally applied technology. This may be up to 30% or more than 1 Mt CO_2/yr for a large power plant. Even though the technology is "routinely used in several countries" (Henderson 2003), this is not the case for non-Annex I countries. There are no signs that in the near future advanced PCC will be implemented in developing countries (Table 2).

5.1.2 Integrated Gasification Combined Cycle (IGCC)

An IGCC uses a fuel gas made up of carbon oxides and hydrogen which is generated under pressurized conditions by reacting coal with steam and oxygen or air. The gas is then cooled, sulphur and particulate matter removed, and the gas fed into a high efficiency combustion gas turbine. GHG emission reductions from IGCC power plants may be substantial. Current achieved thermal efficiencies are already high (43–45%), and there is potential for further improvement. It is expected that IGCC plant efficiencies will reach up to 52% (Lako 2004).

Currently, there are no coal-fired IGCC operating in non-Annex I countries. There are several 250 MW demonstration units operating in industrialized countries, but the technology is not common in newly built power plants. All of the IGCC demonstration units are subsidized. A major incentive for IGCC development is that units may be able to achieve higher thermal efficiencies than PCC plant and be equal with the environmental performance of gas-fired plants (IEA CCC 2005). Emission of SO_2, NO_x and PM are very low.

IGCC is not yet perceived to be a mature technology. One of the main advantages of IGCC is that this technology has an environmentally more beneficial emission profile in comparison to PC technology. IGCC is a process that integrates

Table 2 Typical figures for supercritical PCC plant

Typical size (MW)	400–900
Efficiency (%, current (2020))	44–46 (50–53)
Operating temperature (°C)	540
Specific investment cost (€/kW, current (2020))	811
Implementation Annex I	Standard technology
Implementation non-Annex I	Not implemented
Reduction of air pollutants compared to current practice	None

Table 3 Typical figures for IGCC plants

Typical size (MW)	300
Efficiency (%, current (2020))	43–45 (52)
Specific investment cost (€/kW, current (2020))	1,583 (1,400)
Implementation Annex I	Demonstration
Implementation non-Annex I	First demonstration
Air pollutants compared to current practice	Very low PM, SO_2 and NO_x

a gasification system with a conventional combustion turbine combined cycle power system. The gasification system can convert coal (and other feedstocks) into a gaseous syngas, made of predominantly hydrogen (H_2) and carbon monoxide (CO). The syngas is used to fuel a combustion turbine to generate electricity, while the exhaust heat from this turbine is used to produce steam for a second generation cycle. IGCC technology may not only offer the potential to improve generation efficiency, in comparison to PC plants, but also reduce emissions of carbon dioxide (CO_2), sulphur dioxide (SO_2), nitrous oxides (NO_x), mercury (Hg) and particulate matter (Table 3).

In 2007, the UNFCCC secretariat completed a study reviewing the existing and planned investment flows to identify and develop an effective global response to mitigate GHG emissions using existing IEA scenarios. They found it would cost an additional investment of US$ 200–210 billion to return GHG emissions to current levels with nearly half of that going to developing countries. It was estimated that about US$ 148 billion out of US$ 432 billion of projected annual investment in the power sector would be on renewables, CCS, nuclear energy and hydropower. The investment in CCS would be US$ 63 billion (UNFCCC 2007). Depending on the type of CCS technology the additional cost for a power station could range between US$ 250–500 million. According to the IPCC (2005), the costs of CCS can vary as seen in Table 4.

To illustrate the possible contribution of CCTs to climate change mitigation a simple scenario analysis for the power sector in different world regions was undertaken (Kessels et al. 2007). The technology assumptions are based on the 2004 IEA WEO (2004) and the baseline for unplanned coal-based capacity until 2030 being PCC. The table on regional scenario results indicated the potential GHG emission reductions from different technologies. For each technology a lower and higher implementation share are assumed (the share of the total unplanned capacity replacement and additions to 2030) (Table 5).

It can be observed that the climate change mitigation impact is very substantial for most regions. Naturally the mitigation potential for CCS is larger than for standalone IGCC or SPCC. For SPCC, assuming 30–100% implementation of the unplanned capacity additions and replacement until 2030 for all regions could reduce approximately 600–2,100 $MtCO_2$/yr in 2030, and for 20–60% IGCC, the figure comes to 400–1,300 $MtCO_2$. Application of CCS (10–50%) results in 900–4,500 $MtCO_2$. In the context of global power sector emissions projected to be approximately 17,600 $MtCO_2$ in 2030, this is 5–25% CO_2 reduction by CCS in coal-fired power plants.

Table 4 Cost ranges for the components of a CCS system, applied to a given type of power plant or industrial source (IPCC 2005)

CCS system components	Cost range	Remarks
Capture from a coal- or gas-fired power plant	15–75 US$/t CO_2 net captured	Net costs of captured CO_2, compared to the same plant without capture
Capture from hydrogen and ammonia production or gas processing	5–55 US$/t CO_2 net captured	Applies to high-purity sources requiring simply drying and compression
Capture from other industrial sources	25–115 US$/t CO_2 net captured	Range reflects use of a number of different technologies and fuels
Transportation	1–8 US$/t CO_2 transported	Per 250 km pipeline or shipping for mass flow rates of 5 (high end) to 40 (low end) $MtCO_2$/yr
Geological storage	0.5–8 US$/t CO_2 net injected	Excluding potential revenues from EOR or ECBM
Geological storage: monitoring and verification	0.1–0.3 US$/t CO_2 injected	This covers pre-injection, injection, and post-injection monitoring, and depends on the regulatory requirements
Ocean storage	5–30 US$/t CO_2 net injected	Including offshore transportation of 100–500 km, excluding monitoring and verification
Mineral carbonation	50–100 US$/t CO_2 net mineralized	Range for the best case studied. Includes additional energy use for carbonation

Table 5 Regional scenario results

$MtCO_2$/yr reduction in 2030	SPCC low 30%	SPCC high 100%	IGCC low 20%	IGCC high 60%	CCS low 10%	CCS high 50%
China	193	645	129	387	247	1,233
India	58	193	39	116	74	370
Indonesia	26	88	18	53	34	168
US + Canada	154	513	103	308	237	1,187
EU-25	143	475	95	285	220	1,100
OECD asia	45	149	30	90	69	345
Australia	12	41	8	25	19	95
Total	631	2,104	421	1,262	899	4,497

5.2 *Framework for Protocol*

To provide a structure for the protocol it is suggested to examine the following three options:

- Improving power plant efficiency
- Storage of carbon captured in coal power plants
- Increasing energy security and technology transfer

Improved power plant efficiency. Coal power plants produce currently about one-fourth of all carbon emissions. A large emission reduction would be created if twice today's quantity of coal-based electricity in 2054 were produced at 60% instead of 40% efficiency.

Storage of carbon captured in coal power plants. Carbon dioxide capture and storage (CCS) technology may prevent about 90% of the fossil carbon from reaching the atmosphere. This is a large emission reduction that could be created by the installation of CCS at 800 GWe baseload coal power plants by 2054. For the capture part of this technology, both pre-and post-combustion carbon capture could be employed at coal power plants. In order to achieve this, a policy framework will be required that encourages the commercialization of CCS technology.

Energy security and technology transfer. The Energy Security and Climate Policy Evaluation (ESCAPE) hypothesis suggests that linking climate change policy with energy security of supply could improve climate change policy at the national and international level. An ECN report outlines the ESCAPE approach and its two-fold aim

1. Exploring the extent to which energy security and climate change policy interact and can be linked on a national level, and
2. Exploring the options for linking energy security concerns into post-2012 climate change negotiations on an international level.

The ESCAPE approach explores the interaction between policies of energy security and climate change and the options of including energy security issues into national and international post-2012 climate negotiations. It is suggested that if a protocol is developed that as one of the criterion for a CCT project it directly links its impact on energy security. It is also an option to include technology transfer as well, which I have not yet addressed in detail.

6 Conclusions

The KP does not encourage CCTs and yet this will be one of the biggest growth areas for GHG emissions in the next century. Environmental policy makers, specialists and scientists recognize that the expansion of coal usage faces a number of sizeable barriers. However, it is also recognized that coal will play a key role in providing energy in the short and long term in developing and developed countries.

Coal is the most carbon-intensive fossil fuel and current large-scale coal combustion practices constitute among the prime impediments to implementing effective climate change control regimes. Yet, there is no agreement that allows developed and developing countries to accelerate the use of CCTs and thus to more quickly reduce GHG emissions as well as other gases and particulates.

There is support amongst the G8 and signatory and non-signatory countries of the KP for accelerating the use of CCTs and CCS. The G8 has a target of 20 demonstration CCS projects by 2020. Emissions trading is likely to play a major role in future climate change policies, but its role in promoting CCTs to date has been limited and that role is unlikely to change. Processes to make CCS an eligible activity under the EU ETS were completed in 2009. However, it is still not an eligible activity under the CDM. No CCS projects have been implemented as of June 2009 under the CDM or JI. Reliance on the CDM and JI mechanisms of the KP to encourage CCTs will result in only a piecemeal approach to the problem of climate change and will most likely lead to only a few projects involving CCTs.

The current low price for carbon is insufficient for the internalization of environmental externalities and those imperfections associated with technological change. Therefore, large-scale deployment of CCTs requires the following elements: a long term high carbon price, a policy framework that encourages IGCC and SPCC commercial plants in the short term and CCS demonstration projects in the medium term. A new mechanism is needed to encourage the use of CCS at the UNFCCC level and several proposals are now under discussion and could be approved at Post-Copenhagen conferences.

To accelerate changes will require changes at a national and international level. Until this happens then less efficient coal fired power stations will continue to be built in emerging economies, locking in vast amounts of CO_2 for at least the next 40–50 years. In order for the commercial deployment of CCTs, companies need investment certainty with a policy framework that recognizes the cost and economic risks of long term capital infrastructure investment in SPCC, IGCC and CCS technologies.

To encourage CCTs will require a new approach with a limit to the group of countries involved and excluding smaller countries. This would allow for a more robust, effective and efficient framework for emission reductions. A reliance on emissions trading for the short to medium term will also act as an obstacle unless the price of allowances is consistently high enough to provide an adequate incentive.

This paper outlines the important role that coal plays and how it will continue to dominate world power production during the twenty-first century, irrespective of the contribution of coal consumption to regional pollution and global warming. The KP is not an ideal instrument to encourage the use of CCT or accelerate their use. Therefore it is critical that policy makers recognize that if no agreement is reached in 2010 or new option introduced that allows for CCS then it will become extremely difficult to reach the IPCC stabilization targets.

References

Bohm CM, Herzog JH, Parsons JE, Sekar RC (2007) Capture-ready coal plants options, technologies and economics. Int J Greenhouse Gas Control 1(1):113–120
BP (2006) BP statistical review of world energy 2006. British Petroleum, London
BP (2007) BP statistical review of world energy 2007. British Petroleum, London
Henderson C (2003) Clean coal technologies, CCC/74, IEA Clean Coal Centre, London
IEA Clean Coal Centre (2005) Financing clean coal technologies under the Kyoto protocol, London

IEA (1999) Key world energy statistics. International Energy Agency, Organisation for Economic Cooperation and Development (OECD), Paris

IEA (2004) World energy outlook 2004. International Energy Agency, Organisation for Economic Cooperation and Development (OECD), Paris

IEA (2005) Road mapping coal's future. International Energy Agency, Organisation for Economic Cooperation and Development (OECD), Paris

IEA (2007) World energy outlook 2007: China and India insights. International Energy Agency, Organisation for Economic Cooperation and Development, Paris

IEA (2008) World energy outlook 2008. International Energy Agency, Organisation for Economic Cooperation and Development (OECD), Paris

IPCC (2001) In: Mitigation B, Metz et al (eds) Change 2001. Intergovernmental panel on climate change secretariat, Geneva

IPCC (2005) IPCC special report on CO_2 capture and storage. In: Metz B, Davidson O, de Coninck HC, Loos M, Meyer L (eds) Prepared by working group III of the intergovernmental panel on climate change. Cambridge University Press, Cambridge

IPCC (2007) Climate change 2007: mitigation. Contribution of working group III to the fourth assessment report of the intergovernmental panel on climate change. In: Metz B, Davidson OR, Bosch PR, Dave R, Meyer LA (eds) Cambridge University Press, Cambridge, New York

Kessels J (2008) Economic instruments and clean coal technologies, CCC/142, IEA Clean Coal Centre, London

Kessels J, Bakker S (2005) ESCAPE: energy security & climate policy: evaluation linking climate change and energy security policy in post 2012 climate strategies, ECN

Kessels J, Bakker SJA, Clemens A (2007) Clean coal technologies for a carbon constrained world: the role of power sector clean coal technologies in climate policy. CCC/123, IEA Clean Coal Centre, London

Lako P (2004) Coal-fired power technologies, energy research centre of the Netherlands, ECN-C-04-076

Rosenberg WG, Alpern DC, Walker MR (2004) Financing IGCC – 3party covenant, BCSIA working paper 2004-01, ETIP, BCSIA, John F. Kennedy school of government, Harvard University, USA

Stern et al (2006) The economics of climate change. Executive summary, London

UNFCCC (1992) United nations framework convention on climate change. UNEP/WMO, Climate Change Secretariat, Geneva

UNFCCC (1997) Kyoto protocol to the UN framework convention on climate change. www.unfccc.int

UNFCCC (2007) Investment and financial flows to address climate change. Bonn, Germany

US DOE (2007) Annual energy outlook 2007. Energy Information Administration, Department of Energy, Washington

Van der Zwaan BCC (2005) Will coal depart or will it continue to dominate global power production during the 21st century? Climate Policy 5(4):445–453

World Bank (2008) State and trends of the carbon market 2008. World Bank report, Washington

Post-Kyoto GHG-Offset Project Eligibility Criteria

Brian Robertson

Abstract The post-Kyoto regime (> 2012) requires institutional changes to overcome bottlenecks inherent in the CDM mechanism and the validation/verification standards based on/running parallel to it. Institutional and neoinstitutional theory help explain the adaptation of the standards to the marketplace. Learning by the institutional agents and convergent change towards more technical characteristics of the standards suggests a continuation of the CDM and other auditing standards. A push towards top-down (more technically-based) institutional processes among the hierarchy of agents from the previous bottom-up model (more project-specific based) is already apparent.

Keywords Bottlenecks • clean development mechanism (CDM) • designated operational entity (DOE) • GHG-offset projects • institutional/neoinstitutional economics • post-kyoto • project proponent (PP). • validation/verification standard

1 Introduction

A major question that was addressed in COP15 (Copenhagen) concerns which institutional changes are recommended for the Kyoto flexible mechanisms in the post-Kyoto regime. The Clean Development Mechanism (CDM) has been criticized for its institutional rigidity, involving bottlenecks at all three levels of the project approval process. Because of their inherent complexity, projects under the CDM-guise are also called "boutique" operations. This significantly contrasts with the United Nations Framework Convention on Climate Change (UNFCCC) institutional aim—the creation and proliferation of a globally-recognized project mechanism for small and large-scale GHG-offset endeavors.

B. Robertson (✉)
SolTerra Capital Corp., Toronto, Canada
e-mail: brianrobertson@solterracapital.com

The proliferation of the flexible mechanisms drives the sale of GHG-offset credits. This chapter is limited to project-based credits (earned through the successful implementation and registration of a GHG-offset project with a major global carbon standard) and not allowance-based credits (distributed by a regulatory body, such as the EU-ETS).

The world of project-based credits is divided into two halves, legally mandated reductions (by a government) and voluntary reductions (NGOs and private industry). Several standards have emerged to accredit or certify project-based credits. Most of these standards are based on the original CDM-model for certifying GHG-offset credits. Often sold in the voluntary markets are GHG-offset credits that neither require the credits to undergo a uniform certification or auditing process (called validation/verification), nor register those credits with any central body (Bayon et al. 2007). For this reason, the voluntary market is fragmented, suffers from a lack of impartial information, and is heavily criticized by environmentalists on lack of uniformity, transparency, and registration (Bayon et al. 2007).

On the other hand, private industry criticizes the validation/verification procedures of the major global standards (e.g., CDM, the Gold Standard) for extensive bottlenecks, including administrative dead-ends, lack of transparency and feedback, and most significantly, unpredictable time delays and the need for constant budget increases. The cost of approval, for example, by the CDM Executive Board for a given project still ranges from US$50,000 to $250,000 (Krolik 2006 in Bayon et al. 2007).

This paper examines how the validation/verification standards and the institutional framework of the CDM project mechanism (upon which, directly or indirectly, all validation/verification standards are based) could change in order to alleviate financial/administrative bottlenecks. Institutional and neoinstitutional theory help explain the adaptation of the standards and institutions to the demands of the market for GHG-offset credits. Particularly useful is Scott's research into institutional learning by agents and the convergent change characteristic of new institutions as they develop more technical characteristics.

The chapter will first explain the concepts at play in the project-approval process of a typical GHG-offset project, and how institutional and neoinstitutional theory explain the type of change seen in both the standards, and in the CDM-institution, as they all prepare for the post-Kyoto phase. After clarifying the research methodology, the major validation/verification standards are examined in light of their expected changes. Lastly, the CDM-institution and the standards are seen from the perspectives of the agents from private industry, namely, the auditors and project developers.

2 Background Concepts

Institutional theory deals with the processes by which rules, norms, and structures become formal guidelines or principles that govern the behavior of a given activity (Scott 2008). This applies to any regulatory, political/economic, or market influences, their origins, and their effects. In order to understand the expected changes post-Kyoto for the CDM institution and the other validation/verification standards, the roles or "agents" constituting the institutional field must first be defined.

A GHG-offset credit starts with a GHG-offset project, such as a wind-energy project. A project developer (called a project proponent {PP}) runs the project and documents certain aspects of the project as they relate to GHG offsets. This documentation constitutes a GHG-offset plan. Which aspects the PP documents will depend on the standard (i.e. CDM, ISO 14064) to be subsequently used for validation/verification. Most often, the standard chosen for auditing depends on the market in which the PP intends to sell the GHG-offset credits.

Common to major standards for GHG-offset validation/verification are:

1. The requirement of third-party verification and accreditation, i.e., an auditor will act as the validating and verification entity checking project compliance with specific standard/guidelines
2. A higher authority (often the Standard 'X' Committee) will grant or refuse final approval, basing a decision on the auditor's verification report. (Robertson 2008)

The PP then submits the GHG-offset plan to an accredited third-party auditor (called a designated operational entity {DOE} under the CDM standard). The DOE is a provisionally-accredited (by the Conference of the Meeting Parties {CMP} and the Executive Board {EB}) domestic or international legal entity with two key functions:

1. It validates and requests registration of a proposed CDM project activity;
2. It verifies emission reduction of a registered CDM project activity, certifies it as appropriate and requests the Board to issue Certified Emission Reductions (GHG offsets) accordingly (CDM 2009).

After auditing the GHG-offset plan, the DOE submits the plan to the appropriate authority (e.g. the CDM Executive Board {EB}, the Canadian Standards Association). The authority then checks the completion of work according to the standard in question, makes sure the project meets the standard's requirements, and that the entire procedure is free of conflicts-of-interest. The authority then issues credits to the PP.

Because the PP begins the process and works "upwards" to the other agents (DOEs and authority {EB}), the project-approval cycle is known as a bottom-up approach.

3 Bottlenecks and Institutional Theory

The price mechanism on carbon, set by the Kyoto Protocol, limits the supply of permissible GHG emissions and creates demand for clean energy and GHG-offsetting technologies. The competitive aspect of the marketplace is supposed to drive efficiency (by setting market-based prices) and effectiveness (by proliferating

Table 1 Technical and institutional controls

		Institutional controls	
		Stronger	Weaker
Technical controls	Stronger	Utilities, banks, general hospitals	General manufacturing
	Weaker	Mental health clinics, schools, churches	Restaurants, health clubs, child care

the best GHG-reduction/mitigation projects first). Bottlenecks prove to be a hindrance to this process.

A bottleneck is any resource/process/system whose capacity is less than the demand placed upon it, thereby limiting throughput (Aquilano and Chase 1995). This occurs when the work-in-process (WIP) inventory is maximized (Aquilano and Chase 1995). Bottlenecks occur at all three levels (PP, DOE, and EB) in the bottom-up, project-approval approach.

Neoinstitutional theory gives context to the expected changes to the project-approval process in the post-Kyoto regime. Neoinstitutional theory focuses on the study of economic processes rather than on the purely logical study of equilibrium states, and recognizes that economic systems evolve over time, reflecting, in part, learning by the agents (Scott 2008).

The learning and adaptation by the agents have two characteristics at all three levels of the project-approval process. Firstly, the learning reflects convergent change, change that reinforces and diffuses existing patterns (Scott 2008). The post-Kyoto GHG-offset project-approval process will not represent divergent change or some other institutional break with the previous norms. Instead, it will build upon these rules and adapt, by means of a balancing act, to emerging global GHG-reduction goals and to the demands of the marketplace to best achieve those goals. The bottlenecks represent the most obvious opportunities to improve the CDM process.

The second characteristic of learning represents a push towards technicality. Walgenbach and Meyer cite Scott and Meyer (1991: 124), who explain that "...those who formulate institutional rules strive to make them appear technical in nature" (2008). In the following table, both utilities and general manufacturing (the categories which best represent GHG-offset projects) are found in the forefront of technical controls: ("Technical and Institutional Controls, with Illustrative Organizations" from Scott 2003: 140, in Walgenbach and Meyer 2008) (Table 1).

Scott writes "To be effective, regulation requires clear demands, effective surveillance, and significant sanctions" (2001, p.115). These would be considered the first pillars of the push towards reliable, technical characteristics of the GHG-offset project-approval institution.

4 Methodology

To research the changes expected in the post-Kyoto CDM model (i.e., the learning and adaptation by the agents), the nine major global GHG-offset validation/verification standards themselves (reports, guidelines) were reviewed. Based on

Table 2 Standards, designated operational entities and projects developer

EBs (standards)	DOEs	PPs
1) Clean development mechanism	DNV	1) Climate care
2) Gold standard	TÜV SÜD	2) Climate
3) VCS	SGS	3) Ecosecurities
4) ISO 14064		4) First climate
		5) Natsource
		6) Orbeo

interviews with agents at all three levels (PP, DOE, and EB), the top four standards were sampled and further interviews were conducted with executives of each standard (CDM, Gold Standard, Voluntary Carbon Standard {VCS}, and ISO 14064).

The same process (reviewing, sampling, examination) was conducted with the DOEs. Although the EB of the CDM was considering 30 applications worldwide at the time of writing, both current literature and the interviews conducted with EBs and PPs showed unanimous agreement that three of the eight major DOEs dominated over 90% of the CDM-project based market. Executives from the top three were interviewed.

Lastly, PPs were chosen based on the amount of GHG-offset project experience from a broad sample of investment/fund managers and GHG project-management firms. The table below shows the firms quoted (indirectly, without reference, at the request of the executives) in this paper (Table 2).

5 Validation/Verification Standards and Expected Changes in Post-Kyoto

The CDM standard methodologies are generally accepted as best-practice among the project mechanism validation/verification standards. However, extensive bottlenecks with the CDM (e.g. cost-prohibitive or administrative {project validations from DOEs waiting for EB approval for CDM registration}) cause project proponents to use other standards. Umble and Srikanth distinguish bottlenecks from constrained capacity resources – the latter being any resource which is likely to cause the actual flow of work/product to deviate from the planned production flow (1990). This suggests that the inherent bottlenecks in the CDM standard are likely to be causing the actual flow of work/product to deviate from the ideal, or most legitimate, standard. Colombo and Delmastro explain that "Where uncertainty is high, reputation or other less-tangible results may be preferred" (2008).

Another way of viewing the results of the bottlenecks in the CDM standard is a symbiotic function between the standard and the emerging marketplace for standards to replace/work alongside it. Not only do institutions govern the activities of firms (as firms operate within the market and engage in transactions with others), but they also shape the very environment in which economic activity takes place

(Williamson 2000; Garside 2007). The evolution of other standards (particularly the Gold Standard and VCS) is directly related to the bottlenecks with the CDM standard. Below are the major standards: (Tables 3 and 4).

Of the above standards, the following four were chosen based on their prominence, continuity, and overall development, according to the interviews conducted with DOEs and PPs.

In each of the standards, convergent change is at work, i.e., the changes are built on the original structure set forth by the Kyoto mechanisms. Also, there is a clear shift from a project-by-project basis (bottom-up) to an umbrella (top-down) approach.

5.1 CDM

CDM is a learning-by-doing approach and was never intended by the UNFCCC to be a final solution. Rather, preliminary rules were set to launch a globally-recognized environmental currency. The number of GHG-offset projects using the standard is high and growing, and thus scalability remains an issue concerning administrative efficiency.

Legitimacy plays a role in the CDM's scalability. Not only is the CDM the UNFCCC standard, it is also the pioneering standard, which directs the changes and adaptation of most of the other major standards. Swift decentralization to increase efficiency could have threatening implications to the standard's legitimacy, and in a sense, to the Kyoto regime as a whole.

For this reason, the institution is undergoing convergent change, and its push towards technicality is evident in the shift towards "Programmatic CDM/Program of Activities (PoA)." Organizationally, the shift to a top-down from a bottom-up approach requires clear technical guidelines and thereby can speed administrative efficiency. The PoA mechanism does this by categorizing projects under single administrative units. PPs can pioneer project methodologies in a given area, submit the methodology to a DOE for assurance, and the DOE then submits it to the CDM'sEB. Once approved, the methodology becomes a public good. Any PP performing the same project, in a comparable area, can use this same methodology and merely has to prove alignment and consistency with it. The EB expects PoA to reduce the number of validations/ verifications from DOEs for EB approval. PoA is the UNFCCC's attempt to increase the reach of CDM post-2012.

An example of a potential PoA is Greenpeace's Lightbulb program in India, the Bachat Lamp Yojana Programme, funded through the CDM mechanism. The lightbulb project would be the "core" project that sets a methodology for subsequent projects. The current project is replacing 400 million incandescent bulbs with CFLs in order to save ~55 million tons of CO_2 emissions each year by 2012 (Greenpeace 2009). A PoA- registered methodology would allow other PPs to perform similar projects and streamline the administrative requirements.

Table 3 Institutional setting of different standards (Bayon et al 2007; Robertson 2008)

Standard	Sponsor	Auditing requirement	Approval authority	Verification base document	Registry
CDM/JI	UNFCCC	DNA & DOE/IE	DOE/IE	Requirements of CDM COP/MOP	CDM
Gold standard (based on CDM)	Gold standard organization	UNFCCC accredited DOE verification	Gold standard advisory committee audits the validation	Requirements of CDM COP/MOP	Gold standard database
Voluntary carbon standard (VCS)	IETA, climate group, world economic forum	Accredited under GHG program / or ISO 14065	Verifiers assess claim against VCS 2007 standard	ISO 14064-2 & 3	Caisse des depots, TZI, bank of New York Mellon (BNYM) and APX
ISO 14064	International standards organization	Third-party validation/ verification	ISO 14065 accreditation	ISO 14064-2/3	Regional registries, e.g. Canadian standards association
Carbon financial instrument (CFI)	Chicago climate exchange (CCX)	CCX approved verifier Independent assessment of compliance	CCX Staff & FINRA	CCX guidelines	CCX
VER+	TÜV SÜD		TÜV SÜD acts as validating DOE	UNFCCC based	Blue registry
Community climate biodiversity (CCBA)	CARE, nature conservatory, rainforest alliance, others	Accredited DOE (by the CDM EB) or a FCS accredited certifier	Same CCBA auditor issues validation report	CCBA standards document (version 1.0)	CCBA database
Green-e	Green-e	Green-e energy verification	Network of auditors	Green-e national standard	Green-e climate certified offset registry
GHG protocol	WRI/WBCSD	Verification not required	N/A	N/A	Registries in Brazil, China, India, Mexico, Philippines, North America

Table 4 Key aspects of main standards

Standard	Key feature(s)	Problem(s)	Post-Kyoto organizational change	Post-Kyoto innovation	Potential/current example
CDM/JI	The official Kyoto mechanism with the most legitimacy	Unpredictability repels PPs and potential project financiers. The addition of new rules, alongside the CDM's addition of rules, slows administrative efficiency	Moving from a bottom-up towards a top-down approach	Programmatic CDM / program of activities (PoA)	Greenpeace's bachat Lamp yojana program in India
Gold standard	Based on CDM; emphasizes innovation and flexibility		Moving from a bottom-up towards a top-down approach	"Build-own-methodology" tool	ClimateCare's ® "Improved cook-stoves and kitchen regimes" methodology
Voluntary carbon standard (VCS)	Decentralized and flexible—able to issue 1 year GHG-offset credit streams while PPs work with CDM EB for CDM-based validations or verifications; competition among registries	The addition of new rules, alongside the CDM's addition of rules, slows administrative efficiency; lower-priced GHG-offset credit	Moving from a bottom-up towards a top-down approach	"Benchmark performance standards"	None proposed at time of writing
ISO 14064	No additionality, policy neutral; parallel to CDM	No additionality requirement deters proponents of additionality	Potentially include forestry-related projects	Responsibility of the implementing GHG program	Next mandatory review: 2011

5.2 Gold Standard

The Gold Standard aims to provide a standard alongside the CDM and sees competency as the key cause of bottlenecks in the CDM process. Thus, the Gold Standard seeks to fill gaps left by the CDM that deter PPs from using it. The standard is working closer with DOEs and governments (e.g. Lichtenstein and Thailand), and educating project experts (with full support, no fees) in South Africa and South-East Asia.

For post-Kyoto, the Gold Standard will adjust to fit the shape adopted by the post-Kyoto regime. Overcoming transparency in post-Kyoto is a key priority which the standard will achieve by providing guidance for additionality justification and stakeholder consultations. The standard has no current plans to address forestry projects or further expand its project type eligibility (however, this might change with the upcoming COPs before 2012).

The convergent change and push towards technicality is seen through the standard's development of its "Build-Own-Methodology" tool. The tool shows a shift from a bottom-up to a top-down approach. Essentially, the methodology enables PPs to replicate multiple small projects (and allow the launching of large-scale projects) on the basis of detailed guidance for baseline and monitoring activities.

ClimateCare® used the methodology for large-scale projects disseminating improved cook-stoves. Their methodology, "Improved Cook-stoves and Kitchen Regimes," provides a conservative estimate of what an eligible GHG-offset credit would be. The advantage of streamlined administrative work—documenting each household separately, in the case of ClimateCare's project, would not be feasible.

5.3 Voluntary Carbon Standard

The VCS is also based on the CDM model and sets frameworks for regional GHG programs/initiatives. The standard accredits associations and registries (like DOEs and the EB, respectively, for the CDM), which run the VCS framework for validations/ verifications. The registries verify that processes and norms are diligently followed, then register and issue the GHG offset credits.

Two advantages of the VCS are scalability (the number of VCS Registries can easily expand and attain a wide geographical reach), and preliminary assurance (a VCS registry can issue a year-long stream of GHG offset credits while a given PP works with the EB on a CDM-based validation/verification). The disadvantages of VCS are a lower-priced offset credit and, like the Gold Standard, the addition of new rules is slowing administrative efficiency.

For post-Kyoto initiatives, VCS is moving towards a top-down approach that uses performance-based benchmarks, analogous to CDM's PoA and the Gold Standard's "Build-Own-Methodology." The framework for "Performance-Based

Benchmarks" exists, although at the time of writing this chapter no benchmark standard had been proposed. The benchmark provides technical project performance thresholds. Future, equally-efficient projects may base their performance on the benchmarks and automatically bypass barrier assessments for additionality (the major bottleneck implicit in most validation/ verification methods, discussed in Sect. 6) and streamline administrative work.

VCS has planned the launch of new location-driven registries (i.e. New Zealand, USA, France), stemming from the current registry model. A distinctive feature of the VCS organizational structure is that each registry brings its own organizational background and competes with other VCS registries over processing times, quality, and fees.

5.4 ISO 14064

Unlike CDM, the Gold Standard, and VCS, ISO 14064 runs parallel to CDM and maintains no linkage to the mechanism. ISO 14064 is policy-neutral and decentralized. The ISO committee, formed by both Kyoto and non-Kyoto parties, seeks to develop standards and guidelines (to determine what is required of an audit) for both regulated and voluntary GHG-offset regimes, and leaves the implementation of the standard to those regional GHG programs, frameworks, government initiatives, etc. The "how" of performing a given audit (i.e. the technical, administrative, and policy-based elements) is determined by the corresponding GHG program/initiative. For example, the government of Canada has stated that ISO 14064 will set the framework for its national offset scheme. The specifics will come from the national offset scheme, which will align with Canada's GHG goals and Kyoto commitments.

Another feature of ISO 14064 is its lack of reliance on the additionality principle, the root concept of most bottlenecks in GHG validations/verifications. For proponents of additionality, ISO 14064's lack of additionality is the standard's biggest weakness. For opponents of additionality (or, of the vagueness and lack of transparency concerning its implementation), ISO 14064 (particularly part 3, the verification standard) is regarded as best practice, without competition. In developing ISO 14064, the ISO committees found the definitions for additionality from the UNFCCC to be vague, counterfactual, overly complex, and replete with overreaching assumptions. Instead of additionality, ISO 14064 requires barrier tests (a procedure to determine barriers that would have reduced the likelihood of a given GHG reduction project's implementation). For this reason, and the clear separation of the standard from policy influences, the standard suffers far fewer bottlenecks than the CDM, Gold Standard, and VCS.

Concerning post-Kyoto, ISO 14064 is again an outlier. The standard is reviewed once every 5 years (asking each country/implementing body for systematic and general feedback/concerns) and modified accordingly. The convergent change is implicit in the standard's mandatory, time-driven modification. The push towards specific technical aspects of the standard's implementation are required by the corresponding GHG program/initiative. The standard will not likely become more technical, but the standard accommodates adjustments by GHG programs towards technical specificity.

The standard's last review was March 2006; the next will be 2011. Concerning expected changes in the 2011 revision, ISO 14064 will address forestry-related projects (the standard's accounting framework allows for reservoirs, but experts currently disagree on the degrees of required specificity for such projects). Should the standard tie itself to a government or specific GHG protocol in this period, the standard could experience significant changes.

6 Bottlenecks and Institutional Changes

DOEs and PPs experience different types of bottlenecks with the GHG-offset certification processes; however, lack of both competency and transparency is a concern for both roles.

DOEs referred to four major bottlenecks:

1. Additionality and transparency
2. Greater role and authority for DOEs
3. Separation of politics and markets
4. Competency and consensus for EBs, DOEs, PPs

6.1 Additionality and Transparency

The CDM does not directly define additionality and instead gives a list of barriers that PPs are to use in order to demonstrate that a project would not have occurred without the additional incentive of GHG-offset credits. The vagueness permeates all three levels (EB, DOE, and PP) of the certification/registration process. The lack of transparency concerning the EB's decisions to approve or reject a given project based on additionality dampens DOEs and PPs confidence in the EB's ability to both lead the market and manage its administration. Rejected projects because of the additionality principle require more back-and-forth reviews among the parties than rejections for any other reason, and the solution (if/when reached) is often unexpected and elusive. The guidance provided by the CDM is minimal and both DOEs and PPs relate that, often, a project's compliance with the additionality criterion has more to do with the documents' wording than with the project itself. DOEs suggest that more examples in the CDM's guidance would be beneficial.

Another problem is the convergence/continuation of additionality. PPs complain of waiting 6 months for a reply concerning project registration from the EB, during which time the EB's rules can change, and the project/documents might no longer fulfill the requirements.

Additionality also limits a large number of potential energy efficiency/GHG-offset projects from fruition, not only because the projects don't fit the stated criteria, but also because of the risk of not fitting the vague criteria, or fitting only current criteria.

Sectoral benchmarks (as opposed to project-specific guidance) would increase the technical aspects of the certification/registration process and thereby simplify the rules/norms of the CDM project mechanism. Such benchmarks would simplify baseline justification and project monitoring methodologies. The result would be faster turnarounds at all three levels of the process, ending with a smooth registration at the EB level.

6.2 Greater Role and Authority for DOEs

DOEs want a greater role in project registration at the EB level. An implicit problem is materiality (the threshold of permissible error in monitoring emissions). Like additionality, the CDM manual excludes materiality. Mistakes or accidental deviations by the PPs in monitoring their projects' emissions is almost inevitable. Nonetheless, DOEs must submit all mistakes to the EB for approval. By this rule, materiality bottlenecks pervade the certification process. Clear technical guidance on what constitutes materiality for a specific sector/project-type would eliminate this problem.

6.3 Separation of Politics and Markets

DOEs feel that the EB is reluctant to set clear rules/definitions because of its political influences. Members of the EB are also country-representatives in the COP meetings, and this creates a reluctance by the EB to take a firm stance (which the market wants) and steer the rules in a singular direction. It also means that politicians can and do change rules without liability, which frustrates both DOEs and PPs.

For this reason, a de-coupling of politics and markets is preferred for the EB. DOEs would prefer an EB with clear rules and means of enforcement. Technical, project-specific, and methodology-related issues should be best handled by a technical committee, as is the case with ISO 14064. In other words, the EB should handle leadership, and leave management to a board of technical experts.

6.4 Competency and Consensus for EBs, DOEs, PPs

DOEs feel that PPs often lack understanding of the complexity of validation/verification processes. PPs, likewise, feel that DOEs lack understanding of the complexity required to identify, finance, and develop GHG-offset projects. Clear understanding of all parties' requirements would benefit all parties and minimize regular back-and-forth documentation corrections and adjustments.

PPs cited four major concerns concerning process bottlenecks:

1. Need for more DOEs
2. Competency
3. Speed
4. Liability

6.4.1 Need for More DOEs

PPs want more DOEs, not a new role for DOEs. More DOEs will increase competition and reduce costs (high costs are implicit in the quasi-monopolistic position of the "big 3" DOEs in the market). Malmborg (2008) discusses his findings in *Corporate strategy and the Kyoto mechanisms—institutional and transaction cost perspectives*, namely that using the mechanisms, at a company level, is cost prohibitive.

6.4.2 Competency

More DOEs with the necessary level of competency to achieve EB approval are required. DOE competency depends on experience. Because of high certification costs, when the EB rejects a project, PPs can not simply switch to another DOE—in this case the certification process would have to start anew, therefore increasing the total costs to achieve project registration with the EB.

If the number of DOEs increased, then the EBs would be overwhelmed by project proposals, which would increase project-rejection rates, and therefore further prolong the project registration process. Thus, an expansion of the EBs' capacity would have to occur alongside any increase in the number of DOEs.

6.4.3 Speed

CDM and Gold Standard are seen as the slower standards; however, with VCS's addition of new rules, the standard is also gaining this reputation. Financiers are well aware of GHG-offset project registration bottlenecks and the uncertainty around timelines and deliverables. This makes capital providers hesitant to invest. Validation can take up to 1 year, and registration can take another 3–6 months. EB meetings occur every 2 months, during which the PPs brace themselves, hoping that the rules will not change. Corrections in an already-submitted document usually takes 2 months. The uncertainty increases reluctance among PPs to undertake new, innovative, and potentially, more effective GHG-offsetting projects.

6.4.4 Liability

PPs pay extensive fees to DOEs for validation/verification. Because of bottlenecks and the inherent unpredictability of the process, PPs want DOEs to assume liability if a project's GHG-offset tonnage is challenged during or after the registration process. Liability issues are complex and must address current tonnage, retired tonnage, future vintage tonnage, etc. With more focus on the root causes of the bottlenecks (the need for clearer rules and more technical guidance), liability issues, like symptoms of a bigger problem, would decrease in number. Currently, DOEs and PPs negotiate liability, often in a separate legal contract, before beginning a validation/verification. The goal of the contract/clause is how to share the potential risks of a challenge to a project's tonnage.

7 A New Validation/Verification Standard?

The antithesis of institutional convergence and push towards technicality is institutional stagnation or divergence towards a brand new institution. All interviewees were asked whether the creation of a new standard was likely and/or preferable over the convergence/continuity of the current standards.

The replies were almost unanimous for the continuity and improvement by technical specification of the current standards. The executives expressed that the CDM should be governed differently, particularly, by separating the standard from policy/political influences. The buy-in and support from many countries, along with the strong credibility of the UNFCCC make the CDM a strong, pioneering standard.

Also preferred was the reduction of the current number of standards. Clearer rules within fewer standards would make the resulting GHG-offset trading market more straightforward and with fewer ways around the rules. A new standard could emerge in order to accommodate a greater US/China role in the Kyoto protocol, however the CDM is expected to remain the de-facto standard for Europe.

On the other hand, competition among standards was also considered advantageous. Benchmarking off one another and keeping fees low were of particular importance to PPs. A complication that arises out of such competition is the coordination of linkages between GHG-offset credit registries.

Lastly, the increasingly stringent criteria of the current standards exclude an increasing number of projects (e.g. large-scale hydro or industrial gas projects which do not comply with EU-ETS). A new standard would experience the same problem as improved technical requirements around project criteria require, by nature, specificity. In contrast, the hitherto limited proliferation of smaller projects (because of high costs of auditing and registration) is expected to change with the standards' push towards technicality and top-down approaches, which are expected to allow such projects to flourish.

8 Conclusion

The post-Kyoto regime (> 2012) requires institutional changes for the Kyoto flexible mechanisms. Bottlenecks permeate the project-based mechanisms and limit the proliferation of GHG-offset projects. Unforeseeable timeline changes (prolongations) and unexpected budget increases in project accreditation/registration costs drive PPs and financiers out of the market, to other types of investments and endeavors.

Institutional and neoinstitutional theory help explain the adaptation of the standards to the marketplace. Learning by the institutional agents and convergent change (characteristic of new institutions as they develop more technical characteristics) gives hope and installs confidence in the Kyoto Protocol's continued efforts to reduce and mitigate climate change.

Changes are present in all the major standards. Most common is the push towards top-down (more technically-based) processes among the hierarchy of agents from the previous bottom-up model (more project-specific based).

DOEs and PPs look forward to clearer guidance (i.e. with rules and expectations, especially around additionality, materiality, and roles), greater competency, capacity, and competitiveness in the post-Kyoto regime. There is little to no support for the creation of a new standard. Rather, the preference is for a continuation of the present progress, and a greater emphasis on technical guidelines.

This will not only allow more types of GHG-offset projects to proliferate, but also increase investor confidence and proliferate the current types of successful projects on a wider geographical scale.

References

Aquilano NJ, Chase RB (1995) Production and operations management, 7th edn. Irwin, Chicago
Bayon R, Hawn A, Hamilton K (2007) Voluntary carbon markets: an International business guide to what they are and how they work. Earthscan Publications, Sterling
Colombo MG, Delmastro M (2008) The determinants of corporate hierarchy; determinants of organizational dynamics; effects of organizational design, The economics of organizational design: theoretical insights and empirical evidence. Palgrave Macmillan, New York
CDM (2009) Designated operational entities (DOE). http://cdm.unfccc.int/DOE/index.html. Accessed 4 Sep 2009
Garside WR (2007) Economic growth and development – an institutional perspective, Institutions and market economies. Palgrave Macmillan, New York
Greenpeace (2009) Greenpeace welcomes India's first steps on its climate plan: phase-out of 400 million incandescent bulbs. http://www.greenpeace.org/international/press/releases/india-phaseout-lightbulbs-250209. Accessed: 4 Sep 2009
Krolik T (2006) The Argentine Carbon Fund Helps Developers Dance the Dance. The Ecosystem Marketplace, www.ecosystemmarketplace.com. Accessed 11 July 2011
Robertson J (2008) Voluntary carbon market opportunities. Deloitte, Wellington
Scott WR (2001) Institutions and organizations. Sage Publications, Thousand Oaks

Scott WR (2003) Organizations: Rational, Natural, and Open Systems. Prentice Hall, Upper Saddle River, NJ

Scott WR (2008) Institutions and organizations: ideas and interests. Sage Publications, Thousand Oaks

Scott WR, Meyer JW (1991) The Rise of Training Programs in Firms and Agencies: An Institutional Perspective. Research in Organizational Behavior 13:287–326, Elsevier Limited

Umble M, Srikanth ML (1990) Synchronous manufacturing and integration. South-Western Publishing, Cincinnati

von Malmborg F (2008) Corporate strategy and the Kyoto mechanisms – institutional and transaction cost perspectives. In: Antes R, Hansjürgens B, Letmathe P (eds) Emissions trading: institutional design, decision making and corporate strategies. Springer Business+Science Media, LLC, New York

Walgenbach P, Meyer R (2008) Neoinstitutionalistische organisationstheorie. W. Kohlhammer, Stuttgart

Williamson OE (2000) The New Institutional Economics: Taking Stock, Looking Ahead. Journal of Economic Literature 38(3):595–613

Voluntary Carbon Offsets – Empirical Findings of an International Survey

Stefanie Brinkel and Ralf Antes

Abstract Climate change is one of the greatest challenges of modern times. Businesses are increasingly developing strategies to manage the exposure to climate risk. A robust carbon strategy should focus on a comprehensive assessment of an organization's direct and indirect carbon emissions to avoid and reduce these emissions, and finally to offset the emissions that cannot be reduced further.[1]

Recently, the voluntary compensation of *greenhouse gas* (GHG) emissions emerged as a new business field, which is increasingly attracting public interest. Many different offers for emission compensation have emerged on the market. These offers vary significantly in their concrete design as well as the climate and sustainable development benefits that they yield. This chapter expands on empirical findings concerning worldwide offsetting services.

Keywords Emerging markets • GHG management • quality assurance • voluntary carbon offsets

---

Disclaimer: Research for this report was conducted from May – December 2007. Every effort has been made to ensure that information sourced or supplied from third party material is accurate. The authors accept no liability whether expressed or implied for the accuracy or completeness of the information contained or referenced in this chapter.

[1] See Ceppi 2006; StMUGV 2007.

S. Brinkel (✉)
Martin-Luther-University, Faculty of Law and Economics, Chair of Corporate Environmental Management, Große Steinstraße 73, 06108 Halle (Saale), Germany
e-mail: stefanie.brinkel@wiwi.uni-halle.de

R. Antes
Department of Economics, University of Cooperative Education Gera, Weg der Freundschaft 4A, 07546 Gera, Germany
e-mail: ralf.antes@ba-gera.de

List of Abbreviations

B2B	Business-to-Business
CCX	Chicago Climate Exchange
CDM	Clean Development Mechanism
CER(s)	Certified Emission Reduction(s)
CFI(s)	Carbon Financial Instrument(s)
CO_2	Carbon dioxide
CO_2e	Carbon dioxide equivalent
EB	Executive Board
ERU(s)	Emission Reduction Unit(s)
EUA(s)	European Allowance(s)
EU ETS	European Union Emissions Trading Scheme
GATS	Generation Attribute Tracking System
GHG	Greenhouse Gas(es)
KP	Kyoto Protocol
LULUCF	Land Use, Land Use Change and Forest
MtCO2e	Millions of tonnes of carbon dioxide equivalent
OTC	Over the Counter
REC(s)	Renewable Energy Certificate(s)
UK ETS	United Kingdom Emissions Trading Scheme
UNFCCC	United Nations Framework Convention on Climate Change
VER(s)	Verified Emission Reduction(s)
VCM(s)	Voluntary Carbon Market(s)

1 Introduction

Businesses acquire offsets in a number of ways. A simplified model of the voluntary carbon market's supply chain includes the following stages: After a project is generated (1), the resulting emission reductions are verified to a standard to create carbon credits (2). These are then sold to intermediaries (typically retailers or wholesalers of carbon credits (3)) who finally sell them on to consumers, e.g. businesses (4).

Businesses may purchase carbon credits in order to offset one of the two types of emissions[2]:

- First of all, companies buy carbon credits in order to offset the emissions generated by their facilities and employees in the course of doing business, such as emissions from logistics, manufacturing, energy use etc. These emissions are often termed as "direct emissions" or "internal emissions". Particularly for

---

[2] See Bayon et al. 2007, p. 27.

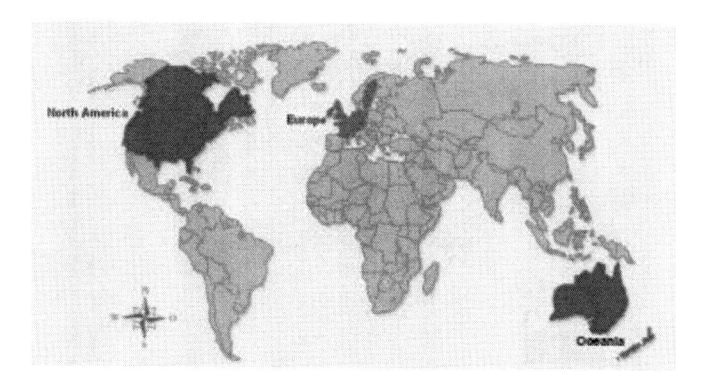

Fig. 1 Overview of carbon offset providers (Own findings)

companies in the non-producing and service sector where GHG reduction measures are only possible to some extent, carbon offsetting offers an innovative means to take action, e.g. for banks.
- Secondly, businesses might swap carbon credits to their own clients by offering climate neutral products.

Quality assurance remains the biggest challenge due to the fragmentation of the market and little regulation. Therefore, this chapter was prepared to analyze and provide information concerning the different offsetting services available with focus on quality[3] assurance.[4] Based on principal-agency theory a number of findings have emerged from the services available.

The research involved a wide-ranging survey with responses from carbon offset providers covering nine countries in three continents. At the time of data selection, 85 carbon offset providers were identified worldwide[5]; 37 in Europe, 32 in North America and 16 in Oceania (Fig. 1).[6]

---

[3]Quality is defined as the level of achievement of objectives (see Müller 2006, p.568). "Achievement of objectives" in this context means that carbon offset projects actually reduce and/or absorb emissions and that trade-offs with the ones who are affected by these projects are avoided.

[4]Neither the evaluation of individual providers nor the ranking of their services are part of the analysis.

[5]In the experts' community 30–40 providers had been assumed by that time. Our research data on existing carbon offset providers was conducted through comprehensive research of reports and studies, current news and web-based search-engines.

[6]Next to the islands of the southern, western, and central Pacific Ocean, including Melanesia, Micronesia, and Polynesia, the term „Oceania"according to the chosen definition encompasses Australia, New Zealand, and the Malay Archipelago; see The American Heritage Dictionary of the English Language (2000).

Table 1 Statistics concerning survey participants (Own findings)

Region	Number of identified carbon offset providers	Number of participating carbon offset providers in this survey
Europe	37	22
North America	32	5
Oceania	16	3[a]

[a]All three participants are located in Australia

Overall, 63 carbon offset providers were contacted.[7] 30 of them agreed to take part in the survey, which implies a response rate of 47.62%. Table 1 presents an overview of the survey participants per region.

Data was collected via comprehensive telephone interviews with the aid of a semi-standardized questionnaire.[8]

The theoretical background of this paper is the principal-agent theory. The assumption made is that information asymmetry exists at all stages of the carbon credit supply chain[9] and that actors are opportunistic.[10] This is particularly relevant as *voluntary carbon markets* (VCMs) face an opaque nature with complex structures.

Next to the above-mentioned supply chain, exchanges may assist in the distribution of offset transactions between buyers and sellers. Retail carbon offset providers may purchase carbon credits from wholesalers instead of buying credits from project developers. Furthermore, project developers may skip stage two (2) and/or three (3) of the supply chain as mentioned above. They may sell verified credits directly to businesses or unverified credits directly to intermediaries or consumers (e.g. businesses like the HSBC bank). Businesses might also swap carbon credits by offering climate neutral products to their own clients.

This leads to an extended supply chain model with an increased number of principals and agents (Fig. 2).

The following market analysis is based on the carbon credit supply chain model.

---

[7]Note on Data: All offset providers identified in Europe were asked to participate in the survey. In order to investigate the variety of approaches available worldwide, offset service providers from North America and Oceania were invited to participate, the selection was done via random sampling.

[8]More than 25 h of interviewing were recorded. The work contains an additional volume of 622 pages that includes the transcription of interviews, the questionnaire, and a table showing the empirical procedure. The individual websites of the offset service providers were also reviewed in order to acquire additional information.

[9]This leads to several multilevel types of principal-agent relationships.

[10]We do not assume that human beings behave opportunistically in every decision (see Zabel 2005). Instead, we focus on the susceptibility of the system against opportunistic behaviour (high-pressure test).

Fig. 2 Carbon credit supply chain (Own construction)

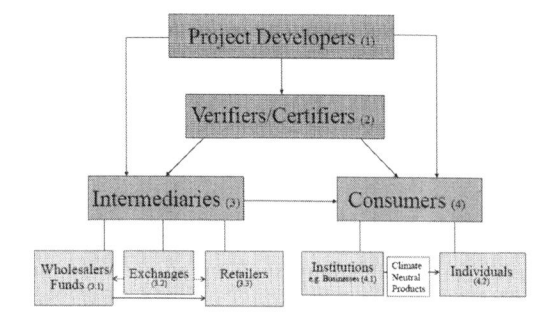

2 Market Analysis

2.1 Market Size and Growth

In analyzing the figures available for global carbon markets (Table 2), there are several points to consider:

- The *Chicago Climate Exchange* (CCX) was launched in 2003. A systematic collection of quantitative data for VCMs was started in 2004 when figures for the CCX were published. By that time, figures for the *United Kingdom Emissions Trading Scheme* (UK ETS) were also available as it operated from 2002 until 2006. Comprehensive data for the voluntary *Over the Counter Market* (OTC) has been available since 2006. This is the point in time when interest in VCMs accelerated dramatically.[11]
- At the time of our investigation, a study published reported a 200% growth in the OTC voluntary offset market between 2005 and 2006.[12] The interviewed carbon offset providers confirmed that VCMs have grown very much during the last two years though most participants in our survey did not dare to mention any figures either for now or the future.[13]
- According to quantitative studies by Carpoor and Ambrosi (the World Bank) and Hamilton et al. (New Carbon Finance and Ecosystem Marketplace), 24.6 millions of tonnes of carbon dioxide equivalent (MtCO2e) were transacted in 2006, 66 MtCO2e in 2007 and 123.4 MtCO2e in 2008. This implies a volume growth rate of 168.3% in VCMs between 2006 and 2007 and a volume growth rate of 87.0% in VCMs from 2007 to 2008.
- The significant growth of volume includes more than a tripling of the voluntary markets' value from 2006 to 2007 (growth rate: 246.74%) and a doubling between 2007 and 2008 (growth rate: 110.12%). In 2008, VCMs were worth 704.8 Million US$.

---

[11] See Bayon et al. 2007, p. 12.
[12] See Hamilton et al. 2007, p. 5. Even a growth rate of 300% is published (Smith 2007, p. 6).
[13] Numbers mentioned by the participants' referred to the findings of Hamilton et al. 2007.

Table 2 Carbon market size and growth (Own compilation according to Capoor and Ambrosi 2006, p. 13 (a); Hamilton et al. 2008, p. 6 (b); Hamilton et al. 2009, p. ii (c))

Markets	2004(a) Volume (MtCO2e)	2005(a) Volume (MtCO2e)	2005(a) Value (US $million)	2006(b) Volume (MtCO2e)	2006(b) Value (US $million)	2007(c) Volume (MtCO2e)	2007(c) Value (US $million)	2008(c) Volume (MtCO2e)	2008(c) Value (US $million)
Voluntary OTC	2.24	1.45	2.83	14.3	58.5	43.1	262.9	54	396.7
CCX				10.3	38.3	22.9	72.4	69.2	306.7
Other exchanges						0.0	0.0	0.2	1.3
UKETS	0.53	0.3	1.31						
Total voluntary markets				24.6	96.7	66.0	335.3	123.4	704.8
EU ETS	8.49	322.01	8,220.16	1,104	24,436	2,061.0	50,097.0	2,982.0	94,971.7
Primary CDM				537	5,804	551.0	7,426.0	400.3	6,118.2
Secondary CDM				25	445	240.0	5,451.0	622.4	15,584.5
Joint implementation				16	141	41.0	499.0	20.0	294.0
Kyoto [AAU]						0.0	0.0	16.0	177.1
New South Wales	5.02	6.11	57.16	20	225	25.0	224.0	30.6	151.9
RGGI								71.5	253.5
Alberta's SGER						1.5	13.7	3.3	31.3
Total regulated markets				1,642	31,051	2,919.5	63,710.7	4146.1	117,582.2
Total global markets	16.28	329.87	8,281.46	1,667	31,148	2,985.5	64,046.0	4,269.5	118,287.0

Motivation

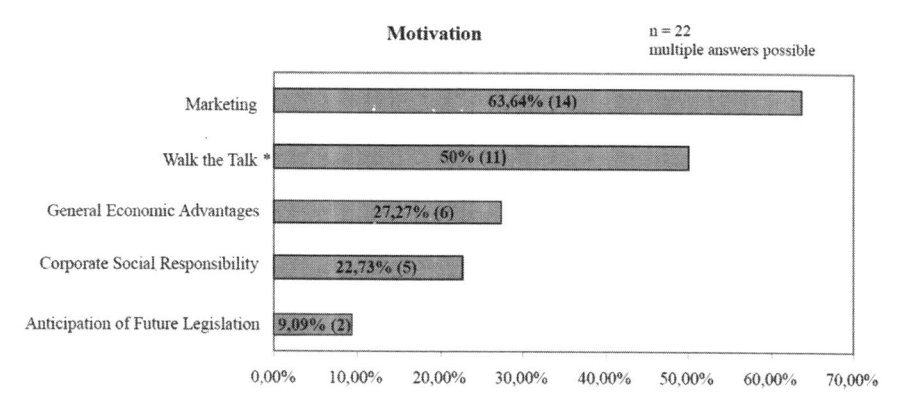

n = 22
multiple answers possible

- Marketing: 63,64% (14)
- Walk the Talk *: 50% (11)
- General Economic Advantages: 27,27% (6)
- Corporate Social Responsibility: 22,73% (5)
- Anticipation of Future Legislation: 9,09% (2)

* "Walk the talk" in this context means to put solutions to combat climate change into practice

Fig. 3 Motivational drivers for businesses concerning voluntary GHG compensation (Own findings)

Although volumes and values in the VCMs are much smaller as compared to regulated markets, VCMs are considered much more innovative and neither restrictions concerning market participants[14] nor limitations to certain kinds of transactions exist. For example, the compensation of GHG emissions through forestry sequestration projects is possible in VCMs. However, the *European Union Emissions Trading Scheme* (EU ETS) according to the Linking Directive currently does not accept *Land Use, Land Use Change and Forestry* (LULUCF) credits of any kind.[15]

According to Ceppi (2006), the main factor for the exponential growth in services for compensating GHG emissions is an increasing awareness of climate change in society.[16] Particularly businesses have recognized the consideration of climate change as an important component of their company's strategy. In the course of the carbon disclosure project, more than 80% of Consumer Discretionary respondents have identified climate change as an economic risk as well as an opportunity.[17] Therefore, it is not surprising that companies see their voluntary steps concerning climate protection measures as a way to differentiate themselves from other companies.[18] Figure 3 shows in order of ranking, factors that offset service providers assume are most likely to motivate companies to take part voluntarily in GHG compensation.[19]

---

[14]The EU ETS is limited solely to energy producing and energy-intensive industries.
[15]See European Commission 2004, p. 19.
[16]See Ceppi 2006, p. 15.
[17]See PriceWaterhouseCoopers 2009, p. 54.
[18]See STMUGV 2007, p. 13; Lafeld 2007, p. 10.
[19]The ranking was done with the response from 22 offset service providers; the highest being the factor that most offset service providers mentioned as a motivational factor.

The answers confirm that marketing is the main motivational factor. Although the anticipation of future legislation could theoretically be a source for the participation in compensation methods, it does not appear as a driving force.

While the demand for compensating GHG emissions rises, barriers for market entry of carbon offset suppliers are marginal. As a result, the growth rate of suppliers is exponentially increasing and comprehensive information concerning market development is not available.

2.2 Compensation Models

Each of the interviewed carbon offset providers shows its very own specific characteristics. The different participants vary in terms of their expertise and message of GHG compensation. From our empirical findings, we suggest the following categorization of providers.

Category 1 (holistic approaches): 11% of the participants offer a holistic approach in the context of climate protection strategies. These providers do not only acquire and retire carbon credits but they also provide measures to reduce GHG emissions (avoidable emissions) before offsetting the emissions that cannot be reduced further.

Category 2 (carbon creditors): Actors in this group are specialized in the acquisition and retirement of carbon credits and do not offer holistic climate strategies. They can act as wholesalers or retailers. 67% of the interview partners belong to this category.

Category 3 (CO_2 absorbers): 22% of the participants belong to this group and are related to the nonprofit sector. They have a similar structure to category 2, the only difference being that, they exclusively absorb *carbon dioxide* (CO_2) from the atmosphere. Their original focus was to preserve biodiversity.

One of the first voluntary investments in compensating GHG emissions took place in 1989 – long before the *United Nations Framework Convention on Climate Change* (UNFCCC) and the resulting *Kyoto Protocol* (KP) were signed and even before the EU ETS had been active.[20] This voluntary investment supported a biological sink project. With regard to the categorization of providers offering GHG compensation, the investment corresponds to the time of market entry of the various categories. All providers whose basic concept is the absorption of CO_2 (category 3) have been active since the 1990s, whereas all other providers, who are not exclusively related to absorbing CO_2 (categories 1 and 2) started business at the beginning of the twenty first century.

Although VCMs are still in the early stages, they consist of a small but growing number of providers: predominantly in the USA and in Europe notably

---

[20]See Hamilton et al. 2007, p. 10.

the United Kingdom and Germany, and to some extent in Australia. According to the responses, we can conclude that providers in Canada, Germany, the Netherlands, Switzerland and the United Kingdom face a seller´s market, whereas the VCMs in Australia, the USA, France and Belgium can still be described as less sophisticated.

2.3 Market Place

We found out that, compensation models are focused on using a project-based mechanism. Offset approaches are idiosyncratic concerning regions in which the different providers are located. Providers in North America offer compensation via the CCX and the OTC, whereas providers in Australia not only use *Verified Emission Reductions* (VERs) from the OTC but also certificates from the Mandatory Renewable Energy Target – a renewable energy trading scheme in Australia which creates tradable units called *Renewable Energy Certificates* (RECs). In Europe, offsetting carbon emissions may be done via VERs or Kyoto-compliant certificates: *European Allowances* (EUAs), *Emission Reduction Units* (ERUs) and *Certified Emission Reductions* (CERs).

2.4 Carbon Offset Projects

Carbon offsets are generated from different project types. In contrast to compliance markets, the OTC encourages innovation by providing a lot of benefit for small-scale projects and technologies that the regulatory market tends to neglect.[21]

With regard to the scale, carbon offset providers generally offer a diversified project-portfolio.

According to the technology, the most common projects are using renewable energy technology, energy-efficiency technology and bio-sequestration. 25% of providers are exclusively offering bio-sequestration as a means of compensation. 50% exclusively rely on energy-efficiency, renewable energy and in some cases methane projects. 25% offer a mixture of projects, which may be, absorbing CO_2 from the atmosphere or reducing greenhouse gases in the atmosphere. At the time of our investigation, none of the participants was using industrial gas reduction projects being used in the compliance markets.

Investigating the overall project portfolios of the carbon offset providers; the following picture can be drawn: worldwide 17% are using methane projects, 35%

---

[21] See Trexler et al. 2006, p.17.

energy efficiency projects, 52% bio-sequestration[22] and 70% renewable energy projects.[23]

Regarding the different project technologies offered in different continents the following depiction can be drawn: In Europe there is clear preference for renewable energy and energy efficiency. Only 37.5% of European carbon offset providers prefer biological sinks in their business portfolio. Noticeably, these providers are categorized as "CO_2 absorbers". In Australia, there is a clear preference for biological sink projects. Providers there rarely use renewable energy technologies. In North America, we found no clear preference for one or another offset technology.[24]

The survey revealed that, the notion whether or not carbon credits from bio-sequestration as well as RECs should be used for offsetting is still a controversial issue for debate.

From a quality perspective, several risks have to be taken into account for the choice of a carbon offset project. As renewable energy, energy efficiency and bio-sequestration projects are the most common ones in VCMs; their associated risks will be considered exemplary.

It has to be noted that, for bio-sequestration projects, the amount of carbon sequestered depends upon a variety of factors. These factors include the age of the trees, their growth rate, local climate and soil conditions. Skeptics specifically reference that these projects risk not being permanent. To be able to realize the full potential of sequestration, a project must last. Mainly natural disturbances and human activities (e.g. fire, pests, insect outbreaks, logging) may destroy a forest.[25] Furthermore, difficulties in quantifying carbon stocks[26] and effects caused through leakage[27] may lead to reduced CO_2 absorption. This must be addressed to ensure the credibility of such offset projects.

Renewable energy offset projects focus on e.g. wind, biomass and solar technologies. To establish the feasibility of these projects one needs to consider the following: economic, geographic, social and political factors as well as legislative hurdles and local opposition to a project.[28] Furthermore, comprehensive capacity and the necessary infrastructure need to be in place in order to make

---

[22]As VCMs are main possible outlet for bio-sequestration credits, the predominance of credits in these markets is not surprising. Compared to Kyoto markets, it is obvious that VCMs play a critical role in financing sequestration projects. In 2010, less than 1% of *Clean Development Mechanism* (CDM) projects that have been registered by the UN are LULUCF projects; see Fenhann 2010.

[23]The universe is 23. Multiple answers were possible.

[24]This might be due to the relatively small universe of North American carbon offset providers interviewed. In addition, it is necessary to recognize that the CCX does not disclose any information in this context.

[25]See Brown 1999.

[26]See Canadell and Raupach 2008, p. 1,456.

[27]See Iverson 2009, p.10.

[28]See Kollmus and Bowell 2007, p. 18.

Table 3 Major standards for VERs and VER providers (See Hamilton et al. 2009, p. 60f)

Standard	Description	Required environmental and social co-benefits	Registry	Geographic scope	Project start date limits
American Carbon Registry Standard	Certification program for emissions reporting offsets, and a registry	No	Registry incorporated	Focused on North-America	On or after 1 January 2002 (forestry projects may start earlier)
CarbonFix	Certification program for forestry offset projects	Yes	Registry incorporated; TZI registry soon	International	After 11 December 1997
Climate Action Reserve	Certification program for offsets and a registry	No	Registry incorporated; powered by APX	U.S. currently; Mexico and Canada soon	After 1 January 2001 (new project protocols excepted)
Climate, Community & Biodiversity Standard	Validation program for offset projects	Yes	Projects on website; TZI registry	International	None
EPA Climate Leaders Offset Guidance	Guidance for companies on voluntary offset use	No	No	Global	After 20 February 2002 (some exceptions)
GE/AES Greenhouse Gas Standard	Certification program for offsets and project developers	No	Yes	U.S.	After 1 January 2000
Gold Standard	Certification for offset projects & carbon credits	Yes	Yes; powered by APX	International	2004
Green-e Climate	Certification program for offset retailers	No	Registry incorporated	Aimed at North-America; International	Varies by project type
Greenhouse Friendly	Certification program for offset sellers & carbon neutral products	No	Australian Climate Exchange registry	Australia	After 18 June 2001
ISO 14064	Certification program emissions reporting, offset projects, and carbon credits	No	No	International	Methodology released in 2006

(continued)

Table 3 (continued)

Standard	Description	Required environmental and social co-benefits	Registry	Geographic scope	Project start date limits
Plan Vivo	Validation program for forestry and agro-forestry offset projects	Yes	TZI	International	Ex-ante crediting only
Quality Assurance Scheme for Carbon Offsetting	U.K. government certification program for offset retailers	No	Not applicable	International	During or after March 2009
Social Carbon Standard	Validation program for offset projects	Yes	TZI registry soon	South America & Portugal	None
VER+	Certification program for offset projects and carbon neutral products	No	TUV SUD Blue registry	International	On or after 1 January 2005
Voluntary Carbon Standard	Certification for offset project & carbon credits	No	Project database; registry provided by TZI, APX, and Caisse des Depots	International	On or after 1 January 2000

sure that the new technology can be maintained and repaired.[29] The use of renewable energy projects which interact with the electricity market (so called on-grid projects which could produce RECs) bear an increased risk that the additionality criteria is not fulfilled, meaning that, real emission reductions are not delivered.

The principle of energy efficiency implies that lower energy losses occurring during the generation, conversion, distribution and use of energy show that energy efficiency is being attained.[30] Examples of energy efficiency technologies include; energy-saving light bulbs and redesigned cooking stoves. Due to the decentralized nature and in some cases small scale of energy-efficiency projects, monitoring and evaluating the projects as well as establishing a baseline and estimating the existent emission reductions can be challenging.[31] Emission reductions are typically calculated by comparing the emissions of the offset project with the emissions of a hypothetical "baseline scenario" which will reflect the business-as-usual scenario. Assuming that actors are opportunistic, then both the host of the project and the investor have an incentive to overstate the amount of emissions reduction yielded by the offset project to enhance their revenues.[32]

To ensure the quality of an offset, verification and certification standards become imperative.

2.5 Standards and Registries

The market is fragmented and has little regulation with a wide range of quality standards emerging internationally. The certificates used in VCMs that have been identified in this chapter, all appeal to different standards, which imply varying degrees of rigid implementation and control-mechanisms for offset projects. This is especially relevant as VCMs face multiple principal-agent relationships. Less rigid verification and/or certification processes increase the possibility of misuse of the system by selling and buying credits without any ecological and social integrity due to information asymmetry (Table 3).

In the USA, the CCX has built up its own rules in order to regulate quality. From our investigation, statements concerning quality assurance received from the survey participants differ a great deal. Whereas some "feel that this is one of the most rigorous tested and verified ways to reducing carbon", others criticize a lack of publicly available information. Furthermore, the interaction of markets for GHG emissions and for electricity leads to enormous lacks of assurance that an energy-related carbon project is additional. Although a conversion from CO_2

---

[29]See Martinot and McDoom 2000; Turkenberg 2000.
[30]See BMU 2009.
[31]See Kollmus and Bowell 2007, p. 19.
[32]See Michaelowa 2005, p. 289–304.

attributes of a REC to a GHG emission certificate is possible, a rigid standard to prove additionality does not have to be followed. An interview partner confirms: e.g. the *Generation Attribute Tracking System* (GATS) allows the conversion but only 50% of REC providers are disciplined enough to follow this standard. A controversial debate among experts is building up. Whereas only one of the interviewed providers uses RECs for GHG compensation purposes, majority of the providers reject the use of such certificates.

In the EU, Kyoto-compliant certificates (e.g. CERs) have to pass a certification process set up by the UNFCCC. The CDM as defined in Article 12 of the KP; implies the furthest developed and most complex mechanism with a detailed project cycle. Nonetheless, it is to state that 25–40% of the projects do not pass the additionality criteria; and although the additionality tool of the CDM *Executive Board* (EB) has been developed further, the additionality proof remains insecure and dependent on subjective influences and judgements.[33]

In principle, the process of assessing emission reductions generated by an emissions reduction project is less rigid for VERs than for CERs. However, in the regulated markets, standards and rules are clearly defined; standards for VER projects are diverse and include different quality characteristics worldwide:

From our investigation, we found out that 36% of the offset providers employ the CDM criteria as a quality check for VERs. The most common VER standards used worldwide are the Voluntary Carbon Standard (used by 20%) as well as the VER Gold Standard (used by 36%).

Mainly in North America and Australia providers indicated that they are currently evaluating all upcoming standards and will adopt a suitable standard later.

With regard to quality assurance, registries are very important; therefore, carbon offset providers were also asked for information about their current use of registries. 42% of them indicated that they are currently not holding credits in a registry. Those who list their credits in a registry sometimes do so via internal registries, which are not audited by a third party. Overall, there is a limited number of carbon offset providers that are using independently reviewed registries for carbon credits.

This situation is leaving enormous loopholes concerning the quality of offsets. Therefore, any screening activities for high profile offers are difficult and require intensive knowledge to succeed in actually offsetting emissions.

2.6 Prices

Typically, supply and demand determine the price. The survey states an enormous variability in prices for voluntary carbon offsets. Determinants for the price per metric ton CO_{2e} contain the type of compensation project and its additional benefits such as community education, the cost of verification and certification of the carbon

---

[33]See Hesselbarth 2009, p. 402.

credits and implied transaction costs. The survey shows that a dependency between the price and legal form of the carbon offset provider company is not given. For offset projects the assumption exists that the more rigid the verification and certification process, the higher the price per metric ton CO_{2e}.[34] Therefore, one could conclude that the higher the price per metric ton CO_{2e} the better the quality (in the sense of emission reduction and social benefit). In the past, free riders used this deduction as an obfuscation; in that case quality and price didn't necessarily correlate. With regard to the survey, interview partners stated that a correlation is being established as the market develops further.

The different carbon offset providers charge the following prices per metric ton of CO_{2e}: CERs are charged approximately 24.50 € per metric ton of CO_{2e} offset, whilst VERs are charged between 0.60 € and 21 €. The price for EUAs depends on the spot price, whereas a credit from the CCX (*Carbon Financial Instrument* (CFI)) costs approximately 5 €. RECs are charged approximately 12 €. As an outlier, there has been one identified carbon offset provider charging up to 180 € for offsetting one metric ton of CO_{2e}.

3 Implications for Businesses

The results lead to the conclusion that it is hardly possible for carbon offset providers – being dependant on project developers – and for businesses – being dependant on carbon offset providers – to gain reliable information concerning the social and ecological integrity of carbon offset offers.

As a clear quality standard is missing, offset providers can exert a pull on low quality offsets by providing lower cost products. The consequence would be that businesses, that are willing to acquire offsets and to develop and market carbon neutral products, face a "buyer beware" market.[35] In order to avoid the poor quality offsets that drive out high-quality offsets from environmentally and socially beneficial projects, businesses need sensitive market information. Otherwise, the enormous opportunity to build emission reduction efforts into ordinary corporate activities would be destabilized.[36]

At this point, notably the provision of required information cannot be taken for granted. Main sources of information are the individual websites of carbon offset providers though the research showed a limited design. E. g. comprehensive descriptions of offset projects are rare to find. Only 15% of carbon offset providers offer newsletters and only 15% publish business reports. This indicates the risk of adverse selection.

---

[34] E. g. the verification and certification process according to the UNFCCC guidelines is much more rigid than the verification process of VERs.
[35] See Trexler et al. 2006, p. 15.
[36] See Trexler et al. 2006, p. 15f.

4 Suggestions for Improvement

To develop the market further, recommended actions can be broadly categorized into increasing awareness and increasing the credibility of the voluntary market. 'Awareness' includes creating awareness of climate change and creating awareness of the existence of offsets as a viable option.[37] In this context, one category can complement the other category respectively. To make the compensation of GHG emissions a reasonable contribution to climate protection the risks involved need to be communicated clearly.

A basic requirement is the full understanding of those risks. Carbon offset providers need to admit their responsibility. Checklists being published at the provider's homepage as well as the establishment of communication platforms are reasonable measures. The establishment of social networks offers an enormous chance to initiate a collective responsible impact. Until now, the self-conception of carbon offset providers for a consistent education of consumers is not necessarily given. Therefore, reports from independent organizations, which show the chances and risks of the concept, clearly are indispensable.

As mentioned, it is difficult for prospective clients to evaluate the quality of offset projects and the credibility of carbon offset providers. A multitude of standards in a fragmented market combined with a lack of sensitive market information still yields a non-satisfying solution. A mutual consent on a few main standards would allow for differentiation of the heterogeneous GHG compensation offers more easily.

To regulate the incompleteness of the effectively available standards for voluntary carbon offsets, the Department for Environment, Food and Rural Affairs in the UK demands a strong focus on standards (for validation, verification and certification) according to the guidelines of the KP. From a quality perspective, this demand seems to be desirable. According to an observer's point of view, this demand might also imply disadvantages; the often-cited innovation of the market might be limited. Typically, less complex verification processes and no limitation to certain offset project types (in contrast to regulated carbon markets) enable investment due to relatively low transaction costs, especially for small-scale projects, which the CDM discounts. In terms of development policy, small-scale local projects need a definite support. A trade-off concerning regulated examination of additionality, permanence and leakage issues on the one hand and the provision for sustainable development goals on the other tends to create controversial discussions among the experts.

In some cases carbon credits (here: VERs) used for compensation purposes do not emerge from genuine projects. To overcome this problem it is necessary to discuss whether to allow credits from projects which strive for registration according to CDM EB, but which have not yet received registration for compensation purposes

---

[37]See Taiyab 2006, p. 22.

only. Considering that the rigid process of registration might take months, it seems appropriate to use those credits, which have been generated before registration of the project and which can be significant amounts, for voluntary compensation purposes.

Furthermore, an argument about the examination of local carbon offset projects in developing countries arises. It points out that, developing countries can hardly pay the transaction costs for project certification by accredited institutions. This suggests that local institutions should conduct examination. In contrast to an examination by internationally-acting certifiers from industrialized countries in the course of "mass processing", this implies the possibility of relatively low transaction costs, the development of jobs as well as the use of existing detailed expertise of typically unique carbon offset projects.

Suggestions for improvement should also include the discussion of forestry projects, which are often disregarded in compliance carbon markets. Given a proper nurturing, these projects can deliver various additional benefits.

In order to secure the quality of GHG compensation measures, it is imperative that the verification and certification of carbon offset projects are reviewed by an independent body. However, according to principle-agent theory, an adequate quality assurance demands additional measures from the agents themselves. To ensure transparency, carbon offset providers should provide comprehensive information; e. g. a provider should publish detailed descriptions concerning all carbon offset projects that are included in a provider's project portfolio. This is important to ensure credibility. Some interview partners argued that this might lead to information overload on the clients' part. This argument loses its importance against the background of existing information asymmetry in the fragmented VCMs.

Typically, carbon offset providers bundle their clients' money acquired through small-scale contracts in order to invest in a project. This particularly affects "small" deals secured through providers' homepages, rather than large orders typically made by companies through other channels. With regard to the investments of those relatively small deals, the actual investment of the money is not necessarily traceable. According to interview partners, the distribution of individual confirmation, that a certain carbon offset project is supported, is not administrable. This might become a problem as providers typically offer projects with different quality standards (downscaling) and might act on several markets. For example, a seller of carbon credits can operate in the CCX market, the OTC market and the REC market at the same time. This creates the risk of concealing transactions and the double-selling of carbon credits. Consequently, one of the involved buyers receives carbon credits for which there is no underlying environmental value. Hot air is traded instead.

Constitutive for the assessment of real emission reductions is the establishment and use of a registry. To be able to trace those complex transactions such a registry would need to include all transactions in VCMs. This demands an international authority. At the moment such a development is not in existence.

Another point to mention is that big companies in particular are responsible for a huge amount of emissions due to their economic activities. Those companies should use their impact. One option for doing so is to bundle their greenhouse gas liabilities for a longer period, e.g. a year, and then issue a tender call to offset the whole year's worth of emissions for all of their business activities. Under the restriction that the company itself is informed about the quality assurance issue and gains expertise in order to evaluate any risks associated with a tender offer, the company could contribute to norm setting and structural policy in VCMs. This can be achieved by being a disciplined buyer and choosing a bidder, who follows clearly-defined and published quality criteria. Considering the enormous amounts of greenhouse gases that businesses could tender in a market where project managers fight for orders, businesses should use their position to set incentives for a credible market and in order to change "the rules of the game" into a direction with quality as the priority.

5 Conclusion

Offers in the relatively new voluntary carbon offset market vary. Whether GHG compensation can contribute to climate protection and sustainable development benefits cannot be answered as a definite "yes" or "no". The answer is dependent on each carbon offset offer. From a quality perspective, a definite satisfying solution is non-existent.

It is positive that the concept of voluntary GHG compensation is accessible to any company that wants to offset its greenhouse gas emissions – in the best case as part of a comprehensive carbon strategy. Additionally, the concept contributes to raising awareness of the sensuously not ad hoc recognizable problem of climate change. This is necessary to develop the motivation for sustainable behavior. It also seems clear that in the short term the market is evolving quickly, creating new economic and environmental opportunities for non-profit organizations, investors and businesses.

References

Bayon R, Hawn A, Hamilton K (2007) Voluntary carbon markets: an international business guide to what they are and how they work. Earthscan Publications, London

BMU (Bundesministeriums für Umwelt, Naturschutz und Reaktorsicherheit) (2009) General information – energy efficiency, Berlin. http://www.bmu.de/english/energy_efficiency/general_information/doc/38267.php. Accessed 22 Jan 2010

Brown S (1999) Guidelines for inventorying and monitoring carbon offsets in forest-based projects, winrock international. http://www.winrock.org/ecosystems/files/Guidelines_for_Inventorying_and_Monitoring.pdf.

Canadell J, Raupach M (2008) Managing forests for climate change mitigation. Science 320:1456–1457
Capoor K, Ambrosi P (2006) State and trends of the carbon market 2006, Washington. http://www.fonamperu.org/general/mdl/documentos/carbonmarket2006.pdf
Ceppi P (2006) The carbon trust three stage approach to developing a robust offsetting strategy, the carbon trust (eds) London. http://www.scribd.com/doc/24771491/The-Carbon-Trust-three-stage-approach-to-developing-a-robust-offsetting-strategy
Commission E (2004) Directive 2004/101/EC OF the European Parliament and of the council of 27 October 2004 amending directive 2003/87/EC establishing a scheme for greenhouse gas emission allowance trading within the Community, in respect of the Kyoto Protocol's project mechanisms. Off J Eur Union L 338:18–23
Fenhann J (2010) UNEP Risoe CDM pipeline analysis and database, Roskilde. http://www.cdmpipeline.org/. Accessed 26 Feb 2010
Hamilton K et al (2009) Fortifying the foundation: state of the voluntary carbon markets 2009, New York. http://www.ecosystemmarketplace.com/documents/cms_documents/StateOfThe VoluntaryCarbonMarkets_2009.pdf
Hamilton K et al (2008) Forging a frontier: state of the voluntary carbon markets 2008, New York. http://www.ecosystemmarketplace.com/documents/cms_documents/2008_StateofVoluntary CarbonMarket2.pdf
Hamilton K et al (2007) State of the voluntary carbon markets 2007: picking up steam, London. http://ecosystemmarketplace.com/documents/acrobat/StateoftheVoluntaryCarbonMarket18July_ Final.pdf
Hesselbarth C (2009) Wirkungen des EU-Emissionshandels als ökonomisches Instrument der Umweltpolitik auf das Betriebliche Nachhaltigkeitsmanagement, Aachen
Iverson C (2009) In search of standards for forest carbon offset projects in BC: a review of Georgian and Californian state standards. http://circle.library.ubc.ca/bitstream/handle/2429/16099/IversonChad_FRST_497_Graduating_Essay_2008.pdf?sequence=1
Kollmuss A, Bowell B (2007) Voluntary offsets for air-travel carbon emissions: evaluations and recommendations of voluntary offset companies. In: Tufts climate initiative (eds) Boston. http://sustainability.tufts.edu/downloads/TCI_Carbon_Offsets_Paper_April-2-07.pdf
Lafeld S (2007) Climate neutral: credibility in the voluntary carbon market through transparency and standardization, presentation carbon expo 2007, Köln 2007. http://www.3c-company.com/uploads/media/Presentation_CE_2007_Lafeld_03.pdf
Martinot E, McDoom O (2000) Promoting energy efficiency and renewable energy: GEF climate change projects and impacts – global environmental facility. http://www.martinot.info/Martinot_McDoom_GEF.pdf
Michaelowa A (2005) Determination of baselines and additionality for the CDM: a crucial element of credibility of the climate regime. In: Yamin F (ed) Climate change and carbon markets, A handbook of emission reduction mechanisms. Earthscan Publications, London, pp 289–304
Müller M (2006) Die Glaubwürdigkeit der Zertifizierung von Qualitäts-, Umwelt- und Sozialstandards. Betriebswirtschaft 5:585–601
PriceWaterhouseCoopers (2009) Carbon disclosure project 2009: global 500 report, London/New York. https://www.allianz.com/static-resources/en/press/news/studies/downloads/downloads_g8/v_1253613990000/cdp_g500_a4_.pdf
Smith K (2007) The carbon neutral myth: offset indulgences for your climate sins. In: Transnational institute (eds) Amsterdam. http://www.tni.org/reports/ctw/carbon_neutral_myth.pdf
StMUGV (Bayrisches Staatsministerium für Umwelt, Gesundheit und Verbraucherschutz) (eds) (2007) Wegweiser zur Klimaneutralität: Klimabewusstes Handeln im Unternehmen, München. http://www.kellendorfer.de/uploads/media/stmugv_app000005.pdf
Taiyab N (2006) Exploring the market for voluntary carbon offsets, London. http://pubs.iied.org/pdfs/G00268.pdf
The American Heritage Dictionary of the English Language (2000), Fourth edition, updated in 2009, Houghton Mifflin Company

Trexler MC, Kosloff LH, Silon K (2006) Going carbon neutral: how the retail carbon offsets market can further global warming mitigation goals, ecosystem marketplace. http://www.ecosystemmarketplace.com/media/pdf/em_going_carbon_neutral.pdf

Turkenberg WC (2000) Chapter 7: renewable energy technologies – world energy assessment – energy and the challenge of sustainability, draft. http://www.undp.org/energy/activities/wea/pdfs/chapter7.pdf

Zabel H-U (2005) A model of human behaviour for sustainability. Int j soc econ 32(8):717–735

Climate Change and the Clean Development Mechanism in Indonesia: An Appraisal

Nicole Dathe

Abstract This chapter provides a detailed description and an up-to-date overview of the Clean Development Mechanism (CDM) market in Indonesia. Indonesia is a country that is both an important contributor to global warming as well as one of its primary victims. Some institutional and policy arrangements in Indonesia relevant to climate change are introduced. The main part of this chapter is dedicated to the state of play of the CDM in Indonesia. The paper compares the CDM in Indonesia with other countries, it elaborates on the Indonesian Designated National Authority (DNA) and sheds light on the country's potential as well as the actual situation in the Indonesian CDM market. Selected players and their activities are mentioned; and recent developments in the national CDM market are highlighted, before a short outlook is provided.

Keywords CDM • climate change • governance • Indonesia

1 Introduction

The Clean Development Mechanism (CDM) is one of three market-based instruments that were introduced by the Kyoto Protocol to help reduce global emissions in a cost-efficient way. It was established through Article 12 of the Protocol and operationalised by the Marrakesh Accords in 2001. This project-based mechanism is the largest offsetting mechanism in the world, accounting for 87% of project-based transaction volumes in 2007,[1] and allowing private or public

---

[1] Cf. Kollmuss et al. (2008). For a comparison of existing mandatory and voluntary GHG reduction programmes and offset mechanisms see Kollmuss et al. (2008).

N. Dathe (✉)
Pfotenhauerstr. 74, 01307 Dresden, Germany
e-mail: Nicole.dathe@hotmail.com

entities in Annex I countries to conduct emission-reducing projects in non-Annex I countries. The CDM is the only flexible mechanism that involves the participation of developing countries in the attempt to limit global warming.

The Certified Emission Reductions (CERs) yielded by the project activity can be used by the Annex I country towards the compliance with its binding reduction targets set out in Annex B of the Kyoto Protocol. The CDM was designed as a market-based, cost-efficient instrument: As climate change is a global phenomenon that does not stop at borders, it does not matter per se where in the world emissions are reduced. Yet marginal abatement costs of greenhouse gas (GHG) emissions are usually a lot higher in industrialised countries than in developing countries where an old and highly inefficient energy infrastructure is often still in place. The CDM therefore has, at least theoretically, a double benefit: Annex I countries can achieve their reductions more cheaply, and developing countries benefit from the investment in clean energy through the CDM and thus from a contribution to their sustainable development.

In an attempt to safeguard the environmental integrity of the CDM, a key concept is "additionality," such that a project activity that reduces emissions would not have taken place without the additional revenue (CERs) from the CDM. Thus emission reductions have to be real, measurable, verifiable and additional to what would have occurred without the project in order to be eligible under the CDM. Therefore the UN CDM Executive Board (EB) oversees the rather complex and often lengthy CDM project cycle (validation, registration, verification, issuance of CERs etc.). Also, the CDM should only be "supplemental to domestic [mitigation] action" in Annex I countries (Art. 12 Kyoto Protocol). Within the European Union Emission Trading System (EU ETS), for example, the use of CDM is regulated in the Linking Directive 2004/101/EC.

This paper provides a detailed description and an up-to-date overview of the CDM market in Indonesia. In Sect. 2 Indonesia is presented as a country that is both an important contributor to global warming as well as one of its primary victims (2.1). Section 2 also examines the institutional and policy arrangements in Indonesia relevant to climate change (2.2). Section 3 constitutes the main part of this paper and is dedicated to the state of play of the CDM in Indonesia. It compares the CDM in Indonesia with the situation in other countries (3.1); it elaborates on the Indonesian Designated National Authority (DNA) (3.2), the country's potential and the actual situation in the Indonesian CDM market (3.3 and 3.4). Also, some selected players are mentioned (3.5) and recent developments in the national CDM market are highlighted (3.6). The paper ends with a short outlook (Sect. 4).

This paper only looks at CDM project types that currently exist in Indonesia. It is beyond the scope of this paper to examine the reasons why Indonesia has no transport CDM projects and no forestry CDM projects. Many of the remarks in this chapter are based on over 20 interviews that I conducted in Indonesia with various CDM stakeholders including government officials, CDM consultants, companies, NGOs and researchers between July and November 2008. During that time, I was doing a field study while affiliated with the German Technical Cooperation (GTZ), a German Development Implementation Agency, within their

"Indonesian-German Environmental Programme (ProLH)" in Jakarta. In addition, I attended several workshops and seminars related to CDM opportunities and barriers in Indonesia, on which some of my comments are based. Finally, I sourced a substantial amount of grey literature,[2] which proved a very valuable source of information on CDM developments in Indonesia.

2 Climate Change as a General Issue in Indonesia

2.1 Indonesia – One of the Biggest GHG Emitters, But Also a Primary Victim of Climate Change

Indonesia, an archipelago comprising five main islands and over 17,000 smaller islands and islets, is Southeast Asia's biggest economy with a gross national income (GNI) of US$ 373 billion and a GDP of US$ 433 billion (2007).[3] It was one of the countries worst hit by the Asian financial crisis in 1997/1998 and was slow to recover. The World Bank classifies Indonesia, which has a GNI per capita of $1,650 (2007), as a lower middle-income country (World Bank 2009, p. 351). GDP growth figured fairly constant at approximately 5% annually between 2000 and 2006, and is projected to keep a level of around 6% per annum until 2010 (OECD 2008a).

Indonesia is the fourth most populous country on the planet, a founding member and driving force of the Association of Southeast Asian Nations (ASEAN) and an influential member of the Group of 77 (G77), the largest intergovernmental organisation of developing states in the United Nations. Moreover, the country is part of the G20, the world's most important industrial and emerging-market countries. Indonesia is also one of the five Enhanced Engagement Countries, along with China, India, Brazil and South Africa, which are "selected, globally important non-member countries" for which the Organisation for Economic Co-operation and Development (OECD) has prepared an Economic Assessment (OECD 2008b). The country is endowed with a wealth of natural resources (natural gas, coal and oil) and is the world's biggest exporter of coal (Mining Journal 2009).

Indonesia's per capita emissions of CO_2 are 1.7 metric tons per year (2004), which is low compared to many developed countries including the United States (20.6 metric tons per capita per year), Australia (16.2 metric tons), Germany (9.8 metric tons), or even compared to China (3.9 metric tons) (World Bank

---

[2]This term refers to papers, reports, technical notes or other documents produced and published in electronic and print formats by governmental agencies, academic institutions and other groups (business and industry) that are not distributed or indexed by commercial publishers.

[3]As a comparison, the GNI of Austria and Belgium was US$ 355 bn and US$ 433 bn respectively, while the GNI of Malaysia and Thailand was US$ 174 bn and US$ 217 bn respectively (World Bank 2009, pp. 352–353).

2009, pp. 352–353). However, due to its large population of around 240 million the country's total emissions are substantial. If emissions from deforestation, forest fires and grassland conversion activities are taken into account, Indonesia is the world's third biggest emitter of GHGs, after China and the US, according to a study commissioned by the World Bank in 2007 (PEACE 2007).

Of an annual output of over three billion tons of CO_2 equivalent, approximately 85% (2,563 $MtCO_2$) stem from land-use change, forestry and conversion activities. Indonesia's total annual emissions from energy, agriculture and waste amount to approximately 451 $MtCO_2e$; equivalent to Germany's allowed cap under the National Allocation Plan (NAP) II between 2008 and 2012, which is 453 $MtCO_2e$ per annum. Even when emissions caused by forests are excluded, Indonesia is the biggest GHG emitter in Southeast Asia and ranks 11th in the world (JICA 2008). Indonesia is therefore also part of the Major Economies Forum on Energy and Climate, launched by the US in 2007 to bring together the world's 17 biggest emitters of GHG.[4]

Indonesia is also likely to be one of the primary victims of climate change, with a recent study by the Asian Development Bank (ADB) identifying Southeast Asia as a region that is more vulnerable to climate change than other regions in the world. The Indonesian archipelago has the second longest shoreline in the world (81,000 km) and is expected to be particularly vulnerable to the consequences of a higher global mean temperature, such as rising sea levels (KLH 2007, p. iii).

More than half of Indonesia's population live less than 25 km from a coastline (World Bank 2009, p. 344) and in some places sea level rises of 8 mm per year have been recorded. Emil Salim, former Indonesian Environment Minister, predicts that Indonesia will lose 20% of its islands. Case et al. (2007) have also identified other impacts of observed and projected climate change in Indonesia including changes in water and food availability, warming sea-surface temperatures with negative impacts on coral reefs, loss of biodiversity and ecosystem services and health impacts such as the spread of vector-borne diseases (e.g. malaria, dengue).

Global climate change models forecast that all parts of Indonesia will face a relatively uniform increase in temperature between 0.1 and 0.3°C per decade over the next 100 years (Case et al. 2007, p. 4). Yet, there are indications that Indonesia may already be feeling the impacts from global warming. For example, in February 2007 Jakarta suffered the worst floods that the country had ever experienced, with flooding in 60% of the Indonesian capital.[5] A study by the Indonesian State Ministry of Environment revealed that flooding in combination with sea level

---

[4]The other 16 major economies and biggest GHG emitters are: Australia, Brazil, Canada, China, the European Union, France, Germany, India, Italy, Japan, Korea, Mexico, Russia, South Africa, the United Kingdom and the United States; see http://georgewbush-whitehouse.archives.gov/news/releases/2007/09/20070927.html.

[5]Agus Sari at the Amsterdam Conference on the Human Dimension of Global Environmental Change, 24 May 2007. For more information on observed and projected climate change as well as its impact in Indonesia see Case et al. (2007).

rise could lead to a permanent inundation of parts of Greater Jakarta, including the international airport, Soekarno-Hatta (Jakarta Post 2009).

Global warming in Indonesia is expected to manifest itself in more severe and frequent weather events, which may trigger economic downturn and rising poverty and thereby impede Indonesia's sustainable development. The ten biggest natural disasters in Indonesia between 1907 and 2007 occurred after 1990 and were mostly weather-related, such as flooding, drought and forest fires. Combined, these events caused economic losses of US$ 26 billion, of which 70% can be solely attributed to the climate (KLH 2007, p. 1). Furthermore, the Singapore-based Economy and Environment Program for Southeast Asia (EEPSEA) reported that of all cities in Southeast Asia, Jakarta is the most vulnerable to the impacts of climate change (Jakarta Post 2009). Hence, Indonesia clearly has a strong interest in the mitigation of GHG that contribute to global warming given the highly detrimental effects for the country.

2.2 The Institutional Setting and Policy Arrangements Related to Climate Change

The State Ministry of Environment (KLH; Kementerian Negara Lingkungan Hidup in Indonesian) was established in 1978, with Emil Salim being its first and longest serving State Minister of Environment to date in Indonesia (1978–1993). Indonesia ratified the UN Framework Convention on Climate Change (UNFCCC) in August 1994, and the Kyoto Protocol in December 2004. As a non-Annex I country, it has no obligation to reduce its GHG emissions. The Convention, however, requires that all non-Annex I countries establish and communicate "a national inventory of anthropogenic emissions" as well as "a general description of steps taken or envisaged by the Party to implement the Convention,"[6] such as actions to mitigate climate change. The country submitted its "First National Communication to the UNFCCC" in October 1999, which draws upon official Indonesian data from 1994 (KLH 1999). Since then, there has been no official data update, but the Second National Communication is currently (as of April 2009) being finalised in Indonesia and expected to be submitted to the UN Climate Secretariat soon.

In December 2007 it became evident that Indonesia is an important player in the fight against climate change, when the country hosted COP13 in Bali, where more than 130 Environment Ministers and over 10,000 participants from all over the world witnessed the adoption of the Bali Road Map. Indonesian President Susilo Bambang Yudhoyono has expressed his commitment to addressing environmental and climate change issues, as reflected in a statement during COP13 where he proclaimed that "there is no need to wait to begin reducing GHG emissions" (Bappenas 2008b, p. 7).

---

[6]Art. 12 para 1(a) and 1(b) KP to the UNFCCC.

The National Council on Climate Change (Dewan Nasional Perubahan Iklim, DNPI) was established in July 2008 based on Presidential Regulation No. 46/2008. The DNPI's tasks are to formulate, monitor and evaluate the implementation of national policies on climate change and coordinate activities related to climate change adaptation, mitigation and financing, and technology transfer.[7] The DNPI is chaired by the Indonesian President and managed by Mr. Rachmat Witoelar, the State Minister of Environment, and is Indonesia's national focal point of global climate negotiations. It is divided into six working groups dealing with issues of adaptation, mitigation, technology transfer, finance, forestry and post-Kyoto aims.

In the Climate Change Performance Index 2009 published by Germanwatch, which takes into consideration absolute emissions as well as trends and climate policy,[8] Indonesia ranks 27th of the 57 countries assessed, ahead of Spain (28th) and the Netherlands (33rd) (Germanwatch 2008, p. 6). The index, however, excludes emissions from deforestation and land use, which Germanwatch estimate to account for about 45% of Indonesia's total emissions.[9] The NGO draws attention to the fact "that these emissions are largely driven by consumption patterns of industrialised and newly industrialised nations" (Germanwatch 2008, p. 9). The Japan International Cooperation Agency (JICA) also emphasises that "Indonesia shows deeper commitment to the climate change issue than other developing countries" (JICA 2008).

Another development indicating Indonesia's commitment to combating global warming is its recent efforts to mainstream climate change. At the COP13 Indonesia launched its National Action Plan for Addressing Climate Change detailing Indonesia's vision to limit climate change and to design and implement a coordinated national policy for this purpose (KLH 2007). The document was prepared under the supervision of KLH but with participation from all relevant ministries. The NAP looks at three major areas: (1) Ways of reducing GHG, (2) adaptation and (3) institutional development. The policies address both global issues (mitigation, adaptation, cross-sectoral aspects), and sector issues (e.g. energy, agriculture, industry and infrastructure). It also highlights the tools available to the government, such as taxation, investment policies, decentralisation and raising awareness.

The NAP has been taken into consideration by the National Development Planning Agency (Bappenas), which incorporated it into the "Yellow Book" released in 2008, National Development Planning: Indonesia's Responses to Climate Change (Bappenas 2008a). This document contains a policy matrix of

---

[7]DNPI meeting in September 2008 in Jakarta.

[8]For a selection of Indonesian climate and energy related policies and measures up to 2006 (incl. transportation, forestry, and clean air) in Indonesia see the website of the World Resources Institute (WRI): http://projects.wri.org/book/export/html/14 or http://projects.wri.org/sd-pams-database/indonesia.

[9]Yet other sources such as the controversial 2007 PEACE study estimate that the share of emissions from deforestation and land use in Indonesia is over 80%.

proposed actions to mainstream climate change into the National Development Plan. The policy matrix lists short, medium and long-term targets and indicators as well as the responsible institutions for the three broad areas of mitigation, adaptation and cross-sectoral issues. Actions and indicators also include the CDM as a crosscutting activity.

The Presidential Decree No. 5/2006 on the National Energy Policy specifies Indonesia's desirable energy mix by 2025. Oil should have a maximum share of 20% (compared to 54% in 2005), natural gas 30% (29% in 2005), coal 33% (14% in 2005), biofuels and geothermal 5% each; other forms of renewable energy should have a share of at least 5% and liquified coal at least 2% (Bappenas 2008a, pp. 22–23). On the one hand, this aspirational energy mix reflects Indonesia's diversity and high potential in non-fossil energy forms whilst at the same time aiming for a huge increase in the share of coal in the energy mix. There are several explanations underpinning this decision: (1) The country wants to reduce its dependency on oil, (2) Indonesia currently produces more than three times the amount of coal that it consumes (BP 2008), and (3) over a third of its population still have no access to electricity (World Bank 2005). The planned doubling of the coal share is worrying with regard to climate change, since coal has the highest carbon emission factor of all fossil fuels with roughly 25 kg carbon per gigajoule (GJ), compared to oil (20 kg/GJ) and natural gas (15 kg/GJ).[10]

3 The Clean Development Mechanism in Indonesia

The following section will look at the development and current state of play of the CDM market in Indonesia and where it stands in the global context. The establishment and work of the Indonesian DNA will be explained, and the potential of CDM in Indonesia as well as the Indonesian CDM project pipeline will be elaborated on.

3.1 Indonesia's CDM Market in Comparison

As of 30 September 2009, Indonesia ranks 9th in the world with regard to the number of projects registered with the UN CDM EB with 30 out of a total of some 1,800 projects (equal to approx. 1.6%) (Table 1) (UNFCCC 2009). Indonesia ranks 10th with regard to the expected average annual CERs (more than 3.6 million, equal to 1.13% of total expected annual CERs) from registered projects.

---

[10] 1 kg of carbon corresponds to 3.67 kg of carbon dioxide; see UNDP (2000, p. 467).

Table 1 Comparison of the CDM market in India, China, Indonesia (as of 30 September 2009) (www.cdm.unfccc.int)

Country	Number of EB registered projects (world total 1,835)	Expected average annual CERs (total 318,942,814)	CERs issued by host party (total 333,068,667)
China	637 (34.71% of total)	188,586,302 (59.13% of total)	153,233,820 (46.01% of total)
India	456 (24.85%)	36,134,925 (11.33%)	71,725,127 (21.53%)
Indonesia	30 (1.63%)	3,609,760 (1.13%)	325,800 (0.10%)

3.1.1 CDM in Indonesia Compared to China, India and Southeast Asia

Many people point to the CDM giants India and China when complaining that Indonesia is lagging behind. However, care must be taken in making those comparisons, since the countries feature different types of industries. For example, India and China have more energy-intensive smelters and coal-fired power plants than Indonesia, and China has lucrative industrial gas projects, such as hydro fluoro carbon (HFC) projects. Since HFC has a global warming potential that is around 12,000 times higher than that of CO_2, it is clear to see why Indonesia does not have the same CER potential as China and India. Also, with Indonesia's DNA established in 2005, the country was a "late bloomer" compared to India (2003) and China.

Compared to other member countries of the ASEAN, Indonesia is the most significant host country for CDM projects in terms of CER potential by 2012 when looking at projects in the pipeline. As far as registered projects are concerned, Malaysia with 65 projects (as of 30 September 2009) and the Philippines with 40 projects registered at the CDM EB rank far ahead of Indonesia with 30 registered projects.[11] However, the expected average annual emissions reductions and thus CERs from these projects are only slightly greater for Malaysia and a lot lower for the Philippines than for Indonesia (Fig. 1).

With regard to the amount of CERs already issued, however, Malaysia, Thailand and even Vietnam with its four registered projects rank ahead of Indonesia. According to one interviewee working in both Indonesia and Malaysia, the Malaysian authorities are more responsive and work faster compared to those in Indonesia which may, in part, explain why it has attracted more CDM projects. It has also been suggested that Malaysia is ahead of Indonesia in the number of EB-registered projects because Malaysia has identified its potential and focussed on it, such that the majority of projects are related to palm oil. By contrast, in Indonesia many report that there is a lot of potential and "we would like to have as many [CDM projects] as possible but we do not focus on the one or two types with the biggest potential,"[12] – a strategy which may deliver better results.

---

[11] Thailand has 24 projects registered with the EB, Vietnam 10, Cambodia 4, and Singapore 1; see UNFCCC (2009).

[12] Interview with Gustya Indriani from the NGO Pelangi.

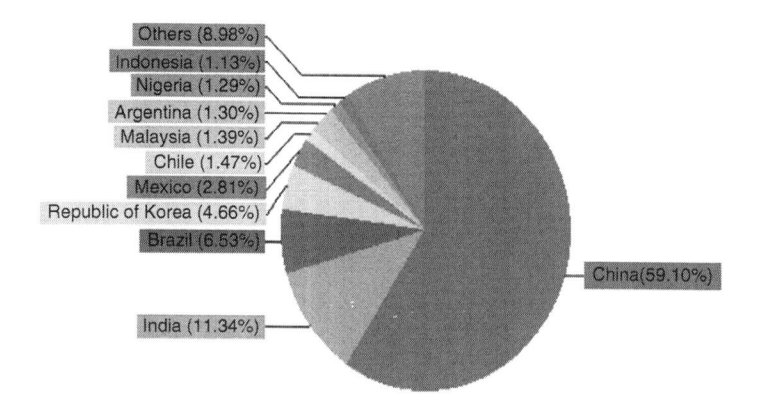

Fig. 1 Share of the CER pie globally

There is currently no accumulated knowledge on CDM in ASEAN, but first steps in that direction are being taken. Theoretically, ASEAN's role in promoting CDM in its member countries could drive clean and green investment in the broad sense. As early as 2004, an ASEAN "Skillshare Workshop" on CDM project development and modes for regional cooperation, as well as a roundtable meeting of representatives from Designated National Authorities in ASEAN member countries, was held at the ASEAN Secretariat in Jakarta (KLH 2005, pp. 23–24). A more recent ASEAN CDM Capacity Building Workshop took place in July 2008 in Bangkok.[13] During this READI Workshop on CDM, success stories, barriers and challenges, as well as the potential role of ASEAN countries in a post-2012 global carbon market were discussed. Interestingly, Liana Bratasida from the Indonesian Ministry of Environment was one of the workshop's key contributors in her different roles as the former chair of the ASEAN Working Group on Multilateral Environmental Agreements, a member of the CDM EB and as a representative from Indonesia.

3.2 The Indonesian Designated National Authority (DNA)

According to UNFCCC requirements, if a non-Annex I country like Indonesia wants to participate in the CDM it has to establish a DNA to approve national CDM project proposals. The initiative to establish the Indonesian DNA started in

---

[13]Personal interview at the ASEAN Secretariat in October 2008.

2003 with the participation of GTZ, CDM expert Axel Michaelowa, and the Indonesian NGO Pelangi. It was not until July 2005, however, that the National Commission for CDM (NC-CDM)[14] was established as the Indonesian DNA by the Minister of Environment Decree 206/2005.[15] The DNA was located at the Ministry of Environment and chaired by the former head of the National Commission for CDM, Mrs. Masnellyarti Hilman. As the CDM is a cross-sectoral issue, DNA members also come from eight other ministries including the Ministry for Energy and Mineral Resources, Ministry of Forestry, the Ministry of Foreign Affairs, the Ministry of Industry, the Ministry of Home Affairs, the National Development Planning Board (Bappenas), the Ministry of Transportation and the Ministry of Agriculture. NGO representatives are also involved. The DNA has technical advisors and consults with external experts on the project proposals.[16] Meetings of the NC-CDM are held at least four times per year and a secretariat deals with everyday business.[17]

Project proponents have to submit their Project Design Documents (PDDs), and may have to attach an environmental assessment report. All CDM project proposals are checked for their consistency with the Sustainable Development Indicators established by the Indonesian DNA. Formally, decisions for and against a project require that at least half of the members or their representatives are present and a majority agreement is reached (Bfai 2008, p. 4). In practice, however, the DNA tries to support the prospective CDM project developers by reminding them of the permits required, both for successful submission and to ensure the project runs smoothly under Indonesian regulations once it comes into operation.[18]

With the recent establishment of the National Council on Climate Change (DNPI), however, there have been institutional changes relating to the Indonesian DNA and today, the DNA is located at the DNPI under the leadership of Mr. Dicky Edwin Hindarto in the DNPI's Financing Working Group.[19] However, the formal procedure for that change has not yet been enacted, thus the Ministerial Decree referred to above will remain valid until replaced by a new decree. There are those, however, that believe the DNPI should not be the institution responsible for CDM and who would have preferred that the DNA remain at KLH.[20]

---

[14]In Bahasa Indonesia the National Commission for CDM is called *Komisi Nasional Mekanisme Pembangunan Bersih* (KOMNAS MPB).

[15]For detailed information on the process of establishing the National Commission for CDM see KLH (2005).

[16]More than 80 local experts are listed as external consultants; see Bfai (2008).

[17]For details on the task, structure, requirements and approval procedures of the DNA, see KLH (2005) or the DNA's website, where a list of the approved projects incl. PDD and status can also be found.

[18]Personal interviews with project developers and DNA staff.

[19]Correspondence with GTZ staff in August 2009.

[20]Personal interview.

3.3 The CDM Potential in Indonesia

As early as 2001, a National Strategy Study on the CDM in Indonesia was conducted by KLH with support from GTZ and the World Bank to look at the theoretical potential of the CDM and the institutional conditions in the country, and to give strategic recommendations for CDM implementation (KLH 2001).

Point Carbon's (2005) country analysis revealed that Indonesia "excels in potential for geothermal power, small hydro and waste biomass from palm oil and forestry operations, and the oil and gas sector could substantially reduce gas flaring. Moreover, Java's large agglomerations could sustain many landfill gas projects. The Active Geothermal Association was the first to recognise the benefits of CDM and has developed several interesting projects, whose additionality is not in doubt" (PDD 2006, p. 14). Point Carbon also assessed that "Indonesia has a relatively vibrant project developer sector, particularly within the energy production industry" (PDD 2006, p. 14).

There is widespread agreement that there are CDM possibilities especially in the renewable energy sector and with energy efficiency projects. According to Gustya Indriani from Pelangi, "a lot of players come from the industry, therefore energy efficiency has a very big potential in Indonesia."[21] In general, however, high-emission heavy industrial companies play a rather small role in Indonesia, unlike in China, which is why the potential CO_2 savings in the industrial sector are rather limited in comparison (Bfai 2008, p. 2). Agus Sari from EcoSecurities also sees great potential for emission reductions in the agro-business, fuels from renewables, and in the oil and gas sector (Sorotan 2008, p. 8).

Numerical estimates of Indonesia's CDM potential vary. However, PEACE (2007) claims that around 235 $MtCO_2e$ could be reduced through CDM projects. This is within the range estimated by the Indonesian Ministry of Environment (125–300 $MtCO_2e$), whilst estimates produced by EcoSecurities suggest higher figures of between 250 and 500 $MtCO_2e$ (Bfai 2008, p. 2).

Even though there is agreement that Indonesia has a lot of CDM potential, there has been criticism by some Indonesian CDM stakeholders that the way this potential is managed needs to be improved. With regard to renewable energy, for example, the promotion, establishment and diffusion of biodiesel, solar and wind energy all need extensive research and effort, yet some feel that the Indonesian government is not giving this issue enough attention. Equally, landfill projects (methane avoidance) are considered to have a big potential owing to their potential contribution towards sustainable development. The question is how Indonesia can use that potential, since from a regulatory point of view there are a lot of technical, bureaucratic and ownership issues. These concern land owners, the land, the rights of local governments and the people living in close vicinity to landfill areas. It is, for instance, debatable as to who owns the CERs if the waste from people in Jakarta

---

[21] Personal interview in September 2008.

goes to landfills in Bekasi, a city on the outskirts of Jakarta, that is managed by the corresponding local government.

The Indonesian company PT. Gikoko Kogyo has been successful in resolving these issues in some of their projects. For example, despite regulatory barriers for landfill projects, Gikoko's Landfill Gas Reduction Project in Bekasi has demonstrated that the successful implementation of a CDM project can also yield multiple sustainable development benefits. This project is exemplary in that it reduces GHG emissions, improves solid waste management and provides funding for local communities in the municipality of Bekasi.[22] The commercial barriers that have previously restricted private sector involvement in solid waste management were removed by entering into a public-private sector partnership between Gikoko and the municipality of Bekasi. Gikoko had already pioneered this private sector approach to investment in municipal solid waste management for the first time in Indonesia through their EB-registered Pontianak CDM project (PDD 2007, p. 2). In the Bekasi project, the municipal government receives a revenue stream from the sales of the CERs, as 10% of the revenue is added to the local budget and an additional 7% goes directly into community development, with the latter being used purely for education and health for the poor. Interestingly, the local communities are to jointly manage the funds, together with the city of Bekasi and the company Gikoko.[23] Therefore, besides reducing emissions and improving solid waste collection and disposal, the CDM project directly involves and provides funds to the community living around the landfill.

Finally, the notion of CDM "potential" has to be considered with care. The hypothetical numbers in studies for potential emission reductions in certain sectors are always based on specific assumptions regarding, for example, future political developments, energy consumption patterns and institutional settings. Fabby Tumiwa, an energy expert who at times also works for the Indonesian DNA, claims that the Indonesian potential is a lot greater than reported figures suggest, as they do not yet contain calculations of the CDM potential related to palm oil.[24] Moreover, it is important to acknowledge that, to date, there have not been any Afforestation and Reforestation CDM projects in Indonesia.

3.4 Indonesian CDM Projects

The calculations and numbers in the following section are mainly based on the UNEP Risoe CDM Pipeline.[25] According to the UNFCCC, each CDM project has

---

[22]Personal interview with John Blair, Gikoko, in October 2008.

[23]PDD (2007, p. 2).

[24]Personal interview with Fabby Tumiwa in October 2008.

[25]The Indonesian National Commission for CDM website also contains a database with an overview and status of the projects submitted to the DNA. However, there seems to be a discrepancy between the total number of projects listed on the DNA website and the higher

to be categorised under at least one of 15 different sectoral scopes. A project, however, can also fall under more than one scope. The UNEP Risoe CDM Pipeline has grouped the projects into 26 different project types, which in their aggregate still correspond to the UNFCCC categorisation.

There are currently (as of 1 September 2009) 94 CDM projects in the Indonesian project pipeline with an estimated potential to reduce around 45 MtCO$_2$e by 2012.[26] Given Indonesia's total estimated CDM potential of around 235 MtCO$_2$e the current Indonesian CDM pipeline taps into just one fifth of this potential. In the global context, Indonesia's share, in terms of numbers of CDM projects in the pipeline, is 2%, whilst expected emission reduction potential is around 1.6%. Interestingly, the National Strategy Study on CDM in Indonesia from 2001 estimated that, for the energy sector, Indonesia's potential global share in the CDM market would be around 2% (range: 1.5–3.5%), generating an expected revenue stream of at least US$ 224 million during the first commitment period (2008–2012) (KLH 2001, pp. xxxi and 52).

From more than 90 projects in the Indonesian pipeline, 55 are at the validation stage, 11 are awaiting registration and 30 are registered with the UN EB. Most of the projects involve methane avoidance,[27] biomass energy and landfill gas (Fig. 2). Given that methane has a global warming potential of more than 21 times that of CO$_2$ it is perhaps not surprising that these three project types, all of which reduce methane, are most common as they will generate most CERs.

However, Fig. 2 also highlights that some project types reduce more GHGs than others. For example, the five geothermal projects, two projects reducing fugitive emissions from fuels and one cement project in the pipeline, are projected to almost avoid the same amount of GHG emissions as would be achieved from over 50 methane avoidance and biomass energy projects (red bars in Fig. 2).

If all of the CDM projects in the pipeline came into existence, they would install an expected 863 megawatts (MW), contributing to the provision of much needed electricity in Indonesia.[28] The CDM project types contributing to this generating capacity are hydro (400 MW), geothermal (318 MW), biomass energy (118 MW), methane avoidance (19 MW) and landfill gas (17 MW) (UNEP 2009).

Of the 30 projects registered (as of 30 September 2009) there are 15 small-scale and 15 large-scale projects. They reduce around 3.34 MtCO$_2$e per year and will yield over 18 million CERs by 2012 if all expected CERs are issued (Fig. 3).

---

number listed in the UNEP Risoe Pipeline. One possible explanation for that difference, other than that the UNFCCC website is -unlike the DNA website- being permanently updated, is that CDM projects may not yet have received the Letter of Approval from the DNA although they are already in the validation process, and therefore appearing on the UNFCCC website. Ulrich Elmar Hansen, UNEP Risoe Centre (personal comment).

[26]These and the following numbers and calculations are based on the UNEP Risoe CDM Pipeline as of 1 Sept. 2009.

[27]This category covers projects producing biogas from manure, wastewater, industrial solid waste, palm oil solid waste, and projects that avoid CH4 by composting or aerobic treatment.

[28]For more information on Indonesia's energy needs see World Bank (2005).

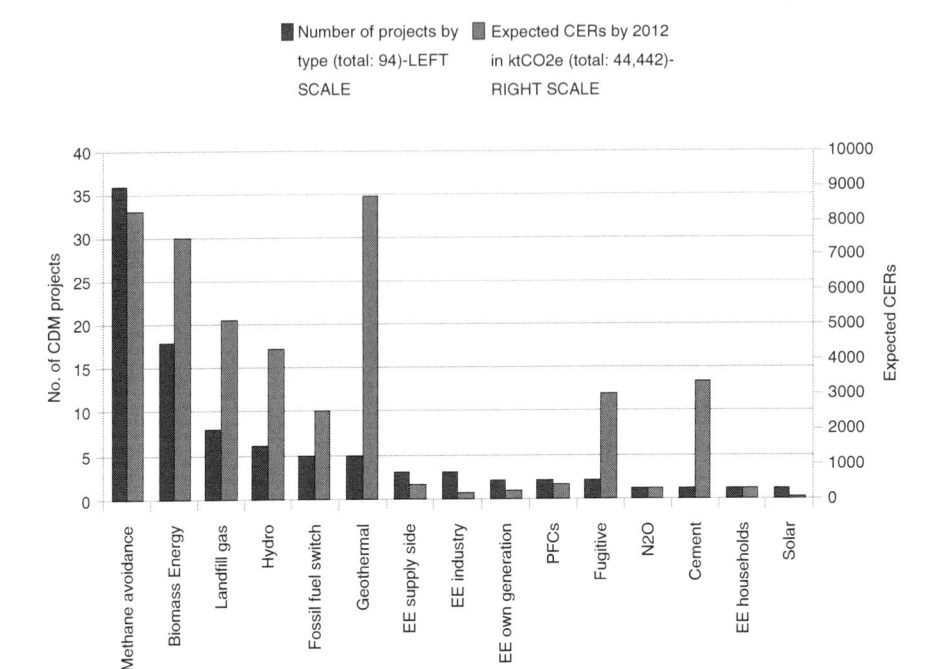

Fig. 2 Number of projects in the Indonesian CDM project pipeline by type vs. expected CERs by 2012 according to project type (UNEP Risoe CDM pipeline, cdmpipeline.org, as of 1 September 2009)

Compared to Indonesia's CDM potential of between 120 and 300 $MtCO_2e$, the expected 18.5 $MtCO_2e$ GHG emission reductions by 2012 seem relatively small.

The majority of registered projects fall into the following sectoral scopes as defined by the UNFCCC: (1) Energy industries (renewable/non-renewable), (13) waste handling and disposal and (4) manufacturing industries (UNFCCC 2009). As was the case with the complete Indonesian CDM project pipeline, biomass energy, methane avoidance and landfill gas projects are still the most common project types among the EB registered projects despite the fact that one cement and one geothermal project combined are expected to achieve almost 40% of the projected 18.5 MtCO2e emission reductions.

So far, only six of 30 projects (of which four were registered in 2006, two in 2008) have received CERs, corresponding to 326,000 t of abated CO_2e. For three of those projects, however, the issuance success (amount of expected CERs compared to the CERs finally issued), was very low at just 12% for the Methane Capture and Combustion from Swine Manure Treatment Project, 18% for the Aceh Solar Cooker Project and 31% for the Indocement Alternative Fuel Project. The Darajat Unit III Geothermal Project and the MEN-Tangerang 13.6 MW Natural Gas Co-generation Project achieved higher issuance success with 65% and 79% respectively. The Tambun LPG Associated Gas Recovery and Utilization Project, on the other hand,

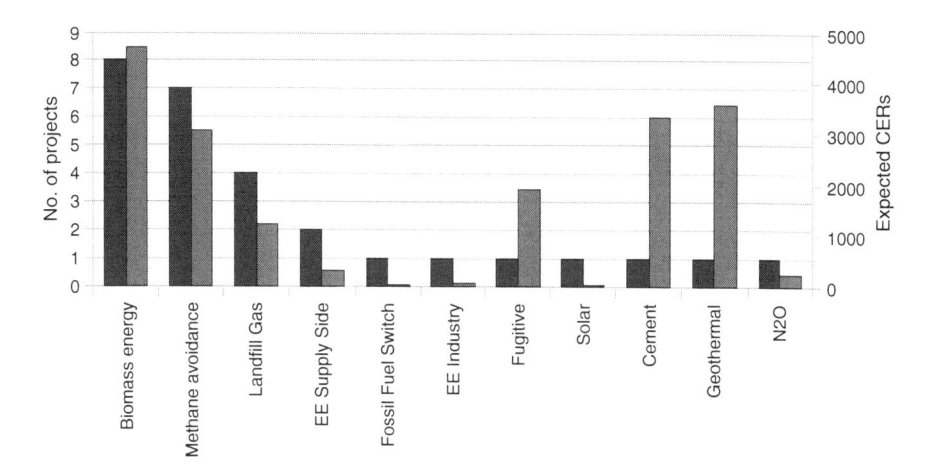

Fig. 3 Number of registered Indonesian CDM projects by type vs. expected CERs by 2012 according to project type (Data from the UNEP Risoe CDM pipeline, cdmpipeline.org, as of 1 September 2009)

received more CERs than expected with an issuance success rate of 154%, higher than the global average of 114% for projects mitigating fugitive emissions from fuels (UNEP 2009). The Indonesian solar project was the first and to this day only CDM solar project worldwide that received CERs. Therefore, a comparison with the global average issuance success rate of similar projects is not possible. As for the other projects, the Indocement Alternative Fuel project significantly underperformed compared to the global average of 89% for biomass energy projects, while the MEN-Tangerang Natural Gas Co-generation project corresponds almost exactly to the global average of 79% for energy efficiency supply side projects.

To date, 17 Indonesian CDM project proposals have been rejected by Designated Operational Entities (DOEs) and one Indonesian CDM project, the PAA Biogas Extraction Project for Heat Generation, was rejected by the EB in October 2008 on the grounds of failure to prove additionality.[29]

---

[29] The EB "could not register the project activity submitted for registration by the DOE (JQA) because the project participant and the DOE failed to substantiate the additionality of the project activity, in particular, by changing the input values of investment analysis submitted in response to the review from those contained in the PDD without any justification, and failure of the DOE to assess the impact of these changes on the additionality of the project." See: http://cdm.unfccc.int/Projects/DB/JQA1205142016.76/Rejection/.

3.5 Selected Players in the Indonesian CDM Market

There are established and well-known players in the Indonesian CDM market, such as the brokers and consultancies Ecosecurities, South Pole and Asia Carbon. The following section identifies other key players and briefly reflects on their contributions and activities.

The most prominent DOEs in Indonesia are DNV (14 of the 30 EB registered projects) and TÜV Süd (9 of the 30 registered projects). If one takes into account the whole Indonesian CDM project pipeline, which includes another 55 projects at validation stage and 11 projects requesting registration, other validators like TÜV Nord, TÜV Rheinland, SGS, LRQA and JQA are also playing an important role (UNEP 2009).

The NGO Pelangi has worked on climate change-related topics since it was founded in 1992, and has been involved in CDM issues from around 2000 when it was the only local organisation working on CDM. Gustya Indriani from Pelangi summarises: "We acted as consultants, as researchers and also as advisors to the government and stakeholders."[30] In the beginning, the focus was on awareness-raising and capacity-building for all stakeholders in the CDM and Pelangi has also supported the establishment of the Indonesian DNA. When Agus Sari (now Indonesian Country Director of EcoSecurities) became Pelangi's director, he decided that climate change would form Pelangi's core remit together with energy and transportation. More recently, Pelangi's portfolio has been expanded to air quality and technology transfer issues. Since 2005, Pelangi has focused on research and policy advocacy and is no longer involved in CDM consultancy. They are, however, working with the community to develop several small CDM-like projects for the voluntary market.

The NGO CER Indonesia (Carbon and Environmental Research Indonesia) focuses on mitigation activities in the energy, waste, and forestry sectors. They conduct CDM-training and studies on CDM-related policies, write PDDs and carry out asset-mapping for potential CDM-projects in the regions.[31] The importance of NGOs for CDM-assistance has been acknowledged by Masnellyarti Hillman, (former) head of Indonesia's National Commission on CDM.[32]

Japan's Institute for Global Environmental Strategies' (IGES)[33] engagement in Indonesia with regard to CDM has proved a success story. With its Integrated Capacity Strengthening for CDM Project in Indonesia (2004–2009), which included the development of a CDM Country Guide for Indonesia (IGES 2006),

---

[30]Personal interview in September 2008.

[31]Personal communication with Syahrina D. Anggraini (Programme Director CER Indonesia) in December 2008.

[32]Masnellyarti Hillman at the workshop "Financial Policies and Incentives for Climate Mitigation Action and Opportunities for Further Development in Indonesia" in Jakarta in July 2008.

[33]The research institute IGES was established in 1998 by the Japanese government.

IGES has certainly strengthened capacity.[34] Evidence of this is provided by the example of Gikoko, a company that is now active in the Indonesian CDM market, which first learned about CDM in a workshop organised by IGES in 2004.[35] IGES' success can be attributed to its cooperation with local institutions and experts, especially KLH (the Ministry of Environment), and the NGOs YBUL (Yayasan Bina Usaha Lingkungan) and CER Indonesia.

The World Bank, a key actor in the governance of clean development on a global scale, has a carbon finance focal point in Indonesia and the Prototype Carbon Fund has acted as a PDD consultant for several Indonesian CDM projects, a couple of which have not only been registered at the EB but also been issued CERs. The World Bank also funded the controversial PEACE study (2007) and conducted workshops on CDM in Indonesia. The World Bank Indonesia is involved in the preparation of several other studies focussed on barriers to CDM implementation in Indonesia, and the production of clean technology by APEC countries.[36] Furthermore, the Indonesian Ministry of Trade has asked the World Bank to examine Indonesia's potential to develop as a producer of climate-friendly goods and services and to assess whether current trade policies encourage or hinder the diffusion of clean technologies. Another World Bank study will look at Indonesia's position in the international negotiations concerning the liberalisation of environmentally-friendly goods and services.

The United Nations Development Programme (UNDP) in collaboration with Fortis Bank has sought to mobilise the benefits of carbon finance for the developing world through the MDG Carbon Facility, which was launched in June 2007 and operates within the CDM framework. This mechanism is designed to support the development and the commercialisation of emission reduction projects. The focus lies on the promotion of projects that contribute to the Millennium Development Goals (MDGs), yielding sustainable development and poverty reduction benefits.[37] In general, UNDP is supposed to work closely with UNEP and the World Bank on capacity development for CDM, as articulated in the Nairobi Framework and in the Partnership Agreement between UNEP and UNDP on climate change (UNDP 2008). Interestingly, the UNDP representative and Carbon Focal Point in Indonesia comes from an investment banking background and seems to look at CDM from a business rather than a development perspective,[38] something that Pelangi has experienced first hand. UNDP states that the MDG Carbon Facility's purpose is to support projects that would otherwise not be pursued due to their inherent risks or low profitability. During Pelangi's discussions with UNDP Indonesia, however, it

---

[34] IGES was honourably mentioned several times by my interviewees. An overview of IGES' activities in Indonesia can be accessed at http://www.iges.or.jp/en/cdm/indonesia.html.

[35] Joseph Hwang from Gikoko in a DPNI meeting in September 2008.

[36] Interview and communication with staff of the World Bank Indonesia Office between September 2008 and March 2009.

[37] See http://www.mdgcarbonfacility.org/.

[38] Personal interview in August 2008.

became obvious that UNDP wanted to have projects with a reduction potential of at least 100,000 t of CO_2e per year. Pelangi was rather incredulous about that requirement, as it would involve dealing with a big company[39] in order to achieve emissions reductions on such a scale. Pelangi, on the other hand, is trying to reduce poverty in Indonesia through its work on small-scale projects.

The ADB's Carbon Market Initiative aims to provide upfront co-financing for CDM project preparation and implementation. ADB achieves this through the Asia Pacific Carbon Fund, the Technical Support Facility and the Credit Marketing Facility.[40] In July 2008, ADB also announced its new Future Carbon Fund, which will use carbon credits generated beyond 2012 to help finance clean energy projects.[41] Although ADB published an extensive Country Environment Analysis of Indonesia in 2005 and has been trying to set up an energy efficiency fund similar to the one in Thailand, it seems to be relatively quiet on the CDM front (ADB 2005 and interview data).

3.6 Recent Developments and Trends in the Indonesian CDM Market

The CDM community in Indonesia is rather small, and most players in the market know each other, with CDM-related workshops and events feeling rather like a "family reunion" of Indonesian CDM players.[42] At the beginning of CDM development in Indonesia, there were still regular discussions with various CDM stakeholders. Liana Bratasida, the former Indonesian alternate member of the EB, usually convened those meetings before and after EB meetings "just to update each other."[43] Since then, the CDM in Indonesia has grown and produced a lot of new CDM consultants, and no such regular meetings take place anymore. The idea of establishing an Indonesian CDM Business Association to unite CDM stakeholders and exchange information was launched in autumn 2008 by EcoSecurities and South Pole in cooperation with the GTZ. However, as of late August 2009, there has been no reported progress on its implementation.

The fact that there is less regular exchange among the CDM community may also be attributed to fiercer competition between project developers. "Sometimes, the consultants have to draw a line, because even though the potential is big in Indonesia, the number of projects that could be developed and the number of

---

[39]Personal interview with staff at Pelangi in September 2009.
[40]See http://www.adb.org/clean-energy/cmi.asp.
[41]See http://www.adb.org/media/Articles/2008/12516-asian-carbon-funds/.
[42]Personal interviews.
[43]Personal interview with Gustya Indriani from Pelangi.

companies that are really interested in getting involved with CDM are not that large and not that easy to find," reports Gusyta Indriani from Pelangi.[44]

The CDM market in Indonesia has gained considerable momentum since 2008. One indication of this is that the DNA approved 46 projects in 2008, compared to 13 projects in 2007, six projects in 2006 and five projects in 2005 (IGES 2009). There has been a growing interest in the Indonesian CDM market from various stakeholders, highlighted for example by the fact that CDM consultancies are hiring more staff. Most interviewees involved in the Indonesian CDM are optimistic and some even describe the CDM opportunities in Indonesia as "great" or "fantastic"[45] and acknowledge an exponential acceleration of developments in the CDM market. Bigger companies, especially foreign investors, are also increasingly interested and active in the Indonesian CDM market (Sorotan 2008). The Indonesian-German Chamber of Industry and Commerce (Ekonid), for example, devoted a 2008 edition of their magazine "Sorotan" to the topics of CDM and energy in Indonesia, entitled More (Cleaner) Energy for Indonesia. It was even mentioned in an interview that although a company might potentially only receive a thousand CERs, they are still interested in CDM for image reasons.

Government entities have also shown interest in learning about carbon financing and the CDM. The Indonesian Ministry of Finance, for example, in collaboration with the World Bank held a series of weekly meetings in the second half of 2008 during which different stakeholders in carbon finance gave expert talks and exchanged views about specific issues. This was seen as a way of enhancing knowledge about the carbon market as well as potential fiscal and financial implications and opportunities for Indonesia. Whilst this has been perceived as a positive step, there remains some scepticism regarding the opportunities associated with the CDM among some members of the Ministry of Finance.[46]

GTZ and other development agencies in Indonesia, such as the United States Agency for International Development (USAid), who have not done anything related to CDM up to now, also recognise its potential. As Suzanne Billharz of USAid put it: "We are aware and informed about its use as a financing tool for lowering carbon emissions. [The CDM] will be taken into account as part of USAid's Global Climate Change assessment, which will shape the mission's strategy for 2009–2013."[47]

Under the auspices of the State Ministry of National Development Planning (Bappenas), the Indonesian Climate Change Trust Fund (ICCTF) was established and launched on 14 September 2009 to mobilise, pool and coordinate the required funding for mitigation and adaptation programmes in Indonesia in the short,

---

[44]Personal interview.

[45]Various personal interviews.

[46]Personal discussion with staff of the Ministry of Finance in October 2008.

[47]Statement by Suzanne Billharz, USAid, in August 2008, passed on through personal communication by Walter North, USAid Mission Director in Indonesia.

medium and long term.[48] The ICCTF is designed to "bridge international financial resources with national investment strategies" (ICCTF 2009). One of the more specific objectives of the ICCTF is to "facilitate private sector investment in climate change" (ICCTF 2009), although they do not explicitly state whether this will involve supporting CDM projects. The strategies and priority areas to be funded through the ICCTF are defined by the 20 Year Indonesian Climate Change Sectoral Roadmap (20-ICCSR), which has identified the energy sector, including renewable energies and energy efficiency, as a main priority for mitigation.[49] It remains to be seen if and to what extent CDM might be affected through the ICCTF.

4 Outlook

It remains to be seen what effect the move of the DNA from the State Ministry of Environment (KLH) to the National Council on Climate Change (DNPI) will have, and if it becomes the "CDM acceleration unit" that Indonesia hopes for. Currently, the DNPI still does not have the legal status that would make it a strong and fully operational institution and a number of issues between the DNPI, Bappenas and the Ministry of Environment are yet to be resolved.

The 2007 National Action Plan Addressing Climate Change set the benchmark of a 400% increase in the number of CDM projects approved by the Indonesian DNA by 2009, compared to 2007 (24 projects). Interestingly, the policy matrix in the NAP has the aim of "doubling the number of CDM projects from the previous period" for the three time frames 2009–2012, 2012–2025 and 2025–2050 (KLH 2007). This suggests that Indonesia not only sees the CDM as a valuable tool, but also that the country is confident that the CDM will remain an integral part of any Post-Kyoto Agreement to be approved in December 2009 in Copenhagen. Recently, hope for new impetus in the Indonesian CDM market has been placed on the concepts of the programmatic CDM/Programme of Activities and the sectoral approach, since the former could help projects especially those on the local level to come into existence. But to date, no concrete results have materialised.

Given the fact that most buyers of Indonesian CDM credits are from Japan, Switzerland, the Netherlands and the UK, it will be interesting to see the effects of changes in the global carbon market, especially that of the EU ETS on the Indonesian CDM market. For example, in its communication of January 2009, the European Commission suggests that "for advanced developing countries and highly competitive economic sectors, the project-based CDM should be phased out in favour of moving to a sectoral carbon market crediting mechanism" (European Commission 2009, p. 11). Yet at the time of writing, there was still no clear

---

[48]The detailed design of the ICCTF is contained in the ICCTF Blueprint document, which is available on the ICCTF website: http://icctf.org/.

[49]Communication from Syamsidar Thamrin, Bappenas, in September 2009.

definition of an "advanced developing country" and "highly competitive economic sectors," so it is uncertain to what extent Indonesia should be concerned about whether the European Commission's suggestions are to be enforced.

References

ADB (2005) Indonesia: country environment analysis. http://www.adb.org/Documents/CEAs/INO/INO-CEA-Aug2005.pdf. Accessed Aug 2005

Bappenas (2008a) National development planning: Indonesia responses to climate change. Bappenas, Jakarta

Bappenas (2008b) Mainstreaming climate change into national development planning. Presentation at the kick-off meeting of Asia pacific gateway to climate change and development, Bangkok, http://www.climateanddevelopment.org/pdf/kickoff_2-1-4_BAPPENAS.pdf. Accessed 23 April 2008

Bfai (Bundesagentur für Außenwirtschaft)/DEG (Deutsche Investitions- und Entwicklungsgesellschaft mbH) (2008) CDM-Market Brief Indonesia. http://www.kyoto-coaching-cologne.net/publikationen/CDM-Indonesien-Endversion-englisch.pdf. Accessed Jan 2008

BP (2008) BP statistical review of world energy June 2008. BP, London

Case M, Ardiansyah F, Spector E (2007) Climate change in Indonesia. Implications for humans and nature. World Wide Fund for Nature (WWF). http://www.worldwildlife.org/climate/Publications/WWFBinaryitem7664.pdf

European Commission (2009) Communication from the commission to the European parliament, the council, the European economic and social committee and the committee of the regions. Towards a comprehensive climate change agreement in Copenhagen. Brussels, COM (2009) 39 final. ec.europa.eu/environment/climat/pdf/future_action/communication_en.pdf. Accessed 28 Jan 2009

Germanwatch (2008) The climate change performance index. Results 2009. Germanwatch, Bonn

ICCTF (2009) Indonesia climate change trust fund (ICCTF). Information brochure published by Bappenas in cooperation with GTZ, April 2009

IGES (2009) CDM country fact sheet: Indonesia. http://enviroscope.iges.or.jp/modules/envirolib/upload/984/attach/indonesia_final.pdf. Accessed Feb 2009

IGES (2006) CDM country guide for Indonesia, 2nd edn. Ministry of the Environment, Japan

Jakarta Post (2009) Jakarta 'most at risk' of climate change. Article by Adianto P. Simamora. http://www.thejakartapost.com/news/2009/01/23/jakarta-%E2%80%98most-risk%E2%80%99-climate-change.html. Accessed 23 Jan 2009

JICA (Japan International Cooperation Agency) (2008) JBIC signs japanese ODA loan agreement with Indonesia. Press release NR/2008-43, http://www.jica.go.jp/english/news/jbic_archive/autocontents/english/news/2008/000105/. Accessed 2 Sept 2008

KLH (Kementerian Lingkungan Hidup; Indonesian State Ministry of Environment) (2007) National action plan addressing climate change. KLH, Jakarta

KLH (2005) Promoting sustainable development in the clean development mechanism in Indonesia: building the national commission for CDM. Final report on the CDM institution building project by KLH, GTZ, Pelangi, HWWA. KLH, Jakarta

KLH (2001) National strategy study on the clean development mechanism in Indonesia. KLH, Jakarta

KLH (1999) First national communication to the UNFCCC. KLH, Jakarta. http://unfccc.int/resource/docs/natc/indonc1.pdf

Kollmuss A, Lazarus M, Lee C, Polycarp C (2008) A review of offset programs: trading systems, funds, protocols, standards and retailers. Version 1.1 October 2008. Stockholm Environment Institute (SEI), Stockholm

Mining Journal (2009) Indonesian coal slows. http://www.mining-journal.com/mining-journal-issues/march-6-2009. Accessed 6 Mar 2009

OECD (2008a) OECD economic outlook. Indonesia, p. 142. Preliminary version. http://www.oecd.org/dataoecd/39/52/41713000.pdf

OECD (2008b) Economic assessment of Indonesia. http://www.oecd.org/document/57/0,3343, en_2649_34111_41014713_1_1_1_1,00.html

PDD (Project Design Document) (2007) Pontianak – GHG emission reduction through improved MSW management – LFG capture, flaring and electricity generation. http://cdm.unfccc.int

PDD (2006) Darajat unit III geothermal project. document version number 3. 14 September 2006. http://cdm.unfccc.int

PEACE (2007) Indonesia and climate change: current status and policies. PEACE, Jakarta

Sorotan (2008) The magazine of the Indonesian-German chamber of commerce and industry. Vol. XVII/1/2008. Ekonid, Jakarta

UNDP (2008) Climate change at UNDP: scaling up to meet the challenge. UNDP Environment & Energy Group, New York

UNDP (2000) World energy assessment: energy and the challenge of sustainability. UNDP, New York

UNEP Risoe Centre on Energy, Climate and Sustainable Development (2009) CDM pipeline; as of 1 September 2009. Monthly updated CDM analysis and database. www.cdmpipeline.org

UNFCCC (2009) CDM website. www.cdm.unfccc.int

World Bank (2009) World development report 2009: reshaping economic geography. International Bank for Reconstruction and Development, The World Bank, Washington

World Bank (2005) Electricity for all: options for increasing access in Indonesia. World Bank East Asia and Pacific Region Energy and Mining Unit and World Bank Office Jakarta

AVR. 2013

CW01180402

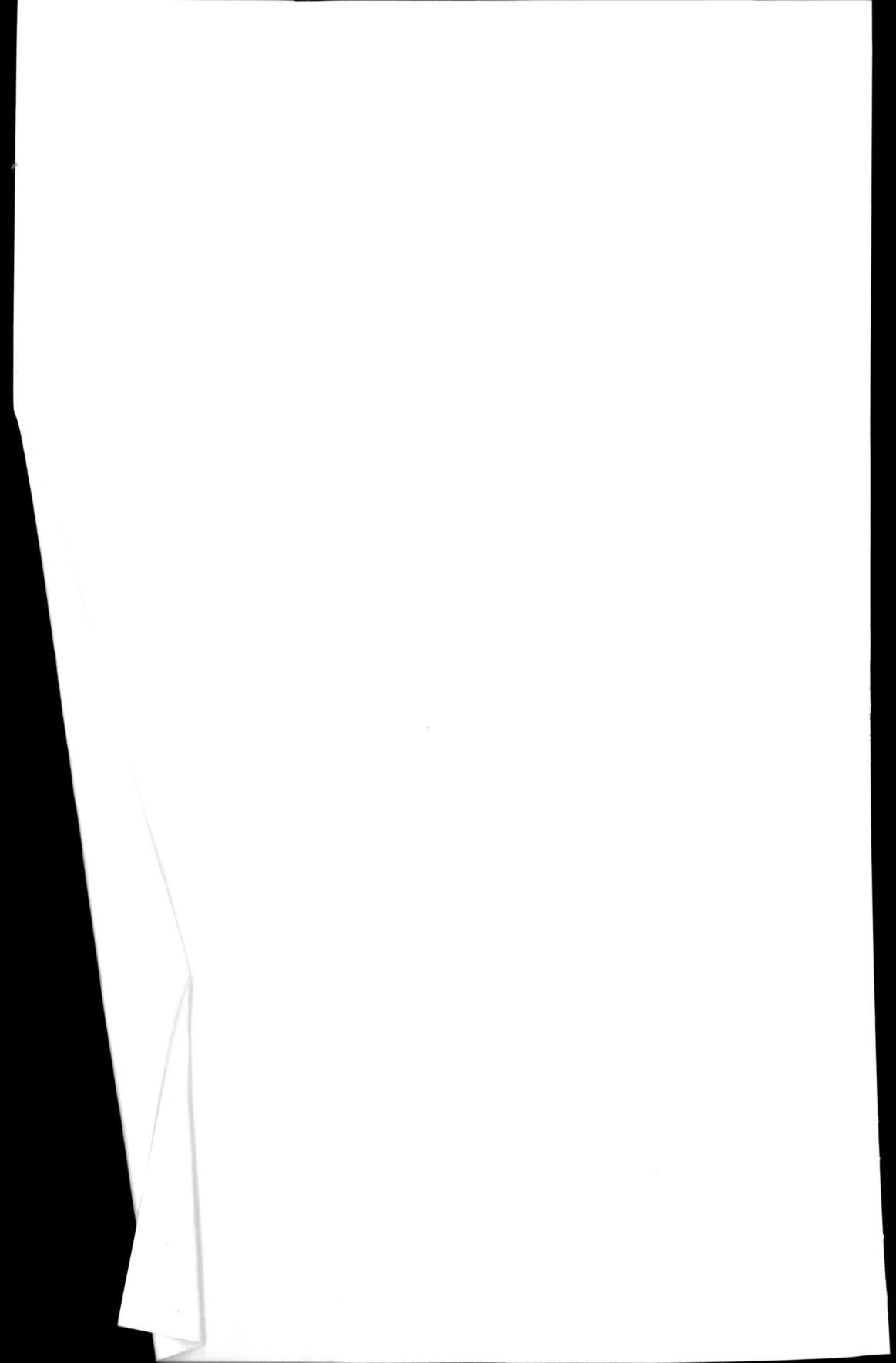

PRODIGAL SONGS

by

Derek Hassack

To Kiri
Everything happens for
a reason :)

Derek x

An Authors OnLine Book

Text Copyright © Derek Hassack
Cover design by © Jamie Day

All rights reserved. No part of this publication may be reproduced, stored in a retrieval system, or transmitted in any form or by any means, electronic, mechanical, photocopy, recording or otherwise, without prior written permission of the copyright owner. Nor can it be circulated in any form of binding or cover other than that in which it is published and without similar condition including this condition being imposed on a subsequent purchaser.

British Library Cataloguing Publication Data.
A catalogue record for this book is available from the British Library

ISBN 978-07552-0630-8

Authors OnLine Ltd
19 The Cinques
Gamlingay, Sandy
Bedfordshire SG19 3NU
England

This book is also available in e-book format, details of which are available at www.authorsonline.co.uk

For Mum and Dad

Acknowledgements

Many people have contributed to *Prodigal Songs*, over a period of years. Not many of them know they have done so.

It would of course be ideal to mention all those who have had some input, directly or indirectly. For example, everyone whom I have loved, and who has shown me love, should get a mention here. However the list would of course be unwieldy, and in any case I would almost certainly omit someone by virtue of my memory, which is distinctly human in its frailty.

So I'll confine myself to acknowledging here those who have made a specific contribution in some way (even if an unwitting one) to the creation/publication of the book itself - those who have given me feedback on some aspect of its content, and/or have offered editorial suggestions and/or, perhaps most valuable of all, have expressed encouragement to continue and complete.

Lion-heartfelt thanks therefore to: Dorothy Atcheson, Marie Batey, Caroline Burr, Juliet Fallowfield, Corrina Gordon-Barnes, Steve James, Julius Lang, Lisa Mitchell, and Sauniere. Much gratitude also to the good people at *Authors OnLine*, in particular Jamie and Gaynor.

Preface

A typical definition of the word 'prodigal' is as follows:

Prodigal: *adj. 1. given to extravagant expenditure; recklessly wasteful 2. of things or actions: wastefully lavish 3. lavish in the bestowal or disposal of things (*Shorter Oxford English Dictionary 3rd ed. 1973)

However, perhaps because it is nowadays almost uniquely used with reference to the Biblical parable *The Prodigal Son*, the word tends to have a broader meaning than that which this definition suggests. For in the parable, the son's prodigality encompasses more than just material possessions or 'things'. The lost son, as he's sometimes known, is wasteful not just of material things and the money he is given, and not even just of his talents. He's wasteful of much more: love, for example, and time, his time on earth as a human being. In being wasteful to this degree, he puts himself at risk of not being the man he could be. He is at risk of wasting his entire life. Thus his subsequent redemption and return to the father figure symbolise his discovery of a meaningful existence.

It's this life-or-death sense of 'prodigal' which the OED doesn't quite seem to capture, but which underscores the use of the word in this book.

Contents

Contents	vi
Introduction	vii
1. Arriving	1
2. Learning	9
3. Feeling	16
4. Moving	19
5. Loving: first steps	25
6. Singing	31
7. Wandering	43
8. Beehiving	53
9. Loving: the promise	59
10. Being Two of Me	81
11. Being One of Me	91
12. Fathering	101
13. Gremlins	107
14. Epiphanies	111
15. Unfolding	119
17. On Being 'Late'	137
Afterwords	141

Introduction

The act of writing has long been a sanctuary for me. Since childhood, I have been able to lose myself in the production of words on a page to such an extent that time has no impact. All other concerns seem to float, powerless, on the extreme fringes of my awareness. In effect, when I am concentrated on writing, self-consciousness loses its grip.

This phenomenon, common to most of us in relation to one activity or another, has always reassured me that writing is one of the things that I should be doing with my life.

From a young age, perhaps six or seven years old, I've made time to scribble words in one format or another: the phrases, poems, short stories and diaries of my youth extended in adult years to include songs, articles, essays, plays, reports, travelogues and, once, a completed novel.

As a teenager, and beyond, I dreamed of being 'a writer', in particular a novelist. I fantasised about emulating my literary heroes, the identities of whom have necessarily changed over time as my own interests have expanded: Isaac Asimov became Henry Miller became Doris Lessing became John Updike, to name a few.

My ambitions in this respect were however formulated quite loosely. Few have been the occasions when I've made a serious, focused effort on getting something of mine published. It's true that I've written professionally, as a free-lance journalist for example. And as a songwriter I've performed a number of my own compositions to small audiences, and have one set of recorded songs on CD.

However, the vast bulk of my written output has been unpublished and, more importantly, un-seen and un-read by others. I haven't had a novel published, and the few newspaper and magazine articles of mine that have been printed hardly constitute a major oeuvre. I can't lay claim with any seriousness to having fulfilled that teenage dream.

And yet I **have** written – millions of words in fact, most of which lie scattered on myriad sheets of paper, in note-books, ring-binders or stored in files on at least two computers and three USB pen drives! Some of my output has been lost over the years, lost forever – thrown out, torn up, mislaid. Years ago, in a fit of frustration and self-reproach, I set fire to the one novel I've so far completed, and reduced it to ashes in a Sussex fireplace.

In more recent times, the propensity to write has been the subject of much reflection on my part. What does it mean that for all the words I've produced, I haven't become a professional writer? What is my writing for, what purpose does it serve? What purpose could it serve in the future? Has my output to date been a waste? Have I been prodigal with a talent? Is it a talent at all, or just a delusion? And, most importantly, what do I do **now** with my desire to write? What should I make of it?

"*Prodigal Songs*' is the first answer to all these questions. It represents my intention to make something coherent out of what so far has been largely amorphous. It starts to give shape to my creative output, at the same time as reassuring myself, and others, that all that has gone before has not been wasted.

On the contrary, all that has gone before has, I now see, been building up to this point. The past has been preparation for the present. This makes '*Prodigal Songs*' the culmination of my creative life to date, as well as the foundation for what follows in the future.

And as I hope you'll see as you read through the book, I've come to understand that the future is a very exciting place.

***

'*Prodigal Songs*' started life as a collection of poetry. The original intention was to bring together in one place as many of my poems as I could find and which were, I considered, worthwhile. However, as the project unfolded, and as I began to perceive more clearly its place and function, I also came to understand that the book didn't have to be 'published', in the normal sense of the word. I didn't need to meet the criteria of any literary agent or publishing house. The project is not about making money or a name for myself. It's about saying something to those who might be interested in hearing it.

I therefore decided at an early stage that I would publish the book myself – with the help of a professional publishing company of course - and that it would by default be a limited edition, at least in the first instance.

This was a liberating decision. It immediately freed me from having to stick to conventional literary genres. I felt more able to play, to be true to my own creative instincts, rather than be confined by the expectations of others.

The explicit result of this is that the scope of *Prodigal Songs* is no longer confined to poetry alone: it also incorporates song lyrics (printed inside bordered pages for easy recognition), and a number of autobiographical prose sections. The book also includes a piece about the Biblical parable commonly known as *the Prodigal Son*, as well as some more general thoughts and perspectives.

As the project unfolded I found that the autobiographical strand started to become increasingly prominent. This in turn affected the book's overall shape and content. The upshot is that most, though not all, of the poems included have been completed relatively recently – within the last five years or so – even if, as is the case with several of them, an initial version may have been written significantly earlier. For my poetry is often subject to an ongoing editing process – which can sometimes start to become a kind of obsessive, habitual tweaking. I suppose this is probably because there has been no formal publication date for them – until now. The songs however have tended to remain in their original condition, presumably because most have been performed and/or recorded soon after inception. These therefore are dated; the poems, mostly, are not.

There is an arc of meaning across the book - a kind of beginning, middle and end – which also dictates to a certain extent the final content. However, as with all creative endeavour the meaning of the book, and of any element within it, is owned wholly by the reader – you! You will take from *Prodigal Songs* what you will. My role has been to write the words, and to put them in a particular order to my own satisfaction. Your role is to make your own understanding of them. In doing that, you will, I sincerely hope, come to a perception of me which is at least in partial accordance with my own.

Having said that, it's also true that there will always be a gap in meaning between what I know and want to write, and what you actually come to understand by what I write. In that respect, all art is always prodigal to some degree.

1. Arriving

All which is temporary is only a symbol
Goethe

I was, I'm reliably informed, late for my arrival. Being several days beyond the scheduled delivery date, my mother - no doubt exasperated by my persistent clinging on inside her womb - employed a typical 'make do and mend' post-war approach to remedy the situation. She chose to increase her levels of physical activity, with a view to kick-starting labour.

Now, she might have gone for a long walk, or perhaps cleaned the windows or such like. However I suspect that a walk might have taken her too far from the security of familiar neighbours and, therefore, the ability to make a quick call to the doctor. And I have little doubt that the windows were already sparkling, along with every inch of wall, paintwork, kitchen item, piece of furniture, nook and cranny in the entire house on Marathon Avenue, Douglas, Isle of Man, the then family home. So instead, my Mum took a more radical approach to the task of getting me shunted out and into the world.

She started to move large items of furniture.

Legend has it that it was the wardrobe that did the trick, although there are no medical records to confirm this hypothesis. Whatever it was, mahogany or oak or pine, with doors or drawers or legs, polished, planed or natural, what was incontrovertible was that something indeed initiated the physiological process of the onset of labour. Waters were spilled, contractions commenced, and soon after, a screaming, red-faced, messy little pink-ish lump emerged into the light.

So 'I' began in the early hours of 21st June 1955.

I've often found it curious that my first moment, like yours, was immediately preceded by a moment when 'I' was not – at least not in that distinct, individuated sense. Whether time will provide the reverse in perfect symmetry remains to be seen. The issue of life-after-death has always been a focus for wonder. "What will I become", we enquire, "if anything at all?"

Sometimes it seems ridiculous that our perspective on the issue of death and the hereafter should shape to such a significant degree our perspective on life. If, before I was born, I had somehow been asked "What do you believe life will be like?" - what possible answer could I have given? How does one describe what it is like to be alive? More especially, how would we describe it to someone who had never experienced it?

Bearing this in mind, do we really think that answering the same question about the after-life could be any more meaningful?! No, there can be no realistic description of life-after-death. Not only do we not have the terms of reference available to us here in this four-dimensional box of existence that could do justice to the experience of not-being-alive, but also, I suspect, not-being-alive-in-this-physical-manifestation is a different experience for each and every one of us.

Just like life.

In any case, like most of us, I have no conscious memory of crossing that greatest of all divides, between being conjoined and being distinct. It must have been a strange experience. I'm told I cried like a baby. And who wouldn't? After all, I had been forcibly ejected from Eden, and was now naked and separate in the universe. Something worth wailing about I think!

So in fact my physical life - in common with the rest of our species through all time - started with a great blessing: a moment of forgetting. In some respects it can be argued that one of life's purposes may be to compensate for that particular memory-loss. We are driven to search for an understanding of what happened when the organically attached growth that is an embryo became a distinct individual person who is apparently much more than just flesh and bone. We are driven to wonder where we actually come from, in the certain knowledge that 'from the womb' isn't answer enough.

***

The phenomenon of 'being late' has been a cornerstone of my life to date. This is not to say that I'm someone who is persistently late for appointments or such like. Far from it: I have long been the kind of person who will be an hour early for a meeting or a date or a train rather than one minute late. I will sit alone in waiting rooms or in the car or wherever those who are early sit, rather than risk arriving even a few moments after the appointed starting time.

This can seem a little obsessive at times, and probably is so, but the characteristic is rooted, at its deepest foundation, in an unshakeable desire to not miss out, to not miss something because I wasn't there.

When I was perhaps thirteen or fourteen years old, I had a dream which I've never forgotten:

I am at school. Nearby, a rocket is going to take off and fly to outer space. Only selected boys are able to go on the trip. The list of the chosen few is posted on a notice-board, typed on paper of a deep yellow hue. I don't see my name at first; others are jostling all around me, obstructing my view. The rocket – which is rather like the Saturn V which was used to propel the Apollo astronauts off the earth – is about to be launched.

The crowd thins out, and then I can see the list clearly. My name is on it! But I only have a few moments to get to the rocket in time for lift-off. I run and run and run…

Now, a young adolescent dreaming of rockets is hardly a unique phenomenon! The dream of course has sexual/hormonal implications, representing typical juvenile fears around physical developments and capabilities.

And yet, like all dreams, its meaning is not single-layered. There are other implications which are very significant, one of which provides the reason for its continued place in my memory: the lucid representation of that sense of 'being-too-late-for-the-stars'. It is this awareness – that it is possible to miss out completely on something that is both wonderful and available – which in turn became a driving force, albeit one that operated for many years at an unconscious level. For although I sensed that, figuratively, I *could* fly to the stars – my name was on the list – I didn't know the way to do it. I therefore needed to keep looking. It's not too dramatic to suggest that this force has been perhaps the most single powerful current flowing under my experience as an adult. The need to change, to keep moving, to keep shedding skin, to keep evolving, can all be sourced in that single principle.

Of course, the dream didn't create the force, it merely reflected back what was already there, in the form of a message from my unconscious. In a sense the dream was acting like a friend, telling me how I was behaving, and why, and nudging me into understanding something of what I was like. I have come to realise that this is the fundamental purpose of dreams (and nightmares) – to show us who we are at any one point in time. For this reason I've tended to view them as allies in life. For a number of years now I've written down my dreams, not wanting to lose the words of wisdom which they sometimes have for me.

In *Prodigal Songs*, I hope to get close to expressing an answer to the stark question that this particular dream raised for me; a question that relates to the most fundamental issues around the purpose and value of my life: will I miss the rocket, or will I get there in time to reach the stars?

***

The poems *'Dear Mum'* and *'Dear Dad'* were given as presents to my mother and father on the occasions of their 88th and 91st birthdays respectively. Two events separated by just five days. The poems represent an attempt on my part to express something of the love and admiration I hold for them, both as parents and as people.

No words can do full justice to this of course, and least not any within my skills orbit. So there is no sense in which I'm stretching in the poems for something wholly true or all-encompassing. Far from it. The poems are straightforward expressions of love, in a familiar and familial context. That they edge on sentimental is deliberate and, given their purpose, I believe, acceptable. Sometimes poetry is precisely **not** the place for elaborate literary technique, innovation or artifice. Sometimes it needs to be simple and direct.

***

My mother and father are remarkable people. Though now in their senior years, they both continue to be mentally alert, generous and supportive. Their playfulness shows itself regularly, and both are still capable of irony and dry wit which can cut down and amuse in equal measure.

Most who come into direct contact with them are appreciative of having done so.

As a couple they exhibit that characteristic of a relationship which I, and many of my generation, will never know – extreme longevity. At the time of writing they have been married sixty-one years. This seems to me to be an awe-inspiring achievement.

I write elsewhere in this book about longevity in relationship as a criterion or otherwise for success, but my parents are supreme exemplars of the 'til death us do part' model of love. What this has brought them is obvious to all who look: a special kind of unity, of bond (as opposed to bondage), which makes the two individuals at times behave like a single entity. They support each other in all kinds of ways. Physically, what one can't do, the other will. Emotionally, when one is low the other will be strong. Spiritually, when one doubts, the other affirms.

Their lives are intertwined at every level. Although they are very different individuals, each with a unique personality, they nonetheless have achieved a kind of union. Time and love have melded them together, and fashioned something which can be seen as little short of sacred.

They have also always been loving and supportive parents. As their eldest son, I've presented them over the years with good and bad moments. For example, I've brought them various challenges and shocks: a serious car accident, dropping out from university, serial romances, financial upheavals, divorce, numerous sudden changes in career direction and home-life status.....and more. Yet through it all they've consistently shown tolerance and patience in the face of what at times must have been, for them, worrying or disappointing developments. They have never dismissed a choice that I've made, rather they've always tried to see it from my point of view. They may not always have totally understood, may not even have liked or agreed with my choices – but they have never, on any serious issue, dismissed my perspective. In doing so, I've been enabled to feel, at a very deep level, a level in fact beyond feeling, that my perspective is of some value. Put another way, my parents have nurtured in me a deeply-rooted sense of self-worth. If there's a greater gift that a mother and father can give their child, I'm not aware of it.

For this reason, *Prodigal Songs*, as with much of my life, is dedicated to them.

Dear Mum

Few are the moments when you're not in mind
Constantly present through all of my life.
You are my maker, the root and the source
I'd be nothing without you (literally of course!).

To me, you're the meaning and feeling of 'home',
the strength, the safety, the not being alone;
and though I've stretched outwards to frontiers quite far,
my true home on earth is wherever you are.

In the core of our empire you make us a house -
the family palace that'll always be ours;
you tend to its workings with fervour and pride
make the stuff and the structures we live our life by:

the smells from the oven, the shine on the pan,
the heat and the sugar, the jars and the jam,
the iron, the name-tag, the knit and the sew,
you make and you manage and everything grows.

But sometimes I catch it, your faraway eye,
and I see there reflected a blue Scottish sky:
for your heart has a tendril in the glens and the lochs
though you long learnt the secret of lidding that box.

And then there's that sparkle, the glint of a laugh
That keen sense of humour, that quiet remark,
The care in your questions, the all-seeing gaze,
(My heart is transparent to you in all ways.)

So this is the wish of a man you helped mould:
understand how much love for you, Mum, I now hold.
I wish you nothing but goodness, happiness, joy -
the true birthday wishes of your eldest boy.

Dear Dad

Few are the moments when you're not in mind
Constantly present through all of my life.
You are my maker, the root and the source
I'd be nothing without you (literally of course!).

To me, you're the meaning and feeling of 'home',
the strength, the safety, the not being alone;
and though I've stretched outwards to frontiers quite far,
my true home on earth is wherever you are.

And you are my model of 'how to' and 'when'
a guide upon whom I can always depend.
You show me the tools that can fix and improve
that bless me with ways to win and not lose:

the workshop, the garden, the oil and the tools,
the caring, the nurture, the tending to rules,
the line and the measure, the cut and the plane,
you make and you manage and everything's gained.

These are the memories that make me complete:
stairs where the queen slipped, a Cup Final treat,
a camera from boxes, a train wood and glue,
a stormy old story, me laughing with you.

And as I grew older I started to see
the private life journey that few get to see
the struggle from Salford through Burma to here -
in awe and respect your son gives a cheer.

So this is the wish of a man you helped mould:
understand how much love for you, Dad, I now hold.
I wish you nothing but goodness, happiness, joy -
the true birthday wishes of your eldest boy.

2. Learning

Only the truth which builds up is truth for you
Soren Kierkegaard

Although given its own section in this book, *'Litter, Litter'* is noteworthy as a poem in only one respect: it's the first creative piece that I can recall writing. I was nine or ten years old, and it was written as a school assignment. My teacher was Mr Weeks, about whom the only other facts I can recall are that he was dark-haired, quite short, had a tendency to wear brown checked jackets, and drove a 'bubble' car. For this he was considered quite daring and modern by my school chums. ('Chums' or 'pals' are what we all had then; 'mates' didn't arrive for several years.)

Primary school was, it perhaps goes without saying, a very formative experience. It's inevitably a source of many memories, most of them positive (as opposed to grammar school which was a very mixed bag indeed). I could of course write a whole book about those years – don't worry, I won't - but for now want to focus on just two episodes which seem particularly pertinent in terms of my later development.

The first involved Gordon Hodges. A lithe, tousle-haired boy of about my height, Gordon arrived in our school in what was then known as 'third form' – year five in today's scheme of things. I would have been about nine years old. As a late arrival on the social scene of the school, Gordon would have confronted a number of challenges, not least the struggle to be accepted. Being 'new' he stood out from the crowd. He therefore, to our juvenile way of thinking, represented both a target and a threat. As I was very much part of the 'in-crowd', the two of us were, in retrospect, on a collision course from the first day he arrived. We just didn't know about such things then.

Halfway County Primary school served the village of Halfway on the Isle of Sheppey. The family home in Western Avenue was within a short walking distance. The annual school intake must have been about thirty, so it was not a large school. In this setting, a bright, middle-class, energetic young boy could easily flourish, and I did so. In effect I became a big fish in a small pool. (A fact I realised with a shock when, aged 11, I started to attend Grammar school where the annual intake was about 120!)

The attempted emancipation of Gordon Hodges culminated (in my memory at least) in a playground fight between the two of us.

Now the word 'fight' doesn't really do justice to what actually happened. For really Gordon and I merely grappled with each other, grabbing each other's shoulders and arms, pulling this way and that, mainly I think trying to avoid being hit rather than making concise efforts to do the hitting. We also made grunting, straining noises and, locked together in this feeble grip, we shuffled about the playground like a drunken, headless llama.

A gaggle of class chums had gathered at a safe distance around us and were in conventional style clapping a beat and chanting "Fight! Fight! Fight!" I suppose this high-pitched scruffy mob were expecting to see something exciting: punches, screams of pain, perhaps even blood. Whatever they wanted I'm sure they must have been disappointed. For what they got was a dismal spectacle: amateurish and ineffective in every way. Gordon and I may as well have thrown soggy biscuits at each other for all the damage we were likely to inflict.

Nonetheless, this was by public definition a 'fight' and therefore there had to be 'a winner'. My place as 'big fish' was at stake. Gordon's rights to be accepted as an equal, or at least as no longer a newcomer, were his to establish.

As we struggled, the aspect of this whole reminiscence which is most vivid for me now occurred. For there was a moment – a few seconds perhaps – when somehow my right arm became free. The top of my head was locked against Gordon's chest and shoulder. I was looking down at his jumper, could see his be-jumpered torso and, beyond, his dusty shoes and the playground tarmac beneath. And my arm was free to move. I knew that this was the time; I would pull my arm back, clench my fist and punch him hard in the stomach. I would hurt him. The fight would end immediately I knew; victory was mine for the taking.

And I didn't.

For at the moment when I might have asserted my dominance by the use of true violence, a different sensibility came over me. It was as if I saw the event, the moment, from afar. I perceived myself, and Gordon, from a distance, and recognised that the whole thing was ludicrous. I was involved in a scenario which was insignificant, pointless, and destructive.

From this perspective – what I've later come to call 'the helicopter view' - the prospect of actually inflicting physical pain was abhorrent. I didn't want to feel my fist smash into his body, and I didn't want to create physical pain in another person.

So instead, I grabbed his jumper and did some more ineffectual pulling. And we two childish combatants carried on staggering about the playground for a few more minutes.

The '*moment-when-I-could-have-punched-Gordon-Hodge*s' is etched very clearly in my memory, I suppose because it is important to who I am. For it was an early example of my own recognition of self-consciousness at work.

This was the only 'fight' I have ever been in. Throughout the rest of my youth, and into my adulthood, whenever the potential for violence arose, I either avoided the situation completely – which included sometimes running away - or talked my way out of it. Having attended a boys' grammar school, and having lived in an urban environment throughout my teenage years at the height of the skinhead era, I think this is not an insignificant fact.

From the helicopter view, a core value was also underlined by that playground confrontation: violence is failure. There are always better solutions. For me, as a nine year old schoolboy, the solution in that situation involved a lot of grappling and pulling of jumpers. And it worked, because somehow, at some point, Gordon fell to the floor and said: "you win!" And, crucially, he wept. This ensured that the outcome was incontrovertible. My status among my peers was assured. And I had achieved it without bloodshed.

The second episode, which occurred at around the same time or perhaps a little earlier, is one snapshot memory in a series involving two other classroom chums: Anne Manners and Barbara Gates. In my memory they were two good friends, and I have grown up thinking of them as a twosome. However I knew even back then that they were very different personalities.

Barbara was blonde and serene and confident, the queen bee among the girls. We brave lads used to cross the line (literally) into the girls' playground just to catch a glimpse of Barbara leading the skipping rope routines, and flashing her stocking tops as she did so! She was bright, athletic, filled with energy, and beautiful - in my then fledgling appreciation of such things.

Anne was small, fragile, quiet. She was a like small bird - a little nervous and very watchful, sometimes prone to sudden movements. I was drawn to her in an unconscious way. I have no recollection of spending any time with her, in or out of school.

However the attraction I held for Anne must have been known by my school friends. I must have spoken about it to somebody. For on one memorable occasion, a group of my classmates, en masse, grabbed hold of her and brought her to me in the playground. She was offered like a sacrificial maiden, for me to kiss. Wriggling and laughing, she was also embarrassed I think. My chums were holding her by the arms, yelling "kiss her kiss her kiss her…" and I rolled up my sleeves – literally! – in order to do just that.

Peer pressure demanded that I couldn't back away.

Yet in truth I was completely abashed and felt little but sympathy for Anne. Unable to lose face and not kiss her, I tried to get the whole thing done as quickly and painlessly as possible. If there was any contact between us then it was fleeting and probably not on the lips. I believe I may have kissed her briefly on the cheek.

"Ay, there's the rub" as Hamlet would say. I didn't have the heart to kiss Anne Manners 'properly' in such fervent and public surroundings, in exactly the same way that I couldn't punch Gordon Hodges 'properly'. On both occasions the separate, detached 'me', who was watching the 'me' in action, took control. I was again both the observer and the observed, and the distinction was placed in stark relief by the intensity of the event in which I was involved. At some point, the observer became the dominant force in me, and as a result my actions were minimised, mitigated, softened. The light of the bigger picture put in shadow the view of the momentary reward.

Put another way, acute self-consciousness was squeezed to the forefront of my personality by the energy of acute experience.

I have never been far from the observer's perspective ever since. On frequent occasions, with a variety of results, this same basic inner process has come to determine key elements of my character, over and over again. What was established empirically in the playground of Halfway County Primary school, became a foundation stone of my subsequent life.

Forty years later, I met Anne again, in a totally wonderful and wholly unpredictable set of circumstances. From that meeting I gained some further and surprising insights into the reality of Anne Manners and Barbara Gates, which I'll return to later in this book.

***

Friends and playground adventures notwithstanding, what I learned in the classroom had of course an equally powerful impact on me, especially around my creative and intellectual interests. The production of *'Litter, Litter'* is a good example of this.

The poem was the result of a whole morning's class-work. We had been asked to produce posters for a litter advertising campaign. I assume there was some kind of national anti-litter promotion at the time, or perhaps Mr

Weeks was simply very forward thinking. In any case, I wrote the poem, and then drew the words in bright colours on a large sheet of paper. I also read the poem aloud in class, and at some point the finished poster went up on the class-room wall.

I was very proud of my work, although somewhat troubled by the ambiguity of the word 'roam'. I realised in the act of reading it aloud that it might be heard as 'Rome'. Now although this latter meaning didn't entirely reduce the verse to farce, it certainly limited its potential breadth of effect, and was, to my mind, an unfortunate distraction. However I obviously didn't, or couldn't, do anything about it and 'roam/Rome' it remains.

I therefore learned a great deal from writing the poem and from the lesson as a whole. For example, I consciously appreciated, probably for the first time, that I seemed to have some facility for word-craft in general and rhyming in particular. Also, I discovered head-on so to speak that meaning could be very dependent on spelling, and that the same word-sound could mean very different things depending on the context. I think I sensed even then that this characteristic of language could be productive. Irony and other forms of ambiguity have never been far from the surface of my written work ever since, at least in my own mind.

I now assign much of my subsequent literary and musical endeavours down to this poem, and that lesson. The experience sparked something that was ready to be lit. It was a good lesson therefore, as is evidenced by the fact that it has, like the poem itself, survived in my memory for over forty years. I doubt that Mr Weeks planned that particular outcome, but the effect of true art is never entirely planned by the artist!

Litter, Litter (1965)

Litter, litter everywhere
In your mouth
And in your hair

So if you go to roam
Please take your litter home

Or put it in the bin
Or keep it in a tin.

3. Feeling

There is a vitality, a life force, an energy, a quickening, that is translated through you into action, and because there is only one of you in all time, this expression is unique. And if you block it, it will never exist through any other medium and will be lost.
Martha Graham

The childhood memory that inspired me to write the poem '*Straddling*' forty or more years after the event to which it alludes, is little more than a momentary snapshot. And even this single frame is uncertain in much of its detail. I *believe* the event occurred in Edinburgh, mainly because one of the protagonists was a Scottish cousin. I *think* the weather was warm and sunny. I *have a feeling* that there was at least one other person playing with us, though I don't recall who this was. I know we played on an expanse of grass, and I see this as a public park of some kind, but I *have no idea* of its size or location. I must have been very young, *perhaps* six or seven years old? But I *might* be quite wrong on this point!

The 'memory' is therefore vague and poorly located in time or space. It seems to hang in isolation, detached as it were from my life; in a solitary bubble of recollection. In this respect it's an unreliable memory; one might therefore ask what value can there be in something so incomplete and uncertain?

The answer is that the value lies in the feeling, not the historical circumstances or, even, the personalities involved. For the image is intense to me. It *feels* vital, even now. It *feels* profound. I have little doubt that this is because something significant shifted in my being at the time in question. The practical details of time and location are unclear because they are not terribly important: what matters is the feeling itself.

I think of the feeling as a movement of energy which broke through me for the first time then, opening up something fundamental in my being. This 'opening up' is the true subject of the poem. Everything else serves merely to contextualise the moment. The physical world was simply a frame for those few seconds of feeling and shifting energy which helped shape me and my life thereafter.

It was the first of a series of such moments, scattered irregularly along my individual time-line.

Straddling

As small children
Our raucous giggles rolled us round the garden
As we ran on and on
Our shirts and skirts fluttered unbridled in the air.

This idyll
captured in my mind
here and there and then and now
is one Eden with one apple and no knowing
and all was first and last
until that one moment
when

I lay on my back
thrilled and panting
the grass scribbling at my neck and legs;
and you fell to me
chuckling your agile legs across me
pinning me to the earth and its unrelenting matter.

For a throat-gripped instant
our roots sparked.

I looked past your sizzling eyes
and young-tanned face
at a new blue sky
suddenly dimensional
dizzying and ached by the sharp pulses
shooting through and from my core.

Your straddling taught a boy
That he would be a man.
Unstained then by conscious knowing
The boy stood and ran
to begin his slow fall
to becoming that man
and to knowing.

He had tasted but did not know
what he had bitten
but still it streamed and rose throughout his lifetime
and even now
is unwritten.

4. Moving

*Search your own heart with diligence,
for out of it flow all the issues of life.*
Book of Psalms

'Home' for me is not a geographical location. It's an emotional experience. As I write this, and consider where my home is right now, several answers feel true. Most obviously, it's where I live now: the small house near a river in a village in Hertfordshire. In an equally real way, home is also where Mum and Dad live: that neat bungalow surrounded by pretty gardens in a quiet village in Lincolnshire. It feels like home even though I myself have never actually lived there, I have only ever visited.

The 'family home', where I grew up and lived with my parents, brother and sister is, well, one of two locations: a house on the Isle of Sheppey near a cemetery and with a large back garden containing, at different times, fruit trees, a willow tree and gooseberry bushes; or a smart detached house on a main thoroughfare in Southampton across the road from a large area of land known locally as 'The Common'.

More subtly, home is also where my children are; or to be very precise, home is where I am when I am with my three daughters. Most often that is here, in my house, but not necessarily: for example a house in the Languedoc where we four once stayed for a fortnight felt very much like home to me at the time, albeit a temporary one.

So when asked the simple question, "where do you come from?", I have no answer except a complex one. For the point is that 'home' for me is a state of being, rather than a place. This truism – or so it seems to me - has probably been reinforced in my own life by the fact that as a boy, my family moved home at key times.

I was born in the Isle of Man, though I have no memory of it as we moved to the Isle of Sheppey when I was six months old. Furthermore, we moved home again when I was eleven, at that critical threshold moment of progression from primary to secondary school.

I unilaterally, as it were, moved again aged 19 when I went up to university (or Polytechnic as it was then) for the first time, in 1974.

There is therefore a mild gypsy element to my youth which no doubt has weakened in me the perceived link between the inner sense of home and the familiarity with a particular building or location.

Interestingly, in recent years, I've felt a sense of home very keenly when spending time in and around the Ariége and the Aude regions of southern France. There are places there with which I identify very strongly, though I don't really know why. A visceral familiarity overcomes me there, one that is as faint and as pervasive as the air, and much older than me.

None of this is negative, it just is. I understand very well that some people do equate 'home' with a special house or town, and that this can be a very powerful connection. Most obviously this is likely to occur if the bulk of one's young history is physically associated with that one place. However I don't envy that experience or feel that I've missed out at all. On the contrary, and without being wittingly contrary, I think moving home as I have throughout my life has given me a great deal. Each move has felt like progress, and carried with it a certain amount of excitement and novelty. In any case, it was all I knew; of course I had nothing with which to compare it.

Most importantly, for my purposes here, I think that the childhood moves go some way to explaining some patterns of behaviour that have asserted themselves in me subsequently. I have, for example, never been particularly phased by moving home. Indeed since the age of nineteen I've taken up numerous residential addresses, sometimes with extraordinary frequency. The act of packing up belongings and transferring them somewhere else has rarely felt a pressure; on the contrary, it has usually felt exciting (although I'm having to express this a little cautiously as there have been times when moving home has been very far from exciting and much closer to traumatic, usually when associated with the termination of a relationship).

And I have always loved travel. The act of being in motion from one place to another, in transit from A to B, can sometimes seem like my most natural way of being. In the act of travelling, I experience both the world and myself in their most relaxed and promising states. In the act of travelling, everything is possible, everything is changing, and everything is fluid. Life flows around and through me, never solidifying enough to cause a significant worry or a debilitating doubt.

The journey is all.

Or rather the journey and the anticipation of it are all, for there are few more exciting activities for me than planning a significant journey. I love the paraphernalia of travel: maps, plotting routes, booking tickets, making preparations to leave, packing. And there is that very special moment, the moment of perfect transition, when preparations are complete and the journey is just about to begin. This has been most acute for me when about to embark on a touring holiday: the car is full, the engine fires, and the journey away from home is about to start. For a brief moment the past is clearly over and the future hasn't yet begun: all is present, all is now. It's a moment of threshold and I have often wanted to mark it as such, perform a ritual of some kind in its honour. However in recognition of the fact that others might not appreciate a mantra or a hymn or the wearing of sacred garments at such a time, and that the mystique in the moment is probably felt entirely by me alone, I limit myself to a moment's silence and perhaps a rhetorical question: "Shall we go to France today?" for example.

Moving has, in a more general sense, been the hallmark of my behaviour and achievements: relationships, careers, world-views, interests, all have changed with sometimes surprising speed. In my youth especially, I rarely stood still, in any meaning of the phrase. More lately I've learned to appreciate the virtues of stillness and peace and being present in the present. I think much of my sense of positivity comes from that simple development. At the same time, I recognise that to live fully means to be in harmony with the process of change. Life is many things, and one of them is movement. To deny change is to restrict life.

In some ways, and as we shall see later, change is what I seem to have to have in order to be fully 'me', fully involved, fully alive. The sea of life is always in motion, the trick I think is to ride the crest of waves, not be submerged beneath them.

***

Cars have particular resonance with regard to the act of movement; of journey; of going and returning; of leaving and arriving. Of getting there.

As a boy, I loved cars; I loved that there were seemingly infinite shapes and styles in which one could be moved about on four wheels. I used to collect toy cars of all kinds, and the manufacturers' names evoke nostalgia and excitement for me even now: Corgi, Dinky, Tri-ang, Lesney, Matchbox…… for a while I must have been a very easy child to buy presents for: a new Triumph TR4, say, or Aston Martin – with suspension, amazing! – was a real thrill and I could hardly get the cardboard box open quick enough to reveal the shine and the unique combination of colour, boot, door, window, bonnet, wheel and roof.

I would take great pride in my knowledge of car makes and models. There was a time, before the mass import of models from the Far East really got underway, when I believed (rightly or wrongly, I don't know) that I could name any and every make and model of car to be seen on British roads: Rover, Austin, Vauxhall, Jaguar, Hillman, Morris held no surprises for me. I could differentiate based on grill-design alone between the Humber Hawk and the Humber Sceptre, or based on tail wing shape, between the Ford Zodiac and the Ford Zephyr.

I had little or no interest in the *mechanics* of the car. I knew engine sizes, and even the significance of the number and style of the pistons' arrangement. But I had little idea about how a car actually was made to move, beyond knowing the phrase 'internal combustion engine'. The science of cars wasn't important to me; what mattered was what they did and what they looked like: their quality in performance and design. Despite an early fascination with Meccano and Lego, I've never been much of an engineer, in fact or in spirit, though I have come to appreciate engineering skills, in whatever genre they may manifest. In fact, I can now see that engineering and art aren't the polar opposites that I might have supposed. My love of great architecture such as gothic cathedrals, the New York skyline and the viaduct at Millau exemplify this.

So in this small boy's back-garden game, where my collection of model cars was lined up to race against each other, and where they moved to the finishing line solely by virtue of the force of the push of my own hand, it was always a joy to me that the most attractive model, my favourite of the moment, would usually come out as winner of the race. Even though I was aware of the game I was playing with myself to achieve this – I would of course actually push my favourite car harder than any of the others – I was still thrilled by the apparent perfect unison of aesthetic and performance. The best looking was indeed the winner! My favourite won and so proved my choice correct!

What a mine of psycho-analytical material there is in **that** childhood game!

The Car

I am the way
I am the head-light
I make the car move
across the face of the floor
faster than before.
I am the way.

Lined up beside
Hillman Husky
Austin Mini
Renault 4
Ford Transit
Mini Clubman
Cavalier
Vauxhall Astra (5-door)
By 306 and 156
Side-by-side and quite assured
are freight
and passenger
foot to floor.
Portland cement lorry
Routemaster bus
A black cab
All await
the hand of force.

A cardboard street map
Dotted white lines
Grey streets
Kerbs
Green spaces
(Where buildings might be)
Zebra crossing
Traffic lights
the furniture of towns
home for cars.

I fold up the town
throw cars in a box
move on to tomorrow
dream a new race.
I am the way.

5. Loving: first steps

Tell me whom you love and I will tell you who you are.
Arsène Houssaye

Of all the features of 'me' to date, the one that perhaps seems most prominent is my tendency to be open to change. Careers, residences, interests, pursuits – all have changed regularly and often. Although more settled in recent years in terms of my understanding of where my strengths lie and what is best for me, everything still seems possible. It may be true that my future goals are clearly established, in a way that wasn't the case as a younger man, but the precise developments required to achieve them are chosen from what seems to be a huge range of options. To put this more figuratively, I know now where I want to go, but I don't have a dogmatic hold on how I might get there. In this respect nothing is fixed, all things remain alive as possibilities. And for me, this is part of what it means to be happy.

The characteristic of change is nowhere more apparent than in the history of my romantic relationships. This is a densely packed story, which has episodes of marvel and beauty, but also of outrage and drama. Starts and endings have sometimes been abrupt, at least as viewed from the outside, and there have been occasions when those close by have been left standing open-mouthed in shock, struggling to comprehend or know what to do. I can't deny that there have been times when I have been selfish almost to the point of cruelty, and yet also times when I have endured almost to the point of self-sacrifice. I feel no pride in either. Rather, if there are moments when I feel regret, it's around these enforced heart-breaks that I most acutely experience it. Yet what can be done to amend what has already been done? Time is remorseless, and 'going back' is never really an option. And so after the event, all I can do is remember, percolate, and move in the direction I believe is forward.

From that helicopter view, it seems that being both a catalyst of love and an agent of despair is an integral element of the modern human condition. We are all, to different degrees, masters or mistresses of the process. What we make of it, what we do with the outcomes, is a determining factor in our sense of self. Too much blame, and we burn. Too much self-pity, and we wither. Too much pride, and we grow lonely.

In retrospect, the light of love with which I've been blessed along the years outweighs the dark mass of despair by a huge amount. Both the light and the dark provide, for me, the strongest impetus to write. I'm never more creative than when in love or in heartache! (From what I can tell, this isn't an uncommon phenomenon. The dark side especially is a renowned kindler of artistic flames.) Hardly surprising therefore that many of the lines in this book are either directly or indirectly about my relationships with women, and about love or its close equivalents.

***

The poem '*Sally*' alludes to my first romantic adventure. Sally Clark, the dentist's daughter, and sister of my good friend John, wasn't strictly speaking my first girlfriend – the sweet Jane Harrison claims that dubious honour - but she was the object of my first serious romantic attachment.

I don't recall where or how Sally and I first met, but I do remember the special heaven that is the first such relationship. It was a massively disruptive yet thrilling phenomenon. I was consumed by it and, I believe, so was she.

For a short time, we two walked though a glorious garden of relatively innocent delights. New kinds of emotions flamed into life, new perceptions and ambitions swung into view, new sensations flowered through me. It was like imbibing a perfect drug that raised each day to a new, more brilliant level of experience.

What we experienced, of course, was falling in love for the first time.

There's nothing like it.

Ours was not a wild, extreme kind of love. In those days, when the issue of sex-before-marriage still carried a moral burden for us all, our adventures were simple and constrained. But they were no less thrilling because of that. We moved forward slowly despite the emotional torrent surging through us.

We also got along well as friends, partly because I put huge amounts of effort into being exactly who she wanted me to be (and to be fair she may have reciprocated in this). After a year or so – a very long time at that age - she had an affair which I discovered by accident and which traumatised me. Suddenly, our relationship ended.

Particularly galling and embarrassing for me at the time was the fact that her betrayal was with John Cunningham (boo hiss), my most immediate rival for the scrum-half position in the school rugby team. It wasn't very surprising even then that he actually replaced me as first choice scrum-half very soon afterwards. That he was a year below me in school threw almost unbearable figurative salt onto the very real emotional wound.

After a few months, somehow, Sally and I 'got back together' but, though we had no clue of this at the time, it was of course almost inevitable that the second attempt was short-lived. I'm pretty sure that I would have been trying to recapture former glories and avoid the pain of loss, and she would have been trying to alleviate her own sense of guilt at having betrayed me.

The fact that I don't recall the details or manner of our actual ending is evidence that the power of our relationship had already passed. What remained was just a husk: the empty working through of a psychological process.

It's been tempting subsequently to assign the cause of some of my later behaviours around women to my experience with Sally, as if it was a kind of blueprint for future love affairs. As if past experience makes present behaviour inevitable.

This is a myth. Notwithstanding the rise of psychoanalysis as a healing tool in our society, the fact is that what happened in the past only has life in the present if we choose to give it life. What makes up our present is, essentially, a matter of choice. Of course understanding yesterday can shed light on today – and this is the power of psychoanalysis and related practices - but the past never justifies or wholly explains the present. Every step we take, we take because we choose to do so, in the way we do so. It's intrinsic to our species that we each make our own life, and where else can we make it except in the present moment? Whatever I am, I am now.

And yet, Sally Clark will always be a critical person in my life. I've often wondered what happened to her. I would love to meet her again, without ulterior motive. I suspect that my residual memory of a beautiful, bright, tender young woman, whilst true, may also be somewhat distant from the truth of my feelings at the end of our relationship – but, now, in the objective, detached clear light with which the passing of time provides us, that really doesn't matter at all. The emotional journey of discovery that she and I travelled together as a young couple remains profound, whatever the actual details of circumstance or historical 'reality'.

Sally

At 16
with eyes closed in rapture
a 3-minute song
might last for ever.

In that darkened dancing party den
'Nights in White Satin'
stuck in the honey-thick air
that squeezed around us
while
thick waves of smoke
breathlessly stroked
our growing pains of attraction

Your fresh-clean blonde hair
straight, straw-sweet
muslin to my desire,
dry against my cheek.
The cool curve
of that musk-drenched
glass-smooth
pale-planed
line
from neck
to shoulder -
a daring waft of flesh against my lips.

We moved as one
front-to-front
called it dancing.
Your silksilksilky brown dress
softly tight
full of you
young to overflowing
full of promise
with eyes closed in rapture
blind to the mystery
of once and future lies.

My newly found desire
my newly bursting heart

my newly living life
surging through my nervous moves -
sixteen years and swept away by feeling
swept away.

Beauty at my throat.

On the edge of air-born
as for the first time
I was born
into love.

With eyes closed in rapture
I could not see that yours
would look away.

Tonight
keyboard-tapping wrinkled freckled hands
are compared
and

I feel you again
my arms overflowing
with what once was.

I cannot distinguish between
the longing for you then
and the longing for then, now.

With eyes closed in rapture
I clearly see
that love is not timed.

6. Singing

A man is what he thinks about all day long
Ralph Waldo Emerson

My sixteenth birthday was significant in at least three ways: it brought Sally closer to me; the party (alluded to above) was the first party I hosted as a young man; and my parents, in a crucial act that helped shape my life thereafter, brought me an acoustic guitar as my birthday gift.

Along with the instrument itself, Mum and Dad had booked a series of introductory lessons. For these, I joined a small group of learners who met on Sunday mornings above a local music shop, to be taught the basics of playing classical guitar.

The teacher was a concert-level performer, and therefore a fine musician. There was much I might have learned from him. But I was a teenager and not very familiar at the time with the charms of classical music. I was listening on my sister's Dansette to sounds of a different kind – pop, heavy rock, and, especially, a new-fangled genre called 'Progressive Music'. My fledgling record collection included albums such as *'This Was'* by Jethro Tull, *'Cream Live'*, and a compilation of new artists called *'Wowie Zowie: the World of Progressive Music'*. This included one song by an up and coming American rock guitarist by the name of Jimi Hendrix. However my favourite track was by a band whose destiny I've often wondered about, Cat Mother and the All-night Newsboys. Surely such a name deserved a more illustrious fate than anonymity!

I owned a few singles too, including *'Stay with Me'* by the Faces, *'I'm a Man'* by Chicago, and – whisper it quietly – *'Hot Love'* by T. Rex!

The combination of this musical pedigree and the fact of my youthfulness, and an impatient streak as wide as the bay of my bedroom window, all contributed to both my itching to play NOW, and to play music which was familiar to me. I had no desire to be a Julian Bream or John Williams – I wanted to play rock! For this reason, I attended only a handful of formal lessons before embarking on what subsequently became a life-long process of teaching myself how to play guitar.

The most lasting skills I learned from the formal lessons, which have actually served me well over the years, were to do with posture and how to hold the guitar properly.

Oh, and I learned how to pick the melody of the Beatles' *'Yesterday'*.

So, armed with a few *'How to play'* type books I was soon practicing basic chords and, fairly quickly, began to imagine all kinds of fabulous futures related to music. Furthermore, I already had a penchant for writing – I had several notebooks full of stories, poems, and general ramblings – so it was a short step from merely playing the guitar to also singing along with it and then to making up my own words to sing.

Because of being predominantly self-taught, I've developed an idiosyncratic style of playing which suits the main intention – to support my voice. For me, the guitar is a vehicle to convey lyrics. I have never viewed it as a musical end in itself. Instrumentalism has never been my forte or strong interest. Songs are, for me, another means of getting words out; another way of expressing myself. The guitar facilitates that, like the pen facilitates writing.

In this way, I became an amateur singer-songwriter-guitarist, a common enough phenomenon in the 1970s. Perhaps less commonly, this form of creative output has persisted to the present time. I still play the guitar (albeit with much less regularity than even a few years ago), I still sing (albeit less easily than I once did) and I still write songs (albeit much more rarely than I used to). Over the course of the thirty-eight years since the day I first picked up my own acoustic guitar, I've written dozens of songs. Some have been performed live, some recorded, others have only ever been heard by the walls of the room in which I sing them, lying dormant on sheets of paper: printed or hand-written words scribbled over with the letters of hand-written chords. The lyrics of some of these songs are included below.

A few years later, and in a very different context, I acquired my first steel string guitar. A friend of a friend, by the name of Bob Bear (or possibly Behr or Bare) was short of money and had put the word out that he wanted to sell his Antoria (a lovely Gibson Hummingbird copy). The word reached me, and for some forgotten reason I had cash to spare. In an act of stunning serendipity, I bought it from him for fifty pounds. The exchange occurred one afternoon in 1975 on the corner of Stanhope Road and Victoria Street, St Albans. I gave him some notes, he passed me the guitar.

I'm not sure I ever saw Bob again, and only subsequently did I discover that his financial shortage was born from a need to purchase amphetamines – he was what we used to blithely call 'a speed freak'. He had sold his guitar to feed his addiction. I'm not sure if I knew about his addiction at the time, but it could easily be argued that there was a potential moral aspect to the purchase. If so, I don't recall that I ever lost sleep over it.

However the story ends happily for I found out years later that Bob had married, had had children and was properly employed and living in Bournemouth. My money had not contributed to a drug abuse fatality. I have wondered how differently I might now perceive this whole incident if it had?

The Antoria was a lovely guitar with a low, smooth action and fine, mature tone. It could be picked as easily as strummed and was a perfect, multi-genre instrument. I fell in love, and this time it would prove to be forever. Over the years it has performed in school halls, wine bars, clubs and pubs, theatres, front rooms, bedrooms, back rooms, staff rooms, waiting rooms, train stations, metro stations, outdoor cafes and plazas, beaches and on street corners. It has travelled with me halfway round the world, and been my one constant companion wherever I've lived and breathed. It's heard my laments and excitements, and felt the force of all my emotions.

More than any person, my Antoria has born witness to my life. As I write now, it sits across the room from me, silent and watchful and – crucially - judgment-free. It has become and will remain that rarest of breeds: my life-long companion.

I've never acquired another guitar, although it is showing signs of age and I've been considering purchasing a new one. If and when I do, the Antoria won't be replaced, merely befriended. Perhaps, like us all, it would benefit from a companion through its later years?

The steel string Antoria really took my musical endeavours to the next level. I soon began playing and song-writing in earnest. Dreams of being a professional musician started to ferment. I teamed up with one of my best friends at the time, John Clement, to form a duo. He was a more abstract, jazzy guitarist and song-writer who had little confidence in his own singing voice. In some respects we were an unlikely musical combination, but my ambitions were poorly formulated in my own mind and I was happy to go with the flow and see what emerged.

Our duo was never formally named. We called ourselves 'Pod Clump Aardvark Clod Pump' for our own amusement (we shared a strange and darkly ironic sense of humour, John and I, but I forgive myself now for being so young and silly), though fortunately it was as 'John and Derek' that we took up a Sunday evening residency at Scott's Wine Bar in London Road, St Albans. We were paid ten pounds each per night, with free wine as perks, and were thrilled to be paid at all for doing something which was such fun.

We mainly performed our own compositions, some Loudon Wainwright material, and one or two 'classics' to an audience which mainly consisted of our own friends and a few hardy regulars. Sundays were quiet nights at Scott's, and I imagine the proprietors were grateful for the extra custom we brought in for them, even if it was small scale. In any event we were only ever acoustic, with no amplification of any kind. Only those nearby could hear us, so we created little distraction to the rest of the bar's occupants. We were easy to ignore, which was probably a mercy all round.

The culmination of this phase of my musical 'career' came about through a mutual friend, Andy. He worked for a London-based PR company which managed various kinds of musical acts. One night, in Scott's, he came to hear us, and later asked if we would be interested in doing a gig at the Marquee club, which was a leading London live-music venue at the time. We would be a warm-up act of course for a more established band. It was, I think, meant as a kind of trial. If we did well, then greater things might follow.

I don't think we bit his arm off, but had we done, it would have been fully justified. Of the very many twists of fate that litter all our lives, this had the potential to be one of the most massive in my own.

***

The lyrics in the following section are some of my early attempts at song-writing. Re-reading (and re-playing) them now, it seems to me that there are some decent lines and phrases contained in some of the songs, and some necessary musical puff. However there is also some uncomfortable phrasing, not all of which can be excused on the basis of changing musical fashion.

No apologies though, they are what they are and seemed to work at the time. I print them here mainly for historical interest, though I still hope there may be some aesthetic impact as well.

Great Expectations (1976)

I want to climb a mountain
Feel the world not just see
Be a man who looks about him
Generally, just be

I want to write a book
Fill it with my very soul
I want to see, feel, look
It seems such a simple goal

But I get in my own way
It's all my fault
I know I have something to say
But it's locked in me the vault

I need to do all I can
As much as my body will take
I want more than any man
All the icing, all the cake.

I want to climb a mountain
To run and never stand still
But the fear inside is mounting
...I'm afraid I never will.

You'd Think By Now I'd Know (1978)

I am going round
Hearing silence in the sounds
I am floating free
Bruised by waves swept by the sea
You know what I am
Hide the wolf, love the lamb
But I don't know which mask to show
You'd think by now I would know.

I am on the fence
Pain and fear as recompense
I hear distant words
Voices straining meanings blurred

Hear me with your soul
Feel what I don't know
Touch me with your eyes
Don't feel any surprise
When my truth turns out to be lies

I could walk ahead
Edging forward living dead
We might rendezvous
Knowing god like lovers do
But I can't see which way to go
You'd think by now I would know.

Talk (1981)

So we talk the night away
Sleep forgets us
Leaves us to our dreams

Still the truth slips away
It won't be held
Rarely what it seems anyway.

How we're longing to be safe
Positively sure
Inside our concrete love

How we have so little faith
In what it means right now
When the present's not enough

Oh but really where are we
And how far have we come
When to even say 'I love you'
is not enough?
And it's hard enough to walk
But still we want to run
And still to say 'I love you'
It's not enough.

We talk of wants and needs
Of heart and soul
Yeah we could talk the night away

But we don't want what we need
C'est la vie
But I'll still love you anyway

Oh but really where are we
And how far have we come
When to even say 'I love you'
is not enough?

Hero the Fool (1981)

I'm a different man every time I tell the truth
Sometimes I'm a cat and sometimes I'm a hot tin roof
I'm a rock'n'roll star I'm a shy boy living at home
I'm the way I'm the goal
I'm the life I'm the soul
I've got so many friends
But in the end I am alone.

I talk to make peace and I'll shout off my mouth at times
I'll try not to laugh or I'll try so hard to cry
I'm society bred or I may be one of Maggie's bad boys
I'm ill or I'm well
I'm like you I can tell
And I get so bored even though I've got so many toys.

You can give me a lot or you can make me stare at my feet
I can be so cold and I can be so sickly sweet
And I'll look behind just to see if there's anything there
And there usually is
But I'll give it a miss
Cos as some might say it's so very rude to stare.

I'm a hero of mine though the man I most hate is me
And I can see quite far though I'm sick when I'm ever at sea
I'm full of religion but can't see god for the proof
I gain by a loss
I serve best when I'm boss
I'm fooled by a joke
My eyes they love smoke
I love you is my best
But it may be just a guess
Cos I'm a different man every time I tell the truth.

Paradise Lost (1980)

I heard a new record on the radio today
It sounded like something old but that's how it goes these days
The DJ said it was sensational, the best around
I'd swear it was a re-make of a re-make of a sixties sound

They say the kids are fighting, they say the kids are alright
But these kids only dream of being 2-tone stars overnight
Their dreams are quick and cheap, they're going for a song
Get the money, get production, get the volume and you can't go wrong

Where has all the music gone and why?
Do we really have to say goodbye?
Has the wind stopped blowing?
Has the river really stopped flowing?
Bye-bye, Johnny, bye-bye

Sometimes it makes me wonder, if it was all in vain
Is the freedom that was won just paradise lost again?
These grunts that they call lyrics seem to me inane
You have to look hard to find the glory that was bound for this train.

We were promised revolution, all we got was loose change
We were promised the lost chord, all we got was new wave
We were promised that the punks and the beats would save our souls
Well c'mon baby light my fire for the heat that made us high has grown cold.

Weekend Fever (1979)

Finished work an hour ago, another week gone by
Days of daydreams all in a row, it's not time it's life that flies
When you're on the run, since life begun
When you're a shallow fool, looking for California fun
Make me believe

Dust and filth and dirt beneath my nails
Take a bath to wash my grins away
No more back-aching for a day or two
I'm in the race but I won't stay
'cos I'm fit to burst, notes in my purse
I'm all psyched up, but here's the worst –
I've got no one to call.

(Chorus)
Got the weekend fever
Ah but this place needs a friend
Got the weekend fever
Feeling sorry for myself again

Hope the phone rings, I'm surprised
Hope someone thinks of me and calls
I hope this fever building up inside
Has a chance to run before it falls
But it's hopes in vain, I can see that plain
May as well cool down, watch TV again, but it's a shame

I know if you or you or you were here
I could make it I could take it fine
I could laugh and smirk at fools like him
Who only live for shallow good times
But it's just no use, go on hurl abuse
I'm cul-de-sacked, got it all to lose
And it really is that bad and I really am that sad
And I've really got no scope, I'm the worst I've ever had
Must be the blues.......

(Chorus)
Got the weekend fever
Ah but this place needs a friend
Got the weekend fever
Feeling sorry for myself again

(Repeat chorus)

7. Wandering

Love can help me know my name.
Seal Adeola Samuel

The Marquee gig never happened.

Instead, in the summer of 1977, aged 22, I went on a camping holiday to France with John. I don't recall much of how we got there; we must have left from Southampton (where my family home was), which at the time ran a ferry service to Le Havre. We then must have hitch-hiked to Paris.

In any event, we found our way to a campsite in the Bois de Boulogne in Paris. There, within a day or two, I met an American woman, Nanette, and we quickly fell in love. I remember the beginnings of our relationship as being completely natural, un-hesitant, authentic and fully-lived.

Nanette was Californian, though she lived in her own home in Richmond, Utah. She was divorced, older than I by four or five years, and seemed at first glance to be very worldly-wise. All of these things gave her a glamour and exoticism that was very appealing. She was also beautiful, almost a stereotype of the 'California Girl' that I had heard sung about in the music of songwriters and bands such as the Eagles, Poco, Jackson Browne, the Beach Boys and many others. I had for several years been a lover of American west coast music and the sun/love-filled lifestyle it seemed to depict. Now, with Nanette, perhaps I had the opportunity to live that dream!

She was travelling in a converted Ford Transit van – with her mother as I recall. Somehow it was arranged that we three – Nanette, John and I – would travel together on through France (Nanette's mother flew back to the States from Paris). This we did, driving south through the Massif Centrale, Provence and on to Monte Carlo and the Riviera. John and I busked the outdoor cafés in Paris, Lyon, Marseille, Nice; Nanette carried the hat around the diners on our behalf. The combination of our idiosyncratic songs, active performance style and (probably crucially) Nanette's glamour earned us a good income, and we lived off these rich pickings for much of the holiday.

For a time we drifted as we pleased. We lived a hippy-lifestyle, going where we wanted when we wanted to, sleeping either in the van or under the stars when ground and sky permitted. I think of those days with unutterable fondness and longing now, though I'm sure of course that the reality at the time was sometimes less paradisiacal.

How it all seemed from John's perspective I don't know – after all, he had come on holiday with his best mate, and ended up holidaying with an amorous couple. Nanette and I must have been annoyingly 'all over each other', being in the first throes of love. Poor John was pure gooseberry.

Strange then that I have no recollection of him ever complaining about that fact. Perhaps my memory has been working hard to delete such difficulties, or perhaps I was blind to them at the time. Or perhaps Nanette and I tried successfully to prevent him from feeling in the way. Or perhaps he was simply a generous spirit. Like much of the past, I will never know the whole truth now.

Later that summer, we returned to Dieppe and all three of us caught the ferry back to England, leaving the van parked near the ferry terminal for later collection. Nanette and I planned to return to it in a few weeks time; we had decided that we were going to travel the world together, starting as soon as possible.

This was not the last occasion when I forsook professional/creative achievement, in the form of the Marquee booking, in favour of romantic bliss.

I have often wondered what fork in the road I denied myself (and John) by the choice of travel with Nanette over that performance. By such decisions is the solid form of a life made. And yet it was no 'decision' at all; I simply followed my heart without a pause for thought. I can honestly state that I have never regretted the path I chose then.

The next few weeks were filled with untying knots that bound me to my life in England: I arranged a year's sabbatical with my remarkably understanding employers (in fact I've experienced several times in my life the extravagant generosity of employers when confronted with my own extravagant requests); ended a pre-existing romantic connection, and terminated rental agreements and insurance policies.

Eventually, Nanette and I drove off from St Albans (where I lived) into the sunset – literally as it happened, for we set off one early evening when there indeed was a most magnificent sunset, which I took to be a very positive sign.

Returning to Dieppe, the van was where we had left it, untouched and driveable (just). From France we plotted a route through northern Europe to Athens. Our dimly realised intention was to get to India. I had £250 and it seemed enough, and if it wasn't we knew we could raise cash as we needed it – part-time work, busking, making and selling jewellery etc. I had such natural confidence in things working out then. Money, or the lack of it, was never an anxiety, only a challenge. I have had to learn to consciously adopt this perspective in recent years, and even now sometimes struggle to find it. I could learn from me back then.

We drove through Belgium, Germany, Luxembourg, Switzerland, Austria, Yugoslavia (as was) and Greece, encountering wonders and adventures of different kinds along the way. We sold the van in Athens (for $100!), hitch-hiked to Istanbul – another novel in that journey – then picked up the Magic Bus to Tehran, and on to Mashad, Herat, Kandahar and, eventually, Kabul. This was a journey full of wondrous landscapes, hair-raising roads (and drivers), exotic music, strange new foods, incredible local hospitality and occasional moments of real danger. The whole was a journey that could not be carried out now, at least not in the same way, in this world so much more extreme in its threat of violence.

As I've said, there were many adventures along the way. I kept a journal at the time. From its pages now vivid incidents and places surge into view. Perhaps one day I may re-package this journal as a full account of what occurred. For now, a few examples will suffice…

> On three separate occasions Nanette and I were held up at machine gun point by special police forces in Germany and Switzerland, under suspicion of being Bader-Meinhof terrorists. Once, asleep in the van, we were awoken in the early hours of the morning by loud shouts, bright lights, and banging on the van door. On opening the door, I was confronted with an alarming sight: five soldiers with severe and slightly anxious expressions. At least two of the soldiers were armed with machine guns which were pointed directly at me. I heard a loud click from one.
>
> Fortunately a passport check and a radio telephone call eased the situation. The guns were lowered, and their frowns replaced with over-enthusiastic smiles and relieved apologies.

***

> Hitch-hiking from Athens we were picked up by a local truck driver. He spoke little English, and seemed particularly interested in Nanette (!) Hoping to make some miles along the motorway towards the north and, eventually, Istanbul, I became a little anxious when we seemed to be heading ever further into rural countryside. He reassured us he knew where he was going. Eventually, as dusk was falling, we came to a large, remote house. There were several other lorries parked outside the house. We were ushered inside with friendly gestures and smiles.
>
> The downstairs room was large and contained a number of men, sat about in a relaxed way, smoking, drinking, playing backgammon.

When we entered, all heads turned to gaze at us. Especially at Nanette. I glimpsed one woman there, at the top of a flight of stairs.

I will never know for sure, but I believe that place was a brothel. I don't think the man, or his associates, were violent, but I do think Nanette was at risk. In any event, she and I made our excuses and left. We were miles from a main road, and concerned that we may be followed. So we walked quickly in a straight line across country, across fields and rough ground, in the direction we guessed to be back towards a main road. It was becoming increasingly dark, but we felt the need to put distance between us and that strange house as swiftly as possible.

After a few hours, tired, hungry and thirsty, we unrolled our sleeping bags and slept on some hard, dry, dusty ground.

In the early morning light, we were awoken by a pack of wild dogs barking nearby. We got up quickly, and found our way back to the nearest main road.

***

A few weeks later, a gunman, shouting hysterically, waved his cocked pistol at me, because I was standing in the wrong queue in a bank in Tehran. He was a Savak officer, the murderous 'bodyguard' corps of the then Shah of Iran.

***

I was one of the last western European tourists to leave Afghanistan immediately prior to the Russian invasion in 1978. I would have left at the same time as most travellers – all of us had been asked by local police to leave the country on the grounds of a forthcoming "special event"! - except that when I got to the border with Iran, I was turned back because I didn't have a properly-stamped exit visa. By the time I had returned to Kabul by bus, acquired the necessary visa, and returned back again to the western border, a round trip of about twelve hundred miles, my only companions on the coach were locals fleeing the country, many carrying belongings wrapped in sheets, and accompanied by the occasional goat. The sense of imminent crisis was pervasive.

***

By the time Nanette and I reached the Afghan capital we had been travelling six months or so. With the time in France and England, Nanette and I had been together for about nine months. We had made many friends along the way, which itself was part of the travelling experience, and most recently with an American couple who were travelling to India as well. After a few weeks in Afghanistan, they were keen to move on and so was Nanette. But I was out of money, and, perhaps, starting to want a break from the road. Nanette was wealthy and offered to support me if we travelled on to India and Nepal. Suddenly, we had come to a figurative cross-roads, not just a geographical one, and we had a decision to make.

I doubt I shall ever know for sure what fed the choices we made then, but one night we agreed that I couldn't live off her money, and that the only thing I could afford to do was to return to England. I think there was a part of me that simply wanted some home-comforts or perhaps just to stand still for a while. Another part of me felt uncomfortable at being 'kept'. Other options – such as Nanette returning with me – were surely discussed but I don't recall. In any event, we agreed to separate – she would travel on round the world, I would return home, and after a few months I would then journey to the States to be with her on her return. That was the plan. In retrospect, this was I suspect little more than a cushion, to soften the blow of separation (a natural and surprisingly common tactic I've since discovered).

'An English Boy Watching an American Girl' is based on a song called *'Like the Woman that You Are'* which I wrote soon after Nanette left our hotel in Kabul to catch the Magic Bus to Kathmandu. Today, as I write this, I can still see the vision of her walking away from me: across the hotel forecourt and gardens, out of the grounds towards the main road, the coach station and beyond….it remains in my mind in high definition. Letting go of love, however it occurs, is the hardest of all things to do. It marks a permanent staging-post in our life, cutting into our memory the deepest of all.

I saw Nanette again, briefly, in St Albans several months later. For a complex set of reasons, her journey round the world had ended prematurely and she was travelling home via England. She had come to see if our plan might still be viable; she wanted me to go to the States with her.

In the days before mobile technology or the internet, the human heart could move faster than an air mail letter sent to a foreign forwarding address. I had moved on, and was closely involved with another woman. I had to let Nanette down.

This, for her, was a shocking discovery. For me it was awful too, but felt unavoidable. Not for the first or last time, I had put myself and others in a position of absolutely conflicting needs and desires. The product of this was pain for both parties.

Fortunately Nanette was a clear-sighted woman, and we managed to hold a friendship together. In fact a few weeks later, I drove her to Gatwick airport to catch her flight back to the States. By the time she walked away again, this time through an airport departure gate, we both already knew that our journey together had actually ended when I agreed to let her walk away in Kabul.

An English Boy Watching an American Girl
(Based on the original song *'Like the Woman That You Are'* written in 1978)

The woman you were becoming
Was strong when you walked away

There were tears on your cheeks
But nothing would happen to make you stay

The morning was virgin
no cicadas spoke
knowing that like your heart
they would go unheard;
your backpack bumped behind you
determinedly making distance between.

I stood in the door
Biting on my lip
Perhaps to keep control
Perhaps uncertain
Perhaps ashamed

Reality's sword
cut my fantasy of honour
into tiny shards

No hero, just a fool
Watching love pour away
down the brook of your gentle face.

And this same sculpted scene
eroded down the years
tear by tear by tear
dripping away down the same angsty path
shaping what once was sharp
Into something smooth and cool
What once was folly
Into routine lies;
Now feels cold and hard against my scarred palm:

The boy become man
still framed by the door
still biting his lip

still full of perhaps

But oh California
You were the golden mould.

8. Beehiving

If a man does not keep pace with his companions, perhaps it is because he hears a different drummer. Let him step to the music which he hears, however measured or far away.

Henry Thoreau

Nanette and I exchanged letters for some time after her departure. I still have them, stored away with other memorabilia in a battered old suitcase in my bedroom cupboard. The letters show how, for a while, we shared mutual sadnesses, and sometimes skirted with 'what if' scenarios. They also contain simple accounts of distant and differing lifestyles. Eventually, she wrote to tell me about her new love, Michael, their marriage, and then her first child.

Any angst I had once felt had long dissipated. She was happy. And I had my Antoria......

While abroad I had had the time and inclination to write a number of songs. My song-writing and poetic interests developed well as a result. Following my return, and over the next few years, my song-writing production was at its peak in terms of quantity and, perhaps, quality. This was reinforced by the fact that I had found an outlet for performance which was more comfortable and supportive than either the public street or the wine bar. I had found the Beehive folk club.

Accommodated in a small hall above a local pub, the Beehive was a long established, live-performance venue. Although called a 'folk club' the music played there crossed many genres; on some evenings traditional folk music could have a very low profile or even be absent completely. Resident amateur singers and musicians took it in turns to host the evenings and were rewarded for their work by being able to take a slab of performance time for themselves. Other acts during the evening would include local floor artists (an 'open mike' evening as it's sometimes now known, though there was rarely any amplification involved, performers were usually unplugged and acoustic) and, very often, a professional or semi-professional solo performer or group. These were paid a minimal fee, covered by the takings on the door contributed by the paying audience.

The main effect on me in finding this outlet was that it gave me a definite motivation to write. I had an audience! Even if this was small, and often comprised of familiar colleagues and, if you were lucky, their friends, it was enough. I had an audience.

The first time I attended the club, I played solo, and was very nervous. Performing to a seated audience who had paid an (admittedly small) entrance fee and who sat in rows to actually listen, was a novel experience for me. I was only accustomed to being either background (in Scott's) or easily avoided while busking.

I was unknown to the organisers and so was put on early; the audience tended to increase as the evening progressed so the reliable performers were often saved for later. On that first occasion, I was allowed two or three songs, and it seemed to go well. The following week I was put on later in the evening.

The first song I ever performed at the Beehive was Loudon Wainwright's *'Motel Blues'*. For this reason, I have a great fondness for the song even now. As my confidence grew, so my inclination to perform my own material increased. Some times I performed only my own creations.

I made a number of friends at the Beehive, all of whom were musical artists, and most of whom remained amateur in terms of remuneration, if not in skill or attitude to their art. Some I recall in particular are Bob Scruton and his Instant Kazoo Band, which was comprised of a foot-operated drum, a semi-acoustic guitar, and a kazoo; his brother Richard who tried hard to sing John Prine and Bob Dylan classics with only marginal success; Hezekiah Slackbandy (aka John O'Dwyer) a witty lyricist in the style of Tom Lehrer; Chris Berry, a smooth guitarist, writer of poignant love songs and friend of the late John Martyn; 'old' George, a local down-and-out who played Christmas carols and army-tunes on harmonica; Tony Haynes, an autoharp-playing truck driver whose traditional folk style delivered narratives of working life in contemporary England; and Steve James, who would subsequently become my close friend and my musical partner in the very slightly famous duo, Tailor's Dummy.
Steve saw in me, I think, an ideal musical companion. His voice, though tuneful, was not as strong as mine. On the other hand my level of musicianship was limited whereas he had a wide-ranging set of skills and interests across various stringed and keyboard instruments.

My former musical partner, John, wasn't living locally any more, and I rarely saw him. In fact it wasn't too long before my girlfriend of the time, Linda, had an affair with him and I lost both of them from my life in one fell swoop! Teaming up with Steve was a synchronous event therefore.

I've come to appreciate that very many significant turning points have born the distinct hallmark of synchronicity. It has always been true for me, that as one door has closed, another one has opened.

Sticks and Stones (1982)

Don't be ashamed
hold your head up don't take all the blame
Don't come on coy
I know you're a girl you must know I'm a boy
They'll say what they will
They'll dream up their clouds
We had our cup filled
Let's not crack it now

I know you well
Seen your heaven felt your hell
Now I feel your pain
Rain on the moon as we waxed and we waned
Hard is the night
strange are these days
Freedom road's a fight
But we both know the way

So don't you touch your sticks and your stones
Even your words are best left alone
There's wind in our sails
But there's a sting in our tails
And although you keep rolling
I know that you're not made of stone.

Feed on the past
the lessons we learn are the lessons that last
Look to the years
yesterday's smiles have tomorrow in tears
There's little that's new
Nothing much to fear
Just now and you
In this one lonely moment here

Going Their Way (1981)

Can't quite believe
Things have worked out this way
Caught in the smoke of their dog-end lies
Don't understand
How some feelings stay
And some become rain in my eyes

It's easy to say 'time will heal'
But can you say which wounds are mine?
It's easy to say 'do what you feel'
But feelings change from time to time

Where's it all gone now?
My confident pose
The way with the world I once knew
I've ground to a halt now
Punch-drunk with the blows
Not a sign, not a smile, not a clue.

Try as I might to keep control
My gasping heart rules my tongue and my head
Forget the lessons forget the role
My loves become hollow and dead

I daren't look at tomorrow
When I can't even see today
Give me a lead and I will follow
Let the blind lead the blind
I'm going their way.

Losses and Gains (1982)

We're all babies to begin
Losing grip on slippery sin
That keeps creeping in and in
And in between us.

We're all children in the end
Acting tough we just pretend
Not to care we bite the hand
The hand that feeds us

But losses turned to gains
Chart the progress of the sane
And our madness turns to rain

And my heart that leaps to you
Fills with thunder at the view
But we rise and seek the new
Love dries us

And the feelings I can tell
Like an iceberg in the swell
It's the tip that I can yell
And yell and yell.......

But losses turned to gains
Chart the progress of the sane
And our madness turns to rain

9. Loving: the promise

Your task is not to seek for love, but merely to seek and find all the barriers within yourself that you have built against it.
                                Rumi

Fifteen years or so after the events of *'An English Boy'*, I recall queuing for lunch in a canteen in Sussex University. Talking with my then newly-found friend Julius, I commented that I saw my life as having been 'structured by my relationships', meaning those that were romantic. Poor grammar aside, the observation seems no less true now, a further sixteen years on.

The *'English Boy'* grew up, sometimes through a process of a sudden tearing apart rather than gentle unfolding. And as with any revolution, personal or social, those in close proximity become at risk of being injured.

***

Like most of us, many things stir emotion within me, many things move me; but the most common and intense source has tended to pertain to love and loving relationships. Falling, making, losing – the holy trinity of the romantic; these are the themes of much of this collection and, by corollary, of much of my life. The poems in this next section range across the spectrum of love (and its close affiliations) and are entirely drawn from my own, direct experience.

Whatever anyone says about love, whatever your own experience of it, whatever its causes and effects, its irrational consequences, its fabulous enlightening of any day, its life-shaping power.......whatever can be done in its name, one thing is certain: there is nothing more important.

My own belief is that love is, in the end, all that sustains. Everything else is product; love alone is cause.

None of which goes any way to explaining or describing the impact of love in my own life. For despite – or perhaps because of – the great abundance of love I've encountered over the years, it remains the great designer, the great architect of action. It still drives me forward at the same time as it tempts me to keep looking back. I yearn for love – to give it and to receive it – more and more and more. It sometimes feels that as each day passes, my longing for it increases. Surely as human beings we are never more alive, never more fulfilling of our purpose than when we are agents of love?

Love of course is often categorised in different ways, into different types: erotic, romantic, familial and spiritual for example. Spiritual love is usually presented as the greatest of these, and who could deny that? Yet at its most intense, romantic love can have a spiritual quality: the act of union between two people can take us to a level of experience which is outside of our everyday sensation of four dimensions. It has a metaphysical quality. And sex can be a vehicle for this union.

Thus, despite the different types that are commonly referred to, it seems to me that there is, in reality, only one kind of love. We simply seek, make and express it in different ways.

Similarly, there's only one reality; it's just that we each perceive it in a different way.

Falling in love is sometimes, in our culture, presented as a purely passive experience. It happens to us, it is suggested, and we can't control it. "I didn't mean it to happen" is a common enough cry in the mouth of the one who has 'found' new love. Sometimes this is even presented as a justification for betrayal, as if it couldn't be helped.

My own view is that this perspective is flawed and self-serving. For the deeper truth is that falling in love starts with the decision to fall in love. It may be subconscious but it is a *decision* nonetheless, like an internal movement towards. We choose to fall in love because at some level we allow that we want it, we know that we are ready, we crave it. We start to look for it, and once we have started to look, it's only a matter of time before an object of love will walk into our lives. Not only that, but the object will bear many of the characteristics that we have been thinking that we need. We meet the next 'right one'. The law of attraction - which states that that to which we give our attention will become manifest – is never more powerfully apparent than in the process of finding love.

Some will object at this point and say that they have been looking for love for years but it hasn't happened. In which case I say that either you haven't been looking as long as you think, or that you haven't actually been looking at all. You haven't actually, deep down as it were, decided. Something in you is saying 'no' and you're not registering it. Deal with the 'no' and love will be found. Life is full of love, we're surrounded by it in infinite abundance; it just needs to be allowed in.

Falling in love always happens when the two people involved want it to happen. There are no victims of falling in love; only perpetrators. Or rather, the victims are never those who do the falling.

However the fact that we decide to fall in love does not guarantee that the relationship it inspires is suitable or will be long-lasting. For one thing, falling in love is a process; loving is a way of being. And love is infinite in its variety of manifestations. It can, for example, fire a connection that lasts just a few hours or a union that endures a life-time; both can be equally pure and profound in their own way. It can fuel relationships which are comfortably inside the dominant social mores of the time, and those which fall well outside of them. If they are honest with themselves and with each other, then there are no constraints on the way love between two people can flourish except those which society tries to impose.

In particular, our culture has for centuries equated 'true' love with permanence. Love, we are led to believe, is only ever successful if, and for as long as, the loving couple are in some respect together. If and when the partnership ceases to exist in a formal, explicit sense then at that point the love that they have shared becomes lost. The relationship is deemed to have 'failed'.

This is a limiting perspective. I have not and therefore never will experience the life-long union so brilliantly typified by my own parents. Yet I don't consider any of my relationships to have been failures, or to have wasted time, even though each has fallen short of the particular marker of permanence. On the contrary, I know now that all my relationships have, at the very least, been valuable. Some have been marvels.

For if nothing else, whatever has happened in my experience on the spectrum of loving - the way that I've loved and been loved, rejected and been rejected - has all taken me to this present moment. And here, now, I've come to understand, at last, that it's all good.

And the same is true for you. One of life's greatest blessings is that this same perspective – 'it's all good' - is available to us all, whatever our circumstance.

***

It's not my purpose here to investigate or explain the details of my love-life after Nanette. That would not be fair, either on myself or on my former partners, some of whom remain good friends. There is too much water that has flowed under too many bridges, and too much heat generated by the burning of some of those bridges, for public analysis to be productive. Especially so when, no matter how objective or clinical I might want to be, an inevitable watermark of accusation or confession would surely be visible.

I will say this though: I have learned that love can fuel demons as well as bring angels. Clear sight of both is essential.

The implications and effects of my experience of romantic love have steadily percolated within me over a period of almost forty years. Love – love of all kinds - has been my greatest, my most persistent teacher. And one clear, strong lesson stands out: everything happens for a good reason, however it happens and whatever the apparent causes. Our lives are driven by deep forces, sometimes deeper than we can know at the time. Sometimes it can take a while, even if we look hard, for the true nature of these forces to become apparent. Sometimes we have to struggle to find a joyful outcome. But it is there, every time all the time, if we choose to see it.

In any case, the best I can say directly about any of it is in these poems and songs. Let it be enough.

By Your Side (1981)

You will be the hour
That gives us feeling
You will be the chimes that never end
You will be the sense when we are reeling
You'll be the love that I defend

I will be the man for all your seasons
I will be the cloak that keeps you warm
I'll be the wind that gives you reasons
I'll be the rock that holds you firm

No no no don't you worry about me
I've never been one to save myself with lies
No no no don't you cry over me
It's more than the fear of being lonely that keeps me by your side

You will be the words I'll be the story
I will live between your lines
I'll fight your ghosts in midnight glory, I'll calm your storm
You'll be my bride
Oh calm my storm, come on be my bride

No no no don't you worry about me
I've never been one to save myself with lies
No no no don't you cry over me
It's more than the fear of being lonely that keeps me by your side

Leaving

He lies
on a bed
on his back
the ceiling
no barrier
between those
wide wet eyes
and the dark
blank night sky.

He feels
creeping cold
a chest plate
of new steel
where feeling
is frozen
in the act
of choosing
his remorse.

He knows
all at once
all in shock
this genie
grants it all
now his bottle
is uncorked
emptied out
as it is.

He pours
himself out
stricken dry
newly snapped
by
the power
of his will
where he lies.

My Wonderful

It was a short summer that year:
three days, two nights, a little more....

Hot. Warm. Full of breath.
Humid very quickly.

My heart-beat noise became
music by your tender touch
as we knew us in long forgotten ways.

Ah, suddenly the sky -
outrageous lapis blue!
The face of the world smiled like heaven!
We sewed a luscious harvest
under that fantastic sun
and smelled the threat of rain with laughter.

Of course of course of course
too soon the storm broke:
our deluge jammed the air we breathed
we gasped and were swept away.

What fed our world
also drowned us.

Now is autumn, inside and out,
memories crackling dry:
the leaves of your hair falling like sadness
through my trembling hands.

One lonely glimpse of spring survives:
your smile
in my heart
if I am old.

Quantum Desire

This desire lives invisible
in between atoms
in the stillness between heartbeats
in the thought of you now.

It flickers from my aura
to the thrill in my throat
from my eyelids
to my animal core
from my back bone
(exactly where I cannot touch)
to my mind games
from my meaning words
to my pumping pumping heart.

What arcs across the quantum
through-leaping time and space
to orbit inside your skin
is Me Here Now.

In a single collapsed instant
I'm inside around you
in your membrane
in your art
in your tenuous grip
(more secure than you allow)
in all things delicate
in your false imaginings
in your pumping pumping heart.

All messages between us
are less instant than our lust
for we inhale the law of attraction
and exhale the power of now.

I go to my centre
and do feel our warmth
and our tightening
and our histories
and our dreamed-of life

(precisely and forever here)
in a Ferrari of love
sleek-engined and fuelled
by our pumping pumping heart.

This desire joins molecules
drives the pull of the magnet
lights up my words
that you read now.

New Light (2002)

I've looked in love's eyes, smelled its perfume
I've opened my wings, flown round the moon
Been lost in the rhythm, the swell of love's tune
I've danced through the night in some beautiful rooms

But I was just waving to ships in the night
You came like sunrise, to shed a new light on my life

I've run from my heart, skipped lessons on the way
I've thought I was safe, but truth finds you one day
I've walked over mountains never looking down
I've breathed in the country, spat out the town

But I was just waving to ships in the night
You came like sunrise, to shed a new light on my life

This kind of love changes history
This kind of love alters memory
Re-shapes the story of the heart
Re-frames the ending
Re-writes the start

Cos I was just waving to ships in the night
You came like sunrise, to shed a new light on my life

Angel

i. Angel Light

You were my sat.nav out of madness;
loved me without strong demand;
are beautiful and now sad
behind a party of smiles.

ii. Angel Rose

The door through which he walked
each evening
was always open.
A mossed path wound through fecund beds
gently curving this way and that
through lawn and growth and writhing colour.
Inside this walled garden
he tends to desire.

His bounteous work
gave flaming life
to the most remote spots of the garden.
His tools rained sun and moon
as his blurred hands flickered across topsoil
with skill and purpose.

And in time he grew a prize:
an abundant rose
of exotic pastel colours
a shocking bloom
at the very breath's edge of decay
its roots brushing under the outer stones of the path
where no growing thing had survived
more than a short summer.

Its fluttering beauty
uncoiling from beyond mortal horizon
its fragrance wafting to senses
suffusing pores
hazing a different sun rise
after nights of darkness.

The garden flourished in the glory of the rose
though none saw it
outside the walls.

iii. Angel Falls

On that one grey morning
blue-skied elsewhere
he chose to build a new path
out of concrete and sweat and dirt
a path which scarred
old-established lawns
and trampled delicate displays.

A small man with small rough hands
and thoughtful eyes
and smiling faces
with a serrated knife
slowly
lopped
each rose head
from its stem.

He crushed stalks and leaves and thorns
beneath steel-capped rough-shod boots
till the life sap seeped
over the petalled thorns
turning summer's long-lived blooms
to a gruel of innards death.

His tears, though tap-dripping on the new earth,
Were knowing and ugly.
They blurred his aim as his white weed-killer poison
sprayed randomly in hope and fury.

Slowly, he dropped all tools
Ambled back up the path
And closed the door.

Gone

That past is a silent hand
in the puppet of our mouths.

It shapes our words
and is dumb to itself.

Dexterity aside
it has no power for life
or happiness
or love.

Air Change (1981)

The air is changing
Will change again
A storm to shake out rusty chains
A face will glow
No face the same
The after-taste of far-flung friends.

Memory lane is a motorway now
Queues of yesterdays at hand
And yesterday
Seemed so simple somehow
When tomorrow seemed so grand.

No regrets for ifs or buts
No claims for right or wrong
Just always never seems to last
Summer's not that long.

Don't need to try
To be right there
In black and white, forgotten grey
When plans were made
and plots were shared
how many saw the light of day?

In times of change
When winds are high
The doors of old rooms are flung wide
And there I sit
Nostalgia's eye
And see a road I never tried.

No regrets for ifs or buts
No claims for right or wrong
Just always never seems to last
Summer's not that long.

Hindsight

One day
We will have had a memorable evening
And be walking home
Hand in hand.

We will have made love
Like we always knew we could
Gently levelling desire
With the kissing strokes of skin.

We will have laughed at each other's drunken dance
And been proud to know us
Our hearts full of the best of our lives
Our sure futures not worth the noting.

We will have walked in the swell
Of our families' contentment
Talked with a knowing that
Made the kindest envy in those we love.

One day
I will not have forgotten or turned my back
I will not have been tangled or caught or lured
I would have been talking
Connected
Holding on
To you in love
To my love.

One day

Not Over

She was lovely:
Enticing alluring
Offering sparkling

But he came home
And cried for you.

She was dazzling:
A gift of just-what-he-needed
At just-the-right-time

But later, softly to his face
He held a picture of you.

She was tender:
Wet passions out-bursting
Full of desiring

But he wanted nothing
But to smell the love of you.

She of a million forms
Can never be you
Who is the one.

You Called

Tonight you called.
Your voice unheard for generations
Crossed my time-slipped broken heart
Held me breathless and foolish once again.

I know you
Hear you more clearly than you hear yourself.

There is no long-distance any more
Just cheap-rate and free minutes bolted on.

Tonight you called
And I performed your old friend from long ago.
I gave you words of comfort soft
And light
Like feathers from a broken wing.

I hear you
Love you more dearly than you love yourself.

"Take care", I said.

And once again
You were gone.

Jealousy

Just below old clouds
I dream the heart of a very black Swann
Watching someone else's shadow
Playing across a dark lake.

The Lady holds Excalibur aloft.

I swoop down in an instant
Fall upon it
My flesh denies the legend:
The sword returns
To a silent quarter.
I can write another line.

Ah, but I cannot swim.

Phoning

My hand is on the phone
Touching the receiver
My fantasy the words
Their effect on the receiver
A moment to speak
Whose impact shapes lifetimes:
Who makes your understanding?

You once were my beloved
Will you be again?
Where is your hand and your phone
What is your fantasy?
The dial tone is loud and full of nothing
No heaven or hell, just flat-line:
Who makes your understanding?

My hand is on the phone
My fingers on the keypad
A single digit's grace or damnation
Staring math-eyed at my heart.
The slight pressure from a finger
And fates are determined:
Who makes your understanding?

I press and press and press again
Eleven times.
The dial tone ceases
A moment's silence
Then the wildest noise
A distant 'hello':
Who makes your understanding?

My fantasy teeters on the brink of real.
My hand is on the phone
As it clicks back
To an unheard dial tone......

Toy Radio

You are radio
All others merely wavelengths.

You play my tune
Transmit my words
Hiss the spaces
In between.

Tied up in one
You pray
In supplication
You speak
My information
You sing
By inclination

You are force
Dispute
Silent obedience.

You magnetise
By abjection.

You must transmit.
You must receive.

You are radio
All others merely wavelengths.

10. Being Two of Me

Conscience doth make cowards of us all
Hamlet in *Hamlet* by William Shakespeare

'Conscience', as used by Shakespeare, is an interesting word. Its derivation is clearly identical to that of 'conscious'. Today, we tend to use 'conscience' when referring to innocence and guilt for example – what we think about what we have done. Shakespeare's use of the word is closer to what we would now call 'self-consciousness' - being aware of ourselves, without necessarily much of a judgemental emphasis.

Self-consciousness, in the sense of being self-aware, is what separates human beings from the animals and other life forms. Our ability to be aware of ourselves as being apparently separate from everything else – in both physical and non-physical aspects - gives us the capacity to learn, speak and change. It's true that other animals can learn to do things: a dog can be taught 'tricks' or to obey its master or to recognise particular signals. But this is the most basic kind of learning, by rote and at a purely organic level. A dog cannot be taught to consider its 'self'. It is not, as Disney might have us believe, a fully formed consciousness frustratingly trapped in a limited, dumb body. A dog is only conscious of things external to itself, and responds only in instinctive or genetic ways. A dog may feel pain, but it doesn't worry about its health; it may be impatient for food, but it doesn't worry about tomorrow.

In terms of a behavioural hierarchy, a trained dog is closer to the plant that has been placed to grow towards the light, than it is to a mature human being.

It's also true that some species, notably the apes, do exhibit some signs of self-consciousness, and this is what makes them closest to human beings in a zoological sense. Yet theirs is a rudimentary awareness of self, far less subtle or agile in its potential than our own.

I mean nothing derogatory by this. Dogs can be devoted beings, acting out of the purest of loves, the unconditional variety. Apes and some other animals can form relationships. Even the growth of a flower can be understood as a form of love. But self-consciousness is the opposable thumb on the hand of the human psyche. It gives us the capacity to change exponentially, and in ways that are beyond even the most exceptional of our nearest life forms.

The signifier of self-consciousness is that an individual has the capacity to be both, at one and the same time, the observer and the observed. We watch ourselves as we act, feel, think. We can reflect on our own performance, not just after the event but in the very moment that it occurs.

But this relentless essence, this most fantastic and promising of human characteristics, is also what separates us from true bliss. In that founding figura of our culture, the story of Adam and Eve, the fruit of the tree of knowledge that Eve bites into is the apple of her own eye, so to speak. In eating what is forbidden, she chooses her own selfish interests over anything else. The apple does not *contain* knowledge; it is the eating of the apple that establishes self-knowledge. From that moment, she has no choice but to see herself as distinctly 'Eve'; she can only offer the apple *to* Adam because she has free will and has become separate *from* Adam. (His own rib is talking to him!) As a result, they become self-conscious, and, symbolically, ashamed of their nakedness. The two have become inextricably amputated from selfless bliss.

Thus the fall from Eden, from earthly paradise, from perfect acceptance without wonder or shame – as in the consciousness of animals - was generated precisely by Adam and Eve's ability to know that they were human beings and to be able to choose what that might mean.

Put another way, the myth of Adam and Eve represents the fact and significance of self-consciousness, and its impact in removing the human species from eternal, un-self-conscious bliss. We are driven to search for union, because we don't automatically have it. We're human instead.

It's a long road back from there.

As intimated above, self-consciousness can be a debilitating phenomenon as well as a liberating one. When out of control it can mutate into shyness, self-blame, anxiety, and aching inertia. We worry about ourselves; we worry what others will think; we question ourselves and, sometimes, become incapacitated by the very questioning.

We can also make some very bad decisions.

When Hamlet, an avatar of self-consciousness if ever there was one, remarks that he has been "thinking too precisely on the event" and it is like the thought is "quartered" into "but one part wisdom and ever three parts coward" (Act 4 Scene 3 lines 43ff), he is simply describing his own inability to act. He's elaborating on his cowardice, yes, but also on his self-consciousness. His inclination to *reflect* is so great, that his ability to *do* is impaired. In the end, he himself as well as Laertes, Polonius, Ophelia and perhaps even Gertrude pay the price for this inertia.

Perhaps this is why I love the play '*Hamlet*' so much? Perhaps I recognise intimately the force of self-consciousness at work and have, at times, like the Danish Prince, felt helpless to do anything about it. The phenomenon feels very familiar to me, as suggested by the following verses.

Me on Me

This swarm of seeing
Buzzes all over me
Never and insistently
Letting me do or say or think
Without question.
The more brilliant my light out there
The more rigorous my questions in here.

I am stung by the truth
And dismantled by clarity.

My ache is the ache of longing to be free of my self.

To find shade from my own burning light
To simply do and make mistakes or succeed
Unhampered by me.

What purpose this swarming, stifling, shimmering self?

And in the moment of beseeching
– let me go, let me go –
We smile at each other
The swarm and I
–– and we know oh we know -
That we neither can answer that prayer.

Something and Nothing

Two broken arms
Encircling empty air
Grasping at a life
The hope for something solid
Amid feeble illusions

On the horizon
Down a stark road
A sky full of sunrise
The promise of completion
In some absolute light

But these ignorant arms
Fall across screwed up eyes
The gesture as proof
That childhood blankets
Separate boy and life.

In nothingness
There is nothing to fear
Because no one to be afraid.

Endlessly hiding boy
Too afraid of holding nothing
To see that he holds nothing
Endlessly hiding boy
Must yearn eternal
For the light of mother-love
To burn through eyelids tightly shut
Endlessly hiding boy
Will yearn eternal for the blast of father-fission
To scatter his dust in certainty at last.

Anything
To escape
Nothing.

Gotta Fight (1990)

Gotta fight this man
The man inside the man
Gotta fight this man
Stop him spoiling my plan

Gotta blow him away
He looks alive but he's better off dead
Gotta do it today
Gotta shoot him in the head

His grass looks greener
But it's the colour of jealousy
His light looks brighter
But it's his shadow that's in me
Gotta blind him so I can see
Oh this man in me

Gotta fight and I daren't lose
He's been the ruin of me too long
Gotta keep only what I can use
Throw the rest away
Like an unused song

Gotta fight this man
The man inside the man
Gotta fight this man
Stop him spoiling my plan

Watching Myself (2008)

I am the observer and I am the observed
Me and my behaviour were separate at birth
I'm full of awareness, of compassion and of tact
But even in my cry of love, there's something of an act

Can't stop watching myself
Can't stop catching my own 'I'
Everywhere I look it's always me
Never any shade from my own light

And when I cry I measure the volume of my tears
I want to speak my truth out loud but first I have to hear
It's always ironic, always once or twice removed
I'm always in between myself and what I want to do.

It's human you say
Not a bad thing
It's what separates us
From every other living thing
In every single moment
In every thing I do
There's only one person present
And it's not you.

I'm capable of anything, and sometimes done worse
Not sure if the heart of me is diamond or a curse
I am my own ending, my own false or happy start
I'm married to me, til death us do part.

Can't stop watching myself
Can't stop catching my own 'I'
Everywhere I look it's always me
It's all wrong and it's all right

Insomnia Infinitas

Memory and tomorrow
serrate this dull scratchy ache
inside the back of my closed eyes.

Minute on minute
the coming day falls darker,
shaded by failing and waste.

I hear it in the dawn's grey reproach –
the rumble of living,
being done by others.

My slowed breaths inhale half-heartbeats;
my flexed muscles stiffen psychic sinews.
No purpose can subdue the tension
of a night without purpose.

Such is the self-sorrow
of dreams without sleep.

11. Being One of Me

The only power the self has is the power to cover up the truth
Sufi proverb

The feeling of loneliness starts with an ache, moving from somewhere near the heart to somewhere near the throat. It is in essence identical to the unmistakeable ache of longing. However sometimes what one is longing for is not altogether clear. It's easy, when feeling the ache of loneliness, to assign the cause for it incorrectly.

With the possible exception of family, romantic love can be the most powerful way of bridging this existential gap. It stops us feeling lonely. Or more precisely, it covers over our essential alone-ness, even if love itself can feel like loneliness; the longing to be *with* the beloved is dissolved utterly in the liquid of separation *from* the beloved.

Friendship and art attempt to do much the same thing.

It follows therefore that when romance dies, or is snatched away for whatever reason, then the most acute form of loneliness can be experienced. The gap yawns loud and wide before us, where once it had seemed almost closed completely. ('Seemed' is important here.) The loss of love opens up the chasm of loneliness very wide. Its sheer precipices can make us dizzy, and fearful that we might fall in.

I believe that much of what we make as human beings – our culture, our social structures, our arts and sciences, learnings and ambitions – are all, fundamentally, efforts to ease the ache of loneliness. The fall from Eden created the most absolute separation – what we now speak of as 'existential isolation'. We are aware of our selves being separate from the cosmos, we know we are each alone in our individual lives. No one can ever truly be in our shoes or experience us as we experience ourselves. We are self-conscious, not alter-conscious, no matter how hard we try or how advanced our sensory perceptions might be.

Put another way, were we in un-self-conscious bliss we could never ever be lonely. Existential isolation is the price we pay for self-consciousness. Sometimes this pours into our experience as a sense of loneliness. It can easily be argued that, as humans, it's our lot to be lonely.

It seems to me that every kind of loneliness we feel, whatever immediate cause may be assigned to it, has a piece of that existential isolation mingled in with it. We may yearn for a friend, a relative, a lover, or a child, but what fertilises that yearning at a root level is the essential longing of the individual to be known, to be in a state of union with something or someone other, to not be alone.

And if, as the Danish Christian philosopher Kierkegaard put it: "there are two types of people: those who are desperate, and those who know they are desperate" then it's surely better to be on the side of those who know. At least then the state of alone-ness can be a starting point for life, not a terrifying end-point. We don't have to be victims of it; we can be wise about it, even if our wisdom is well and truly after the event.

The Real

He watched the TV.
Sunk in the escape that was not an escape.

He walked upstairs watching his feet.
Step
By
Step.
He passed urine watching
it fall.
'Tinkling' they called it.
He walked downstairs
Eyes closed.
Back to TV.

It passed.

No words grazed his dry lips,
cracked and untouched.
He sat, watched and remembered what he wasn't watching.

There was no other person that day.
Nobody talked or smiled or touched.
There was no other body that day.
No person who listened or agreed or shook his hand.
Nobody's lips glanced his lips.
Nobody's eyes caught his eyes.
Nobody heard
What he did not have to say.

They all passed by.

And he knew that it was right.

Regret

In the heart's mansion
Whose rooms are numbered by years
I always live in the newest wing
Where space and matter converge.

My home is mere collections
Of morsels from the past
Pile upon pile of things unfolded
Tightly tight around.

In this suite of rooms
The sadness of objects
Presses hard against my ribs.

An endless seeming party
Roars throughout and around
But
Always outside
The other side of the glass.

In this tiny vestibule
Sounds rebound
Collapse into from where they came
Leaving silence or infinite noise.

All is baggage
All is cramped.
Box after box of previous belonging
Litter the few cubic inches I now inhabit.
Floor to ceiling wall to wall
The things of my life impose upon my now.
The door can never now be reached.
The window is hidden from view.
Immovable furniture covers the light switch.
I am hungry.
I am breathless.
I am hot.
My body aches to stretch
Each limb compressed by solid memory.

Soon, I will be just a pin-point

Beneath things.

All space for me is gone.

The Family Next Door

Doors only close behind us.
We walk through as we desire.

The family man proffers his open hand
No handle to turn, no lock to pick
A threshold to cross.

Their shared points of humour
Their easy knowing of role and response and future
Their quiet guise of source and type and movement
Their language unique, touches unsurprising

All condemn me to keep my laughter to myself.

And all those wide-smiled thresholds I blindly crossed
Hid a cruel joke:....

Doors only close behind us.

When the Plane Left
for my sister

The truth of the departure gate
Is that one leaves
And others miss you.

We couldn't see
Your hand waving
In the tiny window
Above the runway.

Or your tears
On the useless tissue
Gripped painfully
Like a sad blanket.

You couldn't see that
We four held together
On the cold windy top floor
Of the short-stay car park.

Yes, we four held together:
A strange new silver-lining.

And our tears splashed on concrete and white line
And there were those
Among we four
Who wondered and wondered
How we would be five again.

Brave Man
for my brother

You always seemed
To be wanting to catch up.

I have been remiss
In not seeing
Your courage
When you got the letter
And your life would never be
Your life
As you had dreamed it.
When you lay awake and pictured
Conversations with others
Close and far away, as you thought.

Impossible words
Unknown feelings
Death within earshot.
Terror
An intruder
In your blood.

But I was never far away
And never will be
For you have no need to catch up
Being already part of my days.

Welcome.

Not Telling

Silent prompts
Alert us
To verbal response
Thus in stealth
We shoulder our words
Turn away from saying
What is.

In these acts of '*kindness*'
We save us from something un-named
And we two are quiet signatories
To a fragile truce
In which restlessness
Ferments with what we do not tell
Until under the pressure of its own gravity
It erupts into revolutionary action
And is played out in front of our eyes
The one place
Where it cannot be controlled.

War breaks out
And there is always damage.

12. Fathering

*We are such stuff as dreams are made on;
and our little life Is rounded with a sleep.*

Prospero in *The Tempest* by William Shakespeare

In a very real way, and apart from my own birth of course, becoming a father was, is, and always will be the most important event of my life. It's entirely accurate to describe the process of becoming a parent as having a new dimension of experience opened up. There is nothing like it, and no substitute. It's a kind of magic, the hallmark of which is unconditional love.

I've been fortunate enough to have this same event played out on three separate occasions. Three special, unique, and gifted people are in the world because of me (and their mother of course). New and distinct life has been created three times directly from my own body.

My love for my daughters is subterranean, tectonic. It flows through the silent unseen foundations of the edifice of life, within its girders and core structure, rather than being exposed in its decoration or outer surfaces, which are vulnerable to erosion and fashion.

This means that there has never been a question for me about my love for them. There have been, and always will be, questions about what I *do* as a father, about what is required of me etc., and I have of course both made mistakes and acted wisely as a father in a typically human and erratic way. But rarely has this been a source of creative energy for me. My consciousness as a parent seems to inhabit a slightly different psychological and spiritual space to the rest of my affections (and affectations).

Another way of expressing this same point would be to say that my creativity around my children expresses itself in *being* a father, in *doing* fatherly things, and has little need or scope for expression in art. For this reason, I've only occasionally felt the need to write poetically about my children.

On the other hand, they are who I write *for*, they are in the front row of my audience. This means that they are present, behind the scenes so to speak (in a terrible mix-up of metaphors), in everything I create, across my entire experience. In a very real sense, Abigail, Hannah and Martha are with me in everything I do, across the entire environment of who I am.

My daughters bring me recognition of how blessed I am to be alive.

Trinity

You bring a smile to the face
Of every hardened stare.
Like love, you fold our tricks and lies
Into pretty shapes.
You splash through all our ice
As if it were water.
You make our lead
Gold in our eyes.
And you are infinitely more
than you trust to be.

Your rampage is the strident flight
Of sun-bound wings.
Your laughter snaps the strings of sadness
Your passions barge away clouds of mediocrity.
What they see is the frantic paddling.
What I know is the swan.
Sky and water and all the earth
Are your domain.
Flutter your heart gently
And you will fly.

You always knew it would happen.
What you haven't seen
You saw coming.
Your tenderness and wary longing
quiver through you
like dawn's breath
on the tips of blades of growing grass
in this single summer's sunlit dawn.
The day is for you
Though you don't yet know it.

Empty Pocket (1983)

Born in the darkest hour
Still before dawn
You have a name
Ever unspoken.

A page unturned.
A flag forever furled.
I heard your heartbeat
Cruel delusion
Bringer of pain.

The breath of life and
The fortune of war
Just passing moments of solitude with
No tiny hand to hold.

So where does this love come from?
Where does it go?
What means 'you'?
What means 'I'?

Life is movement but
Not one of your moments has passed.
Life is change but
Nothing of you has grown.

I keep you invisible
Close by me in honour.
And though my coat will change its colour
This empty pocket will remain.

The Girls (1984,1986,1990)

You cry in the morning
But you smile when I appear
The ragged sight that I must be
Is enough to stop those tears

So simple and as innocent as the day
You find me lacking love
In every way

Sometimes I don't know what to do
Sometimes I don't know what to do
I've so much love for you

Asleep and I can watch you
Bewildered as I stare
Oh please don't you ever leave
There's too much hurt out there

So simple and as innocent as the day
You find me lacking love
In every way

Sometimes I don't know what to do
Sometimes I don't know what to do
I've so much love for you

And now the mornings don't have you
And you find your own way through each day
Hold on to when I held you tight
And wiped your tears away

13. Gremlins

What's the point of knowing, if I don't do?
Bob Dylan

Gremlins, saboteurs, devils, beasts...we all have them. They are our internal, habitual, negative voices. The voice that questions and resists when we dare to want something different or just for ourselves. The voice that reasons us into inactivity, or resignation. The voice that makes us deride our own desires, and desire our own derision. The voice that encourages self-pity rather than objectivity or action. The voice that says "no!"

Sometimes the voice is familiar, perhaps that of a member of our family or a friend. Sometimes it is so habitual, so ingrained within our psychological normal processes that it doesn't even need to speak - it is just there, behind the scenes so to speak, silently steering us into avoiding the best we can be.

Identifying and objectifying our gremlins is a crucial task if we want to be better than we are. For if we can see the voices of negativity and restriction for what they are – merely voices born of habit – then we can deal with them and move beyond them. Making progress is as much about managing the forces that hold us back as it is about releasing the energy that takes us forward.

These familiar, long-standing, psychic colleagues I call *My Beasts,* though they've been around a lot longer than the eponymous poem.

My Beasts

Pulling me back to the mire
The pandemonium choir
Swinging on grappling hooks
Avoiding my pleading-eyed looks.

Two of them, giants of old:
Devils in modern day mould:
Familiar and yet so abhorred
One pauper, the other a bawd
Swaying like macho old yobs
With filth spewing out of their gobs
Fat flying far from their hips
The dribble of waste on their lips.

Through teeth that may once have been white
They sing out a chorus of blight
No sense of a friend in their tone
The fume of their breath will alone
Ensure that I never would dare
Expect to take wing through fresh air.

The gremlins who run at their feet
Won't slacken to let me have peace.
In the instant I glimpse they are gone
They're crawling all over my bones
Thrilled by their long-lasting skill
In keeping me under-fulfilled.

14. Epiphanies

Time doesn't change us; it unfolds us
Max Escher

In the early 1980s, I was fortunate enough to be invited to be a pupil of Sheikh Abdullah Sirr Dan al-Jamal, a Sufi master based at the time in north London. Alongside the birth of my daughters, the two years or so I spent in the company of Sheikh Abdullah and his other students (known as *murids*), is the most numinous of all my life experiences so far. It seems now to have been like an extended thunderclap which has reverberated across and through the years to the present day. I have no doubt that the consequences of that most fabulous storm will be with me to my death and beyond.

I have no intention of detailing the events or experiences of that time in this volume. Much would not be believed; and in any case some things, it's wisely said, are better left unsaid. Suffice it to say that the Sheikh guided me into, amongst other things, some awareness of my personal potential and powers, a glimpse of the forces of energy that connect all of life, and the beginnings of an understanding of my life's purpose. These are of course profound things, and only the most clear-sighted and wisest of men could have guided me to such places. Sheikh Abdullah was such a man.

However the rigours of the Sufi way were strenuous; the self-discipline and material deprivations involved were, particularly for a young man in his mid-twenties, very demanding (yes, I am forgiving myself now!). Looking back it seems almost inevitable that I would whirl off the Path, and I did. I gave up the practices, gave up the group, gave up my Sheikh.

In the following years I gradually lost sight of the habits and intentions of the Sufi experience, though the memories of it never left me. I often used to hope that somehow I would return to 'the Path' as our study was sometimes referred to, though I could not imagine how. Occasionally I tried (albeit half-heartedly) to re-establish contact with my former fellow *murids*, but even by the time I first did this the group itself had already disbanded. Some leading members had, I later discovered, moved to Australia. Others I could not track down at all. Eventually, some time ago, I discovered that the Sheikh had died.

Then in 2007, I took a course in life-coaching in London. For six weekends in the spring and summer of that year a group of professional and would-be coaches from all over the world met in a conference centre near Regents Park, London, to be trained in some innovative personal coaching techniques.

The course incorporated, for me, a significant strand of personal development, as well as the learning of techniques to be used in coaching work. The course also demanded a depth of honest communication and intimacy with my fellow trainees which in turn founded several substantial friendships. All-in-all it was a wonderful process, and I believe I learned a great deal. However nothing that I discovered about coaching was of any significance at all compared to the – and no other word will do here - epiphany I underwent one Saturday afternoon in a guided coaching exercise in which I was the main protagonist and willing guinea-pig to a specific coaching technique. The event was witnessed by all of my fellow trainees, and some I think recognised that what I experienced was, to me, profound.

Again, the details of the experience are not important here, but the outcome is. For over the space of a few minutes, I re-connected with that part of my being which, for twenty-five years or so, had lain dormant since the 'Sufi years'. Old forces of energy surged through me once more, and I came alive in ways that I had forgotten were possible. I experienced the reality of my self in ways I hadn't done in all those years. Furthermore, I realised, with a great flare of joy within, that my time as a Sufi pupil had not, after all, been wasted. It was possible to once again tap into the same sources and forms of energy of which my Sheikh had made me aware. There was meaning and purpose to my life after all. Nothing was lost, and everything had happened for a reason. The Path – my path - materialised again in front of me, right there and then, in a wholly new form. I stepped back onto it in an absolutely unexpected and ecstatic way.

It was a glorious time for me, and has shaped much of what I have done since. It's not an exaggeration to say that my life changed forever that afternoon. And although it precipitated an avalanche of change (and some trauma) in my personal life, the ripples of which are still present today, it was and is all good.

The Child and the Lion

Close by,
The child has his heart in his mouth
Where the words come out
And is full, achingly full of these longings
All born of the one:

For the touch of true love
That he is free to give and can freely receive;
For the knowing that the thing is done
Not just spent;
For the aftermath which feels fully after
Not just a moment before the next;
For the smile of appreciation that he sees in the mirror;
For the moment when it is the time
To be whole now.

As sensual as her lips are the aches of remorse
As soft as whispered words of the old song
Are the hints of unknown futures.

But
As fierce as the Lion's snarl
Is the energy of truth.
The Boy now rides the Lion with pride
Striding into his life at last.

The Lion walks with you a while.

The Squirrel, the Fish and Two Leaves

One summer
the four of us held hands
told stories
in the outdoor cafés
and air-conditioned bars
in that secluded borough at the river's edge.

We opened – for a moment – the windows in our eyes
And looked far down and in to each other
Without caring.

You, gathering every kernel of insight
Rustling it up onto the page
Snapping the book shut
Carrying it under arm to the next venue.

You, flying over the spray and into the sunlight
Holding your gaze on the birds above you
Still-framed in the bright air of success and faith.

And you and I, drifting there in hope and expectation
Hiding our most silent ghosts of discontent
Never quite daring to reveal our need.

It was beautiful, for a short while
And transforming
Until the press of water moved us on
Under so many bridges some of them burning
and burning still.

Now, here, there are moments
When I look down from a dizzying height
And see us there again,
Sat like friends by a sweet green English river,
and I am smiling throughout.

Who

Who will take me to my self
Who is waiting there for me
Who is the fluttering of a small bird where my heart is
Who is the bird's song in the quiet hour before dawn
Who will breathe life into my soul
Who knows all that I am and can be
Who offers her hand without judgement or regret
Who loves by simply breathing breathing
Who is with me, if I want
Who will heal our quiet ache
The final point of all.

Who.

Our Own Last Supper

Our group personalities
Worked hard at over-pressing our souls
As we tried to recapture
What had obviously gone.

We jarred against each other
The tectonic plate of yesterday
Grinding against today.
Our conversation shuddered
And we looked to other eyes
Not quite in the seat next to us
Searching for what we once had known.

Little scratches on our surface
Marked the time
To say goodbye.

Like a wake that we expected to be a party
We floated over the event
without touching the truth
of what was now
politely inevitable.

The Journey completed
By this threshold dinner
Where we swallowed our sadness
And gulped down our love.

A meal such as this
Our own last supper
enriched us nonetheless.

What is gone is good
And is still gone.

15. Unfolding

A belief is just a thought you keep thinking
Esther Hicks

In the months following the epiphany described in the previous chapter, the outward appearance of my life changed considerably. A long-term relationship ended, the direction of my professional career shifted radically, my waking day took on a new form.

I became truly single – romantically unattached – in a way that I had rarely been before in my adult life. I developed positive, healthy routines around meditation, eating and drinking, and physical exercise. I began to write with purpose again, which included commencing this book. I started in earnest to build a coaching/personal development practice. I made contact with some old friends and took decisions about my free time which were based on what I wanted for myself, not what had been habitual or done to please others.

Psychologically, I experienced a tangible shift in my attitude to my own life – its past, present and future – and found it easy to adopt with consistency a positive, hopeful perspective. In short, I started to live in accordance with the best of me.

As a result, some remarkable things started to happen to and around me. Money – long a particular bête noir for me, the source of a great deal of anxiety and frustration – started to flow into my experience in unexpected ways. Professional responsibilities at work became easier to bear, providing little or no negative stress. Relationships with family and friends became firmer, more open, more honest. Opportunities to develop my coaching work became available out-of-the-blue. And a string of synchronous incidents, some small in scope but important nonetheless, others more significant, entered my experience.

Of these, the most startling – and meaningful at a personal level – involved my former primary school friends, Anne Manners and Barbara Gates. For one day around this time and completely unexpectedly, Anne contacted me. She had found some of my details on Friends Reunited – I had for a short time been a member some years beforehand – and she emailed a friendly enquiry.

As it happened, I'd been considering taking a day trip to revisit the Isle of Sheppey and my childhood neighbourhood. Thus we agreed to meet: outside the front gates of Halfway County Primary school, one cold, cloudy Saturday morning in November 2007.

The school had changed little, nor had the immediate vicinity. The family home in Western Avenue looked much the same, although the willow tree that my father had planted forty or more years beforehand was now large and visible from a distance.

I stood outside the school and Anne arrived at the agreed time. Despite the passing of forty-one years, I was delighted that I could still recognise her! The maturing process could not erase the facial features that most marked her individual identity.

After a quick stroll around the perimeter of the school, we went on a driving tour of the island, to revisit some key sites in my memory. Anne no longer lived on the island, though she still worked there, and as we drove along, she updated me as much as she knew of the lives of some of our former classmates.

I was particularly interested in the fortunes of, and her friendship with, Barbara Gates, but surprised – shocked even – when Anne told me that she hadn't after all been very friendly with Barbara in school. Far from it in fact – the two of them hadn't really got on and there had been some tension between them. My recollection of Barbara as 'queen bee' was correct, but this had been a factor in distancing her from many of the other girls. Anne had certainly not been a member of Barbara's personal 'in crowd'. The twosome in my mind's memory had not been a twosome in real life!

In fact the two of them had had very little contact since leaving Halfway. Anne told me she had seen Barbara working in a supermarket in a nearby town, off the island, but they hadn't and didn't speak to each other.

Later, I would take this news and reflect on its significance in relation to the workings of memory, but at the time I merely expressed my surprise, and suggested we find somewhere for lunch. We stopped at a pub which Anne had heard about but never visited, near the village of Minster.

It was Saturday lunch-time and the pub was very busy. At first it seemed that there were no free tables, but then I spotted an empty one. It was located on a raised area of the restaurant alongside three or four other tables which were all full. There was bright sunlight streaming through a ceiling window which acted almost like a spotlight, shining onto the free table.

We took our seats and ordered lunch. For a few minutes we talked about old times, and about how our lives had unfolded over the last forty or so years. It was a very pleasant conversation.

Then, I noticed that Anne was not really looking at me as I was talking. She appeared to be looking over my shoulder at something or someone behind me. Then she said: "Derek, you're not going to believe this."

"What do you mean?" Out of politeness I didn't turn around to see where she was looking.

"I don't believe it," she said in whisper.

Now I was very curious, and keen to find out what was surprising her.

"What is it?"

"It's Barbara!"

I instantly forgot any instinct for politeness and turned in my chair. There, facing me, at the table immediately behind ours, no more than three or four feet away, and instantly recognisable to me just as Anne had been an hour or two earlier, was Barbara Gates.

She was lunching with a couple of girlfriends, but I cut across their conversation and introduced myself. For a few minutes the three of us giggled and spluttered our way through embarrassment and shock, confirming our mutual recollections. We exchanged brief descriptions of our life circumstances, and one of Barbara's friends took a photograph. It sits framed on a shelf now – me, in the centre, a broad grin, with my left arm around Anne Manners, looking a little nervous – whether this was because of being photographed or because, as was very clear, she didn't feel comfortable around Barbara, I don't know - and my right arm around Barbara Gates, who is smiling serenely.

The pleasure of seeing them both again – perhaps for the last time – was exacerbated by the wonder of the nature of our meeting. Such synchronicity is both stunning and, I believe, highly significant.

To reinforce this, and before we went our separate ways, I checked with Barbara what I had already begun to suspect – she was not a regular visitor to that pub, and, like me, was only there that day because of a sequence of chance decisions and encounters.

***

As intimated earlier, I find synchronicity to be an amazing and frequent phenomenon. I've come to realise that it most often occurs when one's actions are closely aligned to what is best for one's true self. There are many different ways of expressing this idea: notions of being 'true to the soul', of being 'in harmony with your self' of being 'on the right track', 'balanced', 'centred', 'living to your purpose', 'doing God's will' – all connote a similar sense of easy correspondence between instinctive, intuitive, spiritual inclinations and physical, worldly actions.

When this is happening, then external events can seem to conspire beyond physical logic to produce unfathomable consequences. Coincidence is the least profound example of this kind of experience.

We all are familiar with waking up after a good night's sleep feeling positive and happy and full of vigour. We feel 'lucky', like today is our day, as if everything's going to go our way. We feel confident, looking forward to the day's events, keen to live life, happy to experience what the world has to offer. We feel positive, and, if we notice it, we feel energetic and wholly alive. Even the weather seems lovely, whatever the temperature or dryness or cloud cover. Goods things happen. The lights turn green at just the right moment. A long-standing problem at work is suddenly resolved. We experience the kindness of others. 'Coincidences' happen.

(Equally, most of us are all too familiar with the opposite perspective. The day feels difficult, full of problems and obstacles. Negativity is all around us. We 'get out of bed on the wrong side' and everything conspires against us. The traffic lights turn red, the postman doesn't come, a work colleague is off sick, we wonder what we did to deserve this…)

My own experience in recent times is that the positive days far outnumber the negative ones. Synchronicity fills my experience.

And this is due to one, simple reason. I've learned that my experience is ultimately my own to create. I get to choose how to be. I get to choose how I want to feel. What once would have been annoyances, obstacles, bad luck, I now choose to see in a positive light, as much as my strength allows me. Whenever I can, I look for the up side, but have learned that sometimes the silver lining can take time to reveal itself.

A small example of the delayed silver lining would be a minor car accident with which I was involved quite recently. A van ran into the back of me as I was sat motionless in a queue of traffic. Damage was minimal, though I had a sore neck for a day or two. Yet where once I would have berated my bad luck, complained about the idiotic driver, worried about the insurance hassles, the repair estimates, the inconvenience, now I found my reaction was far more equitable. I consciously took the view that something good would come from the incident.

And it did. A few weeks later, I received a cheque for personal injury which made a major contribution to a subsequent summer holiday in France. Without this money, the holiday could never have happened in the way it did. The car crash had been just what I, and my family, had needed!

***

Let me clarify one point: I'm not trying to suggest that my life is perfect! My life is in progress and in process, and far from sorted. I accept that it never will be. For example, there are still times when my gremlins get the better of me. I can still feel gloomy occasionally. I worry sometimes, and money can still pop up as the most acute source of anxiety. I don't yet feel wealthy all the time. I live alone and sometimes this can teeter into loneliness. Boyhood mannerisms of impatience, restlessness and too much rush can still afflict me. The old perspectives have not vanished – they linger under the surface and will jump on any opportunity to express themselves once more. The beasts are still alive and can still be quite dark.

But the times when they dominate are very occasional, usually separated by weeks at a time. The great bulk of my waking experience is now, well, 'happy' is the best word I can find. I feel on track, purposeful, healthy and expectant of the future.

As a result - *'Prodigal Songs'* is not, as with some autobiographies, a reflection on the best of a life. It's an expression of a life so far, a life which is very much a work in progress. It marks a staging post, not a conclusion. It draws a line under the past, if not an absolutely solid one.

And although there is still much to learn, and no doubt some hard lessons to do the teaching for me, one crucial fact has already registered and sits firmly at the front of my consciousness: the best is yet to come.

16. The Prodigal Son

Life continually offers us hints. If we do not take them, then it comes back and hits us.
                        Carl Jung

I am not a true Christian. However I do believe that the historical man we know as Jesus was a unique force of life, and I appreciate that the Bible contains some divine messages.

When I was a young boy, I was fortunate enough to be given a thick, hardback, comic-strip version of the Bible: *'Picture Stories from the Bible'* by M.C. Gaines. Much of my knowledge of the Bible's content comes from that book. I read it avidly, and in awe, several times over a number of years. I have it still on my bookshelf. It covers much of the content of the 'real' Bible in a necessarily simplified manner. It was a book of wonders for one young boy, and can rightly be called an inspiration.

Over subsequent years, I have read much of the 'real' Bible, though it's true to say that I have been selective in what I've read. I have never attempted a cover-to-cover read through. Thus I cannot claim to be an authority on the Bible, though I do know parts of it quite well and, more importantly, I'm very fond of it. It's a marvellous book.

The King James Authorised Version seems to me to be more powerful throughout than any other version I've encountered. Although the impact of other translations may be significant, and their more familiar phraseologies more enabling of transmitting a simple Christian message – though I actually believe there is a dangerous loss in such simplification – the King James Version seems to me to take the Bible's inherent meanings to an altogether higher plane. It's almost as if the King James Bible is more than just Christian – it is, perhaps, Human.

By virtue of its poetic force and strange, semi-opaque language, syntax and imagery, it offers layers of meaning which are as exciting as they are diverse. I sometimes feel that in the Bible, rather like in the best of Chaucer or Shakespeare, there is no solid ground when it comes to meaning; there are always yet more semantic pathways to tread beyond the ones already explored.

But I must repeat, I am not a Christian. I take from the Bible ideas around personal development, not theological or moral dictats. More than anything else, the Bible is a book and so, like any other, is open to personal interpretation as well as literary criticism. In this respect, one of the most interesting accounts that I've come across is by my former professor at Sussex University, Gabriel Josipovici. *'The Book of God'* offers some lucid insights (and some fascinating contextual information), although unfortunately is limited in range to the Pentateuch. ('Unfortunately' only because I'd have liked more.)

There are those – apparently - who take the Bible as being literally true in all respects. This seems unfathomable to me, and rather worrying. On the other hand, there are those who deny it has any value whatsoever. This seems ridiculously ignorant, and not a little sad.

On the spectrum of attitude between absolute literal belief and complete denial, I suppose I sit about in the middle. As will be apparent, I think that some elements of the Bible are profound and have meaning for us (me) today. Other aspects of it are historically interesting, if not spiritually so. Some sections are simply culturally redundant.

Jesus himself is a curious character, not least because he seems so different in the different Gospels, and indeed at times from verse to verse within one Gospel. He is different again in the 'unofficial' Gospels such as those found at Nag Hammadi and Qumran.

I have little doubt that this is because the actual person, Jesus the Nazarite, became a cause célèbre for a variety of political and religious lobby groups who manipulated his life story (or that which was known about it) for their own purposes. The edited (and part-fabricated) biographies we have in the New Testament are predominantly the product of an attempt to re-present Jesus as the instigator of a 'new' religion. The initial driving force behind this movement seems to have been his follower, Paul, who more than any other 'sold' Jesus as a Divine Being rather than as just a wise man or political/spiritual leader. The Pauline lobby group eventually won the argument over other representations of Jesus, and their victory was confirmed by vote at the Council of Nicaea in 325 AD. At this time, any ideas that were contrary (or just different) to those expounded in the newly 'approved' Gospels were deemed 'heresy'. And there the trouble really started!

Let me just repeat that: the Council of Nicaea, comprised of mortal men, *agreed by vote* that Jesus was Divine, the Son of God, three hundred years after the event of his life. (By comparison, it would be as if we today were making a judgement on a man who had died in 1710 or thereabouts.)

And yet even after this heavy-handed editing process, and in whichever Gospel you find him, he still comes across as being a remarkable and powerful man. It would not surprise me were we somehow one day to discover that he actually could perform a miracle or two. He had significant powers and a significant understanding of the human condition. These characteristics provided ripe conditions for actions that would have been wholly mysterious to a contemporary audience – miracles, by any other name.

However, this does not make him the son of God, or even a god. Historical and archaeological evidence is very persuasive on this point. For example, it is pretty clear that the historical Jesus had brothers and possibly sisters. He was almost certainly married to Mary Magdalene, and they almost certainly had children. It seems unlikely that he died on the cross, but was probably substituted, or possibly he simply recovered. It is likely that he and Mary went into exile thereafter, possibly in what is now southern France.

None of which adds much strength to notions of a virgin birth or resurrection.

I appreciate that it's the 'almost' and the 'possibly' which keep the mystery so alive, and allow the faithful a fingertip grip on belief. And the fact that the Q'uran depicts Jesus as being substituted on the cross by Simon of Cyrene, and as being one of the major prophets before Mohammed, is perhaps unlikely to hold much sway with the firm Christian these days.

In Islamic lore, Jesus – or, more correctly, Isa – is known as the Sleeping Prophet, who will return at the end of the world. Most Muslims therefore are familiar with the notion of Jesus' Second Coming. Interestingly, Islam also reveres many of the Old Testament prophets such as Noah, Abraham and Elijah, and accepts that Jesus was the greatest of all prophets – until Mohammed. Far from being in conflict with Christ's teachings, Islam, at its essential core, positions itself on the same theological train of development as Christianity – it just claims to be a bit further along the evolutionary scale.

None of this prevents me from taking a great deal of personal value from the words that are purported to come from Jesus. Whether he said them or not is irrelevant; the actual presence of the words superimposes its meanings on any issues of biographical or sacred fact or fiction.

I find the parables attributed to Jesus particularly fascinating pieces. They seem to offer simple, clear insights into the human condition in ways which few other stories are able to do, at least not with such precision and economy. There is something of a fairy tale quality to them, which has been well-documented. However in the stark simplicity of their narratives, the intense economy of their design, and in their slightly unreal key motifs, there is also a dream-like aspect to them. I have found it productive to understand parables using the same interpretive criteria as I might apply to the interpretation of a deep-sleep dream.

And this is my approach here to the Parable of the Prodigal Son. I want to give it a Jungian twist. But before doing so, I need to explain my motivation for examining this parable in the first place.

***

We all, each of us, carry a song in our heart. By 'song' I mean a set of words that resonate for us in some way; that have a particular and powerful meaning for us in our life at a particular time, usually for a limited period. The song will change as our life evolves and as we grow, and as its personal significance may wane. Some songs stay with us as a pleasant memory for many years, others are forgotten.

The 'song' may not be a song as such – it may be a story, or a poem, or a single line. It may be of literary origin or a snapshot of conversation; it may have been read or heard. It may be from popular culture, high culture, the bus stop or the classroom – anywhere in fact. The wonderful Jungian psychologist and teacher, Clarissa Pinkola-Estes, calls the song "your own myth, your own guiding light" because it "resonates with aspects of your unconscious".

In other words, it means something to you in a profound and personal way.

For a number of years I carried the parable of the Prodigal Son as my song. It resonated strongly with my perspective on my life. For example, I feared that I had wasted my energies, wasted my skills, not used my natural and learned talents to their full, not been the best I could be. I worried that I had spent most of my life focused on the wrong things, had dissipated too much of my strengths. Although there were some successes to point to – notably my daughters – there were too many failures as well, or, more accurately, too many unfulfilled potentials.

There have been times when, emotionally, I could approach that terrible moment when Tolstoy's Ivan Ilych, close to death, realises with absolute horror that "my whole life, my conscious life, has been wrong". The Parable of the Prodigal Son embellishes that emotion and gives it narrative form.

Now, at the time of writing, my song is a different one. The Prodigal Son is history. I recognise its importance to me (and to others of course) but I can view it without angst.

My own song now is probably a line I stumbled across on the internet somewhere, I'm not sure exactly where: "Time doesn't change us; it unfolds us". To me, right now, this line calls loudly to a deep place in my being. It fixes in black and white a growing sense I have had about the nature of my existence now, today, in this very moment. It takes something complex and abstract, and makes it concrete and replete with meaning – for me. It tells my story, the story of who I am in essence in the present and going forward. It speaks to and for my conscious and unconscious self. It is my song for today.

Yet as I have indicated, once upon a time my song was The Parable of the Prodigal Son...

The Parable of the Prodigal Son (or the Lost Son)

From The Gospel of St Luke Chapter 15, verses 11 – 32 (King James Authorised Version)

11 And he said, A certain man had two sons:

12 And the younger of them said to his father, Father, give me the portion of goods that falleth to me. And he divided unto them his living.

13 And not many days after the younger son gathered all together, and took his journey into a far country, and there wasted his substance with riotous living.

14 And when he had spent all, there arose a mighty famine in that land; and he began to be in want.

15 And he went and joined himself to a citizen of that country; and he sent him into his fields to feed swine.

16 And he would fain have filled his belly with the husks that the swine did eat: and no man gave unto him.

17 And when he came to himself, he said, How many hired servants of my father's have bread enough and to spare, and I perish with hunger!

18 I will arise and go to my father, and will say unto him, Father, I have sinned against heaven, and before thee,

19 And am no more worthy to be called thy son: make me as one of thy hired servants.

20 And he arose, and came to his father. But when he was yet a great way off, his father saw him, and had compassion, and ran, and fell on his neck, and kissed him.

21 And the son said unto him, Father, I have sinned against heaven, and in thy sight, and am no more worthy to be called thy son.

22 But the father said to his servants, Bring forth the best robe, and put it on him; and put a ring on his hand, and shoes on his feet:

23 And bring hither the fatted calf, and kill it; and let us eat, and be merry:

24 For this my son was dead, and is alive again; he was lost, and is found. And they began to be merry.

25 Now his elder son was in the field: and as he came and drew nigh to the house, he heard musick and dancing.

26 And he called one of the servants, and asked what these things meant.

27 And he said unto him, Thy brother is come; and thy father hath killed the fatted calf, because he hath received him safe and sound.

28 And he was angry, and would not go in: therefore came his father out, and intreated him.

29 And he answering said to his father, Lo, these many years do I serve thee, neither transgressed I at any time thy commandment: and yet thou never gavest me a kid, that I might make merry with my friends:

30 But as soon as this thy son was come, which hath devoured thy living with harlots, thou hast killed for him the fatted calf.

31 And he said unto him, Son, thou art ever with me, and all that I have is thine.

32 It was meet that we should make merry, and be glad: for this thy brother was dead, and is alive again; and was lost, and is found.

The first thing to state about this story is that the language in which it is couched is crucial. Let's take Verse 20 as an example: *And he arose, and came to his father. But when he was yet a great way off, his father saw him, and had compassion, and ran, and fell on his neck, and kissed him.*

The superficial sense of the verse in terms of the narrative is straightforward: the son travels home where he is greeted warmly by his father. But even a cursory investigation of the detail of the two sentences starts to reveal much more.

'But when he was yet a great way off, his father saw him.'

What exactly, literally, can that mean?

For one thing, consider how far away another person can be before one might start to recognise his or her identity? Fifty metres, a hundred metres? Perhaps a little more if there is something unusual in the person's physical presence or appearance? In any event does that classify as 'a great way off'? If it doesn't – and surely it doesn't - then the meaning of the line is not intended to be literally true.

Of course not, we might exclaim; few of the parables could be said to be literal anecdotes! But if not literal, then again what might this line actually mean? Has the father access to super-visual powers? It would be flippant to suggest that he has the use of a telescope or other visual aid.

No, we are left with something altogether more figurative, or at least a different kind of literalism. The father perhaps 'saw' his son intuitively? Emotionally? If so, this raises another possibility - was the son ever really absent at all? Did he ever actually take 'his journey into a far country'? If not, where did he go? Or did he 'go' at all? ...almost immediately, by virtue of a considered evaluation of one sentence, one phrase in fact, we are beginning to enter a semantic world which feels unstable and limitless. It is fascinating and unsettling in equal measure. It feels numinous, perhaps just like being in the presence of the force behind the words, God himself if you believe.

This is the power and the beauty of the King James Bible in general, and of this story in particular.

Incidentally, the story of the Lost Son is not to be found in Luke's Gospel alone. It is in fact a much older story, a kind of folk tale of the time that would almost certainly have been in its essential elements familiar to a first or second century Judean. And versions of it exist in other cultural histories, most notably in the Buddhist *Saddharmapundarika Sutra* (also called the *Lotus Sutra*) which was composed in the second century AD, probably around the same time as Luke – or the collective of authors known as 'Luke' - was writing. The story in its bare bones is replicated in both traditions, though the respective authors emphasise different elements and extend the narrative in different directions, presumably for their differing evangelical purposes.

In broad terms, the Biblical Parable of the Prodigal Son signifies in Christian terms the potential mercy of God (the father) towards repentant sinners (the lost son). In the Sutra it denotes the struggle of the individual (the son) to find enlightenment and the state of Buddha (the father).

Returning to verse 20 of the Biblical version, I believe that the moment when the father sees his son 'from a great way off' is in fact the defining moment of the story. It is the key that opens a door to a room full of meanings. For if the literal event is denied us then the figurative meaning must take precedent. The idea, surely, is that the son begins to understand where he has gone wrong and to seek redemption, and as soon as he has done that, the father is there, full of forgiveness and love and up for the party.

The son finds his purpose and his fortune through his own understanding of himself. He comes to terms with himself, and is rewarded with love and abundance, much of it provided by his father.

It is not unimportant that the son's speech begging forgiveness and reconciliation is in verse 18, *before* the son actually appears to return to this father. The son *intends* to beg for mercy, '*I will arise and go to my father, and will say unto him...*'; he doesn't actually repent directly to the father.

Put another way, the father 'sees' his son by, as it were, reading his mind. It's the son's intention that counts, his inner state, not the actual external event of physical reunion, and this inward intention is witnessed by the father apparently instantaneously.

The parable therefore is far from just a story of a symbolic event. It is, in my reading, a psychodrama; a symbolic, even allegorical representation of a psychological process - a young man loses his direction in life and struggles, successfully, to find his way back. Through understanding and '*coming to himself*' the lost son becomes found. And the person who finds him is the father aspect of his own psyche. In short, the son finds himself and in doing so is brought into union with his most powerful self, his best self. He is unified. He is, figuratively, re-born, and his life becomes wonderful.

Let me re-iterate this more simply by highlighting the sequence of the narrative:

1. the young man *'wasted his substance with riotous living'*
2. then *'he came to himself'*
3. then he tells himself that he *'will arise and go to my father and will say unto him, Father, I have sinned'*
4. then *'he arose, and came to his father'*
5. and then his father *'saw him, and had compassion, and ran, and fell on his neck'*
6. and then they all party!

This clearly shows that the son achieves self-knowledge first, and following that comes the reunion with the father. I see this story as a symbol of gnostic self-transformation, much more than merely a general representation of the power of God and his mercy.

And of course this is why the Prodigal Son was *my* song for a number of years. I recognised the son in his being lost, and understood the need to be reunited with my internal father, my most potent Self.

My work has been to 'come to myself'. *'Prodigal Songs'* is, I hope, an indication that at the very least progress has been made in that direction.

17. On Being 'Late'

The dream recounted near the start of this book (see page 4) is worth returning to at its end. There is a story to complete.

If you recall, there was no clear-cut finale to the dream — I awoke as I was running to the rocket, not knowing if I would get there in time for lift-off. I have often wondered about the significance of this. Does it mean that I didn't make it, that I didn't fly to the moon? And is that therefore symbolic of the fact that I will never quite fulfil my potential, never quite achieve the heights that being 'on the list' suggested I might be able to achieve? Or did I make the flight after all, and will, therefore, be all that I can be? Will I reach the stars?

The answer to all these questions is: my life. For I see now that the ending of the dream is in fact mine to make. I see now that my life is mine to create, and that actually this is what I have been doing all along. Formerly hidden from view, by virtue of my unfolding — the revealing of myself to myself - the process I've been living through is becoming more visible.

And what is now clear is that my best self has always known where he was going; for my best self is, like yours, pure. Getting my more troublesome self out of the way, with all its attachments and desires and limitations, has been the real challenge, the main task, even when I didn't know it.

I picture this process as being rather like cleaning a mirror — the 'mirror of the soul' as some have called it — allowing the light of my life to be reflected more brightly. The more I understand the true nature of my best self, and the more I live in accordance with it, then the cleaner the mirror becomes.

This 'best self' is the inner force that I, Derek Hassack, give human expression to. And from its perspective, I now see that in fact I've never been late for anything. For my best self there is no such thing as being late, only perfect timing. No such thing as wasted time, or mistakes, or badness, or something wrong. This self has always known that everything happens for a reason, and it's all good in the end.

So - returning to the dream — whether I caught the rocket to the stars or not, I know now that it really doesn't matter. Real success lies in the proportion by which the way I act corresponds to my best self. So I no longer have any need to run for the rocket because the crucial truth is that I'm already flying in it. I made it, because I was already there. I am, and always have been, on my way to the stars.

That I will never quite reach them, is what it means to be alive.

AfterWords

'Advice' as the saying goes 'is just a form of nostalgia'. As such, it should be treated with great caution, by both the giver and receiver. Advice is also very tempting to give - especially when working, as I do, in the field of personal development. And as a father it's almost incumbent upon me to offer it at times, even if it may well be ignored (sometimes rightly so).

'The truth' is also something which needs to be carefully presented. For one thing, the reach of subjectivity is immense and sometimes covert; therefore to insist on a particular version of reality no matter how much evidence seems available, or how specific the topic, is a dangerous move.

And yet...our truths, like our loves, define us. What I see as being real sheds light on who I am. Therefore I feel able to conclude *Prodigal Songs* with a few random 'truths' or pieces of 'advice' or 'beliefs' on the understanding that they are intended to reflect me as much as be accepted by you as undeniably true. They represent some glimmers of the world as I see it, of life as I have come to understand it.

And so, rather like the man who sits quietly and alone at the end of a beautiful and productive summer's day, I take this opportunity to reflect on what has been done so far, and what might be achieved in the days ahead. I take this opportunity to express some of the product of my life, in order to maximise its worth.

I offer my view of the present, partly in order to avoid the risk of being prodigal with my past...

We live in a vibrational universe. Everything, without exception, is a form of energy. All energy vibrates.

It's your life; yours alone. You create it by what you give energy to.

What you truly want to be is in fact the best you can be – but the key is knowing what 'truly' means for you. When you know, do it as if your life depended on it. For in a way it does.

No one but you can make you happy. So never rely on others for your own success. In the same way, you can never make someone love you – or vice versa.

Remorse should have a quick sell-by-date. Mistakes are one of the hallmarks of being human. We must make them to be fully alive.

Understand that old habits die hard by fighting back. Just ignore them when they do this.

Let the sense of longing be a driver not an obstacle.

It's OK to say 'I don't know', if you don't. No matter what the situation, admitting to ignorance is more constructive than pretending knowledge.

Be kind at all times. More than anything else, this means listening and hearing.

Always try to see things from the other person's point of view – but don't necessarily go along with it.

There is a single reality; it's just that everybody sees it differently.

The Self inhabits a body. The Self is self-aware while it inhabits a body. Death is the ending of the body and, perhaps, of self-awareness, but it's not the end of the Self.

Being liked has little lasting value. Being loved is a different matter entirely.

Everybody has a soul. Our purpose is to fulfil the true nature of our soul. One of these purposes, and it's the one for everybody, is to contribute to the general improvement of mankind in the best way we can. As Jung says, we are here to 'light a candle in the darkness'. But this is about more than just

knowledge; it is about consciousness and understanding and love.
We each have our own unique talent to bring to that purpose; we each have our own unique purpose in life. This is true whether we know it or not. The more we can find and consciously live to that purpose then the more we are fully alive and fulfilled.

Consider that word 'fulfilled'. 'Full' and 'filled'. If we live fully to our purpose with what do we become filled?

Love is the only true success.

Everything you need is already with you. You don't need anything that you haven't already got.

Everything happens for a reason, sometimes more than one.

It's so much easier to know the truth than it is to live by it.

Say what you feel, if it feels important. If you don't, eventually there will be unforeseen consequences.

Not expressing your true feelings, even the apparently negative ones, is a kind of infidelity. You are not being true to yourself.

Self-consciousness is what separates human beings from animals, plants and other beings. The gift of self-consciousness enables humanity to understand and to progress in a way that is much, much more than just physical evolution.

Eventually we will become both wholly unique and wholly one. That's our purpose as a species.

Our body exists as a temporary home for our being. Death of the body is not an end to being, but a change in circumstance and, perhaps, in awareness.

The energy that beats in your heart is the same energy that beats in the heart of a star.

Truth is crucial. But not as important as love.

A belief is just a thought you keep thinking.

To Be Continued...

Deepak Chopra
"Life After Death"
"Grow Younger, Live Longer"